Elizabeth Patterson Bonaparte

Elizabeth Patterson Bonaparte

An American Aristocrat in the Early Republic

Charlene M. Boyer Lewis

PENN

UNIVERSITY OF PENNSYLVANIA PRESS

Philadelphia

Published by
University of Pennsylvania Press
Philadelphia, Pennsylvania 19104-4112
www.upenn.edu/pennpress

Printed in the United States of America on acid-free paper
10   9   8   7   6   5   4   3   2   1

Library of Congress Cataloging-in-Publication Data

Lewis, Charlene M. Boyer.
  Elizabeth Patterson Bonaparte : an American aristocrat in the early republic / Charlene M. Boyer Lewis. — 1st ed.
      p. cm.
  Includes bibliographical references and index.
  ISBN 978-0-8122-4430-4 (hardcover : alk. paper)
  1. Bonaparte, Elizabeth Patterson, 1785–1879—Family.   2. Bonaparte, Elizabeth Patterson, 1785–1879—Influence.   3. Bonaparte family.
  4. Aristocracy (Social class)—Maryland—Baltimore—Biography.
  5. United States—Civilization—1783–1865.   I. Title.
  DC216.95.B629L49 2012
  975.2'603092—dc23
  [B]
                                                              2012002585

For my femmes d'esprit:
my mother, Margareta,
and my sisters, Yvonne and Linda

Contents

Introduction
1

Chapter 1
"Nature Never Intended Me for Obscurity": The Celebrity
17

Chapter 2
"The Duchess of Baltimore": The Aristocrat
62

Chapter 3
"A Modern *Philosophe*": The Independent Woman
110

Chapter 4
"Happiness for a Woman": The *Femme d'Esprit*
153

Chapter 5
"So Much Agitated About This Child's Destiny":
The Mother and Daughter
188

Epilogue
"She Belongs to History"
221

Notes
231

Index
271

Acknowledgments
279

Introduction

Early in 1867, at the age of eighty-two, something drove Elizabeth Patterson Bonaparte to pull out her large cache of letters and clippings and read through them again. One can easily picture her: dressed in outmoded Parisian finery, carefully opening the fragile documents with their faded ink, and peering closely at the words and images that surely conjured up memories of more brilliant scenes and glittering occasions. Intriguingly, while she reviewed her life, she also rewrote it. Though she could not change the past, as she probably longed to do, she could analyze, explain, and comment on it; indeed, Elizabeth became the first historian of her life. As she had done in recent years, she added copious comments in the margins of letters, newspaper clippings, and even published works. Like any good historian, she provided biographical details on some of her correspondents and inserted approximate dates for some of the undated letters. But she devoted much of her time to assessing the character and motivations of many of the people who had written to her or were mentioned in her papers. Her goal seems to have been to understand better and to explain how her life had unfolded as it had. She hoped to correct the historical record, at least in her personal archives, by documenting her view of her own life story, filling in the gaps with her own explanations and reasonings. If posterity ever read her saved papers, she wanted no misunderstandings about how she had been treated by the world or why she had made the choices she did.

But, by this point in her life, Elizabeth was an embittered, lonely woman with dashed dreams—and her comments show that clearly. The past haunted her. "Ah! The irrevocable past! The *present* stagnation & the inexorable future," she penned in the margins of one account book; "ah! Could I only shake off the Curse of *Memory*!!"[1] Revisiting the past through her papers caused her pain, and she sought comfort by venting her spleen. She aimed her most venomous attacks at those whom she felt had betrayed her the most—her family members, particularly her father, William Patterson, and her brothers, and her former husband Jerome Bonaparte, Napoleon's youngest brother and one-time king of Westphalia. She remembered her father as "the Plague Sore of my life" and described her brothers as "ignorant, selfish, uncivilized Boors of whom WP was the head." She considered herself to be the "Victim" of these "ignorant Dullards" and their "blind avarice & selfishness" and, therefore, "in strict justice," she had "proportionably despised them!" "An unprincipled, mean souled man" were the words she reserved for her husband. Her hatred of him filled her entirely. "The sentiment of contempt to old Jerome is in my heart, & circulates with every drop of blood in my body. I look upon him as belonging to the lowest type of humanity."[2]

Returning to the old letters and other papers proved too clearly that her life had not turned out the way she had planned. "My life appears a horrible dream," she wrote despondently in her old age, "a terrible delusion."[3] She was supposed to have lived a romantic life in Europe with her dashing husband. She should have been a queen with her own country and court. Instead, she had spent most of her life alone in her hometown of Baltimore, Maryland, deprived of the pageantry and splendor of European life. With great clarity, she blamed much of this on herself, declaring that "the first false step I made in life was" the "absurdity [or] imbecility" of marrying "such a husband." "The consequences," she concluded, "have hung a mill Stone round my neck which I could never get rid of since." But, unwilling to shoulder all of the blame, she also damned her father and her husband—in the same document—for ruining her life: "All the Misery of my life I lay at the door of Wm P & the old Bigamist Gentleman Jerome the double-distilled traitor."[4] Even as it had become clear that she would not achieve her dreams of nobility, she had fervently hoped that her son or grandsons would assume their rightful places in the world of European aristocrats and rulers. But they, too, never fulfilled her high expectations for them. Looking back over her long life seems to have given her little satisfaction, just heartache and disappointment. Her determination to correct how history would remember her, however, reveals much of the character of this tenacious and ambitious woman.

Sadly, history has almost forgotten Elizabeth Patterson Bonaparte. There are no serious scholarly works devoted to her. Indeed, most present-day

Americans, even many scholars of the early republic or of women, have not heard of her. But, in her time and for a few decades afterward, her story captivated the American public. The romance, adventure, and tragedy of her life seemed suited more for fiction than for history. Indeed, the biographies, the novels, and even play and movies about her life made little effort to distinguish between historical fact and imaginative fiction, capitalizing on the already fantastic aspects of her life.[5] Just before Elizabeth's death in 1879, the first published editions of some of her letters appeared. One featured the letters between her and Jerome as well as other pertinent documents concerning their marriage; it began by proclaiming that "the events" surrounding their marriage "find no parallel either in the annals of fact, or the domains of fancy."[6] A second, much larger volume presented a biography of her life and printed numerous letters to and from Elizabeth, highlighting the correspondence with her father while on her European travels. It dramatically declared that "beauties envied her beauty and wits dreaded her wit, kings sought her acquaintance and princes claimed her friendship."[7] The novels, play, and movies that followed in the late nineteenth and early twentieth centuries changed much of her story, of course, sometimes embellishing the beginning, sometimes the middle, and almost always the end to enhance the drama and supply the happy ending that Elizabeth had wanted for herself.[8] This fictionalization is unfortunate, for the real history of her life is captivating and instructive.

While Elizabeth's life is fascinating in its own right, it also possesses larger meanings for those interested in the history of society, culture, politics, and gender in the new nation. Studying Elizabeth Patterson Bonaparte provides a voice from the early republic that offers a very different perspective on the new nation than that of the better known founding fathers and mothers. Personally, Elizabeth was often self-centered and petty, though also amusing. But she reacted to forces and developments that were much larger than her personal situation. Much was still open to debate in American society, culture, and politics during her early years as wife, mother, and later divorcée. Her choices—and Americans' reactions to them—illustrate how much gender roles and expectations were in transition. Her rejection of the emerging ideals of womanhood and, more sweepingly, of the political ideology of republicanism—the belief that people should be governed by representatives of their own choosing—formed part of a wider discussion about the direction that American society should take. Elizabeth's writings and others' writings about her offer valuable glimpses into one of the most important debates that took place in the decades after the Revolution. For a generation or more, Americans vigorously discussed and hotly disputed the form that American society and culture should take: how aristocratic or democratic should it be? Elizabeth was of the generation that had inherited the Revolution and, by the early 1800s, needed to make sense of its goals and ideology and put them into practice. While grappling with the ideological and political issues of republicanism and, later, democracy, as well as with changing gender roles and relations, Americans also had to decide just what constituted *American* character and culture. What kind of society and culture was proper for the new nation? Women, especially those of the upper classes, actively and effectively participated in the attempts to answer these crucial questions. An emerging middle class, dedicated to increasingly democratic values, would also contribute greatly to these discussions, often in opposition to an established elite disparaged by the middle class for its European-style excesses.

Still fearful in the early nineteenth century that the republican experiment might not work and that American culture might become too much like that of monarchical or imperial Europe, many Americans worried about the potentially corrupting influence of European nobility, their manners and ideas. Women were typically seen as especially susceptible to this influence. That might not have mattered so much if women had played only minor roles in the young republic, but they did not. While they were excluded from formal politics (they could not vote or hold public office), women enjoyed real power in both the public and private realms. Long linked with fashion and luxury, and with the corruption and destruction that could accompany them, women, many believed, could mislead men of the republic through their public roles as conveyors of European refinement or their private actions as belles, wives, and mothers.[9]

To many of her day, Elizabeth Patterson Bonaparte embodied these concerns. Her marriage and her son connected her to the most powerful and dangerous man in Europe. Her clothing not only proclaimed her preference for European modes but also scandalized polite society. Her criticisms of American politics and American society were well known in elite circles. Her abandonment and later divorce left her a woman alone, yet still a very public character. Given the long-standing association of women with luxury and corruption, Elizabeth easily served as a lightning rod for those who feared for the success of the shaky republic. She not only contributed to the debates over the correct forms for American society and culture but also was, for a time, a focal point of that debate. Society matrons, her own family, and even members of Congress sought at various times to neutralize her potential power. The threat inherent in her French connections, particularly her possibly imperial son, led Congress to attempt to amend the Constitution in early 1810. The rhetoric of her admirers and especially of her critics was carefully chosen and directly linked to the cultural and political debates about the nature of American society, particularly to concerns about the power and influence of national celebrities, European aristocrats, and disorderly women.

Elizabeth was a rare woman for her time: a transatlantic celebrity. Other than Martha Washington, Abigail Adams, and Dolley Madison, few American women (and not many men) achieved the renown in this period that Elizabeth did. These early First Ladies had become famous through their husbands' elevated position, not by actively seeking celebrity through their own calculations, as Elizabeth had. Marriage to a Bonaparte brought Elizabeth as close to national and international celebrity as was possible for a woman; she then continued to cultivate her reputation through a provocative public appearance centered on French fashions and manners. In the early republic, women had to earn their celebrity in ways very different from men; they could not gain renown through the more obvious and more public military or political avenues. They had to look elsewhere. Causing a great scandal through some sexual act of adultery or bastardy assured a woman's notoriety, but it was not the kind of reputation any woman would actively seek. Elizabeth toed this delicate line and acquired her celebrity through acceptable, if outrageous, means—her marriage, her motherhood, and especially her fashionable style. Through her clothes and manners, she revealed her private self and prepared for her public displays. Like her good friend Dolley Madison, Elizabeth used dress and behavior to participate in the dialogue about the correct character for the new nation as well as to ensure her own celebrity. Her public identity spoke loudly about what she thought the national identity should be in a tumultuous time, when not only the appropriate behavior for American women but also their appropriate attire was contested. The admiration and criticism that Elizabeth's choices produced reveal the importance of fashion, clothing, and the presentation of the body in the early republic.

American society never quite decided how to judge such a celebrity with her French connections—her marriage, possibly royal son, travels, clothes, behavior, and attitudes. Elizabeth was a very public woman but still eminently respectable, and people had to figure out how to respond to such an unusual woman. While many Americans regarded her clothing and attitudes as scandalous, they still admired her beauty, wit, and fame and considered her the height of fashion, granting her status and social power. Party and dinner invitations, and even marriage proposals, rained upon her. But, as both a glamorous celebrity and a potential threat to the republic, she confused Americans from the time of her entrance onto the public stage at age eighteen when she married Jerome Bonaparte. They celebrated her for her beauty and for "catching" such a husband but also disparaged her for her choice of clothing and her preference for aristocratic ways. The choices that she made in her pursuit of a grandiose marriage and a fashionable public persona brought her condemnation, even as they evoked admiration and created her celebrity. This paradoxical view of Elizabeth illustrates the contradictions in American society over the correct character for the new nation.

As her fame and celebrity grew, Elizabeth understandably mattered more to Americans than she had initially. As her national and international importance increased, so did American condemnation of her. Her obvious attachment to Europe and aristocratic culture caused her to be regarded by more people as unpatriotic, immodest, and, more drastically, threatening to the fledgling republic. Such criticism reached its height in the early to mid-1810s as she received an official divorce from the Maryland legislature, negotiated with Napoleon about becoming a duchess, and made her first extensive trip to Europe. Americans started to worry more about her influence when it seemed that her popularity was leading others to fawn over her and even to follow her example; most Americans believed that her versions of womanhood and citizenship—ones that relied on aristocratic values—were unacceptable for a simple republic. Yet Elizabeth cared little whether her compatriots considered her poorly suited for their republic. She was convinced that she belonged in the courts of Europe instead of the parlors of Baltimore.

Elizabeth did not unthinkingly choose Europe and its old aristocratic culture over the United States and its new republican culture. She thought deeply about these issues and selected the political and cultural forms that best suited her beliefs and her self-perception. Her thoughts and actions demonstrate the distinct ways in which women of this era could participate in public culture and contribute to important national discussions. Yet scholars have paid little attention to women's influence on American culture in the first third of the nineteenth century. Judith Sargent Murray, Susanna Rowson, and a few others from the 1780s and 1790s have received attention. And women who influenced the culture of the nation's capital—whether New York, Philadel-phia, or Washington—have been addressed thoroughly and creatively.[10] But, except for the recent works of Rosemarie Zagarri, Mary Kelley, and Catherine Allgor, women have been relatively absent in the historiography of the cre-ation of a national culture in the new republic after 1800. During the early nineteenth as in the late eighteenth century, women, particularly elite women, fully participated in these cultural debates and greatly influenced the forma-tion of a national identity. Culture, even political culture, as many historians have persuasively argued, is a public realm shared by men *and* women. In drawing rooms, dining rooms, and ballrooms, as well as in the halls of govern-ment, American men and women engaged in strident debates over the place of aristocratic ways in the new nation's culture.

Even though they could not vote, women thought about the meanings of republicanism, national identity, and citizenship just as men did. In this pe-riod, citizenship possessed various meanings, not just in strict political terms but also in powerful social and cultural ones.[11] With women recognized as members of the republic and citizens of the nation, though not independent ones, marital and residential decisions, for example, took on new consequences in terms of citizenship. Was a married woman who had been born in the United States an American citizen in her own right? What if her husband was not a citizen? The Constitution and the courts had left this question open for debate.[12] As Elizabeth highlighted, women in this era expressed their ideas about national identity in multiple ways. She was not the only woman who chose a grand European husband or who dressed to display her own particu-lar views about American culture and politics. But, in this period of increas-ing nationalism, her choice to appear as a European aristocrat—indeed, as a member of an imperial family—caused some, including members of Con-gress, to decide that she could no longer remain an American citizen.

Though Americans may have been conflicted about Elizabeth, she was never really conflicted about America. She used her European experiences and knowledge to offer distinctive critiques of American politics, society, and gen-der expectations. She found her native land not only provincial and boring; she also disliked its political structures and, more important, the social limits that it placed on women. Through her sentiments and behavior, Elizabeth tested the boundaries of publicly prescribed gender roles and expectations and presented an alternative model of womanhood for the new nation. While this model was not generally accepted, there were other women like her who found dissatisfaction with the role of republican wife and mother and sought different possibilities for womanhood. She was never content to be the kind of daughter, wife, mother, or even divorcée that American society generally expected of white women.

This work focuses on the first three decades of the nineteenth century—an era of women's history that falls into something of a historiographical gap; it has not received as much attention as the revolutionary era or the mid-nineteenth century. Like "separate spheres" for antebellum America, "republican motherhood" long functioned as the dominant theme in women's history for the early republic, shaping our understanding of the expectations for women's roles during the era of revolution and nation building. This ideal proclaimed that women could best serve the republic in private ways, by marrying virtuous men and raising sons to become good republican citizens. But, as a study of Elizabeth Patterson Bonaparte's life from around 1800 to 1835 proves, this ideal was not the only model available for elite, white women in the first decades of the new republic. At least for women of the upper classes, there were alternative ideas about what their roles could be. While many genteel women did live within the limitations of republican motherhood (and, later, separate spheres), not every woman aspired to become a republican wife and mother. Status and wealth afforded elite women options that were unavailable to their more middle- or lower-class counterparts. These alternatives extended beyond the domestic and familial to the social and public realms, including even an explicitly political dimension. Functioning primarily in the realm of "polite" society, a world that included both women and men, the public and the private, some women focused their energies on bringing refinement to American culture, as opposed solely to raising virtuous citizens. Some women, such as Anne Willing Bingham and Martha Washington, modeled the role of the French *salonnière*; others, such as Judith Sargent Murray and Susanna Rowson, became scholars or writers; and still others, such as Dolley Madison and Elizabeth Monroe, envisioned themselves as cultural arbiters for the nation. At the turn of the nineteenth century, as the ideal of "republican motherhood" waned and before the middle class's "cult of true womanhood" solidified, elite women had choices to make about the social and political roles that they would play and the nature of their relationship to both American culture and the nation.[13]

Rejecting even these untraditional options, Elizabeth presented another model based more on European gender norms. Her marriage to Jerome

Bonaparte and travels to Europe exposed her to different kinds of roles, activities, and beliefs for and about women. She learned that women could behave and think outside the social prescriptions put forward in the United States. Of key importance for Elizabeth, she found that in Europe it was more acceptable for women to pursue their ambitions openly. Their culture was more used to women participating in public in a variety of ways. While in Europe, she formed close friendships with numerous female intellectuals, writers, and *salonnières*. These women, known as *femmes d'esprit*, regularly declared their political and social opinions and knew they possessed influence. They happily welcomed Elizabeth into their exclusive group and encouraged her in her own writing and thinking. She, in turn, felt truly comfortable among these more liberal women. Europe also promised the means for her to achieve her ambitions for her son as well as for herself. Elizabeth embraced European gender norms, as she understood them, along with European aristocratic trappings. In American terms, then, she thought and acted too much like not just an aristocrat, but an *aristocratic European woman*, and that is what often got her into trouble. Americans recognized all of the signs of this type of woman and did not consider her appropriate for their republic. Obvious ambition was just beginning to become appropriate for men in this period, due largely to the growing influence of the middle class, but it was not at all appropriate for women. Similarly, a preference for Europe and its aristocracy over America and its democracy would not be tolerated. Elizabeth never hid her ambition nor her love for aristocratic Europe. She would never be considered an appropriate role model for American women—an Abigail Adams or a Martha Washington—either in her own time or for later generations. Yet she was ultimately adept at finding ways a woman could pursue her ambition without ever destroying her reputation and facing complete ostracism from elite American circles.

Elizabeth Patterson Bonaparte's decades of prominence reveal the intriguing confluence of private acts and public events that took place throughout the transatlantic world long into the nineteenth century. Her marriage, motherhood, and divorce were intimate occasions that had international ramifications. Throughout Elizabeth's life, the private not only became public but also national and even international. Her personal decisions affected two countries—a republic and an empire. During her long life, she crossed the Atlantic Ocean numerous times, making more trips than most women or men of this era. She spent many years living in Europe, yet always—if reluctantly—

called the United States her home. Elizabeth's movement between countries and cultures as she actively constructed a transatlantic life created sharp contradictions for her. Ultimately, she sought and lived a life very different from most of the women she knew, either American or European.

This book is not a traditional biography of a woman's life, covering her birth through her death. It does not, as most women's biographies do, take a strictly chronological approach or focus on the stereotypical roles of daughter, wife, and mother. Those categories and that kind of chronology do not work when trying to understand the significance of Elizabeth Patterson Bonaparte's life. Moving beyond the categories typically associated with women allows us to recast what we know about women and their relationship with the new nation and its culture in the early nineteenth century. Looking at this one woman and her cultural and political significance illuminates the intricate processes of national and individual identity formation during chaotic years when much remained fluid and debated. As a public figure, Elizabeth both reflected and revealed American cultural beliefs and practices, especially those regarding celebrity and fame, aristocracy and luxury, and women's roles and possibilities.

Understanding what Elizabeth Patterson Bonaparte thought about herself and her world would have been much easier had her family members decided to preserve the past instead of protect the family's reputation. Elizabeth always wrote in an honest, straightforward manner. Sometimes she became vindictive, especially when it concerned her father; older brothers ("Bob the Brutal" and "John the Drunken"); former husband, Jerome; and other friends and relations.[14] In one 1867 marginal comment that has survived, she asserted that her father's mistress was in their house "when [Elizabeth's mother] was on her death bed" and that, when her brother Edward got rid of her, she "was succeeded in the same capacity by Somers by whom [her father] had in old age a bastard daughter."[15] While such statements survive, what must have been similar—or worse—comments do not. Letters, her will, and envelope covers all point to the existence of extensive European travel journals, lengthy memoirs that were prepared for possible publication, and a work she entitled *Dialogues of the Dead* (and described as a conversation between Jerome and her father in hell). All of these writings are missing from the manuscript collections that her grandson donated to the Maryland Historical Society after her death. Much to my dismay, she had also kept daily diaries that are nowhere to be found and were probably destroyed, like the rest of the missing material, by her grandson. Lost as well are almost all of the letters she wrote to her confidante and financial manager, Anne (Nancy) Spear. In the 1830s, Spear gave—or probably sold—those letters to Elizabeth's brother Joseph to be used against her in a dispute over their father's will. I like to imagine they are languishing in some old cabinet in a Baltimore law office just waiting to be discovered. What is lost to history (and to this historian) in all of those missing volumes, journals, and papers can only be imagined. If all of her writings had survived, she probably would have been known to us as one of the great literary women of her time—perhaps not for quality, style, or intellect but certainly for sheer output.

Instead of offering a strict chronological narrative, this work is structured around the main themes of Elizabeth's life. Exploring the different aspects of her life—as a celebrity, an aristocrat, a woman in the United States and in Europe, and as a mother and daughter—provides a way to examine different social, cultural, and political issues in the early republic. Each chapter focuses on a particularly important period and theme in Elizabeth's life as she grew from a young to an older woman. The chronological arc of her life, while clear in the progression of these chapters, is less important than the ways in which Elizabeth's actions and sentiments, and the responses to them, illustrate many of the key issues of the period from 1800 through 1835. A short vignette opens each chapter and highlights in detail a specific incident in Elizabeth's life, such as her request for a divorce, to illustrate the themes and arguments in that chapter. The book closes by covering the last decades of her life until her death in 1879.

One last note: deciding how to refer to Elizabeth Patterson Bonaparte throughout this work was not easy. Her last names—the customary manner of reference in scholarly works—are problematic. "Patterson Bonaparte" is both cumbersome and anachronistic. "Bonaparte" seems out of the question since Napoleon laid sole claim to it long ago. "Madame Bonaparte"—the name by which she was known in both American and European society for most of her life—is no less problematic and equally unwieldy. Because she detested her father and much of her family, "Patterson" seems inappropriate as well. While many who have written about her have chosen to refer to her as "Betsy," the name her family used when she was young, that name is also contestable. She almost never used it after her marriage, and few outside of her family called her Betsy; furthermore, as a diminutive form of her name, it implies a dependent girl, not an independent woman. Her husband, Jerome, translated her name into French and called her "Elise," but other than in some letters to him, she never used that name either. She signed most of her adult letters "E" or "Eliz." or "Eliza.," abbreviations of "Elizabeth." That name made the most sense to me, and, in fact, using it alone underscores her position as a woman without a man, her situation for most of her life.

Elizabeth was famous—at times infamous—during her day, and her life inspired novelists and filmmakers into the early twentieth century. But her life and her words have since been forgotten. Similarly, though it consumed Americans in the early republic, the debate over an aristocratic versus a democratic society in the early years of the nineteenth century has only recently begun to receive the attention it deserves.[16] Furthermore, the history of women in this transitional period has needed more examination for far too long. This work hopes to redress all three of those problems. The words and actions of Elizabeth Patterson Bonaparte and the reactions of others to her remind us of the lingering contingency of the republican experiment known as the United States and, equally important, of the active role of women in the creation of American society and culture.

Before examining the significance of Elizabeth Patterson Bonaparte to the new nation, some details about her family and her life before she emerged on the national stage are needed.[17] Elizabeth Patterson belonged to one of the wealthiest families in Maryland. Her father, William Patterson, an emigrant from Ireland, had accumulated a fortune in Baltimore as a merchant and property owner. The early years of the Revolution had found him in the West Indies, already an ardent patriot and engaged in "the Opportunity of Collecting and Shipping Arms and amunition [sic] and almost every thing necessary for Carrying on the War." He remained there for a few more years, acting as a purchasing agent for the Continental Army, and "soon made what was then considered a fortune, say sixty or eighty thousand dollars." "As a prudent Gambler" in the "hazardous and desperate game of Chance" that was international commerce, William decided that Martinique was too risky a base for his trade with the United States during wartime; so he moved his operations to Baltimore in 1778, bringing with him in "fast sailing Vessels, cash and Merchantdize more than a hundred thousand dollars."[18]

William's wealth and his ambition were a perfect match for the burgeoning town of Baltimore. Though bold with his business, he cautiously invested half of his money in real estate, buying properties in the city and the surrounding area. It was a savvy decision in a boom town. The remainder of his fortune he used to set up his business, quickly becoming the leading merchant in Baltimore. The community granted him the honors that came from his remarkable success. When the Bank of Maryland opened in Baltimore in 1790, for example, William was named its first president. He also had access to the best social circles. Here, he met Dorcas Spear, the daughter of a wealthy flour merchant. She would have been around eighteen when they married in 1779. Her sister Margaret had recently married Samuel Smith, who had served as a colonel in the Revolutionary War and was a member of one of the leading Baltimore families. Marriage to a Spear gave William Patterson the high social status to match his financial one; he had become an American success in just a few years.

Children arrived soon after the wedding, as they did for most couples of this era. Elizabeth's eldest brother, also named William, was born in 1780. Dorcas delivered at least twelve more children, with eight surviving into adulthood. Elizabeth, the eldest daughter and fourth child, came into the world on February 6, 1785. Her parents were obviously thrilled with their daughter since they requested the artist Robert Edge Pine to paint an expensive, almost full-length portrait of Dorcas and baby Elizabeth. Little is known about Elizabeth's early years or her schooling. As the eldest daughter, she surely helped her mother in the house, while the brothers closest to her age, William, Joseph, Robert, and Edward, learned the intricacies of the mercantile trade from their father. There is much evidence that she received the genteel education befitting the daughter of an elite, urban family at a private academy in Baltimore, where she would have been a day student with some of the other leading young ladies of the area. She would also have learned domestic skills from her mother and, most assuredly, from the enslaved house servants that her family owned. With some of her mother's family living nearby, Elizabeth grew up surrounded by many cousins as well. Her father kept tight rein over the household, making sure everyone was inside by dark and locking the doors and windows himself. Since her parents were very much homebodies (her father did not enjoy leaving his business), the young Elizabeth seems to have done little traveling beyond the area of her hometown and her family's nearby plantation.

By the time Elizabeth met Jerome Bonaparte in September 1803, the eighteen-year-old was already renowned for her extraordinary beauty and was

Figure 1. Dorcas Spear Patterson holding Elizabeth. Robert Edge Pine, ca. 1786. Image #1959.118.44, courtesy of the Maryland Historical Society.

one of the most sought-after young women in town. Jerome, a lieutenant in the French Navy, had spent the summer traveling along the East Coast with a number of friends and servants. Born in December 1784 in Corsica, he knew little of the poverty and hardship that the Bonaparte family had endured before Napoleon's military successes during the French Revolution moved the entire family up economic and social ladders. In 1800, he had entered the navy—where Napoleon seems to have wanted his youngest brother. At the time, Napoleon, then France's first consul, had warned Jerome that it was better to die young than to "live sixty years without glory, without utility to your country, and without leaving any trace of your passage through life."[19] While learning his new duties as a midshipman, Jerome, who seems to have been a frivolous youth, also began a lifelong habit of reckless spending. Yet Napoleon was determined to turn Jerome into a serious and respected naval officer. He sent him first to Saint Domingue in December 1801, as part of the expedition to put down the slave revolt on that Caribbean island, and then to Martinique in the summer of 1802 as an officer aboard a patrolling brig. Napoleon could not have predicted the trouble that would come from this decision. Years later, Jerome's memoirs would proclaim these years of his life "a veritable novel" for "all of the obligatory vicissitudes figure there: flights, homecomings, wars, shipwrecks, [and] the ephemeral love of an enchantress." "It is around a marital intrigue," the editor explained, "that all of these romantic incidents are grouped."[20]

Ordered to return home from Martinique by the summer of 1803, but worried that he would be captured by the British if he sailed directly for France, Jerome decided that it was safest for him to leave the island on an American ship bound for Virginia and return to France from the United States after a little sightseeing. He landed in Norfolk in July 1803 and did not return to France for another two years. With his friends Alexandre Le Camus, a Creole from Martinique who served as Jerome's secretary, and Jean-Jacques Reubell, the son of one of the five directors (the body that ruled France from 1795 to 1799), Jerome traveled first to Washington, D.C., to ask for money to cover his expenses from the French *chargé d'affaires*, Louis André Pichon. Pichon, who was understandably alarmed at having the favorite brother of the first consul show up unannounced, reluctantly gave Jerome enough funds for a few weeks and begged him to travel incognito. But the secret was soon out, as Jerome toured the area, dined with President Thomas Jefferson in Washington and Vice President Aaron Burr in New York, and attended as many soirees and balls as possible. He and his party soon headed for Baltimore, apparently to wait for a French ship.

According to legend, Elizabeth and Jerome first saw each other in September 1803 at the Baltimore horse races but were not introduced. A few days later, they danced together at a ball and somehow became entangled—quite literally. Whether his watch chain became twisted in her hair or her necklace caught on his gold button, it was love at first sight. Years later, Elizabeth would relate a very different story, telling a friend that she had first met Jerome at a dinner held by the Pascaults, a family of Saint Domingue refugees. Standing at a window with Henriette Pascault, she had spotted Jerome and his friend Reubell coming up the drive. Pascault pointed at Reubell and declared,

"'That man will be my husband.'" Elizabeth said she had answered, "'Very well, I will marry the other one.'"[21] Jerome called on her at home soon after their first conversation, whether at a ball or dinner. By the end of October, they had decided to marry, receiving a marriage license on October 29.

But as the appointed day of November 7 neared, Elizabeth's father received some worrisome information. Elizabeth's uncle, Samuel Smith, asked Jerome if he was of legal age to marry; lying, Jerome assured Smith that he was twenty-one, though he was just nineteen.[22] Pichon, moreover, made it clear that, according to the new French Civil Code, it was illegal for a man under the age of twenty-five to marry without the consent of his parents.[23] More important, Pichon emphasized that this marriage would probably outrage Napoleon. Worse yet, an anonymous letter sent to William apprised him of Jerome's "profligate" character, including tales of several young women that he had "ruined" in France and the West Indies and of a recent proposal to Susan Wheeler (later Mrs. Stephen Decatur), who had had the good sense to reject him. The correspondent, probably someone traveling with Jerome, warned that Jerome would marry Elizabeth "to secure himself a home at your expense" until returning to France and would then "laugh at your credulity."[24] William immediately called off the wedding and sent Elizabeth to stay with relatives in Virginia. There, to her parents' dismay, Elizabeth's feelings for Jerome only intensified. She famously declared that "she would rather be the wife of Jerome Bonaparte for an hour, than the wife of any other man for life."[25] She also let it be known that she was willing to run away with him. Her father, though still very troubled, relented, and the pair married on Christmas Eve in 1803. In an effort to make the marriage as legitimate as possible, the highest-ranking Catholic bishop in the United States, John Carroll, officiated; and the mayor of Baltimore, the French consul, and Jerome's secretary Alexandre Le Camus signed the marriage certificate. Everyone, including her parents, now celebrated the match, though some, including Bishop Carroll, worried about Elizabeth's future.[26]

Chapter 1

"Nature Never Intended Me for Obscurity"
The Celebrity

After their Christmas Eve wedding, Elizabeth and Jerome embarked in early 1804 on a honeymoon tour, spending a few weeks in the capital. Seemingly everyone who was anyone in the city wanted to meet the couple whose romance provided material not just for gossips but even for newspapers. Margaret Bayard Smith, the wife of the editor of the powerful *National Intelligencer* and one of Washington's social leaders, quickly recognized that Elizabeth's husband and, even more significant, her style of dress would make this young woman from Baltimore a celebrity. Bayard Smith even contributed to Elizabeth's growing fame by writing about her daring fashions to friends and family, especially after the sensation Elizabeth created at a winter ball given in her honor and attended by "an elegant and select party" of the Washington elite.[1]

Elizabeth arrived at the house of her uncle, Secretary of the Navy Robert Smith, wearing a sleeveless, backless, white crepe dress of Parisian design that was, as Rosalie Stier Calvert described it, "so transparent that you could see the color and shape of her thighs, and even more!"[2] Elizabeth's thin dress left "uncover'd" "her back, her bosom, part of her waist and her arms." With no shift or chemise underneath, "the rest of her form" was "visible." Not surprisingly, her appearance drew public attention, and a "mob of boys" swarmed around her as she entered the house. Once inside, according to Bayard Smith, Elizabeth's "appearance was such that it threw all the company into confusion, and no one dar'd to look at her but by stealth." Outside, crowds gathered to peer through the unshuttered windows at the "extremely beautiful" and "almost naked woman."[3] Highly offended by Elizabeth's scandalous clothing, "several ladies made a point of leaving the room" and later reprimanded her for the spectacle she had generated, explaining that "if she did not change her manner of dressing, she would never be asked anywhere again."[4] Elizabeth was supposed to attend another soiree the next evening, but her aunt and "several other ladies sent her word, if she wished to meet them there, she must promise to have more clothes on." The rebuke made Bayard Smith "highly pleased with this becoming spirit in our ladies."[5]

But the spectacle Elizabeth created at her uncle's ball also inspired Thomas Law, the wealthy English merchant who had married Martha Washington's granddaughter, to write a few lines of poetry that soon circulated in the elite circles of the capital and its environs. Law's poem—another form of rebuke— was much harsher (and bawdier) than anything a lady could have said with propriety. Interestingly, it condemned not only Elizabeth's clothing and morals but also her lack of republicanism:

> I was at Mrs. Smith's last night
> And highly gratified my self
> Well! What of Madame Bonaparte
> Why she's a little whore at heart
> Her lustful looks[,] her wanton air
> Her limbs revealed[,] her bosom bare
>
> Show her ill suitted for the life
> Of a Columbians modest wife
> Wisely she's chosen her proper line
> She's formed for Jerom's concubine.[6]

Law, known as "a great poet" in the capital area, gave the lines to Rosalie Stier Calvert while staying at her nearby plantation, Riversdale. His poem circulated locally for a few days after the Smith ball before Aaron Burr "wickedly told" Elizabeth that "someone had written some very pretty verses about her beauty." Elizabeth naturally "insisted on seeing them."[7] Law hurriedly scribbled a second part to soften what he had first written that ultimately flattered her:

> Napoleon full of trouble
> Conquers for an empty bubble
> Jerom's conquest full of pleasure

Gains him a substantial treasure
The former triumphs to destroy
The latter triumphs to enjoy
The former's prise were little worth
If e'en he vanquished all the earth
The latter Heaven itself has won
For the ador'd Miss Paterson.[8]

When Calvert sent the poem to her French-speaking family in Belgium, it became an early contribution to Elizabeth's celebrity in Europe. Since the lines were written in English, Calvert directed her mother to "get my brother to read them to you" so that she could "understand all of the humor."[9]

Not all of the public commentary about Elizabeth at this early stage of her celebrity was negative. Thomas Law circulated other odes to her that were much more complimentary in tone than that inspired by Smith's ball. Around the same time as the ball, Jerome and Elizabeth arranged to have the already famous Gilbert Stuart paint a portrait of her to send to France, probably in hopes that Napoleon would accept her after seeing her beauty. Elizabeth's growing celebrity made her portrait a topic of conversation and interest; many made a special trip to Stuart's studio to look at it. Elizabeth's new friend, Sally McKean Yrujo, the Philadelphia wife of the Spanish minister to the United States, viewed the portrait. Many viewers were certainly disappointed that the portrait consisted of three different views of her head—"a full face, two thirds face & a profile"—rather than her full figure. Struck by her beauty, gossips predicted that "upon the portrait's arrival at Paris, the Venus de Medici would be thrown in the Seine." After gazing at Elizabeth's three visages, Law wrote another poem that Yrujo sent to Elizabeth. Though still sarcastic, this one probably atoned for any hurt feelings the other might have caused.

The painter won't oerwhelm the Sculptor's art
For Venus' Statue we no longer fear,
The matchless form of Mde. Bonaparte
Will not by Stewart at full length appear.

But ah! The picture with three heads in one
With so much fervor idolized will be
I tremble, lest our faith should be undone
By this new captivating Trinity.[10]

Figure 2. Gilbert Stuart's three-part study of Elizabeth captivated admirers and added to her celebrity. Copy of original, George d'Almaine, 1856. Image #XX.5.78, courtesy of the Maryland Historical Society.

After these few weeks in Washington in 1804, Elizabeth's celebrity status, both nationally and even internationally, was assured. Through letters and gossip, descriptions of Elizabeth's clothes and way of wearing them fanned out across the countryside and even across the Atlantic. To many, her style of dress was unsuitable for the United States. But the sensation Elizabeth created with her marriage, her fashions, and her portrait captivated Americans and made her one of the most famous women in the early republic.

Many Americans, including military leaders and presidents, were famous in the first fifty years of the country's existence, but few were celebrities. In the early national era, fame and celebrity were not synonymous terms, as they have essentially become in our own time. Both fame and celebrity in this era rested on being widely known and publicly praised. But, unlike celebrity, fame in the early national period came through particularly notable public service that highlighted a person's honor and virtue.[11] Celebrity implied neither public-mindedness nor virtue. A person gained celebrity through acts that often had nothing to do with public service but everything to do with drawing attention to him- or herself, in other words, with becoming popular. Special talents or an especially attractive appearance could make one a celebrity. Dramatic episodes in one's personal life that became public could transform one into a celebrity; so too could the act of marrying someone famous or, better yet, celebrated. Writing for the public, especially travel accounts and novels, and acting on the stage could make one a celebrity as well. Both fame and celebrity required an admiring audience, but those who sought fame had an eye on posterity, on their historical legacy. Celebrity was more temporary, the cultivation of renown during one's lifetime. But both fame and celebrity could translate into power, though fame's influence often came more in politics and celebrity's in the social and cultural arenas.

Another crucial difference separates the two terms: fame, as defined in the early republic, was almost exclusively open only to men; women found it almost impossible to win fame. Just a few women, such as Martha Washington and Dolley Madison, became famous through glorious deeds of public service. Not coincidentally, they were First Ladies and served as models of female patriotism in wartime.[12] Fame, and its concern with a future reputation, was primarily a male goal. George Washington, John Adams, Thomas Jefferson, and James Madison, for example, all had learned that pursuing fame not only provided an acceptable means for pursuing individual acclaim because of its emphasis on public service but also ensured a historical legacy.[13] Women who, despite society's expectations of ladies, also desired influence and acclaim had to seek something other than fame. While the pursuit of fame may have been mostly closed to them, celebrity was left wide open. Ambitious women seized this path to public recognition and social power. Though celebrity was apparently gender-neutral, it may have been especially female in the early nineteenth century.

Men and women gained celebrity in different ways. For men to achieve celebrity, at least before the 1820s, they first needed fame.[14] Famous soldiers, politicians, merchants, bankers, and ministers could then achieve celebrity if they had an attractive appearance and a charming personality to match their feats of public service. For example, Commodore Stephen Decatur, a hero of the War of 1812, earned his celebrity status because of his military exploits as well as his dashing good looks and manners. Conversely, while James Madison was certainly famous as a statesman and president, few would have considered him a celebrity. Indeed, Sarah Gales Seaton claimed that the president, "being so low of stature," was regularly "in imminent danger of being confounded with the plebeian crowd."[15] With professional, political, and martial spheres closed to them, ambitious women found other ways to gain public acclaim by using their beauty, clothes, writings, marriages, or even children, though many of these factors remained linked to men. Decatur's wife, Susan Wheeler, had been celebrated as a belle around Norfolk, Virginia, for her beauty, manners, and conversation while single, but she became a real celebrity only as the wife of a war hero and a widow after her husband's dramatic death in a famous duel.[16] In contrast, whatever celebrity James Madison attained came from his wife, whose appearance and behavior, according to Seaton, "distinctly pointed out her station wherever she moved."[17] Because of her stylish ways and vivacious personality, Dolley Madison surpassed renown and achieved national celebrity—a celebrity, however, that ultimately depended on her marriage to James.[18]

Female celebrity took various forms in this era: great beauty, fashionable clothing, special talents, or bold manners could make a woman a celebrity. It was common in this period, for instance, to speak of "celebrated belles." In 1807, John Quincy Adams informed his wife, Louisa, that a Miss Keene was renowned in Washington, D.C., for her performance "on the Tambourine, with all the confidence and all the graces of a gypsy"; "her dress," he continued, "is as much admired as her person and manners."[19] Yet all of female celebrity began at the same point—with a spotless reputation. In America, unlike in Europe, immoral behavior formed an insurmountable barrier to celebrity for women. The gender standards of the time made private virtue, unlike the public virtue expected for fame in men, a precondition of celebrity in women. Immoral behavior gained women infamy and disdain, not approval and acclaim. Since women were not expected to be widely known, those seeking celebrity had to walk a delicate line between behaving in ways that would gain them attention—that could create spectacle—and in ways that would immerse them in scandal. Female celebrities needed to preserve a reputation for upright behavior to stay in the public's favor. The Englishwomen Mary Wollstonecraft and Mary Wilkes Hayley (the sister of the radical John Wilkes) both suffered rapid declines in their American celebrity status when "immoral" choices they had made in their personal lives were revealed.[20] Women who were celebrated as socialites, writers, or artists were also daughters, wives, or mothers, and were expected to meet the normal expectations for those roles. The stresses of being a celebrity, however, were enormous since such status relied on a whimsical public and a demanding, constant self-presentation. For some, though, the stresses seem to have been justified by the "psychological and social rewards" an exceptional performance could draw.[21] Women had few ways to gain confidence, influence, and power. Being a celebrity was just one more role a woman could play, but one with potentially more rewards than any other for an ambitious woman.

Any woman or man who led a public life in the early republic faced the challenge of negotiating between the private and public self or, more accurately, of presenting a public self that was also the natural self. In the small world of the early United States, anyone who cultivated a public persona, whether political or social, did so on a small stage under close scrutiny. This intense gaze made public personalities constantly aware of how they presented themselves, always careful about the performance of their social and political identity. They had to pay constant attention to which particular self they presented at which particular time since their audiences were not always the same. The theatricality of these public performances of identity, however, was to remain unacknowledged; they should appear natural. Late eighteenth- and early nineteenth-century elites expected the public self also to be the sincere and authentic private self.[22] But this sincere self was to be a genial and affable one; negative emotions, such as anger or sadness, were to remain hidden. In spite of the strictures on permitted emotions, enlightened men and women expected the performance of one's public identity to be a true one, revealing the natural self, not a disguised self. This expectation that the presented self was the true or natural self created many unhappy men and women who discovered just how false these "authentic" identities could really be.

Elizabeth Patterson Bonaparte, one of the nation's first female celebrities, also became one of the best of her day.[23] She achieved and cultivated her celebrity with consummate skill and great éclat (and in ways modern Americans would recognize). She embraced a cosmopolitan identity that transformed her into a celebrity. Her beauty, fashions, and manners, as well as her marriage, family connections, and potentially royal son, all ensured her status as one of the leading American celebrities—a role that gained her popular acclaim in the United States as well as in Europe. Like later celebrities, however, Elizabeth's popularity waxed and waned as she garnered both adoration and condemnation. Her resounding success reveals as well that Americans have long been captivated by celebrities. It is not a new phenomenon or even one that required mass media and a mass culture, though the increase in literacy and in the number of newspapers in the early 1800s surely helped. The engravings, poems, articles, and announcements about Elizabeth that appeared in print increased her popularity. At this time, Americans sought cultural leaders just as they did political ones, and they celebrated them and gave them importance. Perhaps not surprisingly, Washington, D.C., provided one of the best arenas for the cultivation of celebrity, and Elizabeth visited regularly. The public identity that Elizabeth cultivated for herself also served a greater social—and national—purpose as she helped set the tone for fashionable culture. Her role as the nation's cosmopolitan celebrity helped define what kind of culture Americans wanted for their republic and, indeed, helped create the American love of celebrities.

Growing up in the 1790s, Elizabeth could have read about young women who sought a place in the public eye, who desired celebrity and were not necessarily condemned for it. In her 1796 play, *The Traveller Returned*, Judith Sargent Murray allowed her heroine, Harriot Montague, to dream of becoming a "distinguished" woman. Chastising her cousin Emily who wanted to "slide through life . . . without observation," Harriot wished she could "be paragraphed in the newspaper" so that her name would be handed "to thousands, who would not otherwise have known *that I had an existence.*" Emily retorted that "with the knowledge of *your existence,* they would at the same time receive an impression *that would not be to your honour.*" Unconcerned with that possibility, Harriot predicted that the public's *"curiosity* would be called into action" and she would "be allowed *my full share of merit,* and acquire a *prodigious deal of consequence.*" Harriot considered "the very idea [to be] enchanting."[24] The notion that some women desired a life beyond their household and a reputation beyond their locality was available to the young Elizabeth. As Sargent Murray suggested, public renown did not necessarily mean dishonor for women. Having a public reputation could be a positive experience for a woman; she could be celebrated by the crowds instead of ignored or denigrated. And Harriot Montague certainly made it clear that having thousands know one's name translated into acquiring "consequence" or power.

Throughout the 1790s, a number of American women had pursued public consequence, if not outright celebrity, and the power that went along with it. Philadelphia—the nation's capital from 1791 to 1800—was the home of many elite families. Anne Willing Bingham, the wealthy wife of Federalist senator William Bingham, led society in the manner of a French *salonnière*. The lavish dinners and parties she gave, as well as her fashionable clothing and manners, gained her public attention and acclaim. Her name appeared in newspapers and in letters of visitors to Philadelphia. Bingham became a trendsetter—one of the hallmarks of a celebrity. Other women copied her entertainments and her fashions.[25] As early as 1790, Abigail Adams remarked that Bingham had "certainly given laws to the ladies . . . in fashion and elegance."[26] But few outside the nation's elite social and political circles knew of Anne Bingham; she was not a national celebrity. Martha Washington, of course, was the premier public woman before 1800. As a symbol of female patriotism and then as the first First Lady, Washington was beloved by many who purchased engravings of her and retold stories of her courage while staying by the side of her husband, George, during the bleak days of the Revolutionary War and then his presidency. Other women, such as Judith Sargent Murray and Susanna Rowson, although never as well-known as Martha Washington, gained public reputations as actresses or by writing and publishing plays, novels, and essays.

Elizabeth, perhaps influenced as she came of age by these examples from life and literature of women who sought or captured the public eye, clearly felt destined for a grander calling than the simple life of an American wife and mother. As she later explained to her father, she felt that, with her "disposition and character," she never "could have vegetated as the wife of some respectable [American] man in business" since "nature never intended me for obscurity."[27] Perhaps Elizabeth's interactions with the refugee French community in and around Baltimore also convinced her that a cosmopolitan life best suited her. A large number of refugees from revolutionary France, such as the Du Ponts, and from rebellious Saint Domingue (later Haiti), such as the Pascaults, settled in the mid-Atlantic cities of Baltimore and Philadelphia and in the surrounding countryside. They brought with them their language, customs, and fashions—and their claims to being the most cultured people in Europe—that certainly could have dazzled a girl who dreamed of a life beyond Baltimore. Some of the older female refugees opened academies to which American elites sent their daughters for education and status. A Madame La Comte (or Lacombe) from Saint Domingue, for example, opened a school in Baltimore that Elizabeth's friends Mary Chase and Henriette Pascault attended.[28] The daughter of one of the wealthiest men in Maryland, Elizabeth probably received instruction from one of these refugee instructors, perhaps even La Comte, for she spoke, read, and wrote French quite well. Elizabeth probably also learned about European life and aristocratic ways from her French instructor, lessons important to the shaping of her later identity. Her family also owned a 1783 work entitled *Tableau de Paris* that may have inspired her dreams. For most of her early life, events in France had captivated Americans and many, including President Thomas Jefferson and Elizabeth's uncles Robert Smith and Samuel Smith, a senator, still held France in high regard and closely watched Napoleon Bonaparte's growing power as first consul. For a young woman who dreamed of a more glittering existence, France promised a life far different from one in Baltimore.

Even before she met Jerome in 1803, Elizabeth had learned much about how a young lady presented herself in society with the goal of becoming a "celebrated belle." Young ladies competed fiercely, within the bounds of appropriate behavior, for the coveted title of "celebrated." It not only gave a woman high status among her peers; it also made her known throughout her community and sometimes beyond. Small-town and rural belles could become celebrated only by traveling beyond their locale and socializing in the exclusive circles of urban centers: Philadelphia, New York, Boston, and the new capital of Washington, D.C. Creating a sensation at a fashionable resort, such as Saratoga Springs or the Virginia Springs, could serve the same purpose. The names of celebrated belles appeared frequently in conversation, private letters, and newspapers and occasionally even in published travel accounts. Male admirers, both married and unmarried, penned essays and poems describing the character and attributes of the adored woman; these would circulate among their friends and relatives and perhaps appear in a newspaper. Joseph Cabell's "very laboured character" sketch of the "much celebrated" Susan Wheeler circulated "th[r]o various parts" of Virginia in the fall of 1804. Cabell's friend Isaac Coles believed it was "not impossible that you will read it in some of the European prints in less than 12 months."[29] A renowned belle's manners, beauty, and fashions, her flirtations and possible betrothals received close scrutiny and provided much fodder for gossip among her community's elite and, if she were truly celebrated, among the nation's elite and perhaps even beyond. Marylander Catherine Harper, for example, asked her husband to tell her all about the "conquests" and "little flirtations" that Susan Wheeler, who had remained one of the most popular and admired belles for years, engaged in with her many "*lovers*" at parties in the capital.[30] Reaching an audience into the nation's interior, an 1805 traveling exhibit of "wax figures" included representations of "*New York, Baltimore, R. Island, and Friends' Beauties.*"[31] Whenever in public, a belle was constantly on display, hopefully winning and keeping the admiration of her public and also of her prospective beaux—the ostensible purpose of being a celebrated belle. A yearning for celebrity could start early in a young woman's life, and elite society encouraged and even nurtured it. Celebrated belles, however, were supposed to retire from the public whirl and relinquish their love of attention upon marriage. But for many women who desired renown, such retirement could have proven a difficult task to accomplish. Elizabeth wanted a celebrity that lasted beyond marriage. Indeed, a calculated marriage choice catapulted her into the rarefied realm of international celebrity.

Baltimore was already "renowned for the beauty of its women" when Jerome Bonaparte arrived in 1803.[32] A number of these beauties, many of them the daughters or relatives of politicians, increased their reputations and celebrity by spending time in Philadelphia and Washington, D.C. Elizabeth's circle of celebrated belles in Baltimore included not only Maria Chase, daughter of a justice of the Supreme Court, and a Miss Hay, but also the Caton sisters, the granddaughters of the illustrious Charles Carroll of Carrollton, signer of the Declaration of Independence and supposedly the richest man in the country. Marianne (or Mary), Elizabeth (or Betsy), and Louisa Caton shared the public's acclamation—and many of the same aspirations—with Elizabeth, creating a rivalry and jealousy between them that Elizabeth harbored until her death. In 1806, the eldest sister, Mary, married Elizabeth's brother Robert, making one of her archrivals her sister-in-law.

Not surprisingly, given her upbringing and ambitions, Elizabeth saw a sure path to acclaim and renown, both in her own country and abroad, when she set eyes on Jerome Bonaparte. A public and cosmopolitan life could be hers. Young, handsome, and dashing, as well as a brother of the ruler of France, Jerome became the center of attention wherever he went, especially among young ladies. It is little wonder that he and Elizabeth were immediately attracted to one another. Jerome's own celebrity was of a mixed kind. While many feted him or flirted with him as a Bonaparte, he had a reputation for bad behavior with young ladies of the first rank. Early in his stay, he had made a grave mistake by delivering a "gross insult" to Susan Wheeler that had brought him close to a duel.[33] But Jerome's status in elite circles and as a celebrity still remained secure. In spite of the strenuous objections of her father, brother, and many family friends, who doubted the depth of Jerome's love and worried about Napoleon's reaction, Elizabeth determined to become Jerome's wife, openly pursuing him. According to Sir Augustus John Foster, the British secretary of legation in Washington, Elizabeth "declared three Days before Jerome was won that she would have him. It was veni, vidi, vici."[34] Elizabeth's determination is not surprising; Jerome promised her a glittering existence far from dull Baltimore. In turn, unlike some of his earlier conquests, Jerome could possess this great beauty only through marriage. Though many agreed with her uncle that "the risk of her future happiness is beyond calculation,"[35] Elizabeth regarded Jerome as the best chance to fulfill her high ambitions.

At their Christmas Eve 1803 wedding, both Jerome and Elizabeth dressed to produce an effect and proclaim their identity as a fashionable, cosmopolitan couple. Looking unlike most American grooms, Jerome posed as a prince in his "wedding-suit of laced and embroidered purple satin—the white satin-lined pointed skirts reaching to his heels—knee breeches and diamond buckles." Such a costume, with his hair, of course, powdered, "enhanc[ed] his Napoleonic beauty." Elizabeth dressed in a French-style gown of embroidered, lightweight, white muslin. She dressed simply, she said, for she wished "to avoid vulgar display"; yet the thin dress hid little.[36] Alexandre Le Camus, a witness to the ceremony, noted that "all the clothes worn by the bride might be put in my pocket." Another guest described Elizabeth's gown as "a mere suspicion of a dress—India muslin covered with lace."[37] Elizabeth understood fully the purpose of dressing in this mode: "There was little as possible of any gown at all, dress in that day being chiefly an aid to setting off charms to advantage," a display of charms that would capture public attention and cultivate celebrity.[38]

After extracting more money from the French *chargé d'affaires* Louis André Pichon (Jerome had spent sixteen thousand dollars just since landing in Norfolk[39]) and apparently from William Patterson, Jerome and Elizabeth embarked on an extensive wedding tour, which included a visit to Washington. While the happy couple was enjoying the parties and honeymoon, Elizabeth's father turned to President Jefferson, Secretary of State James Madison, and Minister to France Robert R. Livingston to help persuade the fiery Napoleon to accept the marriage of his wayward brother. Because of the husband Elizabeth chose, the marriage, which would normally have been a private event, had an international impact. Like William Patterson and Jerome's advisers, Jefferson, Madison, and Livingston predicted that Napoleon would denounce the marriage, since he had already started marrying off his other siblings to European royalty. With the transfer of the recently purchased

Louisiana not yet completed and with the power of the first consul clearly on the rise, national policy makers wanted to ensure that the marriage of a young Baltimore woman did not place the United States in a difficult diplomatic situation. In an October 1803 letter to Livingston, Madison discussed the consequences of Jerome Bonaparte becoming "smitten" with "a young lady in Baltimore" and a possible marriage. "Considering the relation of one of the parties to a man who has so much influence on the course of human affairs, and whose private feelings may mingle themselves in a certain degree with his public sentiments," Madison explained, "the event is not without importance."[40] Just before the wedding, Jefferson had instructed Livingston to explain that, contrary to what Napoleon might believe, the "Executive of the United States" was powerless to prevent marriages. He also directed the minister to assure Napoleon that Jerome was marrying into a family whose "station" in society was "with the first of the United States."[41] Complementing these official efforts, William Patterson sent his son Robert to France to act as an intermediary for the couple with Napoleon. Jerome and Elizabeth, however, paid little heed to the worries of her family and the administration, even when they received word from Robert in the spring of 1804 that on hearing of the surprising marriage, Napoleon had exploded in anger.[42] Napoleon considered the marriage invalid since it violated the laws of France, and, in late January 1804, he ordered Jerome to return home immediately without Elizabeth. The couple firmly believed, however, that all of Napoleon's objections would evaporate as soon as he saw Elizabeth and witnessed their happiness. More troublesome for the young couple perhaps was Napoleon's declaration that Jerome would receive no more money from French officials in the United States.

To Elizabeth's dismay, during the first few months after the wedding, some of Jerome's brothers, especially Lucien, advised him that the best course would be for him to become an American citizen until Napoleon could be persuaded. Jerome seems to have seriously considered this suggestion, and Elizabeth's family thought it a good idea as well. Remaining in Baltimore with an *American* husband, however, was not what Elizabeth had imagined for her future. A public life on a larger stage than Baltimore had been her dream. When news that Napoleon had declared himself emperor in May 1804 reached Baltimore that summer, any idea of Jerome becoming an American citizen vanished. Both Jerome and Elizabeth yearned for the glory and the glitter that would come as a part of Napoleon's empire, from being international celebrities.

Figure 3. Jerome Bonaparte near the time of his marriage to Elizabeth. Artist and date unknown. Image #XX.5.52, courtesy of the Maryland Historical Society.

But the hereditary monarchy the emperor had established, they shockingly learned, left the rebellious Jerome out of the line of succession. In spite of their "disappointed expectations,"[43] the ambitious couple still believed that Napoleon could be placated; Jerome counted on his older brother to forgive him as he had so many previous times. They merely continued their rounds of parties and visits and waited for more instructions.

During her whirlwind courtship and heady honeymoon, Elizabeth surely relished the public scrutiny and admiration that she and Jerome attracted. Her "position of prestige . . . increased daily."[44] Baltimore and Washington society considered her marriage to the brother of the conqueror of Europe a sterling achievement, a top prize in the female game of husband-hunting—

one of the few honors for which women could openly and fiercely compete.[45] The elite of New York, Philadelphia, and Washington threw parties for them when they visited each city. Everyone wanted to fete this now famous couple. Elizabeth had successfully moved from celebrated belle to female celebrity. Seeing one's name so much in print would have been a mortification to most "proper" American girls, but Elizabeth must have taken great pleasure when newspapers up and down the Atlantic coast reported her engagement, wedding, and honeymoon, while constantly linking her name with Napoleon's and even occasionally calling her a princess. Whenever Jerome and Elizabeth arrived in a new city, newspapers reported the information. Readers were also kept up-to-date on what the couple did—the parties they attended or the theaters they visited. Marriage to a Bonaparte brought Elizabeth as close to national and international celebrity as was possible for a woman in the early republic. In May 1804, for example, English author Thomas Moore considered it most important to let his mother know that among the novelties of New York City, "the oddest things I have seen yet, however, are young Buonaparte and his bride."[46] Conventional wisdom stated that a woman's name was supposed to appear in print only twice—at her marriage and her death; generally, only scandalous women became the subjects of this much public conversation.[47] But Elizabeth's name appeared in newspapers regularly, as well as in circulated poems and private correspondence. Her dress, behavior, and unique marriage set all the gossips abuzz at social gatherings. Celebrity had its costs, however. After a heavy snowfall in January 1804, the Baltimore *Federal Gazette* reported that some "troublesome" youngsters had struck "Madame Bonaparte" with a snowball as she rode with Jerome in a sleigh. An incensed Jerome "offered a reward of 500 dollars" for the "perpetrator" of the "evil," and "several lads [were] taken up by the constables."[48]

Before her marriage, Elizabeth had earnestly desired to be a member of a "public" family in the European sense, those "eminent, titled, and politically well-connected" families that "lived in the great world, constantly in the public eye, their doings reported in the public papers."[49] She wanted little to do with her own family, or with most other American families, who would only be publicly noticed at their marriages and deaths. Her choice of husband ensured that she would be a part of a family who lived in "the great world" and attracted international attention. According to Pichon, soon after the wedding, Elizabeth was "very proud of her position and thinks of nothing but enjoying the glamour that it affords her."[50] His insight was assuredly very near the mark.

Few American women's weddings became the subject of diplomatic correspondence. The international tensions that her marriage caused only added to Elizabeth's celebrity. Decades later, when she saw it asserted in Jerome's memoirs that it must have been "pleasing to her vanity" to think of becoming "a member of a family whose name was echoing through two worlds," Elizabeth wrote "True" in the margins next to this passage.[51]

Elizabeth's clothing alone ensured her a spot in the public eye and in public conversation. Apparently, Jerome had sent for an enormous trousseau for his new wife from one of the most fashionable couturiers in Paris, including a mantilla and dress made of black lace and others of silk and satin.[52] Everything that Elizabeth wore from this shipment would have been *au courant* in France but daringly ahead in the United States. In the 1790s, French styles, in more modest forms, had begun to dominate the American fashion scene. The Grecian-style dresses appealed to American women. Styles modeled on ancient civilizations predominated into Napoleon's reign, and he even caused his own fashion legacy. After his campaigns in Egypt in the late 1790s, turbans became all the rage for female headdress and Dolley Madison's signature fashion feature.[53] American women in the early nineteenth century received their fashion news from a variety of periodicals and newspapers. The *Port Folio*, a magazine published in Philadelphia in the early 1800s, regularly featured a column updating women on the latest fashions.[54] Letters from travelers abroad also chronicled, to the smallest detail, the dress and hairstyles of gentlemen and, especially, ladies. Samuel Latham Mitchill, a Republican congressman from New York City, informed his wife and other female relatives that, in Washington, "the Ladies dress with as few Clothes and as great a display of shapes as ever[;] and their bonnets are worn quite as much askew."[55] Any woman, European or American, who sought attention and status had to stay abreast of the most recent fashion trends.

Fully aware of their effect, Elizabeth consciously and carefully selected her clothes when attending events in Washington, Baltimore, or New York in the months after her wedding. She purposefully decided to follow a French fashion that exposed bosom, arms, and back and barely hid what remained behind thin fabrics that clung to the torso and legs. Benjamin Henry Latrobe, the chief architect of the capitol, attested that, though "Jerome and Madam Bonaparte have amused us considerably for the last fortnight," Elizabeth's dress had "much scandalized the lovers of Drapery and disgusted the admirers even of the naked figure."[56] From Annapolis, Charles Carroll wrote of hearing "strange reports" of "Madame Bonaparte's dress on public occasion" or, perhaps more accurately, *"of her no dress."* Gossip had related to him that she "goes to public assemblies nearly naked, or so thinly covered that all her charms are exposed, and little left to the imagination."[57] Soon after the spectacle at Robert Smith's ball, which became "the general topic of conversation in all circles," Congressman Simeon Baldwin reported to his wife in Connecticut that "Several of the Gent[lemen] who saw her say they could put all the cloaths she had on in their vest pockett."[58] Aaron Burr, a notorious womanizer, was one of a very few commentators who believed that however scantily clad, Elizabeth dressed "with taste and simplicity."[59] As letters detailing her attire spread rapidly throughout the country, her celebrity status was ensured. Louisa Catherine Adams reported to her mother-in-law in Massachusetts that Madame Bonaparte made "a great noise" in the capital, in part owing to her "almost naked" appearances at balls.[60] Catherine Harper, who had known Elizabeth since she was a girl, asked her husband whether he had "visited Madame as yet" to verify "the reports we hear [in Annapolis] respecting her singularity of dress." Harper was "inclined to doubt it unless I read it from some one who saw her." She just could not believe that Jerome would "suffer his wife to appear as they say she has done, if he has any real attachment for her."[61] For Jerome, however, Elizabeth simply dressed like his fashionable French sisters; for Elizabeth, such dress simply elicited the desired social response.

Far from shrinking from public attention, as well-mannered ladies were supposed to do, Elizabeth, like any good celebrity, sought to create it. At the Smith ball, as Baldwin heard, Elizabeth "did not appear at all abashed when the inquisitive Eyes of the young Galants led them to chat with her tete a tete."[62] One 1804 visitor to Baltimore noted that "the much talked of Madame Bonaparte" appeared at his lodging house "either for the purpose of visiting some person of her acquaintance, or to expose to public view, those charms, which, no doubt, she is conscious of possessing."[63] Elizabeth relished her role as a national celebrity and cultivated it in a way that shocked many modest republican Americans. She defied the normal conventions of "female character," which one Philadelphia writer in 1806 characterized as a "modest reserve" and "retiring delicacy, which avoids the public eye, and is disconcerted even at the gaze of admiration."[64]

Choosing the husband and the fashions she did ensured public attention and became two of the main means Elizabeth used to achieve and maintain celebrity. While her connection with Jerome gained her celebrity in an abstract form, using clothing and her body to capture public interest allowed her to cultivate her celebrity in a very visible way. Both historically and today, dress commingles the private and the public in a unique and powerful way. As material objects, clothes possess a symbolic value in a culture, creating and projecting individual and social identity at the same time. The fashions one chooses to wear reflect highly personal choices, but these choices are only evident and understood when one is in public. Then and now, a community commonly understood the multiple meanings clothing possessed. In the early republic, Elizabeth's community—from the rich to the poor—assigned clear meanings to the vast array of men's and women's attire. Certain people wore certain kinds of clothing. The wealthy dressed in luxurious fabrics with exquisite details; those below them dressed in rougher fabrics with simpler details; the poorest dressed in the coarsest woolens and linens. What men and women wore played a crucial role in how they presented their identity in public and, in turn, how the public recognized the status and identity of an individual.[65] Those at the top of society were expected to dress one way; those at the bottom in a different but no less identifiable way. And those who wanted to proclaim certain affiliations or interests did so through dress.

Elizabeth clearly understood the power of clothing since she chose outfits that were guaranteed to cause a sensation, even a spectacle, for public occasions. Her clothing choices reveal a "self-consciously public manifestation" of her beliefs, of what she thought about her self, her destiny, and her country.[66] The cut, quality, and style of her dresses and accessories all mattered. Such reliance on fashion necessarily involved a willingness to have people look at her body. People had to notice her body as they examined her clothing. Female celebrity, so reliant on fashions and appearance, had a corporeal aspect to it that made more modest women blush. Rosalie Stier Calvert informed her mother that though "the clothes [women in Washington] wear are extremely becoming," some of them "display a little too much." "Madame Bonaparte," she continued, wore "dresses so transparent and tight that you can see her skin through them, no chemise at all," while "Mrs. Merry, the new English Ambassadress," was "very fat" and her dress covered "only with fine lace two objects which could fill a fourth of a bushel!"[67] Living in rural Virginia, Huldah Holladay assured her husband, after he had described Elizabeth's clothing and body to her in a letter, that she was "sensible that my ideas of propriety would be thought old fashioned and ridiculous to the fashionable circles in Town," but she declared herself "content to live beyond their influence."[68] A few months after her wedding, a friend sent Elizabeth a poem that later appeared in the Baltimore *American and Commercial Daily Advertiser* that described her body and discussed the potential importance of her marriage. Every part of Elizabeth's body received inspection. The poem rhapsodized about the "Charms which deck thy Form," a voice "like a vernal Breeze," her "speaking Eyes," "thy perfect Face," and "thy Bosom" which the "Whiteness of the Dove impart." An entire stanza was devoted to Elizabeth's new status, linking these physical charms with her marriage to Jerome:

> Thence *he*, whom Queens were proud to claim,
> Proud his imperial Hopes to share,
> Gives to thy Love his glorious Name,
> And finds his happiest Empire there.[69]

When first introduced into the elite society of Baltimore in 1804, Henry M. Brackenridge remembered distinctly that "all eyes were directed toward [Madame Bonaparte] as to the queen of the evening." At the party, Elizabeth carefully positioned her body and clothing to produce the best effect among the crowd: "She stood leaning upon a marble slab under a large looking-glass, and although quite small and delicate, was Venus herself."[70] The presentation of her physical self, cloaked in the appropriate attire, was all she needed to attract attention and promote her celebrity. Jerome figured nowhere in Brackenridge's recollections.

Elizabeth's air of cosmopolitanism, so evident in her dress, became a crucial part of her celebrity image. Both her husband and her clothes were distinctly French. Even before she traveled to Europe, her links with the Continent added to her cosmopolitan credentials. Dressing in the latest European fashions connected any American on the periphery of the early nineteenth-century Atlantic world to its very center. Any woman in Baltimore who had her hair dressed in the same style as a woman in Paris—with "gauze, muslin, cambric, crape, flowers, pearls and diamonds" placed in her hair by Alexander Lavigne, a hairdresser newly arrived from Paris—could claim some degree of cosmopolitanism.[71] But Elizabeth's claims went far beyond those of most other American women. She did not merely dress in American-made clothing that copied European styles, as many of her countrywomen did, but in clothing and jewelry that had actually come from Paris. She had the authentic thing, not a provincial substitute.

Yet the ambitions Elizabeth and Jerome held could never be satisfied on the periphery, no matter how fashionable they appeared to Americans. The pair longed for Paris. In June 1804, after cultivating attention and celebrity in Baltimore, Washington, Philadelphia, and New York City, Elizabeth and Jerome, trying to follow Napoleon's orders, took passage on a French ship. But just outside of New York's harbor, they encountered British ships that they feared would try to claim a wartime prize. Waiting for a safer passage, they continued their honeymoon travels with visits to Ballston Spa, Boston, and Niagara Falls—a journey only intrepid tourists took in this era. Their desperation to return to France drove them to risk their lives twice more. In October 1804, they boarded the ship *Philadelphia*. But an intense storm shipwrecked them in Delaware Bay, and the passengers and crew had to jump into lifeboats (allegedly with Elizabeth being the first to leap courageously overboard) and make their way to shore in heavy seas. That December, they tried again, boarding the French frigate *La Presidente* in Annapolis. This ship had recently brought the new French minister, General Louis-Marie Turreau, to the United States. Turreau carried instructions from Charles-Maurice de Talleyrand-Périgord, Napoleon's foreign minister, that ordered him "to avoid any occasion in which he might find himself in the presence of Miss Paterson" and forbade him "to treat her as the legitimate wife of Jerome." Talleyrand had also sent directions to all French officials in America: "to urge Jerome to return to France" but only on a French ship and only by himself.[72] *La Presidente* provided the perfect means. Jerome arrived in Annapolis with Elizabeth, and the captain of the ship, perhaps unaware of the emperor's orders, welcomed them both aboard. As had been the case six months earlier, though, British ships waited outside of the harbor, forcing the ship to turn around. The couple returned to Baltimore once again.

News from France was worrisome. Napoleon remained strongly opposed to their marriage and had taken steps to end it. Soon after learning of the wedding, Napoleon had applied to Pope Pius VII to annul the marriage formally, claiming—falsely—that it had been hastily performed by a Spanish priest and declaring that, as ruler of Catholic France, he could not have a Protestant among his family. He offered the pope a crown of jewels if he cooperated. Tired of being browbeaten by the hot-tempered emperor, Pope Pius, after establishing that the highest-ranking Catholic clergyman in the United States had married Elizabeth and Jerome, decided that there was no solid reason for an annulment. He boldly defied Napoleon and declared the marriage valid in the eyes of the church. This decision helped produce a huge rupture between the two powerful men. An enraged Napoleon threatened to remove the pope from office and make Paris the center of the church. To his credit, Pope Pius never backed down, and the Catholic Church never annulled the marriage.[73] Napoleon turned next to a body that he could control—his council of state—and had them declare the marriage invalid under French law. Though probably unaware that the pope had sided with them, Jerome and Elizabeth knew they had to get to Napoleon as soon as possible to save their marriage and position.

In early 1805, their frustration probably increased as they read reports, from family letters and in newspapers, of Napoleon's grand coronation ceremony in December (where the emperor had taken the crown out of Pope Pius's hands and placed it on his own head). More disturbing was their discovery that a French civil tribunal had declared their marriage null and void. An enraged Napoleon ordered Jerome back to France, without his "little girl," even though by now she carried a possible imperial heir.[74] Worse still, her brother Robert reported from Paris, in letters sent in code, that Elizabeth might be jailed if she attempted to land in any area under Bonaparte's control. As stubborn as Napoleon, Elizabeth remained determined to accompany Jerome to France and meet her powerful brother-in-law. Deciding not to wait for another French ship, they chose a fast American merchant ship headed for Portugal that William Patterson probably chartered.[75] In March 1805, they set sail, hoping to persuade Napoleon to accept Elizabeth and make them an imperial prince and princess, like Jerome's brothers and sisters. Accompanying them on the voyage were Elizabeth's eldest brother, William; her friend Eliza Anderson; Jerome's secretary Le Camus; a Dr. Garnier (since Elizabeth was about five months pregnant); several servants, including a "mulatto Boy"; and apparently a "Baboon" that Jerome had purchased at some point in his travels.[76]

The ship *Erin* made a fast crossing of the Atlantic (in just twenty-one days), and the anxious newlyweds arrived in Lisbon in early April. Elizabeth's hopes were high as she had finally reached Europe after so many setbacks and a long journey across the Atlantic. Her courage was undaunted, though the trip had been somewhat difficult owing to her pregnancy. Both she and Jerome were excited and afraid. A year earlier, Napoleon had issued a decree that "prohibited all captains of French vessels from receiving on board the young person to whom Citizen Jerome has connected himself" and proclaimed that Elizabeth would "be not suffered to land" in any French territory.[77] When the pair finally arrived in Lisbon, an emissary from Napoleon informed Elizabeth and Jerome that *"Miss Patterson"* could not disembark. Elizabeth allegedly responded hotly, "Tell your master that *Madame Bonaparte* is ambitious, and demands her rights as a member of the imperial family."[78] She managed to get off the ship, spending three or four days with Jerome in Lisbon. Shopping and sightseeing, they planned their next move; but Napoleon ultimately made it for them. An escort sent by the emperor took Jerome as a virtual prisoner to see his furious brother. As they parted, Jerome assured Elizabeth of his undying love and pledged to her and their unborn child that, once he spoke with Napoleon in person, everything would be alright and they would be reunited. Though he expected to send for her first, he suggested that she be prepared to sail for Amsterdam and have their baby there, if necessary.

The story of Elizabeth and Jerome's struggles to cross the Atlantic and contact Napoleon captivated the American public and furthered their celebrity. Every time the couple set sail, newspapers and correspondents up and down the Atlantic coast reported it. Almost every week something appeared about them in a Baltimore, Philadelphia, New York, Boston, or Washington newspaper that would then be reprinted in various small-town newspapers for interested readers who had never seen Jerome or Elizabeth. Their shipwreck and the threat of capture by the British only led to increased fascination with the couple and their fate. Curiosity about how Jerome stood with his powerful brother also kept them a topic of conversation. When the French minister Turreau did not return Jerome's visit, the gossips supposed that Jerome was "in high Disgrace with the Emperor."[79] Nearly anyone could read in Washington's *National Intelligencer* the official letter to Pichon that relayed Napoleon's order cutting off Jerome's money and, more alarmingly, prohibiting French vessels from allowing Elizabeth on board and barring her entrance into France.[80] With Emperor Napoleon, President Jefferson, Secretary of State Madison, and other government officials involved in this romantic affair, Americans could not help being swept up in all of the drama surrounding this celebrated couple. After the pair finally sailed for Europe, another letter from Napoleon that reprimanded Jerome for his disobedience and offered forgiveness only if he returned to France alone appeared in American newspapers. The editor of Boston's *Columbian Centinel* predicted that since "the papers having lately announced that JEROME BONAPARTE, and his fair wife, have embarked from *Baltimore* for *Europe*, it is highly probable they will again become the theme of public discussion." "The manner," he concluded, "in which they will be received materially interests her countrymen."[81] Elizabeth and Jerome's true story of romance and intrigue often seemed like a novel and ensured the pair's celebrity.

But Elizabeth never appeared in Napoleon's court or became an official member of the imperial family. Frightened and worried, she heeded Jerome's directions to sail for Amsterdam with the rest of her traveling companions. But the portmaster there had received Napoleon's orders concerning Elizabeth and, fearing his wrath, would not allow the party either to land or to leave. The ship rode at anchor for eight days, surrounded by gunships and guard boats, as the passengers began to run out of food and grow concerned about Elizabeth and the impending birth. Finally, with the intervention of the American consul, the party was permitted to leave Amsterdam; they headed for England, where Napoleon's decrees held no weight. The welcome Elizabeth received there must have lifted her spirits considerably. At Dover, "Madame Bonaparte, with her suite, landed amidst a great concourse of spectators." According to the newspapers, "the most conspicuous persons" of the area called on her and "vie[d] in the offer of attentions."[82] With no idea when or if she would see her husband again, Elizabeth delivered their son, Jerome Napoleon Bonaparte, on July 7, 1805. She soon nicknamed him Bo.

The trip across the Atlantic with Jerome in the summer of 1805 proved disastrous for Elizabeth's dreams of a life in the glittering courts of Europe. But, on that trip, Elizabeth tasted, though only briefly, the sweetness of Europe's possibilities and international celebrity. Her stay in England lasted just a few months, but, even upon her landing in Dover, crowds gathered on the quay to catch a glimpse of the illustrious and reportedly beautiful woman who had defied Napoleon's orders. "The concourse of persons gathered to see Madame B. land was immense," according to William Stevenson, the captain of the *Erin*, "and it was with great difficulty she could get as far as the carriage." What must Elizabeth have been thinking when she stepped off the ship's gangway to the cheers of such a crowd? She must have believed that she had finally fulfilled her destiny. When a "great crowd was collected likewise at the Inn door and even on the Stairs and entry to get a sight of our fair country woman," Stevenson reflected that he knew "many American Ladies who would have almost sunk under those circumstances." But not Elizabeth. She was "far from shrinking at such a crowd" for she had been ready for such an occasion: she was now an international celebrity.[83] American newspapers kept her fellow citizens informed of her and Jerome's whereabouts in Europe and speculated about

Napoleon's response, Jerome's fidelity and manly honor (or lack thereof), and Elizabeth's fate. Readers in Baltimore, Washington, Boston, New York, and beyond eagerly anticipated each piece of news. Even in the frontier areas of Chillicothe, Ohio, Pittsburgh, Pennsylvania, and Nashville, Tennessee, people could read of the visits made to Elizabeth by "many distinguished persons" and the "attention" paid to her in London, as well as the exploits of Jerome and the most recent edicts by Napoleon concerning the marriage.[84]

Though already a sought-after celebrity in England, Elizabeth discreetly retired to a comfortable house in London to have her son and recover. When it was clear Jerome was not coming for her soon (or ever), friends suggested to Elizabeth that her circumstances would not allow her "to mix in the Gay World" in England. Gossips watched her every movement, and, whether she "mixed" in fashionable society or avoided it, they would make her "subject to the sarcastic remarks of a censorious world." Hoping to help her escape "prejudices that in the end would injure [her] Cause on the other side of the water," her friends advised her to return to the United States.[85] Elizabeth found that her coveted celebrity in England—France's enemy—might cause problems for her with Jerome and Napoleon for, as she informed her father, the English newspapers "often publish that I [have] appear[ed] in public when I am sitting quietly in my room."[86] Returning to Baltimore must have seemed the best course to reunite with Jerome and have her marriage accepted by Napoleon.

Elizabeth had envisioned a beautiful and brilliant future for herself and Jerome at Napoleon's grand court or even in their own kingdom. But the Bonapartes dashed her dreams. The couple had parted in Lisbon, still believing Jerome could convince Napoleon to change his mind and unaware of how angry Napoleon was or of his determination to make a dynastic marriage for Jerome. The emperor refused even to meet with Jerome until he wrote a letter of apology for his defiance. Writing on behalf of Napoleon, the minister of marine cautioned Jerome that if he insisted on remaining "connected" to Elizabeth he would "condemn" himself to "obscurity." "Without distinction, fame, or even fortune, how could you *bear the weight of the name with which you are honored?*"[87] Apparently, Jerome had very little courage or character. His desire for fame and fortune and his loyalty to his brother won out. Even as he continued to write romantic letters to Elizabeth, by mid-May 1805, he had renounced his marriage to her, reconciled with Napoleon, and returned to the navy. By October, he had been made a prince, and Napoleon went looking for a royal wife for his weak-willed brother. Attempting to justify his appalling treatment of his wife and newborn child, Jerome's memoirs later insisted on the sincerity of his love for Elizabeth, while stressing "the shame of two years of inaction [in the navy;] the regret of an important position lost because of his errors; the hope of regaining it; [and] the fear of his brother's anger, anger that he had dared to brave and that made kings tremble in their thrones."[88] For months, he continued to send letters and gifts, including clothing, jewels, and portraits of himself, with assurances of his love and promises of a reunion. But, in September 1805, a dejected Elizabeth and her baby sailed for the only place she could go, her father's house in Baltimore. It would be decades before she saw Jerome again.

By mid-1806, Jerome had sacrificed his wife and child for an imperial title. He consented to a divorce in exchange for being declared a prince of the Empire and promoted to admiral. In October 1806, a French diocesan court proclaimed Elizabeth Patterson and Jerome Bonaparte's marriage null and void, though the Catholic Church never agreed. Ten months later, in August 1807, Napoleon arranged a marriage between Jerome and Princess Catherine of Württemberg, a Protestant, and gave the couple the kingdom of Westphalia (now a part of Germany) to rule. Elizabeth had gambled on a happy, exciting future in imperial France and lost. In November 1806, a year after Elizabeth's return to the United States, the British secretary of legation, Sir Augustus John Foster, quipped that she had not known three years earlier that "she was so near the real Event" when she had announced that "she had rather be Mad[ame] Jer. B. one year tho she was to be nothing afterwards" than marry an American.[89] While Elizabeth never became a princess or a queen, she insisted on retaining the name Bonaparte for the rest of her life.

A dispirited Madame Bonaparte, as most people now called her, returned to Baltimore with her young son in the fall of 1805 to face the people she had denigrated as simple and boring and the town that represented nothing to her but obscurity. Though still a celebrity and much talked about because of her dramatic story, many Americans could not help but gloat over her ruined hopes. While Foster expressed pity for Elizabeth, he reported to his mother that many "illnatured Americans" said "she deserved it—for her Vanity."[90] Even those who felt sorry for her often ascribed much of the blame to her. When Louisa Catherine Adams learned from the Boston newspapers that "Poor Madame B. has lost her Husband," she admitted that she "pit[ied] her from my heart" but thought that "this however is a misfortune which she must have expected."[91] Elizabeth's celebrated ambition now brought her pity and condemnation.

Though cast out of the glittering cosmopolitan world for which she had longed, Elizabeth was determined to make the best of her situation. Her ambition may have been bruised, but it was not beaten. After spending about a year recovering from her pregnancy and Jerome's perfidy, and perhaps also hiding from the gossips (in Baltimore, she remembered, "people are always on the watch"), Elizabeth emerged from her father's house ready to restore her celebrity.[92] As one of her friends admonished her, "nature never put so much beauty & wit together to languish away in obscurity." "Brilliant scenes yet await you."[93] Elizabeth must have agreed; by late 1806, she had recaptured public attention with her fashions and her figure. While visiting from Boston, Sophia May attended a party at Judge Samuel Chase's house and "saw the largest collection of Baltimore Ladies that I have yet seen, some very handsome girls." "Among the most conspicuous," she informed her mother, "was Madame Bonaparte[,] a lovely little creature[;] she was dressed in a Black Lace Robe over pink" with "a compleat and elegant suit of pearl and topaz" that "became her wonderfully." Ballroom gossips said that Jerome had sent the dress and that it was worth an incredible "1500$."[94] Elizabeth quickly returned to the social whirl with even more allure than when she had possessed her husband. She now had to rely solely on her own efforts—her clothing, jewelry, bodily display, and cosmopolitan manners—to cultivate her status and popularity.

Still, it must have been humiliating to read in American newspapers the details of Jerome's grand royal wedding to the Princess of Württemberg in October 1807 and to know that everyone else was reading them as well, not just in New York, Philadelphia, and Washington but in remote sections of the country, such as Russellville, Kentucky. Perhaps she found some solace in those newspapers that headlined the occasion "JEROME BONAPARTE'S BIGAMY."[95] Initially, some people may have been upset with her for marrying the kind of man she did, or they may have even laughed at her misfortune. But when the Bonapartes—a low-born family from nowhere—repudiated one of their own fellow citizens—a moral, if not modest, young woman from an excellent family—the American press quickly took her side. The gentlemen's magazine *The Observer* published a scathing and satirical piece about Jerome's sudden rise to king of Westphalia in December 1807. On the next page, it presented an ode entitled "To Elizabeth," written from Jerome's point of view that assigned him "an aching heart that bled in love forlorn" and a wounded "throbbing breast" that proclaimed "all hopes of thee, O happiness are vain" with "Eliza lost!"[96] Elizabeth seems to have weathered this surely mortifying turn of events quite well. Instead of modestly retiring back into her father's house as an abandoned woman, she presented herself in public by attending parties, visiting friends in Washington and elsewhere, and dressing lavishly.

Whether in the capital or in Baltimore, Elizabeth boldly flaunted her French fashions and Bonaparte connection, modeled herself after European aristocrats, and maintained her place as one of the most fashionable and influential women in the new nation, even after Napoleon's annulment and Jerome's remarriage. Her beauty, wit, European polish, and name formed a powerful combination that ensured her national attention and social popularity. Instead of hiding her tragic fate, as many divorced women did, she flaunted it, and her celebrity status grew. One of her closest friends, Eliza Anderson (later the wife of the architect Maximilian Godefroy), who had accompanied her to Lisbon and had remained with her in England to the end, alerted Elizabeth in June 1808 that "you must know that your celebrity has reached the Inhabitants of Trenton," New Jersey, for "wherever I go, I am questioned about you."[97] Even on a boat to Albany, New York, Anderson heard Elizabeth "very frequently spoken of" among the passengers. She "listened to a million of lies, & a thousand speeches retailed for you which you never made."[98] Elizabeth was now such a celebrity that not only were her life story and her appearance well known but so were her words, even if fictional.

Even without her French husband, she was fully aware that her name and son gave her enormous prestige, especially in the nation's capital. Washington was the perfect place for a woman desperate to assert a claim to public admiration despite having been abandoned. Elizabeth's skills were well-suited for the burgeoning capital as Washington served as a "theater" with "public stages" throughout the city and people constantly making well-crafted appearances and assessing others' performances.[99] It was one of the best locales for an American celebrity to shine. Samuel Mitchill's wife, Catherine, reported from the capital that "here the wise and learned of the nation are assembled, and here too, the rich & the fashionable come to display their equipage and grandeur."[100] The House of Representatives attracted a large audience of women and men for the debates, which offered a chance for congressmen to attain celebrity or even earn a share of fame with the right speech. In the political pressure cooker that was the early capital, semiprivate spaces that included men and women, such as drawing and dining rooms, also served as places of spectacle and stages to create celebrity.[101] Longtime Washington denizen

Margaret Bayard Smith commented that drawing rooms in the capital were "centre[s] of attraction" and "afford[ed] opportunity of seeing all these whom fashion, fame, beauty, wealth or talents, have render'd celebrated."[102]

For much of the decade after her return to the United States, Elizabeth was an attraction in Washington, even during the War of 1812. Usually accompanied by her aunt Nancy Spear, who loved attending congressional debates, capital society awaited her arrival during the winter season. According to one observer, Elizabeth "seem[ed] delighted with Washington and every body here appear[ed] delighted with her."[103] In the fall of 1811, Catherine Mitchill called Elizabeth and her aunt "the two most important personages here at present." The "splendid equipage" in which Elizabeth rode around the capital only added to her celebrity and glamour.[104] Many particularly noted her appearance at all of the important parties and even the horse races. At one of Dolley Madison's famous levees that was crammed with over two hundred guests, "Mrs. Jerome Bonaparte," in Congressman Abijah Bigelow's opinion, "appeared to excite as much attention as Mrs. Madison[;] I thought rather more."[105] Congressmen and cabinet officials often wished to make her acquaintance. Vice President Elbridge Gerry called her his "fair friend and favorite."[106] Delaware's George B. Milligan admitted that "even [Virginia's John] Randolph has ceased to be the 'snarling Cynic' he used to be and gazed on her with delight."[107] Many also attended parties that Elizabeth held in the drawing room of her rented house and spread the message about this fashionable, beautiful, and vivacious public woman. The American minister to Sweden, Jonathan Russell, assured Elizabeth that her "fame" was well known.[108] And European diplomats also sought an introduction, partly out of curiosity and partly from political calculations. Who knew whether this beautiful American mother of a male Bonaparte might ultimately play an important role in Napoleon's Europe?

Elizabeth's friendship with First Lady Dolley Madison also bolstered her celebrity status and ensured her a coveted spot in the inner circle of the capital's exclusive society, regardless of the opinions of some Washington matrons. Indeed, until Elizabeth rented her own lodgings in 1811, she usually stayed with the Madisons in the Executive Mansion while visiting the city. Dolley Madison enjoyed the company of young women and sought close emotional ties with them; so she readily welcomed the young woman from Baltimore who seemed to have been treated so unfairly by life.[109] On receiving news that Elizabeth would once more be back in Washington in late 1813, Madison "rejoiced in the proposal of your return to us," assuring Elizabeth that "such is the interest you ex[c]ite in all who know you, that I trust your time here will glide happily on." While the War of 1812 raged around them, Elizabeth and Madison visited each other and, whenever Elizabeth returned to Baltimore, corresponded about fashions, friends, and Elizabeth's intended trip to France. Both women enthusiastically followed the latest fashions, though Madison more modestly than Elizabeth, and the older woman often relied on the younger to provide her with what was most *à la mode*, especially for her celebrated turbans. "I will avail myself of your taste," Madison wrote to her "precious" Elizabeth, "in case, you meet with any thing elegant in the form of a Turban, or even any thing brilliant to make one, such as gause or lace flower'd with Gold or Silver."[110] Madison's unwavering support of Elizabeth assuredly helped Elizabeth's continued celebrity and public acclaim. Madison controlled some of the most important political and cultural spaces in the capital and, by giving Elizabeth unlimited access to them, guaranteed her plenty of time in the celebrity center.

Continued speculation about the imperial destiny that possibly awaited Elizabeth and her son also fueled public fascination with her and enhanced her celebrity status. Such prospects were rich fodder for gossips, of keen interest to politicians, and of real import to the refugee French who had settled in the United States. "All the Frenchmen in Philadelphia," according to an 1808 report, discussed Elizabeth and her son's future and "agree[d] that there is not a shadow of a doubt but that Bo will be splendidly provided for" and that whatever Elizabeth "asked would be granted." Whether she would remarry also preoccupied gossips for years. At a mineral springs resort in 1808, Eliza Anderson heard and "contradicted most womanfully an absurd report that [Elizabeth was] going to be married to a Mr Black" of Boston.[111] In 1809, Lydia Hollingsworth, who lived near the Patterson household in Baltimore, wrote to her cousin that "Madame Bonaparte makes our street quite gay" by being the focus of attention and speculation. "Betts are made," she reported, as to whether Sir Charles Oakley, the secretary to the British legation, would propose to her since "every evening . . . he takes tea and is with her until ten at night." The neighbors suspected this was an affair of some importance since Elizabeth was "dressed with care every visit he pays."[112] The public, as usual, noticed her clothing and interpreted its significance. The fascination with and gossip about Elizabeth was unrelenting, but that was what celebrity required.

In spite of the scandal that she caused, Elizabeth also continued to attract attention and, more important, to construct her social identity by wearing the French fashions she so admired. She had returned from Europe in 1805 with an enormous wardrobe of morning dresses, evening gowns, hats, jewelry, and more. That same year, even though he had already forsaken her, Jerome sent his "dear, well-loved wife" thirty thousand francs worth of clothes and thirty-two thousand francs worth of jewelry.[113] From their earliest days, Jerome had showered her in jewelry, probably her first extravagant pieces, including a thousand-dollar pair of diamond earrings, a diamond ring, and a double-strand garnet necklace with, ironically, the word "*fidélité*" engraved on the to-paz clasp.[114] Elizabeth was certainly well-equipped, therefore, for her public performances when she reappeared on the fashionable scene. In November 1811, Catharine Mitchill reported on the sensation that Elizabeth caused at a presidential dinner by wearing a dress that "exposed so much of her bosom" and "laid bare" her back "nearly half way down to the bottom of her waist." "The state of nudity in which she appeared," she informed her sister, "attracted the attention of the Gentlemen, for I saw several of them take a look at her bubbies when they were conversing with her."[115] In a February 1812 letter, Phoebe Morris, while visiting Dolley Madison at the Executive Mansion, explained why Elizabeth was adored as a celebrity: she had the whole package. "How I wish you could see Madame Bonaparte in all the splendor of dress, and all the attractions of beauty. I think I never beheld a human form so fault-less. To the utmost symmetry of features is added so much vivacity, such cap-tivating sweetness! and her sylphic form 'thinly veiled' displays all the graces of a Venus de Medicis. She appears particularly lovely in a fine crepe robe of a beautiful azure colour interwoven with silver, in this attire she is truly celes-tial, and it is impossible to look on any one else when she is present."[116] When Elizabeth chose that gown for the occasion, it was undoubtedly for this exact effect. When an invasion seemed possible in May 1813, as British ships lurked off the coast, Elizabeth hastened from Baltimore to her rented house in Wash-ington, D.C., solely to "secure [her] Wardrobe."[117] Her clothing, of course, composed some of her most prized possessions and not only in financial terms. The dresses, jewelry, and accessories were the artillery she used in making such a powerful impact on the public stages of Washington and elsewhere. Her clothing had garnered her much of her celebrity and remained the pri-mary mode for expressing her public and private identities. Her French clothes empowered her, and she wore them with pride, confident that she represented the height of European style and culture. She was still Elizabeth *Bonaparte* after all, at least by her own reckoning. Though nicknamed "Madame Eve" and cautioned that she "must promise to have more clothes on" in order to receive invitations, Elizabeth ignored the warnings, certain that the social force of her French connections, including her clothes, would always gain her admittance into any refined gathering.[118]

Elizabeth ultimately calculated correctly. Though an abandoned woman with scandalous clothes and scandalous opinions, she spent few evenings alone and missed few parties. Indeed, she was one of the most sought-after women in the capital and elsewhere, regularly dining with foreign dignitaries (often aristocrats) and influential Americans. But Americans were conflicted about her: she both scandalized and attracted them. In the same 1811 letter in which she criticized Elizabeth's clothing, Mitchill praised her personality because Elizabeth did "not affect any superiority over others who have been less celebrated than herself." Mitchill even characterized her as "remarkable friendly."[119] Not all of Washington condemned her. One of Elizabeth's many male admirers, Samuel Colleton Graves, "had the pleasure" of hearing some of the capital's elites "speak of [her] in terms of the highest admiration and applause."[120] Poems celebrating her beauty and wit and focusing on her body, many written by lovesick swains, continued to appear in circulated form. One declared:

> My heart's in a blaze,
> When her foot she displays;
> From its Alcove of muslin or dimity.
> But fancy within, From her feet to her eyes;
> Enchanted by Satin and Symmetry
> *Venus* taught these wiles
> By which complasance smiles.[121]

Travelers to Baltimore or Washington longed to meet the famous and alluring American Bonaparte. When her daughter Maria visited Baltimore in 1818, Virginian Hetty Carr asked: "Have you ever seen Mrs Bonapart, & what do you think of her?"[122] On his way from Boston to Lexington, Kentucky, to become president of Transylvania University, Reverend Horace Holley walked "up and down on . . . the principal street [of Baltimore] for an hour [in an effort] to meet Mrs. Bonaparte." When she finally approached, he scrutinized

Figure 4. One of Elizabeth's scandalously thin gowns, possibly her wedding dress, ca. 1803. From A. M. W. Stirling, *A Painter of Dreams and Other Biographical Studies* (New York: John Lane Company, 1916).

her face and then "turned about to see her figure and walk." Holley promised himself to "take some pains" to "be introduced to her" and soon was. During a couple of evenings spent talking with Holley, Elizabeth appalled him with her harsh views of her native land. But he became infatuated with her anyhow—sending her songs about her "faultless beauty" and perfect "form" and informing his wife that she had "a new rival."[123] Holley's descriptive portrait of Elizabeth, sent in a letter to his wife, goes far to explain the public fascination with her and how she cultivated her celebrity. First, he described her body and appearance, revealing the intensity with which he, and assuredly many others, had studied her: "She is not tall, is inclined to corpulency, has dark hair and eyes, a fine complexion and color, a small mouth, pretty lips, teeth not perfect, a finely formed chest, and an admirable play of face and features." Then, he explained why so many people wanted to meet her and spend time with her: "She has full self-possession and command, possesses a great stock of anecdotes about living persons of celebrity in France, speaks French with great ease and eloquence, and is shrewd, quick, and discriminating. She has no stiffness, is not afraid of being addressed pleasantly, is accessible, and playful." When she recommended to him a book written by her friend, the archaeologist and artist Baron Vivant Denon, Holley immediately directed his wife to read it as well.[124] One wonders how Holley's wife felt after reading about such an extraordinary woman. Neither Mitchill nor Holley—nor hundreds more like them—were so outraged over Elizabeth's clothes or opinions that they refused to socialize with, or even admire, her. She represented the height of beauty, fashion, and cosmopolitanism.

Though many considered her scandalous, Elizabeth was a celebrity, and, even in the early 1800s, that status meant she helped set social trends, particularly in fashion and manners. In 1813, the year that Elizabeth received an official divorce through a legislative decree in Maryland, Sarah Gales Seaton, the wife of the editor of the *National Intelligencer*, declared that "Madame Bonaparte is a model of fashion, and many of our belles strive to imitate her . . . but without equal *éclat*, as Madame Bonaparte has certainly the most transcendently beautiful back and shoulders that ever were seen."[125] Elizabeth's image and éclat were so esteemed in American society that women yearned to look like her. Certain that her mother-in-law had heard that Elizabeth "is said to be the most beautiful Woman in the United States," Louisa Catherine Adams reported that a Mrs. Morton preened when told that "Mrs. B[onaparte] is reckoned very like her."[126]

With her scanty clothing, Elizabeth brazenly led a fashion trend among younger women—a trend many commentators found entirely inappropriate for American women and condemned. Many critics noted how the daring fashions not only concealed very little of a woman's body but also seemed to inflate a woman's sense of self. Dining in company with several fashionable young ladies in Philadelphia, Massachusetts senator Jonathan Mason found that the stylish women's revealing clothing should have inspired "more matrimony," but instead "the dress and extravagant ideas of the ladies themselves" scared off men. Most "young men of *our country*," Mason noted, "are not able to support the rank and grade which the ladies assume, particularly in dress." Worse still, for Mason, the dresses made women "so easy of access, so naked in their charms, that they destroy and satiate desire where they would wish to enkindle it."[127] Indeed, matrimonial advice books counseled young women that "a fine woman shows her charms to most advantage, when she seems most to conceal them." Making very clear what he meant by "charms," this author added, "the finest bosom in nature is not so as what imagination forms."[128] Some critiques were quite bawdy. In 1807, Joseph Fay and his male friends toasted "the *breastworks* of the fair Ladies of New York [which are]—like our harbour defenceless—they invite the Enemy."[129] Published criticisms were only slightly less suggestive. One Baltimore editor playfully suggested that "the only sign of *modesty* in the present dress of the Ladies is the *pink dye* of the stockings, which makes their legs appear to *blush* for the total absence of petticoats."[130] Creative minds penned and published numerous odes and poems to the new, more revealing French styles. People in Richmond, Virginia, in the summer of 1806 could read one "epigram" entitled "On Fashion":

> In *fair* Rebecca's *simpler* times,
> That damsel *veil'd* her beauteous *face*
> But damsels, *now*, to shun such crimes
> Scarce half conceal their *breasts* with *lace*.[131]

Abigail Adams considered the new "stile of dress," as she witnessed it in Washington in 1800, "an outrage upon all decency." The thin muslins with "nothing beneath but a chemise" served "perfectly to show the whole form." The "arm naked almost to the shoulder" and the lack of stays or a "hankerchief" across the bosom "fully displayd," according to Adams, the "rich Luxurience of naturs Charms." When Anne Bingham's daughter wore such a dress,

Adams declared that "every Eye in the Room has been fixed upon her . . . and you might litterally see through her." Of course, this had been the young lady's intention, and she had achieved the desired effect. Adams had to admit that the Bingham women were "fine," "in the first Rank," and "leaders of the fashion," but the more staid First Lady considered them going too far beyond "the decent Matron, or the modest woman."[132] After meeting in the capital "a young Lady more than usually undress'd," Senator John Quincy Adams crafted his own poetic lines of fashion commentary for his wife "to describe the effect which their exhibitions have a tendency to produce upon *Sensation*." Exclaiming that fashionable women wore little but a "fig-leaf" and walked about "though naked, not asham'd," Adams continued: "Already how Sally *now* reveals / To view, Back, Arms and Breast; / While a bare Spider's web conceals, / And scarce conceals the rest."[133] This condemnation of women's dress appeared not just in the cities where women of fashion congregated but into the interior of the country as well. In 1806, the *Western American* of Louisville, Kentucky, published a poetical critique of the current fashion and a reprimand to female readers:

> A bosom should remain unseen,
> Hid from the lawless glance;
> No charm there is, so great, I ween,
> Which fancy's dream cannot enhance.
> The scanty robe, and bosom bare,
> Wither the bed of virgin shame;
> The sleeveless arms and forward stare,
> Ill become the virgin's name.[134]

Women's fondness for fashionable clothing and the resulting expenses on temporary fripperies that followed the vagaries of fashion spurred criticism of women as well for valuing ornament over the traditional responsibilities of wives and mothers.[135] Some writers knew that clothing was one of the primary ways women could gain attention and even celebrity and condemned women for that. D. Fraser, in his *The Mental Flower Garden: Or, an Instructive and Entertaining Companion for the Fair Sex* (1807), proclaimed that women set "so high a value . . . upon trifles" because of "the violent desire they have of attracting the eyes of the multitude." If this "fanaticism" entered a woman's head, he warned, "it excludes every other thought: they then love shew and pomp, and live to be looked at."[136] These kinds of women, Fraser made clear, would not make good wives and mothers. Similarly, the editor of Baltimore's *American* saw the current immodest fashions and women's love of display leading only to "the disgrace of our fair country-women." Their shameful "desire to 'shine in the croud'" in their stylish clothing equally revealed their preference for "the gaudy tinsel of the *empty* coxcomb" over the "solid merit" of a republican gentleman.[137] This assessment easily could have been a response to Elizabeth's celebrity and her choice of husband.

The galaxy of celebrated beauties who gathered in the cities to display their fashionable clothing paid little heed to such criticism. Just like Elizabeth, they knew their shocking dress helped attract attention to themselves at balls and parties. Those seeking celebrity were far more interested in the sensation their clothes could create than in following the strictures of more modest Americans. Elizabeth had provided an excellent model for these women and some decidedly followed her. Though often a leader in social trends, Elizabeth still had rivals in the competition for celebrity status, even in Washington; one of the fiercest competitors was from her own environs, Elizabeth Caton of Annapolis. George Milligan considered Elizabeth's "only rival in this part of the world [to be] Betsy Caton." But he made a fine distinction between the two celebrity-seeking women: Caton was "not as much admired" as Elizabeth but was "more esteemed."[138] Apparently, Elizabeth was the better celebrity, but Caton earned more respect. The Reverend Horace Holley went into greater detail explaining the difference between the two well-known women and why a "coldness" existed between them that "began at Washington, and was completed at Paris" after 1815. Elizabeth had aligned herself with "French society"; Caton, a member of "lord Wellington's coterie," became an American representation of "English society." According to what Holley had heard from the gossips, "Miss Caton is said to be the best read, and to have the best [intellectual] powers," while Elizabeth was "said to have the most quickness, shrewdness, & variety."[139]

As the comments above attest, female celebrities were women in public, at a time when the words *public women* usually meant prostitutes. But Elizabeth and women like her, such as Dolley Madison and Elizabeth Caton, were women who not only were out in public attracting attention (like prostitutes) but also possessed public personas. That these women received admiration instead of condemnation certainly reveals much about the intricacies of class, gender, and morality during the early national period. A refined woman's morality went unquestioned until she committed some obvious, serious transgression. These assumptions among the elite allowed the women of their class much leeway in their behavior. They could dress even more seductively than a prostitute for balls and dinner parties at the finest homes without being denied entrance. Indeed, the very gowns that clung to their torsos and legs gained them attention and made them celebrated. And, once celebrated, these elite public women acquired power that they could wield in ways not usually considered "female" without risking their reputations. First Lady Dolley Madison, though wearing the latest styles (but not as daring as Elizabeth's), cultivated a public image of refined, charming femininity in order to help bind the nation together, foster cooperation in the capital, and even gain the personal power to grant political favors.[140] She could hold such power because she never engaged in any behavior that could have been considered immoral. Elizabeth, too, was a public woman who exercised power, was known throughout the country and admired (though never on a par with Madison), and never had her morality questioned—in spite of her scandalous clothing. Both of these successful public women knew how to walk social lines carefully, indulging in excessive behavior without tarnishing their pubic images.

Elizabeth's continuing social successes, notwithstanding the admonishments she sometimes suffered, relied on a variety of factors. Though abandoned and then divorced, she was still from one of the finest families in the United States. That certainly shielded her somewhat. Her close friendship with Dolley Madison probably protected her as well in the capital's social circles. When the wives of European diplomats visited the United States, they reaffirmed Elizabeth's claims to cosmopolitanism and her powerful social influence since they dressed like her and acted like her.[141] Further, the kind of power that American women could exercise—social far more than political—seems to have given them more freedom than American men to emulate European styles. But, most important, Elizabeth had never totally breached society's moral boundaries. She was never tainted with sexual scandal, avoiding social censure and ostracism. In her case, a lack of feminine republican virtue only occasionally was equated with a lack of feminine moral virtue. Elizabeth was charming, witty, and beautiful, and had led a fascinating life—all ideal qualities for an excellent dinner-party guest. She captivated most men and charmed many women. While many who met her criticized her in letters or in whispers, few were so scandalized that they shunned her. When Lydia Hollingsworth encountered Elizabeth in one of her daring dresses at a Twelfth Night

Ball in 1810, she simply commented to her cousin that "Madame Jerome was there as handsome as ever but, a little more in the fashion of uncovering."[142] That she was simultaneously criticized and feted reveals more about Americans' ambivalence and confusion over elite women's place in American culture in the early years of the nineteenth century than about Elizabeth's own views or actions.

Elizabeth knew that the potential for hostility lurked below the surface and that the public could quickly turn against her. When she asked Dolley Madison in late 1814 to find out whether the American minister to the Netherlands, William Eustis, and his wife would let her accompany them on their Atlantic voyage, she cautioned her friend to inquire with the utmost discretion to avoid "the mortification of a refusal." She begged Madison "not to mention in Washington my having written to you on this subject" for the "Public are so malicious & so much pleased when people meet with disappointments that I wish to avoid gratifying them again at my expence."[143] The world had already laughed at her for the "disappointments" of not becoming part of the imperial family of Bonapartes and being abandoned by her husband; she was not going to give the public any more reason to be malicious instead of admiring.

After Elizabeth left the United States for her long-awaited return to Europe in 1815, her name appeared less frequently in newspapers and people gossiped less frequently about her and her French clothing, son, and ex-husband. She probably little cared. Before her departure, she requested letters of introduction from several prominent American men with European ties. In doing so, Elizabeth sought to have her celebrated reputation acknowledged by fellow Americans and her claims to continental celebrity supported. These letters laid the groundwork for the construction of her international public self, the identity that she would present in Europe and that would hopefully win her the acclaim and admiration she enjoyed in the United States. Surely, Elizabeth knew she was stepping onto a grander stage, filled with far more luminaries than in Baltimore or Washington. A national celebrity by 1815, she wanted to guarantee that she would become an international one as well. Wealthy Baltimore merchant Robert Gilmor informed a Madame Liccama of Utrecht that "the interesting history of my amiable countrywoman," "Madame Jerome Bonaparte, . . . would of itself be sufficient to make her friends in Europe." Yet, he made clear that her dramatic life story was not her only claim to celebrity status. "Her own agreeable qualities & distinguished personal advantages will offer a superior attraction," he predicted, and "prove worthy of public attention."[144] John Willink, the American representative of an Amsterdam banking family, wrote to his brother William in Europe that the "beautiful and much admired" Elizabeth was "much entitled to" any "attentions & civilities" that William could afford. Indeed, John made clear that her departure from the United States for Europe was "among the misfortunes which befall this Country."[145] Elizabeth used her familial connections to gain letters from leading American statesmen. Her uncle, Senator Samuel Smith, penned a letter introducing her to the Marquis de Lafayette—a savvy move that ensured her access to some of the best society in France. She even requested a letter from the retired president Thomas Jefferson. While he let her know that most of his French acquaintances had been "all swept off by the violence of the revolution, or have since been withdrawn from life by it," he did provide an introduction to Albert Gallatin, the American minister to France.[146] This introduction would prove the most fruitful for Elizabeth. Not only would the Gallatins secure her entrée into diplomatic and court circles; they became some of her truest friends and even her hosts when she visited Paris.

Elizabeth aimed for transatlantic celebrity. She desired to make a splash at such centers of cosmopolitan culture as London, Paris, and Geneva, not just on the periphery in Washington, Baltimore, and Philadelphia. She felt confident in her abilities, but not all of her countrymen—or even family members—agreed. Washington Irving, once an ardent admirer, worried about whether Elizabeth, "a little star," would have the impact she hoped for in Europe since there were "so many huge Stars & comets thrown out of their orbits & whirling about the world at present."[147] But Elizabeth quickly learned the requirements for fashionable celebrity in Europe. She had expertly cultivated her cosmopolitan image in the United States, and it served her well abroad. Not long after her arrival, she moved out of a boarding house in London and into a rented house beside her "amiable friends, Sir Arthur and Lady Brooke Falkener." Her British friends had "advised [the] move, as people of fashion never live in boarding-houses." And she readily grasped that one needed to befriend only those people who were well-known, for "in this country distinctions in society are so much attended to, that connections with people who are not known, however honest and respectable they may be, are not tolerated." In the fashionable world of Europe, reputation mattered more than character. As she had done as a young woman in Maryland, Elizabeth studied hard and learned the most important lessons for success in these exclusive circles. "All my conduct is calculated," she admitted soon after her arrival.[148] If one word, movement, or expression was out of place, everything in this competition could be lost.

Drawing on her consummate talents and skills, Elizabeth did become a transatlantic celebrity after 1815. That she achieved social success in the most brilliant European circles never astonished her. Knowing she was destined for such environments, it never surprised her that she moved within them so easily and successfully. As she prepared for an exclusive ball in England in September 1815, she assured her father: "I get on extremely well, and I assure you that altho' you have always taken me for a fool, it is not my character here. In America I appeared more simple than I am, because I was completely out of my element. It was my misfortune, not my fault, that I was born in a country which was not congenial to my desires. Here I am completely in my sphere . . . and in contact with modes of life for which nature intended me."[149] Achieving celebrity and renown in Europe—where it mattered most to her—required hard work, but it was work that seemed natural to her. Her efforts were certainly assisted by her reputation. She already was an important enough personage that British newspapers announced her arrival in England.

Almost immediately, as James McElhiney informed her father, "considerable attention is paid to her by Familys of the first Distinction which of course must be gratifying to her."[150] Even the Duke of Wellington became an admirer, paying special attention to her at parties and even giving her a little dog that she reportedly, and ironically, named Napoleon. She had similar scenes when she visited Geneva, where she was again invited to every party, ball, and dinner. Soon after her arrival in Paris, the restored Bourbon King Louis XVIII invited her to appear at his court. The offer must have been tempting—finally a chance to appear on the stage for which she had felt destined—but she politely refused, citing her loyalty to Napoleon despite the unhappiness he had caused her. In France, England, Switzerland, and Italy, aristocrats, artists, writers, socialites of all kinds, and even members of the exiled Bonaparte family sought her company and appreciated her qualities. The fashionable French, including Jeanne-Françoise Récamier and Voltaire's ward and protégé the Marquise de Villette, embraced her as one of their own and hoped to assuage some of the pains that their former ruler had caused her. Talleyrand supposedly praised her wit and Germaine de Staël praised her beauty. Though normally cautious with regard to American visitors, they willingly opened their doors to her. An American who returned from Paris in 1816 described Elizabeth's "doors as surrounded[,] Stairs thronged with Dukes, Counts, Marquis." In this context, he reported, she was "a little Queen, giving & receiving the most supreme happiness."[151] Elizabeth felt finally in her proper element.

It is no surprise that Elizabeth was such a success in Europe. Her beauty, fashionable clothing and jewelry, and tragic story were as compelling in Europe as in America and ensured her celebrity status there, even in a much more competitive arena. But she held her own. Even famously beautiful women, such as Madame Récamier, thought Elizabeth "the most beautiful woman in the world" and told her so. Récamier considered Elizabeth "more beautiful even than the perfect Pauline Borghese," Napoleon's celebrated—and scandalous—sister. To this compliment, Elizabeth wittily replied: "Mais ça est bien impossible, vue que ma belle soeur est parfaitement belle" (But that is impossible, seeing that my sister-in-law is perfectly beautiful).[152] Princesses, aristocrats, socialites, and intellectuals wrote letters of introduction for this beautiful, witty American, so she could meet and charm others throughout Europe. When General Winfield Scott returned to Baltimore from Paris in 1816, he testified to Elizabeth's success among the most exclusive circles, "blazon[ing] forth [her] fame throughout the country." Elizabeth's cousin had heard Scott report that her "levee is crowded every morning with *la haute noblesse* and that the lowest rank admitted is a Lieut. General."[153] By the spring of 1816, a friend in London informed her that she had become so famous there that a publisher was soliciting subscriptions for "a Print of Mrs. Patterson, late Madame Jerome Bonaparte, after half length miniature by W. J. Newton[,] Taken from life." A print on "India paper" would cost one pound; color copies would be "a little more than two."[154] Sir William John Newton, a popular portraitist of the era, had painted Elizabeth while in London "as a Grecian woman collecting the folds of rich purple & gold drapery round her person & contemplating a Bust" that was also "a profile of" her. The image was "said to be an incomparable likeness," and Newton intended including it in an exhibition. She had another portrait of her as "Calypso," the sea nymph who delayed Odysseus on her island for several years.[155] The published engraving was probably one of these images. Not only could Europeans of all classes read about this romantic American beauty in the newspapers; they could also purchase her image as a permanent remembrance and testament of her celebrity.

Just as she inspired some women in cities along the East Coast to follow her methods for seeking celebrity in American society, Elizabeth similarly inspired a more select group of wealthy women to seek celebrity abroad. In 1816, not long after Elizabeth, the three older Caton sisters—her rivals from Maryland—

arrived in England. The trip ostensibly had been planned to improve Mary Caton Patterson's health, but the sisters seemed to hope that a trip to the cosmopolitan centers of Europe would allow them to achieve the same kind of transatlantic celebrity that their neighbor Madame Bonaparte possessed. According to Edward Patterson, Elizabeth Caton's "great ambition" was "to dazzle the Courts of Europe with her charms & accomplishments. . . . There she can be [esteemed] & there she must & will go."[156] Both Elizabeth and the Catons considered Maryland too small a stage for their ambitions. Elizabeth had left London for Paris several months before the Caton sisters arrived to discover her high standing in British society. "I have frequently heard you spoken of with great admiration in this Country," Mary enviously admitted to Elizabeth. The Caton sisters' beauty and wealth made a great impression, and they were soon the talk of England, often being referred to as the "American Graces." The sisters, like Elizabeth, possessed the attributes needed to make a woman a celebrity in Europe and, again like Elizabeth, knew how to compete for acclaim and admiration in international circles. Yet all four of these women had to overcome the surprise some Europeans expressed that they came from the United States. Women with such attributes were supposed to be found only in Europe, not on the other side of the Atlantic. British critics in the early nineteenth century regularly "abused" American women for lacking social graces.[157] Furthermore, women worthy of being "celebrated" in Europe were supposed to be among the aristocracy or, at the very least, the landed gentry. When the widowed Mary Caton Patterson later married the Marquis of Wellesley (the Duke of Wellington's brother), Richard Lalor Sheil remarked after seeing her at a ball that "nobody would have suspected that she had not originally belonged to the proud aristocracy to which she had been recently annexed." "She had nothing of la bourgeoise parvenue," Sheil continued. "She executed her courtesies with a remarkable gracefulness, and her stateliness sat as naturally upon her as though she inherited it by royal descent!"[158] That such beauties with such elegance and grace could be American guaranteed Elizabeth and the Caton sisters much attention on their first entrée into European society. Their success at winning and maintaining public acclaim in Europe proved their skills as transatlantic female celebrities.

The enhancement of Elizabeth's reputation in Europe secured her cosmopolitanism and celebrity for Americans. Though she had left their small orbit behind, American newspapers kept readers abreast of Elizabeth's movements around Europe, noting some of the exclusive events she attended. Now she was truly at the center of all that was fashionable. She had complete access to everything that was *au courant* in terms of people, clothing, behavior, and ideas. Elizabeth had even befriended some of the most celebrated women in Europe, such as the popular novelist Lady Sydney Morgan, the essayist the Marquise de Villette, the iconic Madame de Staël, the renowned beauty Madame Récamier, and the fashionable minor royals, Countess Teresa Guiccioli, Byron's mistress, and Princess Alexandre Caroline Galitzin of Russia. Many of the friends and family she had left at home acknowledged her coveted status at the cultural centers. That Elizabeth was "intimately acquainted with Lady Morgan" and regularly corresponded with her truly impressed the Reverend Horace Holley, and he was even more affected when Elizabeth shared with him some private letters written by other leading European celebrities.[159] Some Americans even inflated her cultural power. John Spear Smith alerted her that "it is very generally reported that you set the fashions in Paris!"[160] Friends and family members repeatedly asked her to purchase clothing, shoes, jewelry, watches, paintings, books, china, furniture, and other items in London, Paris, Rome, or Geneva since Elizabeth had direct access to all that was best and most fashionable.[161] Her aunt, for example, demanded dresses and especially bonnets—"I am distracted to get french Bonnets"—and Elizabeth was at the source.[162] Her brother Edward envied that she was "enjoying all the fashionable amusements of London." "What a contrast there must be," he exclaimed, "between London & Baltimore!"[163] Elizabeth's tremendous impact in the international world of celebrities impressed many on the periphery in her hometown and elsewhere in the United States. Before her sister-in-law, Mary Caton Patterson, became one of the most celebrated beauties in England herself, she probably yearned for similar acclaim when she wrote Elizabeth in late 1815: "They say you are the most lovely woman in the world."[164] Elizabeth assuredly enjoyed reading that report, coming from one of her earliest rivals. Eliza Anderson Godefroy delighted in hearing that Elizabeth was "the cynosure of Paris & that the Conqueror of the Conquerors of the Earth [Wellington] is already a victim to your charms."[165] The arrival of Elizabeth's letters was always an occasion in Baltimore as friends and family gathered around to hear them read. Elizabeth's aunt even met a Mr. Walsh "in the Street" who "entreated [her] to read him some of your letters from Paris." Elizabeth's cousin, John Spear Smith, had told Walsh that one of her letters was "so replete with good sense & sound Philosophy, displaying a Genius at once profound & elevated that he felt a great desire to see more." Her aunt concurred that "it was indeed a very amusing & excellent letter" and informed Walsh that she had kept all of Elizabeth's letters "under a conviction that one day or other they would be published."[166]

Elizabeth's international celebrity, of course, was not the only one to affect Americans. By the end of 1816, Marylanders had also heard of the "distinguished reception of the Catons in England." As with Elizabeth, Baltimore buzzed with excitement whenever one of their letters arrived.[167] Lydia Hollingsworth similarly attested that everyone in Baltimore regarded the Caton sisters as a "success" for their "object is attained!" Meeting the same standards as Elizabeth, they had "been patronized by Fashionable Folks and introduced to Lord Wellington! . . . and all the eclat (we are to presume) has been acquired, that any splendid Belles could receive." Since the Catons were "in high Fashion," their "good Friends" in Baltimore "minutely detail[ed] the particulars" of their successes.[168] Transatlantic celebrity was not an easy achievement, but both Elizabeth and the three Caton sisters managed to attain it, making them even more admired in their native land. Whenever she returned home from her European sojourns, Elizabeth experienced the benefits of her cosmopolitan credentials. With her stylish clothing and manners and her fascinating stories of high society, "she had become very amiable and of course very popular." According to her uncle Samuel Smith, "everyone sought her Society for she is most excellent company."[169] When she appeared again in Washington in 1818, she was often "the object of more . . . attention than any body else."[170] Similarly, while visiting Philadelphia on another brief return in 1825, she "received a great many attentions from the inhabitants."[171]

For much of her life, Elizabeth Patterson Bonaparte attracted public attention both at home in the United States and abroad in Europe. She had a host of admirers who praised her beauty, wit, and stylishness. She also had a host of critics who decried her behavior, opinions, and dress. Many of those who watched and assessed her went back and forth between the two camps, vacillating between admiration and condemnation, considering her both an influential woman of fashion and a most unusual, sometimes even scandalous, woman. They regarded her as a celebrity but also as a woman whose ways should not be followed. But this interest testifies to the strength of Elizabeth's determination to be someone known to the world at large. Like other American female celebrities in this era, she maintained a delicate balancing act, walking the fine line between acceptance and censure—a line that a number of women in the early republic, such as the hotel keeper's daughter and then senator's wife Peggy Eaton and the flamboyant writer and reformer Fanny Wright, crossed to their detriment.

While the fascination with Elizabeth waxed abroad during her long stays in Europe, it waned at home. After her departure for England in 1815, American newspapers and correspondence said less about her over the years. When American travelers encountered her in Europe, they generally reported the fact back home, but fewer people by the 1820s kept track of the events of her life as they once had. During her brief returns, she easily recaptured public attention. But she never stayed long in her native country, returning to Europe usually within a year. As such, her hold on public attention gradually weakened, as did her social influence in the United States. Being a celebrity in America required staying in the public eye, and, before the media age, this was difficult to do if one was not actually in the country, being spotted at fashionable gatherings and discussed in parlors and letters afterward. But, if she had been asked, her diminishing American celebrity would have hardly mattered to her. Being a celebrity with social power at home was not nearly as important to her as being a celebrity in Europe, even if she could only be a small star in an enormous galaxy of brighter luminaries and even if she enjoyed less influence than in her native land. At times, though, she did long for her adoring American audience. Finding herself "in the best society" in Europe, Elizabeth "much deplore[d] the absence of American friends to witness the estimation in which I am held."[172] Elizabeth's dream had been to become a part of a circle of kings, princes, and aristocrats, to be celebrated where it truly mattered. She never could settle for the simple society of the United States and its republican citizens, even if she was one of the greatest celebrities among them.

Chapter 2

"The Duchess of Baltimore"
The Aristocrat

Just a few years after her return to Baltimore with her newborn son, Elizabeth became the center of a debate not in genteel drawing rooms, but on the floor of Congress. By the summer of 1809, rumors swirled around Washington, Baltimore, Philadelphia, and other parts of the United States that Napoleon intended to make his brother's former wife a duchess. After crowning himself emperor, Napoleon had handed out dozens of titles, turning dozens of commoners into noblemen and -women. Yet everyone wondered whether the emperor would actually bestow such a title on an *American* woman living in their midst. Since the previous summer, Elizabeth and Napoleon had corresponded through Louis-Marie Turreau, the French minister to the United States, about Elizabeth's son, Jerome; the possibility of an annuity for his education and other expenses; and a title befitting her position as the mother of a Bonaparte son. By mid-1809, Napoleon, impressed with her confidence and savvy, had ordered Turreau to arrange an annual pension of 60,000 francs (about $12,000) for Elizabeth and her son until they could come to Europe. No promises were made regarding a title, but at some point Napoleon or Turreau mentioned the possibility of her becoming the Duchess of Oldenburg.

As more people learned that Elizabeth Patterson Bonaparte had indeed contacted the emperor and would indeed accept an annuity and title if offered, the rumors grew in number and intensity throughout the fall of 1809 and early 1810. Even abroad, Americans demanded the latest about the possible Duchess of Baltimore. From Stockholm, John Spear Smith wondered whether the rumors were true. Sally McKean Yrujo, wife of the former Spanish minister, informed Dolley Madison that they gossiped about the tantalizing story even in Rio de Janeiro.[1] The arrival of French Colonel Louis Tousard to attend Elizabeth and her son in "their official character," as one newspaper reported in mid-November 1809, made the matter seem a fait accompli.[2] All indications pointed to the establishment of a member of the French nobility in Baltimore, which was to be "the *Imperial and Royal residence* for the present."[3] By November 1809, "no doubt [was] entertained" of "the creation of the Duchess and Prince, by the Emperor NAPOLEON," an article noted as it announced a trip of the "Duchess of Baltimore (Mrs. Jerome Bonaparte)" and "the young Prince" to "honor" Philadelphia "with their august presence."[4] A visitor to Philadelphia notified another newspaper that, while he had initially thought its report "of the New Nobility" "nothing but a joke," he was "now certain it is true."[5]

After much public and private gossiping, curiosity developed into real concern. Wondering whether two Americans might become a duchess and a prince and believing that they already had were completely different. Gossips passed the rumors along as truth, and concern over Napoleon's plans for this new nobility flourished. Margaret McHenry of Baltimore worried that no one yet understood "Bonapartes intentions respecting Madam Jerome Bonaparte & her son." All McHenry knew was that Elizabeth was "much pleased at the idea of being a Duches and her sons being a Prince." She also noted that Elizabeth was "very anxious to go to France . . . and expect[ed] soon to receive orders to that effect."[6] By conferring on "Madame Jerome the title of Duchess of the House of Napoleon and her son Prince of the French Empire" as well as "an annuity of forty thousand crowns," the "Emperor Napoleon" afforded Philadelphia, the capital, and other cities not only a "great field for conversation" but also "*much apprehension of french influence*."[7] The newspapers echoed these concerns. Federalist newspaper editors, long convinced of excessive French influence over the Republicans, leapt at the opportunity to detail the dire implications of having *American* members of Napoleon's court. One prophesied that not only would Napoleon regain Louisiana but that "the little limb of French royalty at Baltimore" would reign as "The Emperor of the West." Another predicted that "*all of America* would fall to monarchical tyranny." Republican editors fought back, calling Federalist claims "nonsense" and drolly asking: "What court officers would 'the puissant little baby' require? A Master of the Rocking Horse?" They also insisted that administration officials could not be held responsible "for a [marital] connection which they neither sought nor promoted," for, as everyone knew, "women will bestow their hearts and their hands where they please."[8]

Even though Elizabeth had confided to a few friends that, "tho' Napoleon supports them now," "neither she or her son . . . has a title yet," the fear of Napoleon's influence through the two soon spread beyond newspapers, letters, and drawing rooms to Congress itself, engaging some of the preeminent statesmen of the era.[9] On January 18, 1810, Republican senator Philip Reed of Maryland introduced a resolution calling for an amendment to the Constitution that became known as the "Titles of Nobility Amendment." The proposal that emerged from a committee for Senate consideration in late January stated that either the acceptance of a title or marriage "with any descendant of any emperor, king or prince, or with any person of the blood royal" would cost a person "the rights and immunities of a free citizen of the U.S."[10] The committee had targeted two of Elizabeth's presumed betrayals of the republic. By mid-February, a revision to the proposed amendment added her third: no citizen could accept a present, office, or *pension* from "any emperor, king, prince or foreign state."[11] Clearly, this amendment meant to neutralize the domestic and diplomatic threat presented by Elizabeth and her son.

Senator Timothy Pickering, the staunch Federalist from Massachusetts and a member of the committee that revised Reed's motion, never doubted that Elizabeth and her son were directly responsible for the proposed amendment. "Every one's eye is doubtless turned to the case of Mrs. Bonaparte and her son" began his notes for a speech in support of the amendment. According to Pickering, many believed that little Jerome was "undoubtedly" "destined by his imperial uncle to a throne," perhaps even to become "the imperial successor." Since "neither [Elizabeth's] ambition nor her maternal affection [would] permit her son to be torn from her & carried to France," the two were expected to remain in the United States or go to France together. Pickering and other senators feared that "a lady of this character" and her "so connected" son could not "with safety be allowed to reside within the United States" and desired that the amendment be expanded to prohibit persons "of imperial or royal blood" from residing in the United States. In his musings over possible objections to the resolution, he asked: "What danger can arise in a republic from the residence of a solitary woman & her child?" His answer was: "Much every way." Pickering clearly believed that "this member of the imperial family & his mother" posed a threat to "Republican Government." He thought that a key step toward disaster had come when Elizabeth received "the homage of the officers & representatives of this nation." The next step in Napoleon's diabolical plan, according to Pickering, was "the establishment of a Court, which in splendour, [would] outshine, & in expences & attentions, surpass, the palace of the first magistrate of our nation." Then, Pickering logically argued, "our eyes are to be introduced to the gorgeous scenes of royalty . . . till at length, seduced & corrupted by the charms . . . & the promises of royalty, the citizens of these republican states are to be prepared to receive a king." Elizabeth and her son would be the beginning of the end of a republican United States. He "entertain[ed]" no doubt that Napoleon had "already contemplated the erection of a throne in Washington on which his nephew is to be placed. . . . Such expectations should receive no countenance from our forbearance," Pickering concluded.[12] For Pickering, the republic would not fall to an aristocracy if the Constitution was amended to protect Americans against examples of royal lifestyles.

The two decades after 1800 were full of uncertainty and anxiety for Americans. Many remained concerned about the stability of the federal union and the success of the republican experiment. "*Four* memorable evils," Richmond *Enquirer* editor Thomas Ritchie warned in 1806, still threatened the "unexampled *freedom*" of the United States: "war," "party spirit," disunion, and "luxury."[13] Between 1800 and 1820, each of these "evils" appeared at one time or another. Scholars have fully examined the divisions of the first party system and the diplomatic challenges that culminated in the War of 1812. And they have recently turned more serious attention to the fears of disunion.[14] But they have said very little about the widespread concerns about luxury and Americans' complex ideas concerning this "memorable" evil.

Unlike their colonial and revolutionary ancestors, early nineteenth-century Americans were no longer ambivalent about refinement.[15] For most elite men and women, refinement was acceptable, even necessary, for the new republic. It gave polish—even legitimacy—to republican society and those ladies and gentlemen who led it. But luxury corrupted. Luxury threatened the republican experiment since it could, in Ritchie's words, "unnerve the zeal that would watch over the public welfare."[16] By 1800, Americans had drawn a distinction between refined manners and ideas, which were suitable for the republic, and luxurious behaviors and possessions, which went beyond the bounds of suitability and could corrupt or destroy the republic. Though their colonial forebears had drawn directly on the English court and gentry for their ideas about refinement, early nineteenth-century Americans explicitly linked luxury with aristocratic behavior, ideas, and objects and regarded aristocratic luxury as the opposite of a desired republican simplicity. Yet, problematically for Americans in this era, the definitions of what constituted refinement and luxury were not clear and therefore subject to much debate.

By the early 1800s, Americans had imbued their acceptance of refinement with feelings of nationalism. While refined manners and minds might have drawn upon courtly antecedents, good republicans would no longer celebrate them as such. "The permanence and practical blessings of republican liberty," the *Enquirer* emphatically declared, "essentially depend upon the gradual and eternal extinction of those fatal and factitious propensities" toward luxury, especially "the passion for the alluring and expensive, but useless and pernicious refinements in dress, equipage, building, furniture, and the luxuries of the table." These dangerous cultural articles served only "to excite the admiration and wonder of the giddy multitude, and gratify the pride of opulence." Such examples of "phantastic refinement and expensive splendour" belonged to the "polished littleness of regal titled Europe" and "despotic government." Therefore, American "virtue and national happiness," as well as the "manly simplicity" of the republic depended on the abandonment of this love of corrupting and feminine luxuries.[17] At an ideological level, most elite Americans could agree that aristocratic luxury imperiled republican simplicity, while believing that refinement was compatible with the republic. Indeed, they set out to create an *American* version of refinement. Courtly ways would still have a place, albeit a limited one. Americans looked to refinement as a way to celebrate the nation, not the European court.

For most historians who have looked at the debates over how democratic or aristocratic American culture should be, the 1780s and 1790s are the crucial decades and 1800 provides the final resolution. But Thomas Jefferson's election to the presidency can serve as the endpoint of this ideological struggle only if it is seen in narrowly partisan terms, pitting the more elitist Federalists against the more egalitarian Republicans.[18] Even those historians who do not view this debate primarily as one of party politics and political leaders but instead as one of national culture and intellectual leaders have often seen 1800 as the conclusion. Those Americans, such as Noah Webster and Hugh Henry Brackenridge, who favored a social hierarchy and a culture that incorporated some European, even aristocratic, forms apparently no longer had the energy to fight for their beliefs and let a more popular, less elitist culture take hold.[19] But the "culture wars" over the degree of European luxury versus American simplicity, aristocracy versus democracy, in American culture were far from settled with Jefferson's election. For a generation after 1800, Americans argued with each other over differing ideas of the proper nature of American society and culture. Certainly, the Federalists and the so-called great men did not have the same political power as before 1800 (though the persistent power of Southern planters challenges even this assertion), but even the Federalists still helped shape American culture long after their national political defeat.[20] Elite men, including those writing dictionaries and plays, may have catered more to popular demands, but they still dominated culture, if not politics. Through this elite, which included numerous influential women, aristocratic European ways continued to influence American culture. These men and women refused to give up imported luxuries and continued to see an important role for the "privileged" classes to play in American society.[21] But those Americans who regarded aristocratic culture as too luxurious and therefore too corrupting for a republic debated the issues vigorously. American cultural forms were in flux after 1800; a democratic and egalitarian culture did not reign supreme. While Americans grappled with the ideology and politics of republicanism and democracy into the 1820s, they also struggled to decide just what constituted an *American* character and culture.[22]

The debate over the nature of American culture took place within a transatlantic context. In spite of their political independence, the image of "Europe," though not specifically London, still shaped ideas of culture and fashion for Americans.[23] While they constructed their culture and their national identity and even while they traveled in Europe, Americans sought to redefine the old, colonial division between American provincial and European cosmopolitan. Europe remained the yardstick by which Americans measured their cultural attainments—and they often suffered feelings of inferiority in doing so. But, for Americans, Europe also represented corrupting luxury. When they thought about the nature of American character and culture, many Americans feared the influence of European individuals, manners, and ideas; many dreaded that American culture might replicate that of monarchical Europe. In the 1780s, for example, the Society of Cincinnati, an organization of the officers of the Continental Army, came under heavy fire from American citizens for its hereditary membership and wearing of a badge (an eagle with a ribbon)—both of which seemed too aristocratic in their demands for distinction and deference. The society's opponents feared the creation of a military aristocracy whose members, in their desire for economic and political privilege, would "spread [foreign] opulence and luxury in America" and "supplant republican institutions with a nobility."[24] Similarly, the Boston Tea Assembly, called the Sans Souci ("without care") Club by its critics, provoked a public uproar over the members' exclusiveness and penchant for dancing and card playing at their meetings. Appearing too much like European landed aristocracy, the speculative claims of large landowners in Maine and other frontier areas also incited popular reaction, including rebellion. Monarchical models of politics and economics that the Federalists, under Alexander Hamilton's leadership, had put into place in the 1790s also generated fierce conflict and helped produce Jefferson's election in 1800. Moreover, beginning in the late 1780s, great debates raged over how much pomp and ceremony should surround the president, such as whether he should be called "his excellency" and whether his social events should be modeled on those of a court.[25] But these worries and concerns over the unsuitability of European models for the American republic did not disappear when Jefferson became president; instead, they extended more deeply into the arenas of culture and gender, as the reactions to Elizabeth clearly demonstrate.

Given Americans' deep concerns over the dangers of luxury to the new nation, women, who had long been associated with fashion and luxury, seemed especially worrisome. The author of *The Mental Flower Garden: Or, An Instructive and Entertaining Companion for the Fair Sex* (1807) warned that "the luxury of women, alone, makes the men fearful of uniting themselves with them."[26] Women could reward aristocratic fops instead of virtuous republican suitors by agreeing to marry them. Worse, since women controlled the realm of refinement, setting and enforcing its standards, they could lure men into luxurious and ruinous extravagance. As they had proven in aristocratic Europe, women could also sow "disruption and disorder" in America.[27]

During the early decades of the 1800s, Elizabeth Patterson Bonaparte symbolized the menace of aristocratic and even despotic excess for those who feared for their virtuous republic. Too much about her seemed threatening. Her marriage to Jerome had linked her to the most powerful ruler in Europe, a man with global ambitions. Her child, Jerome Napoleon Bonaparte, was potentially in line for a European throne even though he lived in Baltimore. After her abandonment in 1805, Elizabeth remained a public character. Her clothes and appearance proclaimed her preference for European fashions. And her European sensibilities and later experiences led her to criticize many aspects of her native land and society, which she did openly both at home and abroad. Simply put, Elizabeth believed a monarchy was superior to a republic. She despised the increasing democratization of America and longed for the strict social hierarchies of Europe. She found American society insipid and stagnant, lacking in "imagination, feeling, taste, [and] intelligence," when compared with the excitement and elegance of European circles.[28] Because of her aristocratic ways and ties, Elizabeth was not content—nor fit, according to her detractors—to play the republican wife or mother. Her French connections and the French imperial image she cultivated, even as her country labored to shape a new republican culture, caused many Americans to fear her and seek ways to limit her influence.

In the public arena as a celebrity, Elizabeth had turned her back on her provincial American upbringing and reinvented herself as a cosmopolitan—one who embraced the metropolis of Europe and its fashions and manners. Increasingly, the identity she presented was at odds with the emerging national identity. She therefore served as a point of contention in the debates over American culture and the lines between republican refinement and aristocratic luxury. She existed, even flourished, at the boundaries of acceptable behavior for her class, thereby helping Americans define their national culture and character in this period. Through her husband, clothes, and behavior, she avidly played the role of the cosmopolite for Americans who were struggling to overcome their cultural provincialism as their nation gained status in the transatlantic world. Since she unashamedly represented the metropolis of Europe for them, Elizabeth received both social power *and* condemnation. She personified all that Americans admired and envied as well as all that they feared and denounced about aristocratic Europe. Many adored her, but many also found her a threat to the republic with her desire to gain some place in an empire or monarchy and her clear preference for all things aristocratic. Some even sought to suppress the sources of her influence. Her personal choices became political ones as Americans analyzed and judged her in this era of fierce cultural debate. Elizabeth's celebrity never waned; she continued to attract attention and receive invitations to almost every party in Baltimore and Washington, D.C. But as it became clear that she and her son would live not in France with the Bonapartes but in Baltimore with the Pattersons, her critics intensified their criticism and shifted their focus from her clothing and immodesty to the much graver threats that this ambitious woman and her imperial son presented to the republic. By around 1810, some of the most powerful men in the country had turned against her.

By the time Elizabeth married Jerome in December 1803, Americans' opinions of France had changed significantly from the early days of its revolution. The fierce partisan tensions and unfolding international developments of the 1790s had shattered Americans' previously positive views of France and its revolution, leading to political decisions and divisions—for both sexes. Women as well as men took a political stance, either Republican or Federalist, when they declared themselves pro- or anti-French.[29] With the Quasi-War of the late 1790s, when France seized hundreds of American ships, refused to negotiate with American ministers unless they paid a bribe, and forced President John Adams to prepare for war, the ranks of pro-French Americans thinned. Napoleon's coup d'état in late 1799, which made him first consul, diminished them even further. The peace settlement with France in October 1800 and Jefferson's election soon after eased much of the partisan intensity associated with attitudes toward the French. With the French Revolution seemingly over and Napoleon moving toward imperial rule, France came to appear to many Americans by the early 1800s as a dangerous threat. Disappointed Americans believed French citizens had drastically swung from being "violent republicans" who "rais[ed] altars to reason and liberty" in the mid-1790s to a people who "pull[ed] down those altars, creating and supporting a new dynasty and huzzaing to all its pageantry" by 1805.[30] On hearing that the Bonapartes and their supporters were "going to plunge into" royal titles "with the all the fondness of children for a new rattle," Massachusetts senator John Quincy Adams remarked: "Was there ever so horrible a tragedy concluded with so ridiculous a farce?"[31]

Concerns about Elizabeth's appropriateness for and impact on the republic centered initially on her choice of husband and the larger significance of an American marrying this particular Frenchman at this particular time. In January 1804, just a few weeks after their wedding, but obviously with no knowledge of that event, a letter appeared in London's *Gentleman's Magazine* and then in American newspapers that was purportedly penned by Elizabeth herself. Arguing that "it would not be *love* but *madness*" if she allowed Jerome to visit her again "after all that I have heard and know of you," she "dismissed" him. Emphasizing the superiority of her pure republic to his decadent nation, she then ordered him back to France where "such *lovers* and such *politicians* may be in requisition." Finally, she "thank[ed] God!" that in her country "we can continue to do without them."[32] The writer of this piece remains unknown, but it is fascinating that someone chose Elizabeth to express these sentiments. For this writer, at least, it clearly was how Elizabeth should have responded to Jerome's overtures, rejecting a corrupt Frenchman instead of agreeing to marry him. Others were initially unsure how to view the "hymenial conjunction" between Elizabeth and Jerome in terms of the future relations between France and the United States. South Carolinian Ralph Izard Jr. believed that "our land must [derive] advantages from the affair no doubt."[33] But, given the political concerns about France by 1804, many saw Elizabeth as a mere pawn in her family's, especially her uncles', grab for greater glory. Commenting on Jerome and Elizabeth's recent marriage after spending an evening with them, John Quincy Adams rightly predicted that, though Maryland senator Samuel Smith "swells upon [the marriage] to very extraordinary proportions," the union "undoubtedly will be broken," as everyone knew that it was "a marriage against many laws, many usages, many opinions, and many prejudices, personal, official, and national, of the First Consul" Bonaparte. In Adams's opinion, "the lady's parents" and "the whole family of the Smiths" possessed "such an *inconceivable infatuation*" for the match that "it was really the young man who was seduced."[34]

Her uncles' political and social aspirations notwithstanding, Elizabeth's own desire was to be married to a titled—or even royal or imperial—European. In the first months after her marriage, this dream seemed to be coming true. With Napoleon's ascension as emperor of France, Jerome adopted a "mode of living" and "act[ed] the part of a prince of royal blood."[35] Elizabeth played her part as princess, wearing gowns that Jerome had ordered from Paris at the time of their wedding and riding around in their coach and six accompanied by several servants. Indeed, some immediately considered her a princess. One French official on the Canary Islands commended "His Imperial Highness The Prince Jerome Bonaparte" on his marriage to "the lovely princess you have thought worthy of your choice," who, he had been told by a visitor who knew Elizabeth, "will shine in Paris."[36] Locals even considered her royalty. In July 1804, the Baltimore *American* announced that "our little Baltimore beauty has of course been elevated by her marriage, to the sudden and unexpected dignity of a Princess."[37] Reports from Paris, however, did not support this vision. Napoleon's displeasure with the marriage was soon known. Lucien Bonaparte believed that the couple's destiny lay in the United States and not France. He warned his brother that, as such, he needed to live like a republican, not a prince, and try "not to think of himself anything more than he really is, and to strive as soon as possible to assimilate himself to the *plain and uncorrupted* manners" of the United States. As long as Jerome stayed in the United States with Elizabeth, Lucien expected him "to live on *equal* footing with your most respectable citizens, but never *beyond* any of them."[38] That certainly was not what either Jerome or Elizabeth had in mind, especially once they heard of Jerome's brother-in-laws and even family friends receiving imperial titles. Elizabeth's "womanly ambition dreamed of the future," as Jerome's published memoirs would note years later; Elizabeth confirmed this statement by writing "true" next to it.[39]

Elizabeth was not the only American woman in this era who desired a European—even a titled—husband. Since the creation of the new nation in 1787, a number of young American women had met and married visiting European diplomats, secretaries, and consuls. Cornelia Clinton, the daughter of New York Governor George Clinton, married the minister from revolutionary France, "Citizen" Edmond Genet, even after he had caused a diplomatic scandal in 1793. Hannah Nicholson, of the politically powerful Nicholson-Livingston family of New York, preferred the Swiss-born Albert Gallatin, who had immigrated to the United States around 1780 and became a congressman and later secretary of the treasury under Thomas Jefferson and James Madison. Anne, the eldest daughter of the wealthy Philadelphians Anne and William Bingham, married Alexander Baring, a successful British banker and the first Lord Ashburton. Her younger sister, Maria, scandalously ran away to marry the Comte de Tilly, a dashing but debauched Frenchman, who was soon paid to divorce her. While secretary to the British legation, David Montague Erskine, later Lord Erskine and then British minister, married Frances Cadwalader, daughter of General John Cadwalader of Philadelphia. Most like Elizabeth was Sally McKean— the vivacious daughter of Thomas McKean, the chief justice and later governor of Pennsylvania—who fell in love with and married the titled Spanish minister Carlos Fernando Martínez de Yrujo, becoming the Marchioness de Casa de Yrujo. Perhaps not surprisingly, she and Elizabeth became good friends. Both relished their elevated status and ties to important European families. One of Yrujo's letters to Elizabeth began, "The Marchioness de

Casa de Yrujo's compliments to Madame Bonaparte & would be happy to know how she is this morning."[40]

These women's marriages to foreigners, especially titled ones, seem to have started a trend among young American women who were supposed to desire virtuous republican men. In 1811, Catherine Mitchill noted that the newly arrived, handsome, unmarried French minister would attract female attention in Washington "as some of our Girls are very fond of foreign alliances." "They will try to conquer France and unite it to America," she foretold, "not however in a national point of view, but a matrimonial one."[41] Elizabeth's nemeses, the Caton sisters of Annapolis, would all marry titled British men after 1815. Elizabeth had not set a very good example at all for young women of the early republic. William Eaton, who would soon lead the marines onto the shores of Tripoli, predicted from Gibraltar in 1804 that Elizabeth's worrying example might "set all our handsome daughters a tip-toe to be running away with Corsicans."[42]

After being abandoned by her French husband and returning to Baltimore in 1805, Elizabeth never felt truly American. She found herself caught between two worlds—living in the one she hated and excluded from the one she desired. She had to negotiate as satisfactory as possible a place for herself and her son on her own terms. Her opinions of republican government and society ensured that she would always remain an outsider, even if a celebrated one.[43] Though she always called Maryland her home and returned to Baltimore often to oversee her American rights and properties, Elizabeth never embraced her homeland; in fact, she felt that being born in America had been the fatal blow to her destiny. As soon as she married Jerome, perhaps even before, Elizabeth decided to eschew anything American, considering its ways too provincial, and embrace Europe. She turned her back on her American upbringing and, keeping Bonaparte as her last name, reinvented herself as a cosmopolitan.

The Baltimore to which Elizabeth returned in 1805 was not truly the backwater town she decried. While not approaching the dazzling cities of Europe, Baltimore, with a population of just over 26,500 in 1800, was coming into its own as an important commercial city, and its citizens actively sought to display their increasing refinement.[44] On his way to Washington in 1804, Massachusetts's Jonathan Mason stopped in Baltimore and found a city "growing in extent, in wealth, and in luxury," whose diverse inhabitants took great pride in themselves and in the city's "prospects." He judged Baltimore's citizens to be "not so refined in their manners as the Philadelphians, [but] more so than the New Yorkers." He noted the "many handsome women" but also the scarcity of "young men to match with them." But the city had "not much to amuse a traveller" in his view, just one library and one assembly room.[45] Mason must have missed the race course and theater. John Melish was more favorably impressed when he toured the city in 1806, when Elizabeth was becoming one of the tourist attractions. "The whole city exhibited a very handsome appearance, and the country round abounds in villas, gardens, and well-cultivated fields," Melish enthused. The "upwards of 6000 dwelling-houses" were "mostly built of brick, and many of them are elegant." In addition to the assembly room, theater, and library, there were thirteen "places of public worship, a courthouse, a jail, three market-houses, a poor-house, the exchange," and an observatory. A Female Humane Association to help poor women had been established in 1801. The manufactories in Baltimore were "considerable" and consisted "chiefly of ships, cordage, iron utensils, paper, saddlery, boots and shoes, hats, wool and cotton cards, &c." Even in 1805, readers could subscribe to a half-dozen newspapers. Since the city was "the great through-fare between northern and southern states," visitors on business and pleasure added interest to the scene as did a glimpse through a window of "a very handsome lady with her child . . . the wife and child of Jerome Bonaparte."[46] But for Elizabeth (and other visitors), Baltimore still lacked the multitude of cultivated spaces and people that marked elegant metropolitan life in Europe. Her negative attitude toward her hometown helps explain why she would spend so little time there in the decades after it became possible for her to return to Europe.

Effectively exiled to Baltimore, Elizabeth faced constant reminders of the imperial life that had been denied her. As she sat in her parents' house in Baltimore with her infant son, Jerome's early letters promised that "the time is not far, I hope, when we will be reunited" and that he "fel[t] certain" that he would "refuse . . . the Emperor if it becomes necessary to choose between he and my wife."[47] In the fall of 1807, she had to read again and again—and know that everyone else was also repeatedly reading—the details of Jerome's opulent royal wedding to Catherine, the Princess of Württemberg. Visitors to Europe related to Elizabeth their encounters with Jerome. The wife of the American consul in Genoa informed Elizabeth that she "had frequent Occasions of seeing and Dining at the Table of your Husband, the present King of Westphalia," where Elizabeth "was no less frequent the Topic of our conversation." According to Anna Kuhn, Jerome "speaks of you as the only woman he ever Loved or ever shall Love tho' united to another much against his Inclination, which the Emperor . . . cruelly imposed on him." Kuhn also reported that "the Grand Duchess of Tuscany, the Vice King of Italy, the Prince Borghese and others of the [Bonaparte] family are extreamly anxious to see you and have made me repeated enquiries."[48] It must have been heartbreaking for Elizabeth to learn that Napoleon's imperial family wanted to know about her and her son but did not let her become one of them. By 1810, she could have regularly read in newspapers and magazines about Jerome and his second wife's glamorous life in Paris and at their court and their participation in Napoleon's growing empire.

Denied the gilded life of a royal or aristocratic existence, "the gew-gaws and tinsel of usurped nobility," as one newspaper called it,[49] Elizabeth determined to utilize her ties with the Bonapartes to create her own aristocratic, cosmopolitan image in simple Baltimore, triggering a national discussion about how much aristocracy the new republic could bear. Elizabeth knew well the requisite trappings—or "gew-gaws and tinsel"—of an aristocratic life and spent large sums of money to look like a Bonaparte. In her earnestness to overcome her enforced provincialism, she eagerly displayed the clothing and other accoutrements that would mark her as aristocratic and cosmopolitan, that would link her to the centers of fashion and culture. All aristocrats traveled in style to display their status and wealth; so Elizabeth's neighbor, A. M. Hollingsworth, expected Elizabeth to "set up her carriage etc. as becomes a member of the imperial family."[50] Hollingsworth knew her well. Shortly afterward, Elizabeth ordered a luxurious carriage with the Bonaparte family crest, purchased a set of horses "handsome enough for" it, and had her servants outfitted in new livery of "drab coloured cloth with scarlet trimmings."[51] She furnished her house with items that Jerome had purchased for her during their courtship and marriage, many of which were suitable for a palace: gilded Louis XIV armchairs, a large wardrobe, a Sheraton-style ladies' writing table with a marble top, ceramic jars with painted landscapes and gilded handles, a silver-plated chest, a dinner service of almost two hundred pieces with some pieces in green with zodiac designs and others in black with gold trim, and even a mahogany-and-brass traveling bidet with a silver-plated basin.[52] For her personal adornment, Elizabeth possessed her substantial French wardrobe and numerous pieces of expensive jewelry, luxury items that aided her presentation as an aristocrat in the midst of republicans. Her choices of jewelry were those of a queen, not a simple American wife who might boast a single string of pearls. She wore tiaras filled with amethysts, pearls, and other gems. She had necklaces of emeralds, garnets, pearls, coral, and diamonds, as well as thick gold chains, and rings of small and large diamonds, emeralds, rubies, and turquoise. Her collection also included gold bracelets and bracelets with garnets, opals, pearls, and other precious stones; bejeweled hair combs, lockets, and perfume cases "striped with emeralds & diamonds & rubies"; and "a garnet and pearl comb & necklace & earrings" that she wore when she had her portrait painted by Firmin Massot.[53] When outfitted in her jewels and gowns, she looked like any aristocratic European woman.

Through her clothing and jewelry, Elizabeth constructed not only her social identity as a celebrity but her political identity as well. In the early nineteenth century, clothing was one of the most visible markers not only of gender and class but also of the wearer's acceptance of or divergence from the new nation's ideals. Fashion was strongly linked with national as well as personal identity and played an important role in the construction of American nationalism in the early republic. Indeed, historically, dress has often served a crucial function while a nation establishes or contests its identity.[54] As with men, women's choices of clothing and accessories could make them political actors, even though disenfranchised. Clothing had long served as a material manifestation of a person's political loyalties. In the colonial era, fashion provided the most important means through which elite women "expressed their relationship to imperial culture."[55] During the Revolution, wearing homespun had served as a very visible way of supporting the patriots; conversely, not wearing it demonstrated loyalty to England. Similarly, in the partisan battles of the 1790s, some Americans donned special clothing and accessories that proclaimed their loyalty to the Federalists or the Republicans, as well as their opposition to or support for the French Revolution.[56] Choosing what one would put on for the day could be a very conscious political act, even for women.

The French revolutionaries took the connection between clothing, political identity, and women's bodies to even higher levels. Artist Jacques-Louis David designed symbolic images, many based on the female form, for the new republic for display in parades, pageants, and paintings. The use of these images quickly shaped new fashions for women such that the new republic was displayed on women's bodies. David outfitted women in gowns and hairstyles that hearkened back to ancient Greece, linking that great republic to France's, and made dressing *à la grecque* the height of fashion for women throughout the

Figure 5. French women who dressed *à la grecque* hid little of their bodies beneath the clinging, thin fabrics. Circle of Jacques-Louis David, *Portrait of a Young Woman in White*, ca. 1798. Chester Dale Collection, courtesy of the National Gallery of Art, Washington, D.C.

Revolution and Napoleon's reign. As one way to assert a continuity between the French Republic and Napoleon's new empire or, perhaps as one historian of the French Revolution has argued, to "lure men to attach deep romantic longings to the state," Empress Josephine, Napoleon's sisters, and many elite French women all dressed in this simple but "seductive" republican style, with plunging necklines and thigh-high splits in the skirts.[57] It could also be that these women chose these fashions simply because the dresses, without hoops, bustles, panniers, or often even undergarments, were easier to wear than anything they had worn previously.

Just as in republican and then imperial France, material culture provided important symbols in the United States during the late 1700s and early 1800s. Monuments, national insignia, the designs on national currency, and other images all played crucial roles in evoking the idea of a United States and loyalty to it.[58] As yet another sign of national identity, fashion was crucial in this period. How one constructed and presented the self in public, through behavior and clothing, mattered immensely in this era for both men and women. Fashion was not a uniquely feminine pursuit after 1800. As they had in the 1780s and 1790s, political men in public knew that their appearances would be carefully monitored and that they had to dress the part of a republican citizen; no pretentious European fashions would do.[59] Yet politicians were not the only men using fashion in the public arena. Though American men no longer wore brightly colored silks, cascades of lace, and shiny silver buttons and buckles with powdered hair, a number of them still took great pride in their clothing and followed the latest fashions. Men who publicly displayed their fashionable selves in the early decades of the nineteenth century were often denigrated as "dandies" or "fops" and censured for their apparent lack of republican virtue.[60] Even General Winfield Scott found it difficult to protect his reputation and professional future because, for a time, he indulged in "so many absurd European fashions that people [were] quite disgusted with him." Some feared he would "blast his prospects" for "behaving so ridiculously."[61] Americans would not tolerate an excess of European behavior, not even from their military heroes. Women's love of fashion was regarded as even more threatening to the republic and its virtuous citizenry. One supposedly female writer to the Baltimore *Republican; or Anti-Democrat* firmly stated in 1803 that "it is the improper dress of our sex which has, if not alone, at least in great measure, worked the innovations which have turned the world topsy turvey." "It will be seen on examination," she concluded, "that most of the great alterations which governments have experienced of late, have been attended by an alteration of female dress."[62] What would it mean to the fate of the American republic if its women adopted French imperial fashions?

By the early 1800s, visibly linking one's self to republican America, not aristocratic Europe, should have been the desired goal for all citizens. Elizabeth perfectly understood the symbolic power of fashion, which she had used to gain her celebrity status, and wielded it skillfully in creating her "self-narrative"—the way in which society was to understand her.[63] In Elizabeth's case, national identities clashed in her dress. As Thomas Law's poem made clear, Elizabeth Patterson Bonaparte's clothing and marital choice projected her attitudes and beliefs about the United States: a woman with "limbs revealed" and "bosom bare" was certainly "ill suitted" as a republican's wife but not as "Jerom's concubine."[64] It was not just that her clothes revealed so much of her body; it was that they were so *French*. Congressman Simeon Baldwin of Connecticut reasoned that "having married a Parissian," Elizabeth "assumed the mode of dress in which it is said the Ladies of Paris are cloathed—if that may be called cloathing which leaves half of the body naked & the shape of the rest perfectly visible." She consciously shaped her appearance to construct an identity consistent with her marriage choice and at odds with the early republic's values. While in public or receiving visitors, she constantly made clear how she thought of herself and her place in American society. No one could have misunderstood the message: Elizabeth regarded herself as a member not only of the finest French circles but also of the imperial family into which she had married. The style of her clothing—as well as her diamond tiaras and decorated coach—publicly signaled that she had chosen France over the United States, an empire over a republic. By continuing to wear these dresses to public functions, she showed that she was unconcerned that provincial Americans considered her too daring and immodest. Her image was ardently European, foregoing the republican modesty prescribed for women by many American writers. With her strong attachment to courtly ways, Madame Bonaparte proudly presented herself as unsuited to be a "Columbians modest wife." Though "condemned by those who saw her," Simeon Baldwin found Elizabeth's fashions "astonishingly bewitching." Still, he wondered "what shall be" when such mesmerizing styles "shall remove all barriers from the chastity of women?"[65]

Commentators found Elizabeth's fashions, followed by so many younger women, threatening to the virtue of the republic. After erecting a republic that seemed inspired by that of America, the French had descended into chaos and emerged as an empire. The revealing French fashions had been a part of this process from the beginning; they seemed too radical and too immoral for many Americans. Obviously, not every woman who wore French dresses wanted to signal that she preferred a European empire over an American republic, but that was how some Americans, who worried about the fragility of the republic, understood it. One newspaper editor pleaded with "the ladies of this country" to reject "the destroying evil" of French fashions and return to "a fashion of dress which should be truly American, healthful and decorous."[66]

Figure 6. Elizabeth's celebrity in Europe led artists to paint or engrave her image for sale. In this miniature, she is depicted in the fashionable, yet revealing, attire of elegant French women, such as Madame Récamier. Augustin, ca. 1814. From Mary Caroline Crawford, *Romantic Days in the Early Republic* (Boston: Little, Brown, 1912).

Evidence that the pursuit of fashion and the influence of French modes could corrupt the virtue of republican citizens appeared everywhere in the early 1800s. Even at a moment when simple, republican virtue should have prevailed, during the waning days of the War of 1812, Lydia Hollingsworth was shocked to discover that Baltimore was "gay . . . almost to dissipation!" As evidence of this antirepublican activity, she pointed to luxurious "dinners on dinners; parties on party's," and, most scandalously, "the Belles [being] more french in the[ir] dress and manners then heretofore."[67] As Elizabeth completely understood, social commentators feared what the dress and behavior represented more than the clothing itself.

Paradoxically, those very attributes—the French connections—that gained Elizabeth status and even popularity caused some to perceive her as a threat to the republican experiment. As they wrestled over the precise nature of their culture, many Americans regarded Elizabeth as inappropriate for the new nation. She had willingly chosen to be affiliated with a European empire. They admired her beauty, style, and courage, but worried about her European manners and views and her excessive cosmopolitanism. In a letter to his wife, Huldah, Waller Holladay gushed over "the charms" and "perfections calculated to captivate the brother of the first Consul," including Elizabeth's "beautiful, well-turned Ancle" and "the more gorgeous display of a breast, luxuriantly rising under the hand of nature." He then conceded, however, that if he were her husband, "I should like to see her contented with a more modest exhibition of her beauties."[68] After reading her husband's flattering—and quite sexual— portrait of Elizabeth, Huldah responded that Madame Bonaparte's celebrated charms were "better calculated to encite momentary admiration, than lasting respect and admiration," since she was "deficient in modesty & female delicacy." And couching her comments in the language of American simplicity versus European excess, Huldah further concluded that Elizabeth was "no doubt *charming* in the eyes of a *French*man," but would be better off in Paris "where the manners & customs of people would be quite congenial to her taste."[69] Such a woman seemed out of place in the new nation.

Many Americans regarded the fashionable life pursued in cosmopolitan centers, even those in the United States, suspiciously. Dolley Madison expertly designed social events that avoided appearing "overtly monarchical" during her reign as Washington's premier hostess, but many still found her social rituals too luxurious for good republican citizens.[70] The "splendid" parties Elizabeth threw in Washington during the War of 1812 inspired Virginia congressman William Burwell to ruminate about happiness in a republic. As he explained to his wife in 1813, true happiness could only be found "in the pursuit of virtue, and the discharge of duty[;] in a life actively and usefully spent." He approved that his wife did not "envy the enjoyments of the gay[,] . . . the brilliant display of drawing rooms & the whole pageantry of show" in Washington. The "frivolity & insincerity of town Inhabitants" only created "poorer people of fashion . . . tormented by jealously, & vain rivalship."[71]

Expressing sentiments like Burwell's, Margaret Bayard Smith admitted that she grew weary of the "many tedious evenings" she passed "in what is called *gay company*." "Much pleasanter were the evenings we spent at home" in her small family circle around the fireside. She dreaded "to live in the fashionable circle, to live in a city," where she had "to part with ones liberty" and spend days in ways that neither "interest or duty would have dictated."[72] Explicitly associating the dangers of cosmopolitan life with women, Joseph Cabell of Williamsburg, Virginia, advised his friend Isaac Coles, private secretary to Jefferson in Washington, "not to be captivated by the glittering accomplishments of those *sea-port* girls, to whom the movements, and pleasures of large cities have become physical wants." "A brilliant, fashionable wife," he cautioned, "is a very pretty thing, like a rainbow; of no use very often but to delight the eye, and its beauties vanishing with the first change of scenery."[73]

Some worried Americans came to see Elizabeth's dramatic life as one that might tempt other young women. They publicly regarded Elizabeth as an unacceptable model for the republic both in terms of gender and citizenship. Poems, such as Thomas Law's about her dress at the Smith ball, that simultaneously praised her beauty and attacked her modesty and republicanism, quietly circulated among the elite; some even appeared in newspapers. One ode admired the "charms which deck thy form" and "the graces of thy soul," but then linked her with a "despotic empire reign."[74] Echoing this ambivalence, newspaper articles celebrated her beauty, acknowledged the importance of her European connections, and even came to her defense on occasion, while also adding criticisms of their own. Boston's *Columbian Centinel* took great affront at Napoleon's rejection of a woman who was "of superior rank and virtue" to most of the "little low Corsican-born we know not of whom" Bonapartes. Similarly, Baltimore's *Telegraph and Daily Advertiser* raged that the "mock emperor" and his unmanly brother had cast aside "an amiable and virtuous wife" from one of the "most respectable" families in the country.[75] But editors also attacked Elizabeth's vanity and questioned her appropriateness for a republic, mocking her desire for a "sudden and enexpected [*sic*]" elevation to royal status.[76] Like elites in the capital and elsewhere, these editors responded to Elizabeth with a mix of admiration and disdain as they judged her impact on American society and simultaneously revealed their own struggles over the appropriate standards for American culture. And when Elizabeth's dramatic life took another turn, when she apparently had become a duchess and her son a prince, she presented the American public with another occasion to discuss and debate her appropriateness for the republic as well as the place of certain aristocratic elements in American society.

The furor over the possibility of Elizabeth becoming a duchess and Bo a prince reveals much about American culture and politics at the time, as the social identity of Elizabeth collided with her political identity. The cosmopolitan image she had created through her clothing, behavior, conversation, and marriage had not only cultural ramifications but political ones as well, as the Titles of Nobility Amendment shows. While Elizabeth's ambitions were social when she sought titles for herself and her son, many of the men around her (especially those in the nation's capital) worried that such titles could carry real political, even geopolitical, power. The debate over the Titles of Nobility Amendment illuminates a particular moment during the early republic when concerns about women, France, the stability of the republic, and the threats of luxury and aristocracy all came together.

If Napoleon had not annulled the marriage between the Baltimore beauty and his impetuous youngest brother in 1806, Elizabeth might have reigned as a queen, if not in Westphalia then somewhere. Instead, she had returned to Baltimore with her infant son, facing what she believed would be a life of "suffering & ennui" in the fledgling republic. After a few years in her "cruel exile," Elizabeth could no longer stand being cut out of the Bonaparte family's rise to fame, fortune, and power.[77] But she was stunned in May 1808 when Jerome, now ruling his own kingdom with his new German wife, sent a member of his royal court, along with letters to Elizabeth and her father, to bring three-year-old Bo back to Westphalia so the boy could partake of the "brilliant destiny . . . reserved for him" and be "brought up . . . in the rank which belongs to him."[78] Elizabeth refused to let her child go. Instead, she turned to Napoleon. After a friend informed her that the French consul in Philadelphia had assured her that "little B. would be splendidly provided for" by the emperor and that she would "*obtain any provision [she] would demand*," Elizabeth wrote a long letter to General Turreau intended for Napoleon in the early summer of 1808.[79] She was firmly convinced that the emperor could help her much better than her unreliable and inconstant former husband. She let Napoleon know that her and her son's destinies lay in his hands and essentially offered him her son with a few conditions: that she accompany him if he went to Europe and, in order to raise him properly for his possible imperial position, that she receive an annuity for his education and other expenses. Then, she asked, if the emperor agreed to these terms, could he also give her a title befitting her station?

Napoleon was impressed with her proposal and demeanor; he also had heard the rumors that Elizabeth had been proposed to by Sir Charles Oakley, the secretary to the British legation in Washington.[80] The prospect of a British stepfather for a possible heir to the French empire must have seemed mortifying. In fact, Napoleon and Turreau discussed the possibility of the latter marrying Elizabeth, after divorcing the wife he hated and regularly abused. In a letter to Turreau, Napoleon told him to assure Elizabeth that the emperor would receive young Jerome "with pleasure" and would "be responsible for him." She "may count on my esteem and my desire to be agreeable to her," he noted, adding that "when I refused to recognize her, I was led to do so by reasons of high policy." Napoleon made clear through Turreau that he was "anxious to secure for her son the future she would desire."[81]

When Jerome discovered that Elizabeth had not only refused to relinquish their son to him but had contacted the emperor regarding provisions for her son and herself, he exploded. "What necessity was there for you to address yourself to the Emperor," he asked in November 1808. "Am I not a good enough Father, & friend, & powerful enough to give my son & to his Mother all the titles & all the Fortune which they may desire?" He then offered her a proposition: "You will possess at Smalcanden [Smalkalden], which is 30 leagues from Cassel [the capital of Westphalia], a residence, which is handsome, commodious, & worthy in every way of you. I will give to you, as well as to our child, the titles of Princess & Prince of Smalcanden with forty thousand dollars a year." Since she would be so near, he slyly added that he could visit "twice every month." He closed the letter by assuring her that he waited "anxiously to see your letter to the Emperor, & his answer, & the propositions which have been made to you by general Turreau" and, in usual form, that he "remain[ed] for life your devoted Jerome."[82] Though offered the title of a minor princess, she refused, declaring that Jerome's offer was "abject and shameful" and that his tiny kingdom was "not quite large enough to hold *two queens*." She chose instead to rely on Napoleon, stating that she would rather accept "refuge under the wing of the Eagle in preference to suspending myself to the Beak of the timid Goose."[83]

By mid-1809, the emperor had ordered Turreau to arrange an annuity of 60,000 francs (about $12,000) for Elizabeth and warned her against marrying any Englishmen. In her letter of thanks, she made clear her preference for a residence in Paris or any other city in the empire that the emperor thought appropriate and reiterated her desire for "a name and a title." As Turreau correctly surmised, Elizabeth's "ambition" made "her more anxious for the éclat of rank than of money," and either he or Napoleon dangled the possible title of the Duchess of Oldenburg in front of her.[84] The emperor and his minister had their own demands should Elizabeth receive a title that included "never to marry without the consent of the French government," to "renounce forever the idea of going to England," and to "renounce the United States & go to Europe."[85] To live in Europe with an exalted title and an annuity from the most powerful man on the continent—what more could one desire? Renouncing the United States—a place she loathed and regarded as "a desert"—would be easy.[86] She quickly sent off a letter to John Armstrong, the American minister in Paris, directing him not to "disclaim" anything concerning her if the emperor discussed her situation with him. "Should I be offered a title & Pension I will certainly accept them," she assured Armstrong. "I prefer infinitely a residence in France to one here."[87]

In the fall of 1809, when Turreau, with Napoleon's later blessing, sent Colonel Louis Tousard, vice consul at New Orleans, to watch over Elizabeth and Bo for the emperor, he also sent, under Napoleon's direction, "an allowance which would permit [Elizabeth] to maintain an independent and suitable existence." Tousard's orders were to "pay scrupulous attention to the conversations of Madame and her son; to guarantee her safety is the first of your duties or rather it includes them all," for the emperor was still fearful that the British "plan of seizing Madame and her son and carrying her and her son to London has not been abandoned." Tousard was to "live under the same roof" as Elizabeth and Bo, "eat at the same table and in a word never leave Madame and her son except when propriety requires it."[88] To have her own courtly protector and to have others acknowledge this imperial mark of her standing must have pleased Elizabeth immensely. And others were well apprised of her new situation. In early 1810, Kentucky congressman Richard Johnson heard that "Madam Jerome Boneparte," who might soon be "tendered" a "title of nobility," was receiving "40,000 crown annually . . . to be expended by her, in Courtly Style," to educate her son Jerome "in princely style," since it was "not improbable that he may [be] assigned some high station in France if he should have intellect when grown."[89] A Massachusetts newspaper reported at the end of November that "Gen[eral] Toussard" had arranged rooms at the Philadelphia City Hotel "for the Dutchess of Baltimore and Prince Napoleon" and had signed the registry as "Governor of the Prince Napoleon."[90] Hundreds of miles away, in Savannah, newspapers reported on the "certain arrangements made in Europe respecting Mrs. Bonaparte and her son," including that she was "to have a pension of sixty thousand dollars per annum and to be a dutchess" and that her son had been "created a prince of the French empire" with "a princely allowance" given "for his education." The newspaper also noted that "colonel Toussard, who served during our revolutionary war, is appointed governor of the prince."[91]

Elizabeth's ambitions for a title led many to question her morality. In Europe, the title of duchess was "the usual stile of a French King's mistress"; in that light, many Americans regarded Elizabeth's willingness to accept that specific title "as consenting to be considered in the rank of a mistress."[92] Former Navy Commodore Thomas Truxton agreed, proclaiming that, if she accepted, he would hold "the most contemptible opinion of" his old friend's daughter. He thought Elizabeth should have married Sir Charles Oakley, instead of choosing "$40,000 per annum to be [Jerome's] mistress."[93] This particular title served to reemphasize the sexual and physical dimension that had earlier appeared in the critiques of her clothing. Amused by the whole situation, Senator Henry Clay suggested that what Elizabeth needed was not a title or a fortune, but "a good strong back[ed] Democrat" since she looked "as if she wanted very much the services of such a character."[94] As usual, however, opinions regarding Elizabeth revealed Americans' ambivalence over their cultural boundaries. Some admired her rise to possible titled glory and others criticized her. From Baltimore in the spring of 1810 in the midst of congressional action, Margaret McHenry reported that some envied "her agrandizement," while others "pit[ied] her" or said "that she deserves to be punished for her folly."[95] Elizabeth's actions once again had proved her unworthy of the republic but still a captivating figure.

As the rumors about Elizabeth and Bo's titles gained strength in 1810 and more and more Americans became convinced that a real aristocracy and, worse, a legitimate appendage of the powerful Napoleon now existed in their midst, Elizabeth's national celebrity transformed into something darker. She was no longer merely a fascinating and celebrated woman. She now, for some, represented a real threat to the survival of the republic. For these Americans, her French connections symbolized not attractive cosmopolitanism but the danger inherent in luxurious aristocratic and royal influences.

Given the prevailing gendered notions of the time, it must have seemed implausible that a mere woman could create such a threat to the republic that Congress felt forced to respond to the danger she and her son seemed to pose.

Senator Timothy Pickering acknowledged the apparent ridiculousness of the situation when, as we have seen, he answered the question of what possible "danger can arise in a republic from . . . a solitary woman & her child?"[96] Yet women had long been associated with the downfall of nations. Their supposedly innate love of luxury and fashion, the reasoning went, was symptomatic of the ills that befell countries when they slid into dissipation and corruption. Indeed, women's love of luxury could *cause* the ruin. But Congress acted not on general fears of women but on particular fears raised by a single woman—a cosmopolitan one with potentially dangerous imperial connections. Its response to Elizabeth reveals not only continuing insecurities about a fragile new republic but also a new sense of the danger of kinship and family ties. Women's familial connections could be dangerous, especially through marriages to unsuitable foreigners. Thus, the Titles of Nobility Amendment can also be seen as a way to subdue women's power of kinship. Through her uncles and her husband, Elizabeth's kinship ties made her seem threatening since she and her son could become a conduit for ideas and power that threatened the republic.

American concerns about rank and titles had not disappeared after the Revolution. While most Americans never desired a society without status distinctions or marks of refinement, they had long opposed the notion of citizens receiving titles and the creation of an aristocracy. In 1787, the members of the Constitutional Convention had attempted to protect the nation by including in the Constitution statements that "No Title of Nobility shall be granted by the United States" and that "no Person holding any Office of Profit or Trust, shall, without the Consent of the Congress, accept any present, Emolument, Office or Title, of any kind whatever, from any King, Prince, or foreign State" (Article I, Section 9). As originally adopted, the Constitution said nothing about private citizens accepting titles or funds from foreign monarchs. Thus, when Elizabeth and her son appeared to have accepted the titles of duchess and prince, Congress felt the need to act.

Legal historians have long debated the motivation for the Titles of Nobility Amendment. Most agree that "no particular event precipitated the introduction of the amendment." Instead, they argue that a "general animosity to foreigners" on the eve of the War of 1812 produced overwhelming support for the proposed amendment among both parties.[97] A few have suggested some link between the amendment and Elizabeth, Jerome, and their son by noting erroneously that Jerome himself was in the United States at that time or correctly that he had married "a Maryland lady" or, as one scholar called her, "a prostitute."[98] But even these scholars have been quick to dismiss any real connection to Elizabeth and her son as mere rumors, not direct causes, returning to the "animosity toward foreigners" theory as the "more logical explanation."[99] They have drawn this conclusion despite admitting a paucity of sources concerning the proposed amendment. Neither contemporary newspapers nor the *Annals of Congress* reported the debates in detail. But a careful examination of the private letters and papers—and even one published circular letter—of congressmen make it perfectly clear that the Titles of Nobility Amendment resolution grew out of the fear of Elizabeth, her possibly imperial son, and their potential impact on the new nation.

As forceful symbols of the debate over European luxury and monarchy, Elizabeth and her son soon provoked reaction that crossed party lines. At first, Federalists had used the rumors about Elizabeth possibly becoming a duchess as a way to attack the Republicans; in turn, the Republicans, especially newspaper editors, had initially downplayed Federalist fears and presented the matter simply as a case of a misled woman and a harmless child. But Republicans in Congress eventually reassessed the political climate concerning Elizabeth and baby Bo and joined the movement to neutralize their threat.

Congressmen in both parties supported the amendment for various reasons. Some seem to have regarded Elizabeth as an annoyance rather than a source of real concern. Kentucky Republican Richard Johnson charged that "some people" in Washington "effect[ed] to be frightened at this infant being allied to Napoleon," since the emperor had no children and his brother Louis's only son was "sickly & not very promising." But, while Johnson himself feared "neither Napoleon, nor King George nor their power" because Americans' liberties "depend on no such despots, nor their Creatures," he was pleased that the Senate had the "very proper amendment before them . . . disfranchising a Citizen who shall accept letters of nobility from Foreign Potentates."[100] Others had grown suspicious of the connections that Elizabeth and her son formed between her uncles—the powerful senator Samuel Smith and Secretary of State Robert Smith—and Napoleon. In early February 1810, Samuel Taggart, a Federalist congressman from Massachusetts, characterized the visit of "the newly made Dutchess" and her son to Washington as a trip "to familiarize the citizens of America with the view of their future soveriegn." Taggart saw a worrisome significance in the willingness of "the heads of department and other gentlemen" of Congress who called on Elizabeth "to pay their respects." He also fretted that this attention was directly related to the "various reports" he had heard "about a projected alliance with France," which "some members of Congress . . . openly" favored. Taggart wished, as others surely did, that "both she and her offspring were safe in Westphalia" instead of threatening the republic in its capital.[101]

Others genuinely believed that the presence of the Duchess of Baltimore and her son could bring down the republic. Along with Senator Timothy Pickering, these people worried that the example of her luxurious, aristocratic lifestyle could corrupt citizens into no longer desiring a republic. They were alarmed and saw, as General William Eaton had even before the resolution, "political annihilation and voluntary transmigration into reptiles" in Napoleon's plan to make "his well beloved nephew DON JEROME PATTERSON NAPOLEON" into the *"King of these States."* Only if Americans "put on our armor" and "resist[ed] the lure and fraud of a blood stained son of rapine," Eaton proclaimed, could they "be loosed from the shackles which depress the nation."[102] Under the pseudonym of "Mutius," Republican curmudgeon John Randolph of Roanoke published a letter to President James Madison, outlining the history of the "beautiful American woman" who had married "the brother of the emperor of France" and seemed "destined again to become (with the un-offending fruit of her womb) the sport of avarice and ambition." As Taggart had hinted, Randolph feared her politically powerful relatives even more than Elizabeth herself, "the disconsolate mother." Randolph linked Elizabeth's uncles, his hated enemies, not only with James Wilkinson and Aaron Burr's plot to sever the West but also with Napoleon's plan "to make use of [the Smiths] through his nephew" to "obtain possession of the government of the United States." All the evidence that Randolph needed could be found in the fact that just after "Madame Bonaparte" was "created a duchess, and her son a prince of the empire, . . . the councils of the United States after a momentary fluctuation accommodate[d] themselves, at once, to the views of France!" "The inference," Randolph concluded, "is irresistible."[103]

In Maryland, Republicans especially wanted to distance themselves from this explosive issue. In fact, the proposed Titles of Nobility Amendment originated with a Republican Marylander, Senator Philip Reed, perhaps backed by Elizabeth's uncles. The Smiths may have been concerned about their reputation since they had already provoked criticism and concern by supporting Elizabeth and Jerome's marriage and seemingly seeking to benefit from their new ties to Napoleon. That the men in Elizabeth's family had permitted her marriage to the brother of Napoleon and then reveled in the status and attention that followed caused their party loyalty and even republican commitment to be questioned by at least a few. Randolph especially saw a plot by Napoleon to control the presidency through the untrustworthy Smiths, warning President Madison that he was about to become a "victim" of the dangerous Smith "junto by whom you are surrounded." Randolph feared that "the government of the United States" would "submit itself to the proprietary rule of the *new Lords Baltimore*" since "Bonaparte must make use of the tools [now] in our councils."[104] Someone in the Smith camp, possibly Virginian Wilson Cary Nicholas, struck back at Randolph, declaring that no "proof exist[ed] of the French Influence in our Councils" and that Randolph had put forward only "idle and contemptible insinuations" that "every man in the nation knows . . . to be false!" Randolph had taken the "very natural and very harmless" story of a "young and lovely girl, accustomed to admire the manners of France," and a "little and helpless child" and turned it into "unworthy suspicions" of the most "miserable" kind.[105] The Smiths may have outmaneuvered their enemies by arranging for the amendment to be proposed and thereby distanced themselves from the scandal Elizabeth and her ambitions had created.

By early 1810, those inside and outside of Congress could not ignore the geopolitical context that made the prospect of a titled nobility tied to Napoleon in the United States a serious concern. Most Americans objected to the creation of any European nobility within the United States, but a French one was especially troubling. Napoleon Bonaparte was the most dangerous man in Europe and might pose a real threat to the United States. At a time of rising Anglo-American tensions, Napoleonic France might prove an essential supporter, if not ally, but no one knew for certain. One newspaper worriedly reported that "Madame Jerome has already observed to some of her acquaintance, that *in her son they beheld* THEIR FUTURE EMPEROR!!"[106] Referring to Elizabeth's son, one Boston editor declared: "The Emperor of the French has now very kindly laid a young nobility upon the *stocks* for us. Fall down, grateful Americans, and worship the *rising Sun!*"[107] "*Our liberties in danger!!*," the *Raleigh Register and North Carolina Advertiser* proclaimed in March 1810, blaming "Mr. Jefferson" and his interest "in the appointment of little Jerome Bonaparte to a princeship." The newspaper had pieced together that Jefferson was actually distantly related to Elizabeth and therefore to Napoleon, and warned its readers that "ERGO, Mr. Madison is under 'FRENCH INFLUENCE!'"[108] Similarly, a Savannah, Georgia, newspaper declared that the Bonaparte family sought to "[extend] their limbs and branches over the whole civilized world" and worried that "a scion [Bo] is now acknowledged to be shooting up in the United States." Couching his concerns in the language of virtuous republicanism versus corrupting luxury, the writer "suspect[ed] that our habits, manners and institutions will be found unfriendly to its growth in that luxurious style which the head of the family thinks necessary in all its members."[109] New Englander William Jenks was one of the first Americans to fear the consequences of the presence of an imperial heir in Baltimore. In a work published in 1808, he used the story of Elizabeth and Jerome Bonaparte and their young son as an essential component of a tale of national disunion and destruction. Believing that the southern states might secede from the union with the help of France, Jenks predicted that Napoleon would demand that the "Southern Division of the States" come under "the future care of a son of [the] Imperial family," his nephew Bo, who was already "allied to the Americans by blood and every tender consideration."[110]

The tremendous anxiety many policy makers felt over the future of Spanish America intensified the problem of the American Bonapartes. Napoleon's decision to place his brother Joseph on the Spanish throne in 1808 had ignited American fears about the future of the New World. If Spain's colonies remained loyal to the new king, Napoleon would gain a powerful foothold in the New World—one that extended to the uncertain borders of the United States.[111] Elizabeth and her son often seemed to be part of a larger Bonapartist incursion into the Western Hemisphere. One newspaper even predicted that the Louisiana territory would be returned to France and that Elizabeth's son would become its "Emperor."[112] The British minister Sir Augustus John Foster surmised that it was "not improbable too that [Napoleon] might have entertained some such vague intention at that time of making use of the boy in his Spanish intrigues" or, more ambitious still, of finding a place for him in some "gigantic plan for North America that along with other visionary projects he was never allowed to ripen."[113] Spanish diplomat Luis de Onís mistakenly reported to his superiors that President Madison's obvious preference for France had led him to heed a request from Napoleon to consider "erecting a monarchy in the United States" for the emperor's nephew.[114] This geopolitical context helped make the Titles of Nobility Amendment a nonpartisan issue that provoked little debate in either the House or the Senate. Indeed, few congressmen voted against it.

In its final form the proposed amendment read: "If any citizen of the United States shall accept, claim, receive, or retain, any title of nobility or honor, or shall, without the consent of Congress, accept any present, pension, office, or emolument, of any kind whatever, from any Emperor, King, Prince, or foreign Power, such person shall cease to be a citizen of the United States, and shall be incapable of holding any office of trust or profit under them, or either of them."[115] It easily passed the Senate on April 26, 1810, and the House of Representatives five days later. It was then sent out to the states for ratification to become the thirteenth amendment to the Constitution.

Even while the amendment was being considered for ratification, Elizabeth did not curtail her aristocratic behavior and still awaited her title. At parties in Washington, she acted the part of the duchess at court, wearing "the most superb dress" Robert Bayly had "ever beheld" and "a crown on her head sent by the emperor of France, which . . . cost $15000." In such regal attire, she reminded Bayly "very much of Burke's description of the Queen of France."[116] "*The pretty little Duchess of Baltimore*" outshone "all the Ladies here for the splendour and elegance of her dress," Catharine Mitchill related in 1811. "Even Mrs. M[adison] cannot sport Dimonds and pearls in such profusion."[117] Is it any wonder that so many saw Elizabeth as capable of seducing republican Americans into monarchical subjects with, in Timothy Pickering's words, such "gorgeous scenes of royalty?" Her public conversation fit her appearance. Far from assuming a retiring pose during the firestorm of public debate, Elizabeth flaunted her connections to imperial blood as well as her cosmopolitan clout. In November 1811, Samuel Smith reported to his daughter that her cousin "Madame B.," with her "$12000 p[er] ann:" from Napoleon, "laughs and talks, defends the Emperor and hopes he will destroy all his enemies."[118] Instead of feeling cowed or embarrassed by the amendment, Elizabeth considered it "injurious to my future prospects and vexatious in every point of view." Though she had thought about "seeking to avert its future pernicious consequences," "after mature consideration," she decided "to see it pass into effect."[119]

Elizabeth's aristocratic credentials and pretensions had gotten her into trouble with concerned congressmen and with staid matrons, but they still made her powerful in polite circles. Delaware's George B. Milligan recognized her continuing influence and power. Writing from Washington in 1812, he noted that "sover[eigns] seem to send their ambassadors here less to negotiate with the Government than to pay their adoration to her," while "the wise legislators of the nation (Senator & representatives) seem to have forgotten their errand to the capitol & their wives at home to pour forth their admiration to her beauty."[120] Even as the Titles of Nobility Amendment was being debated in Congress and the states, she received invitations to all of the important parties and balls during the capital's social season and threw parties herself that were well attended.[121] Her uncle declared that she continued to have "great attention paid her[:] rides, walks, visits, and talks."[122] Dolley Madison, the reigning queen of capital society, never abandoned her, and Elizabeth remained a fixture at the Madisons' levees. Elizabeth's behavior may have been condemned by some and regarded as threatening by others, but, ultimately, her role as a cosmopolite—as the personification of European culture and fashion—proved more powerful. Americans continued to admire her, not shun her, as they continued to admire European aristocratic culture and not entirely shun it. Elizabeth marked the boundaries of acceptable refined behavior; that was the function she served for Americans struggling to define the appropriate characteristics for their culture. Neither her abandonment and divorce, nor her scanty clothing, nor even a constitutional amendment in Congress directed at her personally could bring down the woman so many regarded as the height of fashionable style. As Elizabeth haughtily asked her father in 1815, "If people do not approbate my conduct in America, what is the reason they paid me so much attention?"[123]

Ultimately, the Titles of Nobility Amendment failed to become part of the Constitution. Between late 1810 and early 1811, six states rushed to ratify the amendment; six more did so by the end of 1812. Then, the momentum ran out just two states short of ratification.[124] The War of 1812, Napoleon's downfall, and Elizabeth's departure for Europe at the war's end dissipated the initial support for the amendment (though, for decades, many assumed, even in published works, that it had become the thirteenth amendment).

Even while legislators at the federal and state levels were acting to contain the threat she posed to the republic, Elizabeth made plans to leave her hated native land. Before the outbreak of war in June 1812, she waited in vain for an invitation from Napoleon. Then the war with the British prevented her from crossing the Atlantic. Even before the war ended, however, she had revived her plans in response to Napoleon's abdication. "The obstacles which the Emperor Napoleon opposed to my continual desire of residing in Paris," she related to Dolley Madison at the end of 1814, "have ceased with his Power."[125] She began planning in earnest for what she regarded as her destiny. She asked Madison's help in finding a respectable escort for her voyage. And she made other necessary arrangements. Friends who either lived in or had visited Europe informed

Elizabeth that a lengthy stay in Paris and other European cities would be expensive. Jonathan Russell, the minister to Sweden, counseled her that she would need about $6,000 a year to support her lifestyle.[126] But she had already prepared herself financially for this adventure. The 60,000-franc annuity from Napoleon continued until at least March 1815, nearly a year after his abdication and the restoration of the Bourbons.[127] Elizabeth had invested the money wisely and believed that, if careful, she could live well and happily in Europe. Her son would not add to the expense since she had decided to leave nine-year-old Jerome in Baltimore with her father to continue his tutoring there.

As soon as the war officially ended in February 1815, Elizabeth finalized the details for her trip, hoping to sail in early summer. With her son, escort, and funds secured, she saw to other precautions as well. Though convinced of her "unimportance [to] the actual French Government," she had heeded "the prejudices of some timid friends" by having an acquaintance ascertain "beyond all doubt" that she should "enjoy in Europe exactly the same privileges with any other American Lady who finds it agreeable to travel there: & that Paris like every other Place is quite accessible to me as to other People."[128] But by the time she sailed from Boston for Liverpool in late May or early June 1815, Napoleon was back in power. Her escorts, William and Caroline Eustis, had strongly joined in "the universal sentiment" that she should not "go [to Europe] at this time, and [that] there would be great impropriety in her going with" them; "in the present uncertain state of politics there are possible embarrassments which might occur which would be mutually unpleasant." Caroline Eustis believed Elizabeth would "doubtless defer her visit to Europe untill she can hear from France," showing how little she knew her.[129] Elizabeth was determined to begin her long-anticipated journey, with or without the Eustises. One wonders what she thought and the expectations she might have had given Napoleon's return to power and Jerome's presence in Paris as she boarded her ship with a Washington friend, Mrs. Ashley, rather than the Eustises as her escort.

The earlier furor over the Titles of Nobility Amendment had not propelled Elizabeth to Europe in 1815; her desperate desire to be at the center, not the periphery, of fashionable aristocratic life did. Her 1805 trip with Jerome had provided her first glimpse of European society and culture. Though in Lisbon for just a handful of days, she had toured grand cathedrals, ancient convents, and royal gardens, as well as purchased exquisite jewelry.[130]

Her longer stay in England, where she had given birth to her son, had exposed her further to cultural sites and aristocratic ways. Lords and their ladies had called on her and welcomed her into their circle. What she had experienced on that six-month trip had confirmed her belief that women with her qualities belonged in the glittering and convivial salons of Europe, not the insipid and simplistic parlors of America. Since her return in 1805, she had remained thoroughly unhappy whenever she was confined to her drab hometown. It was not where she longed to be—that is, in the glamorous, European, aristocratic world. For Elizabeth, and probably for many Americans, "European" and "aristocratic" seemed almost interchangeable words. Europe, for her, meant castles, chateaus, and villas; crowns, tiaras, and diamonds; salons, parties, and balls; and dynasties, lineages, and titles. Exclusivity and superiority characterized her meanings of Europe. Those words also meant "Europe" for many Americans and had led Elizabeth's appearance, behavior, and sentiments—those of Europe's aristocrats, not its peasants or bourgeoisie—to seem dangerous in a republic. With little regard for her native country and with great anticipation, she sailed in the summer of 1815 for her long-awaited arrival in the city she assumed she had been destined for, Paris. Napoleon's actions once again deferred that dream, but only momentarily.

Wisely, Elizabeth did not travel immediately to Paris on her arrival at Liverpool sometime in late June or early July 1815, probably because Napoleon, with Jerome by his side, had met defeat at the Battle of Waterloo on June 18 and abdicated four days later. Elizabeth must have decided to extend her visit as the newly restored Louis XVIII decided the fate of her imperial former brother-in-law and her royal former husband. She happily bided her time in England, traveling to London, where she ironically received invitations to the Duke of Wellington's parties. "Treated with the utmost distinction" at one of his balls, she declared it "the happiest moment of her life."[131] A letter of introduction to the already famous artist Benjamin West allowed her to visit his gallery and make his acquaintance. Writing to her father from Cheltenham, England, where she was taking the waters for her health (the reason she had given for going to Europe), Elizabeth noted that the "political state of Europe is still fluctuating. France is a volcano, from which occasionally are emitted sparks of fire which threaten alike all parties." By late August, Napoleon was exiled to the island of St. Helena and the rest of his family was permitted to reside in Italy. "Louis XVIII remains at Paris," she reported, "protected by the combined forces of Europe," but Napoleon had "left behind him a reputation which adversity has not subverted."[132] Though assured the "same privileges" as other American travelers in late 1814, Elizabeth received a warning soon after her arrival in Cheltenham in September 1815 that, in Paris, "the Police Officers are watching for the moment of your arrival."[133] The warning did not deter her. By November 1815, when the Bonaparte chaos had settled, Elizabeth moved on to Paris, her dream.

After leaving Baltimore for Europe in 1815, Elizabeth stayed abroad for almost twenty years with just a few short return trips to the United States during that time. For example, she returned briefly to Maryland in late 1817 to check on her son. She worried that the Pattersons, especially her ardently patriotic father, had too much influence over Bo and were ruining him for the aristocratic or even royal future that she hoped awaited him in Europe. Elizabeth would soon spend several years in Geneva, Switzerland, where she enrolled her son in school. After returning home in 1824 for less than a year to visit Bo, who had left Europe earlier, and to look after financial matters, Elizabeth soon sailed again for Europe in June 1825. Though she had intended to return to the United States the following year, Elizabeth would remain in Europe for the next nine years, often spending the summers in Paris and the falls and winters in Geneva and Florence. Over these years, Elizabeth became even more European and aristocratic in her views, and every trip confirmed her strong belief in the superiority of monarchies over republics and of luxurious aristocratic ways over simple republican ones.

By waiting until 1815, Elizabeth arrived, much to her advantage, in a new Europe where the old lines of wealth and aristocratic prestige had been scrambled. The Atlantic world of a generation earlier had been greatly transformed, first by revolution and then by Napoleon. The France that she visited was neither that of the *ancien régime* nor that of the Bonaparte empire. Social hierarchies had been redrawn but not in completely new ways. There were still aristocrats who possessed grand estates and dominated society, but the definition of who constituted an aristocrat had been rewritten. Aristocrats with a long lineage now mingled, intermarried, and shared social and economic power with aristocrats of recent vintage and far more mundane backgrounds. The newcomers were treated as legitimate nobles. The Bourbon restoration actually intensified aristocratic culture, though in an altered form, and encouraged salons through its blending of the old and new.[134] That it was a new aristocratic world mattered little to Elizabeth. If the aristocrats with whom she socialized were not only of the old guard but also those with little or no lineage—those Napoleon had "picked . . . out of the mud and made . . . rich and noble"—she little cared; everything looked aristocratic, and she was now in the middle of it.[135] In fact, this new order made her entrée into society and claims to status even easier. The welcoming reception that she received reinforced the exalted views she held of herself and European society, as well as her negative views of America as hopelessly provincial. Cosmopolitan aristocrats, whether new or old, and their fashionable way of living were what she had sought, and she now found herself in the center of what she had longed to experience.

The revolutions and wars in Europe between 1748 and 1815 had fostered national sentiment and patriotic loyalty in many European nations. This nationalism demanded a new kind of European cosmopolitanism. Cosmopolites before the French Revolution and Napoleonic wars had defined themselves differently than post-Napoleonic cosmopolites would. Eighteenth-century "citizens of the world" had primarily been men of enlightened education and refinement—philosophers, scientists, naturalists—who had made connections with others like themselves primarily through letters and print. The postal system and printing technology had allowed a "republic of letters" to flourish throughout Europe and even in the Americas, spreading Enlightenment ideas and discoveries and joining them together in an imagined, but meaningful, community of intellectuals that extended across geographical and political boundaries.[136] At royal courts, at universities, and at leisure sites, a roaming community of courtiers and nobles had constructed a different, but intertwined, version of cosmopolitanism. The French Revolution and the Napoleonic wars had transformed those cosmopolitan communities. Many aristocrats lost their properties and some their lives. Bonaparte's replacement of ruling families with his own brothers, sisters, and relatives in France, Austria, Italy, Spain, Germany, and the Netherlands, as well as his devastating wars, reconfigured who held power and wealth throughout Europe. Equally transformative, most of the men of the republic of letters—key figures of the eighteenth-century cosmopolitan community—embraced the growing nationalism of the early nineteenth century and became some of its most vocal proponents. In other words, their enlightened cosmopolitanism, their sense of belonging to a community of citizens of the world that was above and beyond local identities, had been replaced by patriotic nationalism, a strong sense of identification with and love of country. Their writings increasingly contributed to and fostered nationalistic pride in their own country's culture and politics.[137]

By 1815, what characterized and who constituted the community of cosmopolites had changed in the face of a transformed ruling hierarchy and emergent nationalism. No longer a republic of letters composed primarily of well-educated men or of landed aristocrats centered around royal courts, European cosmopolitans developed into a broader community consisting of old aristocrats who had withstood or accommodated to the challenges to their place, new aristocrats who were struggling to prove they deserved their recently elevated status, and a large, roaming group of displaced aristocrats, royals, and other wealthy elites—émigrés—who moved around Europe, gathering at fashionable resorts, urban centers, and country estates and villas.[138] This last group perhaps played a central role in the reconfigured circle of cosmopolites and in shaping new definitions of cosmopolitanism in the new nationalistic world. Cosmopolites became more mobile, less rooted. As American author Washington Irving noted in 1815 on a trip to Europe, "there are so many huge Stars & comets thrown out of their orbits & whirling about the world at present."[139] The face-to-face interaction among cosmopolites made possible by their travels increasingly became the measure of membership in the community, challenging a cosmopolitan community based on letter writing and the spread of the printed word. French was the language of this community and fashionable French clothing and behavior its hallmarks. The new cosmopolitan community, moreover, was not only more open to women but even dominated by them. They seemed to have controlled much of its life and identity.[140] Writers, such as Germaine de Staël, Madame de Genlis, and Lady Sydney Morgan; *salonnières*, such as Jeanne-Françoise Récamier, the Comtesse de Rémusat, and Madame de Rumford; and fashionable celebrities, such as Princess Alexandre Caroline Galitzin, the Russian Princess Potemkin, the Marquise de Villette, and the divorced Lady Westmeath, apparently controlled the contours of and admission to the cosmopolitan community. Elizabeth Patterson Bonaparte's style of cosmopolitanism and her background perfectly fit with this newly formed version. She had arrived in Europe at the perfect time.

In Europe, especially in Paris, the aristocrats—new and even old— embraced Elizabeth as a transatlantic celebrity. Her tragic story and the cosmopolitan image she had so earnestly cultivated for herself gave Elizabeth access to the aristocrats traveling around in Europe. "My misfortune," she informed her father in 1815 from England, provided "a passport to the favor of the great," while her "talents and manners" seemed "likely to preserve their good opinion."[141] Her close study of their lifestyle paid off with intimate friendships with numerous aristocrats, including Voltaire's protégée and adopted daughter the Marquise de Villette, a "great friend" with whom she dined "three times a week"; the celebrated novelist Lady Sydney Morgan, whom she saw "every day" and with whom she toured the sights of Paris; and such émigré Russian royals as Prince Nicolas Demidoff, Princess Caroline Galitzin, and Princess Potemkin. She formed affable acquaintances with many more, including Germaine de Staël, Madame Récamier, Lady Westmorland, and the Countess d'Orsay, whose balls she attended weekly. Many of the aristocrats she encountered and befriended considered her one of them because of her marital ties and cultivated appearance. A number of titled men—including the Duke of Wellington, Lord William Russel, the Grand Duke of Mecklenburg-Schwerin, an impoverished French count, and a son of the Duke of Sussex, who professed he "was one of [Elizabeth's] captives"—fell in love with her; some may have even proposed to her.[142] The Prince of Württemberg, Jerome's second wife's uncle, was rumored to have said that "Jerome had made a great mistake in deserting so charming a woman." The Russian prince Alexandre Gortchakoff, whom Elizabeth first met in Florence and remained friends with, exclaimed, "Had she been near the throne, the Allies would have had more difficulty in overthrowing Napoleon." Even Talleyrand allegedly remarked, "If she were a queen, how gracefully she would reign!"[143] Her celebrity and reputation was such that the restored King Louis XVIII regretted that she would "not come to [his] Court."[144] Writing to her family, Elizabeth took pride that "people of rank and distinction . . . are willing to notice me."[145]

She found Geneva especially appealing, perhaps even more so than her beloved Paris. Foreign aristocrats and royalty of all sorts swarmed Geneva in the early 1820s, and Elizabeth quickly gained access to the best of European society there. She considered this quite a triumph since "it is more difficult to obtain access to [elite Swiss] society than in any other country." "For whatever cause," she was "better received than any other stranger of greater rank or infinitely greater wealth has ever been."[146] Bo also found a place in the social whirl. Writing to his grandfather in Baltimore, he described a "superb feast of eight hundred persons, where there were rockets and all kinds of artificial fires" and added that "Mama goes out nearly every night to a party or a ball." But the son was not nearly as enraptured with European society as his mother. "Since I have been in Europe," he acknowledged to his grandfather, "I have dined with princes and princesses and all the great people in Europe, but I have not found a dish as much to my taste as the roast beef and beef-steaks I ate in South Street" (at his grandfather's house).[147] Bo's preference for an American instead of a European lifestyle would soon place him at odds with his mother.

During her lengthy stay in Europe, Elizabeth began talking and writing about Americans and their society with an intensity she never had previously. Before 1815, Americans had subjected her to endless scrutiny and judgment; after 1815, she scrutinized and judged Americans. Her antipathy toward American society, politics, and culture colored her letters throughout these years, and they offer especially eloquent testimony to her thinking about her relationship with the American republic and her fellow countrymen and to the still-open question of whether a republic without aristocratic elements was desirable. Europe, in her view, bested the United States on every point. Soon after her arrival in England in 1815, she enthused: "Europe more than meets the brilliant and vivid colors in which my imagination had portrayed it. Its resources are infinite, much beyond those which can be offered us in a new country." But Elizabeth had arrived at a time when European interest in America was high; to her chagrin, "American institutions, government, manners, climate, etc., etc., have become the subject of inquiry and concern" in elite European circles. She felt compelled by "fashion" to display "patriotic feelings" and "draw a veil over the defects of my country." But she never performed that feat very well. She did "feel some little complacency" in declaring herself "an individual of a country which every one seems to think will one day be great"—a view she did not share. "The British are," she readily concluded, "the greatest nation in the world," since they defeated "the man whose talents menaced their existence."[148]

Elizabeth was not the only American of this era who scorned American simplicity and embraced the glamour of European society instead. Charleston-born Margaret Manigault longingly declared to her close friend Josephine du Pont of Delaware that "only in France can one enjoy life."[149] Elizabeth's girlhood friend, Henriette Pascault, who had married the Frenchman Jean-Jacques Reubell around the time of Elizabeth's marriage and had been to France, "still sigh[ed] after Europe & its pleasures" years after her return to the United States.[150] Elizabeth's kinswoman, Elizabeth Caton, traveled to Europe soon after Elizabeth to escape the mundaneness of the United States and "dazzle the *Courts* of Europe," where her "charms & accomplishments" could be better "estimated" than in her dowdy native land.[151] His grandaughters' presentation at the French royal court in 1817 "delighted" Charles Carroll, who bragged about it to all who would listen back in Annapolis.[152] Other Americans, including a number of American ministers and their families, shared the sentiments of both Elizabeths, preferring the delights of European cities over the simplicities of American society, and chose to stay in Europe, if not for their entire lives, then for lengthy visits. Laura Hughes, the wife of an American minister to Sweden, and Elizabeth's cousin Mary Mansfield, who married a titled Englishman, "both agreed that neither of them [could] ever live in America again."[153] Hannah Gallatin and her children, especially her son James, dreaded their return to the United States after years abroad. While on a return visit to New York in 1815, James Gallatin complained that "I honestly feel I would much prefer to live in either France or England—all is so crude in this country." Just two years in Europe, he believed, had already "unfitted me for America." Facing the prospect of moving to the home his father had built in western Virginia in 1822, Gallatin confessed that his mother "detests" the United States and wondered how his father could "expect" the family "to live in idleness in the backwoods of America" after "lead[ing] a life absolutely different from that at home"—a life he described as being dedicated "to simply wasting my time in an everlasting routine of enjoyment."[154]

The admiration, respect, and friendship that Elizabeth found in Europe, especially France, reinforced her anti-American attitudes. She criticized not only the lack of true refinement in American culture but also the direction in which the United States, its society, and its gender roles and expectations were headed in the early decades of nation building. Like some other American travelers, including James Fenimore Cooper on occasion, Elizabeth disparaged American society for being too democratic and disorderly. She saw little merit in a republican government or society based on ideas of equality, liberty, and popular participation, and never hesitated to share her views with friends and family. She found it entirely impossible, as she informed her father, "to be contented in a country where there exists no nobility, and where the society is unsuitable in every respect to my tastes."[155] Refined republicans were not enough. She made it clear to her cousin that in France she remained "much more contented then I can ever expect to be in my own Country," and then spat: "Oh! That country can claim no gratitude from me for I never experienced its favors. Bitter are its recollections, deplorable the anticipation of returning to it."[156] She even believed that her dog, Le Loup, was happier in

Europe, where "he had been used to drawing-rooms and fine ladies" and "to much attention" (including an invitation to "a large evening party," which he attended), than in Baltimore, where he found only cold floors and "black faces in the kitchen" that "must have frightened him."[157] "What can I say," she confessed to her dear friend, Prince Alexandre Gortchakoff, "monarchy just suits me better than republican vulgarity: the republic has repelled me from the day I arrived in the world."[158] Her admiration for Napoleon's empire never waned—even when he shunned her and deprived her of a husband and her son of a father. Her only criticism was that he had "hurled me back on what I most hated on earth—my Baltimore obscurity."[159] Even then, she fully understood Napoleon had acted for his empire. It was Jerome she hated—intensely and until she died—for not fighting for her and finding some way for her, too, to have become a part of the grand imperial court. When Napoleon's empire crumbled, she took solace in the restoration of the Bourbon monarchy.

Elizabeth's upper-class status and even higher aspirations drove her views of where the American republic seemed to be heading. She clearly regretted the direction American society had taken since the 1790s. Like other social conservatives, including a significant number of Federalists and other privileged Northerners and Southerners (those who styled themselves an "American aristocracy"), Elizabeth despaired of elites losing their influence in society as the public sphere of politics and business incorporated more people from the middling ranks and grew more important. Many elite families in the South and in northern cities firmly believed, well into the first half of the nineteenth century, that those "who enjoyed wealth, sophistication, education, exposure to the wider world, and other privileges ought to receive deference from those who did not."[160] According to Harman Blennerhassett, Mary Randolph, a near-relation of Thomas Jefferson's, "uttered . . . treason" as "she ridiculed the experiment of a republic in this country" for its "vices and inconsistency of the parties and the people."[161] As early as 1806, Benjamin Henry Latrobe lamented the kind of society a government of *"an unlettered majority"* had created, one that "put down even that ideal rank which manners has established." With no titles of nobility to give status, all "importance [was] attached to wealth." This "state of society," Latrobe concluded, must "present a very unpleasant picture" to "a cultivated mind, to a man of letters, to a lover of the arts."[162] James Gallatin concurred. He found that he had "nothing in common with the young American men" for, in addition to their "horrible chewing of tobacco," they "are all absorbed in making money" instead of pursuing a life of "luxury and excitement."[163] The few times Americans pleased Elizabeth was when she encountered some in Europe who "had sense and good taste enough to feel that [she] had risen above them, and always treated [her] with the respect and deference due to a superior."[164]

By the 1820s, American society had grown more democratic, both politically and economically, and American capitalism had allowed the middle class to displace the hold that elites once had on society and culture. These transformations caused the United States to appear even further removed from the centers of cosmopolitanism. James Fenimore Cooper confessed in print in the late 1820s that "as a people" Americans were "beyond a question, decidedly provincial, but our provincialism is not exactly one of external appearance." While American men were "negligent of dress," women "dress remarkably near the Parisian *modes*."[165] So, for Cooper, American provincialism must have been internal—a mixture of republican and, by this time, middle-class beliefs and behaviors. Elizabeth detested the attempts of the American middle class to adopt the appurtenances of the elite when they did not possess the wealth, the attitudes, or the refinement for such a lifestyle. She was convinced that the "fine house and the extravagant mode of living" her uncle, General Samuel Smith, had "introduced into Baltimore caused the ruin of half the people in the place, who, without this example, would have been contented to live in habitations better suited to their fortunes; and certainly they only made themselves ridiculous by aping expenses little suited to a community of people of business." Businessmen and their wives only appeared foolish and ended up bankrupt when they tried to live in large houses and follow a genteel lifestyle. Elizabeth "hoped that in [the] future there will be no palaces constructed" in American cities since she could "not recollect a single instance, except that of [William] Bingham, of any one who built one in America, not dying a bankrupt."[166] For those from Elizabeth's social and economic circle, the growing democracy was a situation to be lamented, not celebrated. To her sister-in-law, Mary Caton Patterson (who would eventually marry the Marquis of Wellesley), she violently declared: "I hate, I abhor America. I can never exist there."[167] Likewise, she emphatically informed her father that her "happiness [could] never be separated from rank and Europe."[168]

While Elizabeth occasionally wished more Americans were in Europe to witness her triumphs in its exclusive, aristocratic circles, she interacted with only a select few of the Americans who did visit Europe, including John Jacob Astor, the American fur baron, and the Gallatins. To her "great annoyance," "quite a Baltimore society," including her brother with the Caton sisters and some other relatives, landed in Paris during the winter of 1816.[169] As she made clear to her cousin, "my object is French Society." She stayed as far away as possible from her provincial "compatriots," who tended to congregate together rather than visit "in either French or English Houses" as she did.[170] Indeed, Elizabeth had successfully transformed her identity into that of a cosmopolitan aristocrat and surrounded herself with them, not with provincial Americans. "Dukes, Counts, Marquis" filled Elizabeth's drawing rooms, where she reigned "as a little Queen."[171] Elizabeth quickly perceived that American travelers often sought to use her to gain admittance to select gatherings. But, not wanting to be linked with boorish Americans, she refused to play this role. American visitors had looked to Elizabeth, their own cosmopolitan role model, to provide entrance into the exclusive circles of European aristocrats. She found it offensive, however, that visiting Americans considered her "business in Paris to be Introductrice des Americains." "Not being paid by the United States for so troublesome a place," she sarcastically noted, "I declined the honour & ceremonies of the Office & left my fellow travellers to present themselves in the societies of Paris." This infuriated a number of Americans who, on returning home, spread the word about how "very ungrateful & unamiable" Elizabeth had become. In this, as in other matters, though, she little heeded the criticisms of her fellow Americans. She had been granted access to the centers of culture and fashion, and, once she entered, she had overcome her own provincialism and been accepted. But her achievement would be threatened if she regularly played the role of "introductrice" and let any other than worthy Americans into that circle. She admitted as much to her cousin, telling him how she had "offended Major Mercer" when she "refus[ed] to present him at Mde. Recamiers." Mercer had been woefully mistaken, in her opinion, when he "thought the circle would be agreeably enlarged by his presence, & that if an American woman [Elizabeth] was admitted, she might get a countryman squeezed in." But Elizabeth "dared not monopolize two places in such company" at Récamier's salon, fearing that her place "should be withheld for my indiscretion" and that she "should be left to sit at home with the Gossiping Major."[172] Elizabeth staunchly guarded the aristocratic persona she had created for herself and the privileged place that her image had gained her among the cosmopolites.

Furthermore, she believed she knew the real reason visitors wanted to enter aristocratic circles. Many elite Americans traveled for the cachet a trip to

Europe would gain them at home and knew that socializing with aristocrats would increase their cultural capital. That seemed to be why so many of them desperately wanted Elizabeth to get them access to aristocratic circles. Her brother Edward agreed with her that "most" American travelers desired "admittance into the high circles" because they possessed "high pretensions" and that ultimately most found "disappointment" in their "failure" to enter exclusive society.[173] Brother and sister both regarded these visiting Americans' quest as foolish. Indeed, when Edward's neighbors, merchant Robert Gilmor, his wife, Sarah, and a young female relative, prepared for a trip to Europe in 1817, Edward wrote to Elizabeth in Paris that "the people in your part of the world must think Baltimore a very stupid place as so many of its inhabitants migrate in pursuit of amusement or admiration," without a hint that he included his sister in this indictment. When in Paris with Elizabeth, South Carolinian William C. Preston concurred with her opinions about visiting Americans. "Our countrymen have preëminent and indecent propensity to thrust themselves upon exclusive circles, to seek the acquaintance of distinguished and above all titled people," he recorded in his travel memoirs. He, like Elizabeth, found the American "indulgence of this appetite" quite boorish, as the visitors "often trample upon rules of propriety and expose themselves to disparaging remarks."[174]

By the 1810s and 1820s, however, American travelers also used a trip to Europe to develop or deepen their sense of national pride while traveling abroad, assuaging their feelings of provincial inferiority while at the metropolitan center by comparing their country's republican simplicity to Europe's aristocratic luxury.[175] As Elizabeth explained to her cousin, Americans "sought to know" European high society "for the virtuous purpose of being disgusted with vice and [being] confirmed in [their] primitive simplicity & republican opinions."[176] As American men and women traveled through Europe in increasing numbers throughout the 1820s and 1830s, they assessed its society and politics, often convincing themselves of the superiority of their homeland. While on a visit to Italy in 1836, American Fanny Hall recorded her belief that, although the United States lacked "marble palaces, adorned with crimson and gold, and embellished with exquisite paintings" and "public gardens on a scale of royal magnificence," what it did have was "infinitely preferable": "laws which respect equally the rights of the poorest peasant and the richest citizen."[177] Though Elizabeth tried "dissuading" Ann and James Brown from leaving Paris after the end of his tenure as American minister to France since "no happiness is to [be] found in the United States which can compare with the pleasures of European society," the Browns felt "assured" that, although they had "seen a great deal of society under its most attractive forms," they could be "happy in our native country."[178] Similarly, one of Elizabeth's friends wrote to her in Paris that, while in America they did not have "Parisian splendour," the "simplicity & good nature of the golden age are all our own." "We have no scandal b[l]acklisting nor ill nature," she continued her rhapsody, "no *envy* hatred nor malice: who . . . would not delight to dwell in such scenes of sweet unsophisticated Nature."[179] This woman on the periphery obviously tried to make clear to one at the center that America trumped Europe in its virtues if not its charms.

Elizabeth fully understood the cultural work that a trip to Europe performed for Americans, whom she recognized as "offended & complaining Moralists," in the early decades of the nineteenth century. She "found their whinings so uninteresting [about] the corruption of European morals" and tired of their hypocritical "growling at my selfishness for engrossing these corrupt people to myself."[180] She knew, perhaps better than the tourists themselves, that Americans came to Europe to condemn it and, in turn, to fuel their growing sense of native pride and overcome their feelings of inferiority, even as many of them secretly adored it. Elizabeth was fully acquainted with the language of moralistic nationalism—of American simplicity and virtue versus European luxury and corruption—that Americans regularly employed in their comparisons. She also completely understood they felt superior when confronted with the luxurious culture of aristocratic Europe. She herself had struggled so much to get there and then to stay there.

Her complete dissatisfaction with the United States, while perhaps not surprising to historians, surprised many of her contemporaries—men and women who enthusiastically supported and firmly believed in republican ideals and the promising future of their new nation. Some who knew Elizabeth "loath[ed]" her country were willing to forgive her "for the crime of visiting foreign countries" if she would just return to live in the United States and stop being so negative.[181] But others were less charitable. Her old friend Eliza Godefroy scolded Elizabeth in 1817 for being "so impolite as to abuse your own country as you do." Even though Godefroy herself considered zealous "Love of Country" "a fashionable cant" of the era, she wanted Elizabeth to know that her comments had been regarded as "nothing less than treason." "All the Americans come back" from Europe, Godefroy reported, "furious against you." "Be witty as you will," she warned, "but for God's sake chuse some other subject or I am afraid if you ever come back you will share the fate of Ovid amongst the Goths."[182] But having found a society that valued her particular ideas and admired the qualities she possessed, Elizabeth did not take such warnings seriously. In her view, her Baltimore neighbors were merely envious of her "elevated situation" or embarrassed because "they know that their daughters might come here and never be known." She believed she could prove their envy: "Look how they run after the poorest sprigs of nobility, and then you will [truly] know what they think of my standing in Europe." In a clear reference to the Caton sisters, who were planning a trip to Europe, Elizabeth proclaimed: "Let them come and try which is of most consequence, they or me!" She was confident that "all their government stock, insurance stock and real property could never put them" in a "rank" equal to hers.[183] While the Caton sisters, in fact, succeeded in the highest circles in England and eventually married aristocrats, that only proved that Elizabeth was not alone in her valuing of European above American culture.

During Elizabeth's long and repeated visits to Europe between 1815 and 1834, counts and countesses, dukes and duchesses, and princes and princesses from France, Russia, Germany, Italy, Poland, and Switzerland—the roaming cosmopolitan aristocrats of post-Napoleonic Europe—all befriended her. Surrounded by titled cosmopolitans, she never failed at fitting easily among them and never once was regarded as an interloping provincial. Through economical living and fortunate friendships with generous noblemen and -women, Elizabeth spent her days in grand country estates, splendid palaces, and elegant townhouses and dressed at the height of fashion in her exquisite jewelry. She traveled Europe confidently and comfortably, avoiding only Rome where, according to James Fenimore Cooper, Jerome and his second wife lived "in a good deal of style, and enjoys his ancient reputation, which is none of the best."[184] Though she relied primarily on her self-created status, not on that linked with her unfaithful husband, Elizabeth was a triumph in aristocratic, cosmopolitan Europe.

In the first third of the nineteenth century, Elizabeth Patterson Bonaparte's image, literally and figuratively, came to embody Europe as a cosmopolitan center. Even when she was most celebrated at home, she considered American ideas of refinement to be a poor substitute for European luxury. She paraded her stylish French fashions and exploited her glamorous connection to the Bonapartes. Given the new, more fluid definitions of aristocracy in Europe,

Figure 7. Dressed in stylish clothes, Elizabeth had this portrait painted soon after her arrival in Europe. François-Joseph Kinson, 1817. Image #XX.5.72, courtesy of the Maryland Historical Society.

her French connections and aristocratic sentiments gained her public fame and social power in American as well as European social circles. But her adoption of European in preference to American notions of fashion, society, and politics also earned her criticism and condemnation. Americans recognized that she chose to act more like a luxurious aristocrat than a refined republican and feared what such a woman could do to their republic. The proposed Titles of Nobility Amendment clearly encapsulated the threat Americans saw in Elizabeth and her son. Elizabeth understood that in her native land, a new country actively working at building a nation and creating a distinct culture, "they consider me an apostate from the Republic, an impudent & successful imitator of high Life, which they [profess] to dispise[:] in short[,] a bad Citizen."[185] But she had never wanted to be an admired member of that republic or a good citizen; nor had she ever desired to play the role of a "Columbian's modest wife." She had wanted acclaim and to live in Europe's aristocratic circles—at the cosmopolitan center, not the provincial periphery. Her "ideas soared too high for anything in [her] own country," her financial agent in London perceptively understood, "which of course must have given offence to all around" her in the United States.[186] But she little cared. Elizabeth had become a social success in first America and then Europe, garnering social and cultural power because of her cosmopolitan status, family connections, and even scandalous clothes. Yet her behavior, ideas, and connections also offended and worried Americans. She was an extraordinary woman who presented a model of womanhood few Americans could understand.

Chapter 3

"A Modern Philosophe"
The Independent Woman

During the final months of 1812, in the midst of a war with Great Britain that was already going poorly for Americans, the members of Maryland's House of Delegates discussed a divorce for "Madame Bonaparte." One issue that had to be decided was whether Elizabeth would appear before the House and "exert the blandishments of her beauty and address to induce a favorable impression."[1] Many delegates "express[ed] great anxiety to *see* you *here*, saying they are sure your presence would remove every scruple," according to Delegate William B. Barney. But Barney thought her presence unnecessary, notifying Elizabeth: "I will not consent to your indignifying yourself so much."[2] Elizabeth's petition for a divorce from Jerome Bonaparte caused some acrimony in the House and provided new fodder for gossip in social circles.

Some time that fall, Elizabeth had decided to pursue a formal divorce from Jerome. Why she chose this moment, seven years after Jerome deserted her and five years after his marriage to Catherine of Württemberg, is somewhat unclear. Some gossips busied themselves guessing at her motives. When he heard of the divorce petition, William Burwell surmised that "Madame Bonaparte . . . must have some scheme of marriage on the taps" since "she has given up all desire to be united with the King of Westphalia."[3] Jerome had recently pressed hard for his son to be sent to Westphalia, so Elizabeth may have wanted to establish her control over her son and her future. There may also have been financial considerations. Decades later, in 1857, she stated that she had obtained a divorce from the Maryland legislature "to enable me to acquire & hold property, or to perform any act in relation to property: in fact to make any Contract or agreement binding on others or on myself in the ordinary transactions of life."[4] In other words, she wanted to become what was known in legal terms as a *feme sole.* Whatever her reason, Elizabeth seemed ready for the divorce, being "cruelly disappointed [at] having attained neither" the "honor [nor] profit" she had expected "from the marriage."[5]

Though Napoleon had pushed an annulment of her marriage through a French diocesan court in October 1806, few, including the Catholic Church and Elizabeth, considered that act legal. Elizabeth wanted to end the marriage formally in an American court. As such, by November 1812, clearly with the help of a lawyer, she drafted a petition to Maryland's General Assembly. At the time, a divorce was a legislative rather than judicial act that required the passing of a bill. Elizabeth began her petition like hundreds of others, stating the simple facts that she resided in Baltimore and that she and Jerome had been "united in matrimonial alliance" in 1803. Then, she unfolded her striking story. "Since that period," her petition continued, "Mr. Jerome Bonaparte departed from this country for France, where, on his arrival, his Brother [the] Imperial Majesty, the Emperor Napoleon of France, thought proper to consider the marriage between your Petitioner and the said Mr Jerôme as null." It further stated that Jerome had "since united himself in marriage with a German Princess, and been created King of Westphalia." Everyone who read her petition would already have known her story—a story so different from that of other divorce petitions. Tales of desertion and even bigamy were not uncommon. But a desertion ordered by the French emperor and a bigamist who had become king of a European country made Elizabeth's petition unique. Elizabeth then returned to the more common language of petitioners, stressing the "delicacy of her situation" and her reliance on "an enlightened Legislature" to grant her "the necessary aid to dissolve an union contracted and maintained under such circumstances." She closed her petition with the recognition that while "the marriage contract" should be of an "indissoluble nature," "cases may and do occur, where the happiness of Individuals may be consulted without sacrificing the permanent good of society."[6]

Elizabeth's petition was turned into a bill by a committee, quickly passed the Senate on November 18, and had its first reading in the House of Delegates soon after. The proposed bill, "An Act Annulling the Marriage of Jerome Bonaparte King of Westphalia and Elizabeth Bonaparte of the City of Baltimore," relied heavily on the language of the petition. It detailed in its preamble the date of the marriage, the desertion, and the remarriage of Jerome, as well as the role Napoleon had played in the annulment, Jerome's marriage to the German princess, and his elevation to king of Westphalia. Since "the prayer of the petitioner appear[ed] reasonable," the bill pronounced:

> Be it enacted by the General Assembly of Maryland that the Marriage of the said Jerome Bonaparte, King of Westphalia, and Elizabeth Bonaparte of the City of Baltimore heretofore solemnized, be, and the same is hereby declared to be absolutely to all intents and purposes Null and Void; and the said Jerome Bonaparte and Elizabeth Bonaparte are declared to be divorced "a Vinculo Matrimonii"; Provided, nevertheless, that nothing in this act contained shall be construed to illegitimate the Child born of the said Jerome Bonaparte and Elizabeth Bonaparte, any law to the contrary notwithstanding.[7]

Elizabeth's supporters worried about the second reading of the bill and the ensuing vote because of the "*known* opposition intended to be made by many *Fed[eralist]s*."[8] They discussed whether it would be useful to have Elizabeth address the legislature in person in order to remove any opposition with her charm and beauty. That turned out to be unnecessary. A few Federalists did make some "feeble" attempts to defeat the bill, and one opposed it from the floor. William Barney later stressed to Elizabeth that, "without every caution which was used on the occasion[,] the Bill would have been lost," including holding off "a malicious attempt . . . made by a Mr. Crabb, at a time when the friends of it were out of the House."[9] But some "friends of the Bill" did object to the first section of the bill, detailing Elizabeth's reasons for the divorce, and to the references to Jerome as the King of Westphalia. Barney and another legislator quickly led a vote to strike the objectionable preamble and words and then moved for passage of the bill in its amended form. It passed the House by a vote of 44 to 31, owing, according to Barney, to "good management alone."[10] He was confident that the Senate would accept the bill in its amended form.

Perhaps to escape the pressure in Baltimore, Elizabeth left with her aunt Nancy Spear for Washington, D.C., where she had rented a house. There, Elizabeth waited anxiously for the General Assembly to decide on her divorce. When she arrived in the capital at the end of November, everyone knew that a bill "to divorce Mrs. B. From her Royal Husband" had already passed the Maryland House and was before the Senate. Washington society kept abreast of the happenings in Maryland's assembly and filled letters and conversations with not always accurate news. On December 16, John Mifflin, having heard that the Senate had denied her petition, wrote that he felt sorry for "poor Madame B." "They cannot justify it," he insisted, considering it "some political measure, to which she is made a Sacrifice."[11] Four days later the correct news reached Washington. William Burwell quickly reported to his wife that "Madame Bonaparte has been divorced by the Legislature of Maryland."[12]

On January 2, 1813, the governor signed the divorce into law. Finally, almost eight years after Jerome deserted Elizabeth and six years after he married the Princess of Württemberg, their marriage legally ended. Rather than go into seclusion, as many divorcées did in this era, Elizabeth threw parties. William Burwell reported in early January that "Miss Patterson . . . has her parties once a week. Last night she received company & I understand the audience was numerous & splendid."[13] Elizabeth simply would not accept the role of a rejected or somehow unworthy woman.

Between 1800 and 1830 or so, as Americans worked on inventing and stabilizing their republic, the character of politics, the economy, and society remained in flux. In fact, the parameters and definitions of American institutions continuously shifted in this era. Not surprisingly, gender roles and identities, especially for women, remained in flux as well. Over time, the expectations for women that had been established and accepted in the 1780s and 1790s no longer carried as much weight—expectations based on notions of women as "republican mothers," "female politicians," and key participants in civil society.[14] But the powerful Victorian (and middle-class) notion of "separate spheres" that would come to characterize women as morally superior, wholly dependent, and primarily domestic creatures had not yet shaped gender conventions, as it would by the 1830s and 1840s. The early decades of the nineteenth century constituted a period of gender transformation; it was not a smooth one. What roles women would perform at home and in society, in private and in public, in the community and in the nation were open to discussion and debate.

The definitions of womanhood that came out of the Revolution had begun to unravel as both men and women revised their ideas about the proper place for women in American society. The Revolution had provided women with acceptable ways of taking part in party politics in the 1780s and 1790s. Those opportunities changed ideas of femininity and women's roles. During those decades, "women's opinions, issues, and needs" became an essential part of the new nation's identity.[15] This gender ideal of more independent women and the specific political roles crafted for them declined after 1800, however. By 1830, as Americans became more aware of the transformations in women's roles and women's growing identity as political beings, a conservative, "revolutionary backlash" spread throughout society and brought forth a definition of femininity primarily based in the domestic and maternal realms and one that formally removed women from partisan politics. Yet some strands of the earlier gender definitions continued, especially the emphasis on women's involvement in civil society, now as moral reformers rather than political actors and as contributors to public opinion.[16] During these few decades of flux, before a more lasting and more powerful set of gender conventions reigned, competing ideals and models of womanhood flourished. Some models hewed more closely to centuries-old, entrenched notions of femininity that emphasized dependence, inferiority, and domesticity. Some models struggled to maintain the relatively new ideal of the political and independent female that had arisen during and just after the Revolution. Other models, such as that presented by Elizabeth Patterson Bonaparte, strayed from or even completely broke with any of these notions. Suspended between two eras with dominant gender ideologies, this transitional period allowed women, especially elite women, to play with definitions of womanhood and experiment with a variety of gender roles. They did not have to rest content with their roles as wives or mothers but could seek alternative ways of being women, accepting those gender forms they liked, discarding those they did not, or even inventing new ones.[17]

These alternative versions of womanhood actively involved women in the development of the new nation. While political leaders debated the meanings of republicanism, national identity, and citizenship in the decades around 1800, women joined them. These political ideals had an impact on women's place in the republic and women understood that. Though they could not vote, women did not always shy away from politics. Indeed, women formed an important part of the public and, in their roles as citizens and women, they "ratified and legitimated the proceedings of the new national government."[18] Many women strongly believed that they could not only participate in politics but also help shape the identity and culture of the new nation. In fact, many considered this a necessary role for elite women to play in the republic.

Women of the upper classes in the early republic, including Elizabeth Patterson Bonaparte, constructed and navigated complex social positions as they
sought ways to participate in American society and culture outside of the domestic and familial spheres traditionally accorded women. The realm of "civil
society" existed beyond the household and family and offered multiple ways in
which women could function in the public world. While not overtly political,
civil society was also not domestic and private; it "blurred the lines between
state, family, market, and culture."[19] For Americans in this period, civil society meant any public arena (except organized politics) inhabited by private
persons. In general, such arenas were wide open to women. Civil society was
not male or female but a heterosocial place that bridged the gap. While civil
society encompassed all classes and the contests among them, "polite" society,
a phrase used at the time, was more exclusive. Those ladies and gentlemen who
possessed the ideas, behaviors, and accoutrements associated with gentility
and refinement constituted polite society. Though still within civil society,
polite society operated somewhat differently. It offered a transgressive space
that could confer power on its female members; in fact, women came to control much of it. Their crucial involvement in polite society made them public
figures in their own right in the new nation—social and intellectual equals of
men, if not political ones. Men accepted their influence and control, regarding
refinement and fashion as natural characteristics of women and crediting
women with leading humanity's progression from a rude to a civilized state.[20]
Ironically, then, women's long-standing association with luxury gave them
power in the public cultural arena of polite society. It also meant that women
could do more than raise virtuous sons for the republic or locate their identity
in the domestic sphere. Polite society created spaces where elite women could
focus their efforts on bringing refinement to American culture and actively
contributing to the public debates about the proper character for the nation.
The contested nature of gender boundaries in this era, along with the freedom
of movement provided by polite society, allowed elite women, such as Anne
Bingham, Dolley Madison, Judith Sargent Murray, and Elizabeth Patterson
Bonaparte, realistically to envision themselves as cultural arbiters for the
nation.

Elizabeth grew up with one set of gender expectations in the 1780s and
1790s and eventually had to accommodate herself to another set of expectations by the time she reached middle age in the 1820s and 1830s. It was between these periods that Elizabeth made important choices about marriage,

motherhood, and lifestyle—choices that help illuminate the shifting notions of gender across these decades. Like other women, especially elite women, Elizabeth spent these years actively constructing her female identity, accepting some gender conventions and challenging—explicitly and openly—others. Her negotiations among gender conventions shaped the ways she constructed her roles as a celebrity and an aristocrat. As Elizabeth crafted her own identity, she also contributed to the larger debate about the appropriate roles for women in society and in the nation as her sentiments and behavior tested the boundaries of emerging gender expectations. She was not alone in her dissatisfaction with the prospect of being limited to the roles of wife and mother, and she was not alone in her pursuit of a different, more liberating definition of womanhood. Yet most women accepted the gender limitations imposed on them by American notions of womanhood, even when they privately resented them. Instead of keeping her complaints confined to letters and diaries, as so many other women did, Elizabeth chose to break from the expected conformity. While many women failed to adhere to proper gender codes out of necessity, whether poverty, widowhood, or something similar, Elizabeth's situation gave her the freedom to make a choice. Unlike the vast majority of women in the United States, she was in charge of her own financial affairs, had full control over her son, and could live how and where she wished.

Events in her life ensured that Elizabeth would not follow the typical path of most women. She had moved very quickly out of the traditional dependent states of daughter and wife to spend most of her life as an independent woman. And even in this role she forged her own way. After 1805, Elizabeth occupied a relatively rare situation for her day and class. She had no husband but was neither a spinster nor a widow. She had no husband but had a child. At a time when other such "manless" women were typically poor, she had family wealth and a steady income, giving her a great deal of independence. This independence allowed her to pursue other feminine roles, such as social leader, female politician, or businesswoman, that lacked clear definitions and remained more open to experimentation and adaptation in this period before "separate spheres" reshaped gender conventions. As a woman fully in control of her own life and not content to play the role of the modest wife and mother, Elizabeth represented a very threatening version of womanhood at a time when men were growing "anxious about out-of-control women."[21] In this era of competing models of womanhood, she offered a peculiar version based on ambition, confidence, independence, and European concepts of gender and fashion.

The example she presented was a threatening, if alluring, one and eventually was deemed unsuitable for the republic. Elizabeth would never serve as a model for American girls to emulate. Her unconventional life certainly defied the growing nationalism of the era and the growing domestication of ideal womanhood.

Born in early 1785, Elizabeth benefitted immensely from the impact of the ideological changes that came with revolution. After the Revolution, genteel families generally agreed on the importance of education for the girls and young women of the republic. In addition to learning the customary subjects for girls, including reading, writing, ciphering, French, drawing, and dancing, young women schooled after the Revolution increasingly learned subjects previously taught only to young men: history, geography, science (often astronomy and botany), geometry, rhetoric, and, in a few progressive academies, even Latin and Greek.[22] This education, while intended to prepare them to become good republican mothers, also opened up new ideas about women's potential and the roles they might play in society. They were exposed to the possibility that educated and political women could have public roles and greater independence. Large numbers of educated young women prepared themselves to become key members of civil society and even influential contributors to public debates in the new republic.[23] Elizabeth seems to have imbibed deeply these ideas about women's independence and significance in civil society.

Like many other young women of her class, Elizabeth became an avid reader. And, like most other genteel young women of the late eighteenth century, she developed a penchant for novels and English poetry. But she also read more serious classical works at an early age, including those by Homer, which marks her education as typical for an elite, young woman. Increasingly, by the late eighteenth century, classical learning was required for any young lady who hoped to participate brilliantly in polite society.[24] Elizabeth read widely. According to a later biographer, at ten years of age, she could recite portions of her favorite books, such as Edward Young's collection of poems entitled *Night Thoughts* (1742–45) and François de La Rochefoucauld's *Maxims* (first published in 1665).[25] When she was twelve, Elizabeth received Henry Brooke's sentimental novel, *The Fool of Quality; or, The History of Henry, Earl of Moreland* (1765–70), a three-volume work that put forth Enlightenment ideas in the tradition of Rousseau. Surprisingly, even at an early age, Elizabeth was also reading more radical works by Germaine de Staël, giving her, like other girls who read De Staël, a model of a literary female and of a strong, public-oriented woman.[26] Even more radical were the works by Mary Wollstonecraft that Elizabeth read as a young woman in her teens and that, along with works by De Staël, certainly shaped her thinking about the appropriate roles for women and their relations with men. Combating the model her mother provided of a docile and submissive wife were the proto-feminist ideas Elizabeth absorbed from Wollstonecraft's *A Vindication of the Rights of Woman* (1792), which advocated equal education for women and marriages based on equality and companionship. She also owned Wollstonecraft's posthumous novel *Maria; or, The Wrongs of Woman*, published in 1798, whose heroine suffered under the social, economic, and legal restrictions of married women. According to Rosalie Stier Calvert, by the time Elizabeth was eighteen, she was known around Baltimore as "a most extraordinary girl, given to reading Godwin [Wollstonecraft] on the rights of woman, etc." "In short," Calvert declared, many considered Elizabeth "a modern *philosophe*" at a young age.[27] The education Elizabeth received, the lessons she took from it, and the gendered notions about women's roles circulating in the 1790s did not prepare her to be merely a wife and mother happy to play hostess in genteel circles. Several years after Elizabeth's rejection by Jerome, a friend wrote: "How fatal was the system of education pursued with you—it has made you like an exotic that is transplanted from the rich soil where it imbibed its vivid colours & fragrant odours, into a poor Earth in which its sickly existence is maintained by artificial heat."[28]

Participating in the heterosocial world of young elites in Baltimore and its environs also contributed in important ways to Elizabeth's "education" as a young woman in the late 1790s and early 1800s. Genteel society brought men and women together in convivial heterosociability. The later notion of separate spheres for men and women was not an ideology these Americans would have recognized. Home was not yet known as a "refuge" or "haven" from a "heartless" public world; it was not yet considered separate from the public. Without the gendered ideals that would later assign them to different spheres, men and women came together in polite society and considered each other equals in reasoning and affection.[29] Elizabeth was a full member in Maryland's heterosocial circle of elite young adults and took part in the flirtations of mixed-sex conviviality. When a female cousin visited Georgetown, near the nation's capital, in 1802, and attended its balls and other entertainments, she carefully alerted Elizabeth to each occasion when a man spoke of her. One beau "talk[ed] so much" of his "great wish to see Miss P[atterso]n." Another "remarked how much" Elizabeth would "enjoy" the *"grapes & jellies"* they ate at an "elegant" supper. Another of Elizabeth's admirers included a postscript to her cousin's letter, full of the overly romantic sentiments that were a ritualistic part of heterosociability among young people. When he spied Elizabeth's address on the letter, he enthused dramatically: "Ten thousand inexpressible sensations croud impetuously upon me. . . . Were I surrounded by brilliants— pen[n]ed in by Diamonds fronted on all sides by every thing that was curious & interesting—yet would all these remain by me unnoticed provided I saw the name of Miss Patterson."[30] Expressions such as this proved how well young men and women had learned the rules of polite society.

Polite sociability extended into the political realm as well. Elizabeth came of age in an era where it was not at all uncommon for women to act as political beings. Women participated in political parades, heard speeches, and even joined in toasts to "the rights of women." They read political newspapers and tracts and discussed political issues with their husbands, male friends, and each other at parties and dinners and in letters. One of Elizabeth's young female friends "adore[d]" "talking politicks" with men at genteel gatherings and seemingly attracted no censure for doing so.[31] And Elizabeth's aunt Nancy Spear was a classic example of a "female politician." Spear enjoyed the heated political contests of this period and would become a regular attendee at congressional debates in Washington, D.C. Political women were easily visible in the early decades of the republic.

By the time she reached marriageable age, Elizabeth had convinced herself that she was destined for a grander calling than a simple American wife and mother; she would not become like her mother, Dorcas, who dutifully fulfilled society's expectations as a submissive wife, delivering a child every other year or so, obeying her husband's dictates, and "leaving a numerous family to bewail the loss of one of the best of mothers" when she died at the age of fifty-three in 1814.[32] Elizabeth had observed around her and read about women who not only contributed to but also led polite society. Her upbringing had thoroughly exposed her to the idea that women could play crucial roles in the social sphere and in setting the tone for a nation's culture. The young Elizabeth also believed that her contributions would be made on a stage much larger than her hometown of Baltimore.

Elizabeth showed early signs of the influence of the feminist works she had read and of the fierce independence and stubbornness that would characterize her later years. Her choice of Jerome Bonaparte for her husband at the age of eighteen and her open pursuit of him did not fit within the usual standards set for young women of marrying age. Around 1800, Eliza Southgate, of Scarborough, Maine, complained to her cousin Moses Porter about the "inequality of privilege between the sexes" when "choosing a partner in marriage." Women only had "the liberty of refusing those we don't like, but not of selecting those we do." A woman "of taste and sentiment" had to rely on "fortune's random favor" to end up with a man "she could love."[33] A young lady could modestly encourage the attentions of a gentleman, but usually waited for the man to call on her and, if all was agreeable, for him to ask for her hand. If her parents objected to the match, proper young ladies knew to end it. Elizabeth followed neither course. In the fall of 1803, she took a very active role in courting Jerome, with little regard for the rules of female propriety. She was calculating and ambitious in her choice of a spouse. Her uncle Samuel Smith considered her "conduct [to be] abominable" as she seemed "as anxious to possess" Jerome "as when a baby to possess a rattle or doll."[34] And she defied her parents. In November, Rosalie Stier Calvert heard that the Pattersons had only accepted the marriage when Elizabeth had "threatened to run away with" Jerome. Then, Calvert reported, "the evening before the wedding [Elizabeth] was driven off to one of her relatives in Virginia under a chaperone's custody."[35] But, while in Virginia, Elizabeth remained stubborn and made clear she only wanted Jerome and would not relent. Their Christmas Eve wedding came out of her tenacity and willingness to defy her parents.

Marriage placed her in the legally dependent role of wife. But, given Elizabeth's early reading and experiences, she probably hoped for a happy union of companionate equals—an increasingly popular notion—instead of expecting a marriage like that of her parents with a patriarchal male and a submissive female. The sources reveal little about the actual marital relationship between Jerome and Elizabeth before their fateful trip to Lisbon, but it appears to have met her expectations. They socialized together and frequently traveled as a pair, Jerome rarely leaving Elizabeth behind. No matter how uncommon their marriage appeared under the norms of the time, Elizabeth did follow the traditional standard of becoming pregnant within a year after the wedding. It looked for a while that Elizabeth just might be following her mother's example in terms of quickly bearing children, if not in other ways.

When the troubles with Napoleon over the marriage ensued, Elizabeth's family and husband expected her to act as a dutiful wife. While in France trying to meet with Napoleon, her brother Robert reminded Elizabeth that it was her "duty" as a wife "to retain and increase the affections of her husband" and that "her exertions ought, if possible, to be doubled, from the peculiarity of her situation."[36] After he left her in Lisbon, Jerome similarly assumed he could exercise his powers as husband, ordering her, on her return to Baltimore, to "live in your own house, . . . keep four horses, and . . . live in a suitable manner, as though I were to arrive at any moment." Further, he exercised his powers as father by instructing her to "take the greatest care" of their "ill-starred" baby and to "teach him to love and respect his father."[37] Jerome desired that Elizabeth "especially make a Frenchman of [their son], not an American," and teach him to know "early that the great Napoleon is his uncle and that he is destined to become a prince and a statesman."[38]

Though it would not be an easy start, Elizabeth's abandonment by Jerome marked the beginning of her life as an independent woman. She initially received little support from the community on her return from England. While still pledging his undying love and repeatedly claiming that he "preferred" her "to a crown," even Jerome displayed no sympathy for her incredibly difficult situation, counseling her in May 1806 merely to "let the silly girls and the evil tongues of Baltimore say what they please."[39] The story of Elizabeth's marriage and betrayal never seems to have been presented as a sympathetic "seduction" story, like Samuel Richardson's fictional heroines Pamela or Clarissa or any of the real women who had foolishly let some rogue take advantage of their innocence and cause their downfall. Elizabeth had been too much involved in her own downfall, perhaps even considered by many the instigator of the entire relationship, simply to play the victim in this romantic drama. A writer in the *Scioto Gazette* of Chillicothe, Ohio, smugly reported after her return that he had been told by an acquaintance of Elizabeth's that she had declared that "she would rather enjoy a year of glory than an age of usual scenes in Baltimore." "Happiness attends the Happy," the editor sarcastically concluded.[40] Where her story paralleled Pamela's or Clarissa's was in the casting of it as a cautionary tale and, even at this early date, as an example of womanhood that should not be followed. According to one newspaper editor, "the history of Miss Patterson has pointed [at] a moral which seemingly her successors have failed to observe to their profit. She was and is foremost in the ranks of those whose ruined lives have been the consequence of too implicit faith in foreign fidelity."[41]

Life with her family on her sad return must have been unbearable for a young woman who had longed for the brilliance of a public life in Europe's courts. Looking back on the days she spent in her parents' house as an abandoned wife, Elizabeth bitterly reminisced in 1861: "My position under the paternal roof of the opulent Mr. Patterson after my repudiation by the Emperor & by the husband was painful. It was without pity, sympathy, or consolation. [Fate] had nailed me between an incredibly unnatural Parent & a faithless husband."[42] To Elizabeth, returning to Baltimore—to "obscurity [and] isolation to mere solitude to Poverty"—constituted a "revolt against [her] destiny." It was, she reflected, "torture to my love of Eminence & of Society" and to the "ambition in me."[43] During her son's early years, Elizabeth increasingly despaired of her situation; her friends watched her begin to sink under the weight of her disappointment. Years later, she would confess to her father, perhaps spitefully, that she "hated and loathed a residence in Baltimore so much, that when I thought that I was to spend my life there I tried to screw my courage up to the point of committing suicide. My cowardice, and *only* my cowardice, prevented my exchanging Baltimore for the grave."[44] In 1808, her stalwart friend Eliza Anderson ordered her to "let not the gloomy Monster take possession of so fine a mind as yours. Call forth every latent spark of energy, & exert its faculties to them." Anderson suggested "a stile of metaphysical reading in which I delight," consisting of "Smith's moral sentiments, L[or]d Kaimes' sketches of Man, his principles of Equity, Paley's moral philosophy, the 1st volume of Bacon, Helvetius on Man & on the mind." These would all help Elizabeth "learn new powers of charming," according to Anderson.[45] Obviously, both women were serious and prodigious readers, and not just of the sentimental novels that women of this era were so often ridiculed for preferring. Elizabeth certainly accepted her friend's advice, even if not the reading list, and increased her "powers of charming" to turn herself into an even brighter celebrity, as we have seen, than during her marriage.

Finding sympathy among her neighbors and family may have been rare on her return, but her situation soon improved. Elizabeth was determined not to suffer through a "ruined life." She emerged from this scandal not only with her personal reputation almost unscathed but also with public acceptance as a highly admired celebrity—a testament both to Elizabeth's amazing abilities to transform herself and to the cultural flexibility of gender norms in this period. Many members of the communities of elite women in Baltimore and in

Washington, who had initially used their "evil tongues" against her, turned into some of her staunchest supporters. Women's historians have shown that female kin played crucial roles in the lives of early nineteenth-century women, reflecting and reinforcing these women's sense of themselves.[46] But, except for Nancy Spear, Elizabeth was not very close to her female relatives; indeed, she was often at odds with them, especially her Smith and Caton cousins and in-laws. Instead, over the years, Elizabeth sought out unrelated women who could better support her sense of herself. By the time she became a young woman, Elizabeth had crafted her own identity and then sought out women who were either similar to herself or accepted her version of womanhood. Even as her identity changed from belle to wife to mother to manless woman, from an American celebrity to a would-be European aristocrat, Elizabeth always had a solid circle of women, almost none of whom were relations, who reflected and reinforced her sense of self. She relied heavily on female friends for support, comfort, and companionship throughout the unsettling years of her abandonment, the Titles of Nobility Amendment, and her divorce. Girlhood friends, such as Henriette Pascault, stayed loyal into adulthood. Eliza Anderson, who later married the architect Maximilian Godefroy, served as one of Elizabeth's strongest pillars of support and staunchest allies during these years. Anderson accompanied Jerome and the pregnant Elizabeth on their trip to Europe in 1805 and remained with Elizabeth in England through Bo's birth. She always vigorously defended Elizabeth whenever gossips criticized her dear friend and regularly offered counsel, though little heeded, concerning Elizabeth's life choices. Other women, some personally unknown to her, also helped Elizabeth during these very trying years. The Marchioness of Donegal used friends in Europe to carry letters and news between Elizabeth in England and Jerome in Genoa. Lady Elgin, whose husband was being held as a prisoner of war in France, risked sending letters, gifts, and money from Jerome to Elizabeth back in Baltimore. Elizabeth had turned to James Monroe's daughter Eliza in Richmond when she had been sent to Virginia to get over Jerome and relied on that friendship again during her stay in England, where James Monroe was minister. Once the Monroes left London for Paris in the summer of 1805, Elizabeth asked her friend to "sometimes write me & communicate what occurs" since Monroe's new residence "afford[ed]" her "an opportunity of being acquainted with many circumstances interesting to me."[47] During these difficult early years of motherhood and abandonment, as well as throughout her life, Elizabeth turned to these female friends and others she would soon meet, including Dolley Madison, far more than to family members for support and guidance.

When she returned to Baltimore without Jerome, Elizabeth might have accepted a return from dependency on her husband to dependency on her father. That approach was certainly the one traditional mores advised. Taking this more socially acceptable view toward abandoned women, James Monroe deemed her return to her father's house the "measure best calculated to preserve your own honor & reflect credit on your son." Casting Elizabeth as a submissive, dependent female, Monroe continued: "It was in your father's house that your husband became acquainted with you" and he "led you from it." It only made sense in this patriarchal world that "it was to that safe and honorable asylum that it became you to fly, as soon as he withdrew his protection from you." By doing this, Elizabeth had "increased the regard" and respect Jerome, the Bonapartes, and "every other person" had for her.[48] But Elizabeth chafed at such social restraints on her position. Instead, she gradually claimed an entirely nontraditional position as an independent woman who was dependent on neither husband nor father to determine her actions or to define her legally. The legal limbo ended with her divorce in 1812. After that point, coverture no longer formally applied to her as she took on the legal category of *feme sole*. But she had been acting informally as a *feme sole* for many years, as most abandoned women did, rich or poor. Legally, financially, and socially, she was a "manless" woman. This condition differentiated her from most women she met, American or European, and shaped the course of her remaining life.

A woman without a husband, Elizabeth was also a mother without her child's father. Like many widows, but unlike most divorcées who rarely gained custody of their minor children, Elizabeth felt heavily the responsibility of her child's future, a burden she believed she bore alone. But in 1808 when Jerome, as king of Westphalia, presented the opportunity for his son to achieve a brilliant destiny, Elizabeth balked. She understood this was one of the biggest decisions in her and her son's life. This episode reveals the kind of power that came to "manless" women. Though few mothers in American society had to make such calculations, women without husbands enjoyed far more control over their children's futures—where they would live, how they would be educated, what kind of religious and moral upbringing they would have—than dependent wives. Elizabeth had this control, yet consistently maintained that her own ambitions never influenced the decisions she made regarding her son.

Writing to James Monroe, to whom she turned for advice as she weighed her choices, she declared that her "maternal duties certainly prescribe a total dereliction of all self-interested motives." Regardless of whether Monroe believed it, Elizabeth presented the issue as one where her duty as a mother took precedence over her own wishes. She claimed that her main concern was whether the *"prosperity* or *personal safety* of the child" could be "ensured" and sought Monroe's opinion on that issue.[49] Monroe cautioned her against sending her son to Jerome because of the potential danger that might await him, not from Jerome who was assuredly "sensible that he owes much to the claims of a child" or from Napoleon who "must be aware too that the attention of the world has been drawn to him by his conduct in that transaction." The danger, for Monroe, could come from "the wife of Jerome, or some of her connections," who would not find "pleasure" in the reception of Bo by his father and might regard him as "in their way." "Such things happen in courts," he warned. As before, Monroe offered a standard American prescription for her situation. He pointedly asked Elizabeth to consider another question before she made her decision: would the "surrender" of Bo, if he was not in danger, "likely contribute more to his happiness than an education in the respectable circle of his maternal family, conformable to the principles of his country?"[50] In other words, would her son ultimately be happier in an imperial court or in a republican home? Unlike most women and mothers in this era, Elizabeth had the sole power to choose between these very different courses for her son. She ultimately informed Jerome's agent, Auguste Le Camus, that her "determination is never to let my Son go to Europe without me" or "without the full & entire approbation of the Emperor, signified to me officially."[51]

Elizabeth mastered the art of drawing from the variety of feminine images that this period of gender flux created. When she wrote to Napoleon expressing her expectations for an annuity for her son's upbringing and her desire for a title, she interestingly adopted the more submissive (and hopefully more persuasive) tone of the distraught female and dedicated mother instead of that of the independent woman, the tone she used with Jerome and her family. To Napoleon, she characterized herself as a mother "who owes her misfortune to circumstances over which she had no control, and who, disappointed in her high hopes without reason to blame herself, is reduced to weeping over the birth of a son whose status and whose very means of subsistence remain uncertain even though he seems born to enjoy esteem and happiness."[52] In a later letter to the emperor, she continued to play the, for her, unusual role of submissive female. Referring to Napoleon as "the greatest of mortals" and herself as "the humblest of women," she thanked him for his "interest in" their "fate" and reminded him that "the blood and the talents that are the inheritance of my son and the name that distinguishes him are incompatible with a humble upbringing or an obscure existence." "I owe it to him, to the world, and above all to Your Majesty," she exclaimed, "not to miss the opportunity to place him into a situation where, taught by the most enlightened men of the greatest nation in the world and protected by the most August sovereign, his mind, his genius, and his virtues will acquire all the power of which they are capable." She assured the emperor that she "would consider it amiss to place my destiny into other hands," such as her former husband's. "Whatever will be Your Majesty's orders concerning the establishment, the residence, and the conduct of my son and myself," she concluded, "we shall do our utmost to comply with them."[53] In her later memories, she characterized herself as "poor & homeless" when she "accepted from the Emperor a pension of sixty thousand francs per annum." But she recalled no submissiveness, just strength, writing that she had accepted the pension "on my own conditions however, & never on those of relinquishing his name, which I invariably signed to all receipts for the same." She regarded the annuity as "a recognizance of some of my rights & some of the claims of my Son."[54]

With the French minister to the United States, Louis-Marie Turreau, she took quite a different tone, largely because she despised his conduct toward her, which she characterized as "insulting" and "offensive." Once again, she presented herself as the strong, independent woman. She knew her "determination" was "irritating to Genl. T," but insisted that she did not deserve "his taunting manner & language." During one conversation, she had "to remind him that my situation did not permit me to suffer myself to be treated by him in the way a *fille entretenue* [a kept woman] might be."[55] If she had been Jerome's wife instead of an abandoned woman, Turreau never would have treated her as a cast-off mistress. One of the drawbacks of being a "manless" woman was such treatment. But Elizabeth had learned how to respond.

By the middle of 1811, with Napoleon's money, Elizabeth moved out of her father's house and set up her own household, physically declaring her independence even before her formal divorce. Many other manless women chose more modest lives and often lived in the homes of parents, siblings, or relations, as her aunt Nancy Spear did. But not Elizabeth. She did not like her family and could afford her own quarters, unlike many women on their own.

She quickly chose to spend some time in Washington, staying first in the boardinghouse of William O'Neal, whose daughter Peggy would later become infamous, and then renting a house of her own. This private action of Elizabeth's—moving to the capital—became another international event as her relocation posed a diplomatic and social problem for Louis Sérurier, Turreau's replacement as minister. Sérurier wrote Napoleon that Elizabeth's decision "to take up an establishment here will embarrass me greatly, for I cannot act toward her in the way the great title which she has had for a moment would require, and on the other hand[,] I cannot refuse her the respectful attention which her conduct, her position and her misfortune deserve and which also attach her to France."[56] Few manless women would have voluntarily made the choice to live on their own, though many ended up alone because of abandonment or their husband's death. These women often suffered since they could not conform to early nineteenth-century American notions of womanhood that, no matter how varied, rested on adult women being wives.[57] But their unconformity came out of necessity, not inclination, as with Elizabeth.

Elizabeth's uncertain marital status between Napoleon's annulment in 1805 and her legislative divorce in 1812 did not stop men from regarding her as perfectly available in the marriage market. Her seasonal residence in Washington placed her in one of the supreme spouse-hunting arenas in the new nation. Until her departure for Europe in 1815, she stayed in Washington for almost every social season, even during the war years when the British threatened the capital and despite her divorce in 1812 and her mother's serious illness in the winter of 1814. She entered with relish the capital's demanding game of calling upon and receiving visitors, maintaining old friendships, such as with Anna Thornton, and creating new ones, such as with the author Washington Irving. Like the Baltimore of her youth, this was a heterosocial world, where men and women eagerly came together for socializing and even some politicking. This social arena included married men and women of various ages, not just single, young adults. Therefore, Elizabeth's collection of admirers and friends included numerous married men, especially among those politicians who had left their wives at home. With so many lonely men congregated in one place, flirting and courting easily mixed with intellectual and political discussions. While in Washington trying to repair a reputation tarnished by the recent Burr Conspiracy, the recently widowed General James Wilkinson confessed that women were "the subjects of my Matins & Vespers," including "my very dear friend Miss Spear & the divine little legitimate

Queen of Westphalia."[58] American and European men were besotted with Elizabeth. Even ardent republicans acted like noble courtiers in their devotions to her. Her beauty, wit, and the ease with which she interacted with men made her "charming" or "enchanting" in the almost magical sense of those words. She captivated men—married and unmarried—and they often recognized her power, though they may not have enjoyed it. In Washington especially, where there were far fewer women than men, many fell under her spell.

Elizabeth received numerous professions of undying love and many proposals of marriage after Jerome abandoned her. Samuel Colleton Graves was the first to propose, in May 1808. Declaring that he understood her "situation is peculiar," Graves professed that "when I first saw you, your beauty won my admiration, & since that you have acquired most truly (to call it no other) my esteem & my regard." Regretting that "seclusion and dereliction should be the los[s] of youth and beauty," he "determined to require your hand in marriage."[59] Graves penned innumerable love poems to her, including one after seeing her Stuart portrait and one after sleeping in a bed in which she had once slept. Even after she rejected him and he returned to England, he continued to profess his enduring love. A year later, gossips reported that Sir Charles Oakley, the secretary to the British legation, had become "devoted" to Elizabeth. He already had a scandalous past, though, since he had "elop[ed] with the Queen of Prussia's sister, then a married woman." All of Baltimore, according to Lydia Hollingsworth, was making bets on whether Oakley "will offer [and] if so, whether she will accept or decline."[60] Even Bishop John Carroll relayed to his sister the intriguing news that Oakley had "transferred his attentions to Mad[am]e Bonaparte" and wondered whether "they will be married."[61] Elizabeth rejected Oakley as well; her brother Joseph assumed she had merely "made use of O." to get Napoleon and Turreau to agree to her demands for an annuity.[62]

Another in the long line of suitors was Virginia's Henry Lee, Jr., who squired Elizabeth during the War of 1812. In March 1813, Lee declared how much he "adore[d]" the "most lovely Madame B." and encouraged her to "discountinence" her "diplomatic dalliances" with the new French minister Sérurier and "get married." "If *my sex* be worth thy winning, Think oh! think it worth enjoying," he slyly concluded.[63] William Johnson, Jr., an unmarried Supreme Court justice, fell victim to Elizabeth's charms, too. Drawing on characters from William Shakespeare's *A Midsummer's Night's Dream*, Johnson called Elizabeth his "Fairy Queen." He hoped to please "my Titania" and hear "some of the inimitable Passages utter'd by her to the adorable Nick Bottom during her Love-fit." "You recollect I appraised you of my Designs upon you," he reminded her, "should I ever succeed in procuring the potent Drug so successfully applied by the facetious Robin Goodfellow. What a victory to make a Fool of her who has made Fools of half Our Sex." Johnson knew he was just another in a long line of suitors who would find their romantic hopes dashed. Nevertheless, that did not stop him from including at the bottom of his letter two poems in praise of his Titania's charms.[64] The author Washington Irving was one of Elizabeth's admirers as well. He missed out on his opportunity for a romance, however. There had been plans for him "to have been introduced to her, and to have gone on a little *moonlight* party at Masons Island . . . a favourable opportunity . . . for sentiment & romance." But Irving had "dined with a choice party at the Speakers, drank wine, got gay, went home, and fell asleep by the fire side, and forgot all about Madame Bonaparte until this morning."[65]

The qualities that attracted all of these men to Elizabeth highlight how transitional this period was in terms of gender definitions and relations. Elizabeth was not the industrious housewife of the eighteenth century who, through her hard work in and around the home, would make a family successful, as the Maine midwife Martha Ballard so crucially did for her family. Nor was she a republican wife of the 1780s and 1790s whose efforts would support her husband's work for the new nation, as Virginia's Elizabeth Wirt beautifully did for her husband the attorney general.[66] And certainly none of the men who courted her would have expected her to play the role of the wife by the fireside, making her home into a restorative haven for her weary husband on his return from the heartless public world, as their counterparts a generation later would. The emphasis in civil society on heterosociability, on men and women coming together as social equals, and on companionship in this era could make women with Elizabeth's attributes appear an ideal wife. Of course, her romantic history, her renown, and her family's wealth made her a woman of interest, but they saw so much more. Her schooling, reading, and traveling allowed her to converse easily on many subjects. Her ready wit offered constant amusement. Her ability to interact easily with men, talking about subjects they found interesting and flattering them throughout the exchange, set her apart from women who were not as comfortable in a heterosocial circle. Another master of such heterosocial interaction, Aaron Burr, delighted in her company and thought Elizabeth possessed "sense, and spirit, and sprightliness."[67] New York's Pierre Van Cortlandt, Jr., reported that he agreed with one of his fellow lodgers at O'Neal's boardinghouse who thought Elizabeth "possesse[d] all the qualities that render the female character angelic," which, for him, included "a great ease & urbanity of manners, qualified by a great good sense . . . [and] much knowledge of the world & great good breeding." In short, she was "a sweet little person that *Cupid* could not have found more to his taste."[68] Elizabeth's beauty and clothing seems to have distinguished her the most. The men who wrote to and about Elizabeth always started with her beauty. None of them ever seem to have considered what married life with Elizabeth would really be like; they just wanted to possess this extremely beautiful, engaging woman who had so charmed them.

Married men, no doubt missing their wives, could not resist Elizabeth's charms either; their comments about her attest to a gendered environment that readily permitted married persons to engage in flirtatious banter with no harm to their reputations. Senator Jeremiah Mason told his wife that he found Elizabeth "very lively and facetious, accomplished of course, and very handsome." The two got along well, and Elizabeth invited him "to come and see her as often as I please," which seems to have been quite frequently.[69] Vice President Elbridge Gerry relished his close friendship with Elizabeth. He called on her frequently, and the pair took carriage rides together to visit other friends, such as General Steven Mason on his island in the Potomac—all of which Gerry reported to his wife in letters. Gerry and Elizabeth enjoyed conversing together, with Gerry characterizing one of their conversations as "interesting to herself, and pleasant, very much so to me." He considered them true friends, telling his wife that "the more I see of this lady the more I like her, and so would all our family. She is amiable, unaffected, unassuming, sensible and altogether free from a disposition to censure."[70] The married Reverend Horace Holley got caught in Elizabeth's web as well, writing her lengthy letters and penning poems about her beauty, "vivacity," "intelligence," and "accomplishments." He charged himself with relieving her of her constant ennui and making her happy after she returned from Europe in 1818.[71] And, in spite of their often tense relationship, General Turreau ended up falling under Elizabeth's spell too, regarding her as "a young lady who is distinguished by her honorable and pure conduct as well as by the quality of her heart and mind, worthy of the brilliant destiny which awaits her."[72] This affection for Elizabeth may have cost Turreau his position. Napoleon recalled him in late 1810, leading to speculation in Washington "that the Emperor does not ap-

prove of his proceedings with Madame B."[73] Some years later, Elizabeth noted
that she had found out "subsequently that General Turreau contemplated divorcing his wife & marrying me himself & getting the Title of Duke thereby
from the Emperor."[74]

Captivating women like Elizabeth could also be considered potentially
dangerous to men. Commenting on the effect Susan Wheeler (later Mrs. Stephen Decatur) had on some men, Catherine Harper believed she "must indeed
be a most dangerous woman to be [in love] with, for old & young, married &
single, they are quite *fools* on her subject."[75] Eliza Godefroy saw something
similar in her friend Elizabeth, calling her on one occasion "a peerless Spider,"
and wondering "how many more poor Knights are doomed to beat their hap-
less wings in thy fine spun web."[76] In Washington, Elizabeth certainly distracted men from the important business of the government. According to
Virginia representative William Burwell, during the 1812–13 social season,
Elizabeth "exercise[d] all her wit upon the Gen[er]als who have been selected by the Govt to conduct the war."[77] Years later, General Winfield
Scott and his friend both got caught in her web when they met her in Paris.
Writing to Elizabeth, Scott's friend declared that he thought "much of you, and
always with the tenderness of a Brother—more I dare not—tho' 'twoud not be
strange for few escape you, either married or single." Her power to attract all
kinds of men impressed him as much as it worried him. "Indeed 'twere a poor
and ordinary conquest, that of fiery headed young men who blaze at every
thing, but to turn the heads of the most sedate as of all others can only [be] the
effect of such advantages and excellencies and charms as you possess." Though
fully aware of her power to ensnare men, this admirer pathetically begged at
the end of his letter, "when you have no one else to spend a thought on, think
of me."[78]

Elizabeth enjoyed the heterosocial whirl and her flirtations with men. She
certainly appreciated their attentions and probably even their proposals. But,
even though everyone wondered during the years after her return to Baltimore
whether she would marry again, or at least fall in love, or even reunite with
Jerome, by the time of her divorce, she had already rejected several serious
marriage proposals from likely prospects. She seems to have decided that she
would never marry a second time for fear of it harming the future of her possibly imperial son—as well as her own ambitions. As she informed her first
serious suitor, Samuel Graves, in 1809, "my time & attachment must be devoted exclusively to my Son, from whose destiny whether inauspicious or the

reverse, I can never divide myself. The resolution of consecrating to him every sentiment & action of my life, is irrevocable, which must with other circumstances *peculiar* to *myself*, will ever preclude a change of my situation."[79] Other women might have regarded marriage to any one of the men who had proposed to Elizabeth as a way of providing security and companionship. For Elizabeth, however, marriage to any of these men could have closed off opportunities for herself and her son. On the occasions when she did think of remarrying, she rarely discussed love but frequently status and money. To her father, she declared that she "never would marry without rank, or God knows I might have got money enough by marriage."[80] She also seems to have not only grown accustomed to being an unmarried woman but also preferred that state that allowed her to live her life as she pleased. While she confessed that at times she felt "induced to accept *very respectable* offers" out of loneliness or "*ennui*," she preferred "remaining as I am to the horror of marrying a person I am indifferent to."[81] The loneliness of her independent existence sometimes made her wish for a companionate marriage, but those wistful moments were rare.

To some women, however, Elizabeth's single status appeared enticing. Recently married Eliza Anderson Godefroy envied Elizabeth's "Independence"—"that premium mobile of comfort"—as well as her "beauty, wit & fascination." Indeed, Godefroy regarded female independence as one of the "*primary* ingredients" for happiness.[82] Godefroy's views suggest that independent women were not yet regarded by all of American society as failed models of womanhood, social pariahs, or threats. Obviously, some women, like Godefroy, longed for the state of comfortable independence that Elizabeth had constructed.

The fluidity of possible identities as Americans sought a solid definition of womanhood allowed women like Elizabeth to stretch what was considered appropriate for women. At the same time, the fluidity also created multiple ways of perceiving Elizabeth's version of womanhood, which some deemed acceptable and others regarded as unacceptable or even threatening. Different aspects of Elizabeth's identity could combine in powerful ways. Her roles as a woman without a husband, as the mother of a possible prince, as a female representation of aristocratic culture, and as an alluring celebrity with considerable social influence came together in the Titles of Nobility furor of 1809–10. Even in an era of gender flux, only a woman who had gone too far could have caused such a national—even constitutional—response. Marriage and motherhood usually locked women into positions under the control of men—

but not in Elizabeth's case. Her confusing marital situation and her possibly imperial son only added to the challenge posed by her celebrity status and her aristocratic ideals. As an ambitious woman with well-known aristocratic aspirations, the men in Congress could not count on her loyalty to the republic. She was a public woman, a celebrity, whose choices and independence presented a model of womanhood far from accustomed notions of female submissiveness and modesty. As a manless woman in control of her own and her son's destiny, no one could predict how she would respond to Napoleon's strategies. In the same way, her divorce petition highlighted her various identities as an ambitious but abandoned woman, as the wife of a bigamous king and mother of an imperial heir, and, concurrently, as a supplicating female in need of the protection only the assemblymen could grant. Of course, the petition also requested a permanent legal identity for her as a single woman.

Though divorces became easier to get and somewhat more acceptable in society after the Revolution, as those inspired by its ideology emphasized the importance of "freedom and happiness," a divorce was still an unusual event in the early republic.[83] Receiving a divorce through a legislative assembly required great skill and savvy, for more petitions were denied than granted. Most states required their assemblies to enact divorces on a case-by-case basis, just like a piece of legislation; the courts had little control over marital separations. It would take a full three decades after Elizabeth's divorce before Maryland legislators assigned the courts jurisdiction over divorces. It also remained quite difficult to receive a full divorce allowing for remarriage, the kind Elizabeth requested, as even republican assemblies were reluctant to separate permanently a husband and wife. It was easier to receive a divorce "from bed and board," which only allowed the couple to live separately. Legislators believed this form of separation better preserved the social order. In 1810, the North Carolina legislature granted only one full divorce out of twenty petitions.[84] Exceptions were rare. The Pennsylvania legislature, for example, granted Anne and William Bingham's daughter Maria a full divorce from her profligate husband, the Comte de Tilly, probably because Maria was only fifteen at the time of her clandestine marriage and Tilly had been paid off to give evidence against himself. Observers generally believed the divorce had been "obtained by influence."[85] In 1807, Maryland legislators allowed one wife a full divorce because her husband continuously threatened to kill her.[86]

Elizabeth was fortunate to receive a full divorce. If she had only been granted a divorce from bed and board, she would not have regained complete *feme sole* status, which allowed her legally to act as an independent business-woman, collecting rents and controlling her real and personal property. And if Jerome reappeared in the United States, as rumored when the Bonaparte empire began to crumble, she would have had far weaker claims to both her money and her son. The full divorce granted by the legislature ensured Elizabeth's economic and personal independence.

Elizabeth apparently did not have to go through the ordeal of divorce alone. Not only did she have supporters in Maryland's assembly, but even the community of women in Washington and Baltimore gathered around her, seeing her probably as a victim of an uncaring husband instead of as a scandalous woman. One report told of a number of Baltimore women, "particularly Mrs. Barry and Mrs. Caton[,] who are industriously electioneering in behalf of Mrs. Bonaparte."[87] These women obviously believed they wielded some influence with the men in the assembly. And they may have contributed to the petition's success. The broad support she received probably also explains why Elizabeth emerged from what should have been a scandalous process relatively unscathed and with her reputation untarnished. Where many other divorced women in this time faced damaging scandal and financial hardship and found it difficult to hold their place in society, Elizabeth's celebrity and men's attraction to her only increased.

When Elizabeth's longtime friend Eliza Anderson received her divorce in 1808, she did not fare nearly as well in society. But her story was far more cloaked in scandal. Anderson's first husband had left her years earlier, and the two had been living apart, though still legally married, ever since. By 1808, the French architect Maximilian Godefroy, who helped introduce the neo-Gothic style to America, had fallen in love with Anderson. Many suggested that Godefroy and Anderson had already engaged in an adulterous affair, but an exasperated Anderson vigorously defended herself, asking Elizabeth in one letter why Godefroy would have formally asked her father for her hand and why she would have bothered to get a divorce if she "had already sacrificed honor."[88] Unlike Elizabeth, whose husband's perfidy everyone knew, Anderson could only obtain her divorce "by giving proof" of her husband's "infidelity." After her lawyers failed to find her husband or news of "whether he was alive or dead" in Albany, New York, with letters, Anderson "resolved courageously to go to Albany myself." She boarded a steamboat, one of the first in the country, "amidst a heterogeneous crowd" and headed up the Hudson River. She found her husband at Ballston Springs, where he was now a fisher-

man. Amazingly, she persuaded him to write a letter acknowledging his infidelity, though he refused to include the names of "any of those *'good women
who had a kindness for him.'"* He finally agreed to give "such references to a
physician" in Baltimore as would "ensure success" for her petition.[89] Anderson
finally received her divorce and married Godefroy. But despite her insistence
that nothing dishonorable had occurred, she did not come out of her divorce
unsullied. Many in her social circle shunned her, and even Elizabeth cooled
the relationship between them. In later years, her increasing drunkenness led
even her old friends to "[determine] to give her up." According to Elizabeth's
brother Edward, Godefroy had appeared at several parties "so much intoxi-
cated that the hostesses were obliged to put her to bed." And, even at one of
her own parties, "she was so far gone that the company was obliged to retire."
By 1817, the Godefroys were in wretched economic circumstances—"almost
in a state of starvation," according to Edward.[90] While polite society could accept those in genteel poverty, it could not accept those who flouted social
rules. A publicly drunken woman, especially one already marked by a scandalous divorce and remarriage, was completely unacceptable. They would "give
her up," and so did Elizabeth apparently. By 1818, at the latest, Elizabeth had
"entirely discarded" her old friend.[91]

Faring more like Elizabeth through the social trials of divorce was Eliza
Parke Custis Law, the step-granddaughter of George Washington. She divorced her adulterous husband, Thomas Law, and seemed to have weathered
the scandal well, retaining her elite position after an initial period of gossip.
Around 1804, Catherine Harper shared with her husband that "the cause of
Mrs Laws separation from her Husband was owing to him keeping publickly
a mistress & still does so."[92] Elbridge Gerry reported that the couple had "dis-
agreed and separated."[93] The divorced Law, who went by Mrs. Custis, was rumored to have received a settlement of $1,500 per year from her ex-husband,
allowing her to live "where she pleases."[94] Their daughter lived with her father,
though she frequently visited her mother; gossips hoped that she would "in no
way suffer for the folly of her parents."[95] Elizabeth knew Custis somewhat and
wrote of seeing her at a party where she "appeared as gay as I ever saw her."[96]
A crucial difference, of course, between Eliza Godefroy and Eliza Custis and
Elizabeth was the elite status of the latter two. That Elizabeth and, especially,
Custis came from families of the highest standing certainly shielded them
from the worst social condemnation, and their great wealth certainly protected them from the worst economic repercussions of a divorce. Their elite

status likely caused legislators to look more favorably on granting their divorce petitions as well; women from the lower orders were not as successful as those from the top ranks in receiving full divorces.[97]

The urban environments in which Elizabeth, as a legally manless woman after 1812, chose to live seem to have provided a more accepting atmosphere for women on their own. Cities held a wider variety of people than the countryside and permitted a wider variety of behavior. The political, social, and economic flux of the era that fostered the fashioning of multiple identities was most evident in urban areas. Furthermore, in the cities along the Atlantic coast, single women—whether never married, widowed, or divorced—gathered in greater numbers and therefore likely attracted less censure than their counterparts in rural areas.[98] Urban areas also offered women more ways to make a living on their own and, for wealthy women like Elizabeth and Custis, provided greater opportunities for mixed-gender socializing and entertainments where elite women, whether married or not, held sway. Atlantic coast cities served as the best environments for polite society. Not surprisingly, women who sought a life beyond the roles of wife and mother within polite society congregated in the cities. The nation's capital surely attracted Elizabeth precisely for these reasons since its congressional halls, presidential drawing rooms, and even boardinghouse parlors contained perhaps the closest approximation to European culture in the new nation.

The lack of clarity in gender definitions in the early decades of the nineteenth century allowed women, especially elite women, to experiment with various versions of womanhood as they sought to find ways in which they could contribute to the new nation and to the shaping of its culture. In fact, American society expected women to "engage in the cultural work of nationalism."[99] The education of women was not only for themselves and their children but also for the general improvement of American society and the nation. Women served along with men as cultural arbiters, creating, debating, and enforcing the rules of American culture in this period. While some individuals worked through published writings and plays, many women grounded their influence in the "institutions of sociability"—the tea tables, dining rooms, parlors, and other spaces of civil society—that not only included women but often were controlled by them.[100] Such institutions acted as important sites of public opinion and even politics in the early republic. The cultural work of nationalism combined with the era's fluidity in gender roles and relations to provide clear means for elite women in the capital and other cities to seek, possess, and enjoy cultural and, at times, as a number of historians have shown, political power. Some of these women even chose to become "female politicians" who firmly "saw themselves—and were seen by others—as political actors in their own right."[101] The spaces that women created for socializing (and politicking) in the public sphere allowed them to play significant roles in the new nation beyond wife or mother. By influencing and critiquing American manners, style, and culture, and by participating in the polity, these women helped shaped the nation.

Well-educated, wealthy, and, often, well-traveled, these women claimed to possess the credentials for setting the cultural tone for the nation. Long accustomed to looking to England, in particular, and Europe, in general, for cultural cues, elite Americans were open to the idea that those men and women who had traveled to Europe had valuable insights. Such American women acquired a unique opportunity to contribute directly to the debate over the nature of American culture. While often pleased with their own country, some of these traveling women attempted to use their ties to and experiences with Europe's aristocratic ways to influence or improve the character of the new nation. In the 1790s, the renowned American *salonnière* Anne Willing Bingham, for example, recreated French modes of entertaining at her Philadelphia mansion in an attempt to impart a certain cultivated style to the ruling class of the new republic.[102] In her elegant home with its European furnishings, Bingham, dressed in the latest French fashions, modeled herself after Parisian *salonnières*, reigning over a drawing and dining room that prized amiable conversation, witty repartee, and the display of elegant manners among men and women. To some, Bingham's "exuberance of sprightliness and wit" and her more daring fashions (and even rouge) defined her as "quite a French woman."[103] But she was "a French woman" who wanted to transform American culture. Many genteel American women who had seen Europe or felt connected to it, including Dolley Madison, chose this public role as their special province with such a goal in mind.

Engaging in the cultural work of nationalism offered many genteel women not only respite from their domestic toils but also a sense of importance in the larger world. After complaining in her diary about the chores that consumed her entire day—food to prepare, clothes to make or mend, a house to put in order—Margaret Bayard Smith decried that "limited circle which it is prescribed for women to tread"; a woman's life seemed "like that of the horse chained to the mill."[104] Smith found escape in the fashionable circles in Washington, though its demands were often at odds with her domestic "interest or duty."[105] Yet she never stopped entering into the public whirl or bringing it into her home. Not surprisingly perhaps, many of Elizabeth's friends who played the role of cultural arbiter for the nation were childless, such as Anna Brodeau Thornton, or women whose children had grown into adulthood, such as Dolley Madison. Few were actively raising young children; serving as a cultural arbiter or female politician was too difficult to engage in while birthing, breastfeeding, and rearing young children. The women who could pursue such a public life in polite society, then, were almost all at a certain point in their life, of a certain class, a certain education, and a certain mindset.

Such women's gender and class supported their concerns with cultural forms and encouraged their cultural "borrowing" from Europe. Perhaps more so than American men at this time, elite American women in the capital and in major cities seemed convinced that their new republic could have elements of aristocracy or luxury without becoming corrupt. In fact, they believed these elements could only elevate the culture of the fledgling country. As First Lady, Martha Washington led a growing network of female-headed salons, including that of Anne Bingham, centered in the then capitals of New York City and later Philadelphia. While Washington's gatherings may not have boasted the same luxuries as Bingham's and while Washington did not dress in the latest French fashions, she still found herself attacked by ardent republicans who charged that these salons were intended to create a national governing class. There may have been some truth to the charge since Martha Washington herself was responsible for brokering at least sixteen marriages between congressmen and women from leading families, including that of James and Dolley Madison.[106] These marriages and the salon culture that fostered them did make it look as if some elements of a European aristocratic culture had taken root in the new nation and reaffirmed the accepted link between women and luxury. But these women had sought to use certain aspects of aristocratic culture, such as salons, to improve the new nation, not to corrupt it; patriotism and nationalism motivated them. Later First Ladies Elizabeth Monroe and Louisa Catherine Adams, each of whom had spent years at various European courts, as well as Dolley Madison, who never traveled to Europe, saw the adoption of some European ways at the Executive Mansion as a means of giving grandeur and authority, and European-style refinement, to the nation's capital.[107] This is what good republican women were supposed to do in the late eighteenth and early nineteenth centuries. Like any good American citizen, they were expected to prefer the United States and its forms of government and society to those of any other country and to work, both at home and in society, to improve the republic and its citizens. For American women who had traveled abroad, efforts at improvement often included adopting European aristocratic forms of refinement to an American milieu. But the end result was still supposed to be one that celebrated the new nation over monarchies and empires, that brought courtly luxury safely within the bounds of republican simplicity. That was not Elizabeth's goal, however.

Fashion, interior decoration, the arts, and literature became specific vehicles by which these women could display the cultural forms they considered suitable for the American republic. Elizabeth and other leading elite women, such as Dolley Madison, Margaret Bayard Smith, Anne Bingham, Elizabeth Monroe, and Louisa Catherine Adams, "navigated the transition from Roman asceticism to Grecian luxury" in American culture in the early decades of the nineteenth century.[108] Their Grecian style in personal dress and parlor decorations not only displayed their knowledge of current European fashions but also encouraged Americans to embrace a level of refinement, even luxury, that seemed compatible with their republic. Those women who had their portraits painted in this period, including Bingham and Madison, used the opportunity to display the fashionable and somewhat daring Grecian style of dress as a mark of both their cosmopolitanism and their republicanism. Often dressed in Grecian robes of sumptuous fabrics and bedecked in stunning jewelry, some of these women, such as Louisa Adams, even posed *à la grecque*, reclining languidly on a *klismos* chair, similar to a chaise longue, evoking simultaneously their femininity, elite status, cosmopolitanism, and cultural sensibility.[109] While Elizabeth certainly contributed to this shift in American culture, she was not completely like these women. Though also painted by Gilbert Stuart, like Bingham and Madison, and also attired in Grecian styles, like many of these women, Elizabeth embodied a different politics—that of revolutionary and imperial France, not republican America.

Through their appearance and behavior, women not only publicly displayed their desired version of American cultural forms but also tested what was considered "appropriate" and even "scandalous" for ladies. In this era of unsteady gender definitions, what was "ladylike" dress and comportment easily shifted. For Elizabeth, early nineteenth-century Grecian fashions perfectly symbolized the freedoms that European women enjoyed. For her friends, they more likely evoked the classical Greek republic that the United States sought to emulate. In either case, these fashions not only publicly marked these women as cosmopolitan but also offered more private benefits as well. The simple, columnar dress in the Grecian style, with its "empire waist" that fell straight from under the breasts, required no metal hoops or layers of heavy petticoats (or even underwear, depending on the wearer). While some of Elizabeth's more modest American counterparts chose to wear long stays (or corsets) to achieve the columnar look,[110] even with the stays women literally enjoyed more freedom to move in these dresses than in earlier or later fashions. Further, the light and soft fabrics felt pleasing on the body and added to the sensuous presentation. Given the real freedom these Grecian dresses allowed and the behavioral freedom they symbolized, it was no surprise that many Americans, men and women, considered them immoral. Fashion and women's political place in the republic were undeniably linked. One newspaper editor sarcastically remarked that "the change in the female dress of late must contribute very much to domestic bliss; no man can surely now complain of petticoat government."[111] In fact, some did complain about the obvious influence of such women, not within the home but within civil society.

Not everyone in Washington and elsewhere endorsed the heterosociability of polite society and the reign of women over it. New Hampshire senator William Plumer complained that there were simply far too many women in the capital, local women as well as "many from other parts of the United States," who came to the city "to see & be seen, to admire & be admired." While they dressed "richly & splendidly," he thought that few deserved his admiration. Women who ruled polite society had created far too much "pomp & parade & artificial politeness," in Plumer's opinion.[112] While New Hampshire's Jeremiah Mason thought highly of Elizabeth and called on her often, he similarly assessed the conversation around her tea table—a center of polite society in early Washington—as "of that tinsel kind, which is not even very interesting or instructing, and will not wear long." Interestingly, he blamed this shortcoming not on the hostess who presided over the table but on the "fashionable old and young men" who "surrounded" Elizabeth.[113] Elite men recognized the kind of women who sought a larger role for themselves beyond the household, and not all of them approved. Isaac Coles had "never seen a more elegant & accomplished woman" than one he met in Philadelphia in 1807. But, though he admired her, he decided he would never marry her. As he reported to his friend Joseph Cabell, she was "a woman of the *Great World* & rather possessed of those qualities which are calculated to shine in the brilliant circles of fashion" instead of qualities that would "fit her to pass thro' the varied scenes of life, & to discharge all the duties which may hereafter belong to her as a wife or mother."[114] This comment could have been easily made about any number of women who chose to participate in and lead polite society and seems particularly suited for Elizabeth. In *A Series of Letters on Court-ship and Marriage* (1806), the male author wondered whether his younger sister could "associate with those who are called the polite and well bred, the gay and fashionable ladies of the present day, without assuming their manners, and adopting their free and forward airs?" He worried most about her following their example of "admitting the gentlemen among your acquaintance, to liberties, to familiarities which, if they are not criminal, are at least inconsistent with that modesty, and chastity of manners which constitute female charm." His advice had a mixed message, however, for he also wanted her to have "an intercourse with the world" so that she could "acquire just that ease and presence of mind, which is necessary for your own satisfaction, and to prevent your being embarrassed" in "company."[115] Clearly, there was uncertainty over the accepted boundaries of behavior for women in polite society and whether their engagement with the public world made them less suitable wives.

Like other elite American women, Elizabeth "participated actively and creatively in [the] debate about national character and destiny."[116] But her opinions differed from theirs in critical ways on the most important issues. Like them, she enjoyed presiding over the tea table or parlor and attending parties, balls, formal dinners, and plays. Like them, she relished polished manners, fashionable dress, and witty conversation with educated people. Like them, she also firmly believed that women had crucial roles to play in the shaping of culture and society. And, like them, her celebrity and prominence helped define acceptable American social rules and limits. But, unlike her counterparts, Elizabeth never viewed her European experiences and sensibilities as a way to help mold a republican culture. Instead, they formed the basis on which she denigrated it. Her anti-Americanism intensified with every trip abroad. And whether at home or abroad, she saw only the positive aspects of aristocratic European culture and the negative ones of republican American culture. While her friends and acquaintances used their energies to help create an elegant society in their republic based on ideas of taste and style that drew on European influences, Elizabeth never shared their goal and received criticism for it. She simply went too far in her preferences for aristocracies and

Figure 8. Dressed in her most aristocratic clothing and jewelry, including a tiara, Elizabeth had this portrait painted during her long stay in Europe. Firmin Massot, 1823. Image #XX.5.69, courtesy of the Maryland Historical Society.

monarchies. Here, as in other places, she helped define the boundaries of proper American behavior and sentiments.

Unlike Anne Bingham or Elizabeth Monroe, Elizabeth never tried to bring the metropolis to the provinces, to re-create a Parisian salon in her American dining room, even though she possessed all of the requisite "aristocratic" attributes of beauty, wealth, ease, "droll maxims, uncommon eloquence, and an admirable fund of new things to say."[117] The American situation, in her opinion, was simply too hopeless. Except for an exclusive few with whom she interacted in mid-Atlantic cities, Americans, in her opinion, knew nothing of the art of living. "The waste of life which takes place with us shut up in our melancholy Country Houses where we vegetate for months alone is happily not endured" in Paris, she informed her cousin in 1816. "Those long, wearisome winter Evenings varied only by the entrance of the Tea Equipage, mending the Fire & handing round apples & nuts do not form any part of the 12 months in happy, wise France. No Family ever spends an evening without society." Outside of the nation's capital, Elizabeth believed a cosmopolitan salon of refinement, grace, and intelligence was an impossibility in the land of "apples & nuts." Though Americans imported expensive material goods to impart a sense of European refinement to their living environments, Elizabeth saw through what she regarded as a misguided attempt. "One would suppose," she cuttingly remarked, "the dullness of life in America was to be charmed away by superfluous expense in furniture of Houses & Table equipages." In Paris, in contrast, "there is less waste of money & greater enjoyment in living. Society[,] that blessing which is refused to all our [American] exertions[,] can be had in Paris without effort."[118] Living on the periphery, American men and women lacked the necessary elegance and wit. Far too many men were focused on their business affairs and far too many women on their children to discuss genteel subjects. "Commerce," Elizabeth explained to her friend Lady Sydney Morgan, "may fill the purse, [but it] clogs the brain." "Beyond their counting houses," the men of America, she insisted, "possess not a single idea." And housekeeping and nursing children, while "useful occupations," did not "render people agreeable to their neighbors."[119] Moreover, she insisted—probably alluding to her father's household—"all people living in the same house with each other" could never "be society for each other." After a while, "they exhaust their topics, their curiosity, their activity of intercourse, and nothing but ennui and contention remains."[120] Instead of trying to improve American culture by re-creating her European experiences at home, as many of her friends did, Elizabeth drew upon them to condemn American society.

Elizabeth also divided such social activity from the political purposes it served for many American men and women. Female leaders of polite society in Washington and in cities along the Atlantic coast excelled at creating *political* spaces where men *and* women came together for genteel discussions of local, national, and international matters. Like the French salons of the eighteenth and early nineteenth centuries, these mixed-gender gatherings of the wealthy and educated became "an acknowledged part of political society" and therefore ensured some women a recognized and meaningful part in the political culture of the early republic, at least until the early years of the 1800s.[121] As a number of women's historians have shown, the world in which Elizabeth moved allowed women to act as political beings and possess political identities.

Though these possibilities may have been closed by the mid-1820s with the triumph of a separate-spheres ideology that relegated women to more domestic and familial concerns (if not actually keeping them in the house), Elizabeth grew up, married, divorced, and spent much of her life in an environment that accepted women's involvement in some forms of political life.

Political females surrounded Elizabeth. Her aunt, Margaret Smith, the wife of Senator Samuel Smith, often attended congressional debates; only the rare event could keep her away. "Mrs. Smith has not gone to Washington," Elizabeth's sister-in-law reported in 1816, because her daughter was ready to deliver a child.[122] Another aunt, Nancy Spear, was widely known for her passion for politics and especially for attendance at debates. When Congress was in session, Spear left Baltimore and became a fixture in the ladies' gallery. Visitors counted on seeing her there.[123] Spear, however, was an unusual woman. In 1811, Catherine Mitchill described her as "a Maiden, between 45 & 50 years of age, but dresses as youthful as a Girl of 18. She is called very sensible, and as proof of it she prefers the company of gentlemen to that of her own sex. She is also celebrated for being a great politician, and is withal very satirical." Spear rarely concerned herself with the details of fashion or the gossip of the day. Her favorite topics of conversation were books, business, and most of all politics. She considered herself a staunch Old Republican, and she not only frequently voiced her political opinions in letters and discussions but also acted on them. After her kinsman Robert Smith's dismissal as Madison's secretary of state, Spear, "having espoused his quarrel," would "not visit at the Presidents" or even call on Elizabeth's friend Dolley Madison, and she never missed "an opportunity to abuse Mr. Madison."[124] Spear was regarded as a serious political being by male politicians. Senator Jeremiah Mason believed she possessed "a shrewd masculine understanding, has read much and thought more." He considered her the "opposite" of Elizabeth, though they were "rivals in nothing."[125] In 1827, minister to France James Brown simply assumed that "Mrs. [Margaret] Smith and Miss Spear" would accompany Senator Samuel Smith "to the seat of Government next winter."[126] Politics captivated Spear so much that, in 1828, "the interest she [took] in the approaching Presidential election and its probable result . . . had an unfavorable influence on" her health and spirits.[127] Still a loyal Republican, Spear detested Democrat Andrew Jackson and those who elected him.

In the early republic, women who so chose could participate in politics and have politics be a part of their lives. Like men, they possessed their own opinions and ideas about politics. This role could easily become part of their sense of themselves as women. In 1806, Catherine Mitchill reported that the "debates in the house of representatives" were "quite a fashionable place of resort for the Ladies." She found attendance at them "a very agreeable way of spending the morning" whenever there was "any interesting subject of debate."[128] And when Frances Few visited her uncle, Secretary of the Treasury Albert Gallatin, during the 1810–11 season, she regularly attended the debates and often stayed up late "talking politics" with men in the government.[129] Elizabeth herself attended Congress occasionally when in Washington, sometimes with one of her aunts or other women. Mary Mason, the wife of the New Hampshire senator, asked her husband Jeremiah "to write [her] some politics" in his letters home. He happily obliged, and the two engaged in detailed political discussions. In November 1814, for instance, after Mary had expressed "surprise that Mr. C. Cutts should be chosen Secretary of the Senate," Jeremiah provided her with an explanation, though it was "*for yourself*" only.[130] Women in Elizabeth's milieu assuredly knew that property-owning, single women in New Jersey had the right to vote and exercised it before it was taken away in 1807. In elite circles, women with political interests and identities were common, and they were not generally treated as violating the bounds of acceptable behavior for ladies. At times, though, the strength of women's political identities could prove unsettling. The British diplomat Sir Augustus John Foster speculated that the New Jersey state assembly had taken away women's voting rights because "the men they chose were thought to be too aristocratical, for ladies have the reputation of hating democracy as well as demagogues."[131]

While widely considered "too aristocratical," Elizabeth did not deploy the same kind of political identity as some of her female friends and family. There is no evidence of political engagement or interest before she connected herself to Jerome. After her marriage, she became greatly concerned about the political fortunes of Napoleon and the other Bonaparte rulers. But her extant writings do not dwell on political news or propound views on political subjects. Correspondents often assumed that she was interested in politics, frequently writing to her with the "public & private news in circulation," especially political happenings, while she was abroad. In addition to Spear who constantly kept her abreast of the political situation, Elizabeth's sister-in-law informed her in one letter that "Mr. Munroe is to be the next President, Mr Dallas or Mr Pinckney will be sent to the Court of France. *Dick Rush* is to go minister to Russia . . . General Smith is in Congress," and "Uncle Harper is Senator."[132] Though she read newspapers, Elizabeth does not seem to have followed politics with the passion her aunts Nancy Spear and Margaret Smith did. Perhaps like many women in this period, she seems to have been more than willing to discuss politics in social situations, participating in a kind of political sociability at heterosocial gatherings. For two decades after her marriage, though, she generally seemed more interested in the wars and politics of Europe—events that could have a direct impact on her and her son's future—than on elections and political parties in America.

It is impossible for us to categorize Elizabeth as a female politician like her aunts, but it was easy for Americans of her time to see her as unrepublican. Interestingly, Elizabeth seems to have been one of the only women to have been publicly labeled unrepublican, as Thomas Law did in his circulated poem. Elizabeth did not bestow her sexual favors on those who qualified as good men for the republic; she did not court or marry a republican man; she did not act politically through her husband or son; and she did not support the republic in her words or behavior. She certainly had no desire to raise her son as a virtuous republican citizen. While female politicians may have been regarded by some as unladylike, they were never considered unrepublican. Conversely, Elizabeth was never regarded as unladylike for being unrepublican. By the early 1800s, the "republican wife" and "republican mother" that have been so compelling to historians seem to have survived only as abstractions; few wrote about them in their private letters or diaries. While these concepts remained a topic of national conversation, women seem to have discussed them little, and few women were identified as good examples of republican motherhood. Instead of being attached to specific women or specific characteristics, the general concepts seems to have persisted in this era of gender flux, ultimately becoming a key part of the characteristics of womanhood in the mid-1800s. Elizabeth's failure to perform the roles of republican wife and mother had little impact on her socially, further suggesting the weakness of these gender definitions in the early decades of the nineteenth century.

After 1830, amidst the political changes of Jacksonian democracy, Elizabeth appears to have become more interested in American politics. But her new interest seems to have derived from the links between her personal financial situation and the nation's political challenges. When Jacksonian fiscal policy paid off the national debt and eliminated government bonds as one of the main sources of her income, she paid attention. Indeed, her financial adviser noted that the situation "deranges the affairs & incomes of many who live on capital & are unable to make interests of their money." It "presses with peculiar severity," he continued, "on retired individuals and on widows, other females, & minors."[133] As a single woman in control of her own financial future, Elizabeth could no longer ignore politics. The Nullification Crisis of 1832–33 especially attracted her attention since it was a political crisis over a financial issue. Her financial adviser in Baltimore was astonished that Elizabeth had "not only turned Politician," but supported the South Carolina nullifiers during their standoff against President Jackson over protective tariffs and states' rights since her "station" was "not of the common mould" but "distinguished and aristocratic." Someone normally so opposed to democracy, her adviser believed, should not suddenly become "a leveller" this late in life.[134] Her puzzling support of the nullifiers also shocked Nancy Spear, who hated Jackson and loved Henry Clay and who had enough experience to know that possible political and financial chaos was never good for business. "You have jumped from Aristocracy to Jacobinism," Spear told her.[135]

Though few young women in the 1830s would have followed their example, Elizabeth's aunts still clung to an increasingly old-fashioned definition of womanhood that included female politicians. Elizabeth's financial agent, John White, wrote her in the midst of the Nullification Crisis and Jackson's attack on the Bank of the United States that "Miss Spear . . . has a continual feast presented to her in the existing political warfare" and that it was "unfortunate" that "Mrs [Samuel] Smith does not go to Washington this Winter so that she will be prevented from [figuring] at this important era upon the grand Theater."[136] Spear fully understood the complicated and thorny issues and thought the nullifiers were in the wrong. "How could you suppose it possible that any administration woud suffer them to nullify laws & yet live under the protection of the government?" she asked Elizabeth. Blaming the whole crisis on Jackson, Spear argued that he "had fostered this spirit in the South." Sounding like an earlier generation of Republicans, which she was, she considered Jackson "ignorant without a single statesman like quality." Her class status easily came to the fore on this issue. What could one expect, she argued, from a president "elected by the 'rank scented many' who can only judge of something gross & palpable like war." Sounding much like Elizabeth, she declared that while England's "glory & greatness" rested on "a fearless & a high notiond aristocracy," the United States had "a bad system in which the publick functionaries are incessantly changing by the breath of the common mouth & Where the very paupers in the streets are carried up to vote." She agreed with Elizabeth that "our Utopia will not last ten years." Spear especially regarded

Jackson's attack on the Bank as "silly & atrocious," especially since recharter-ing it "would have been worth a hundred & fifty dol. a share."[137] Class status and politics remained intertwined for these single women.

During this era of shifting definitions of womanhood, political women found acceptance for a time, but businesswomen still struggled for fair treat-ment and social recognition of their expertise. Far more than those with politi-cal interests, women who expressed a keen interest in commercial and financial issues often met with a difficult reception among both men and women. While society accepted the widow who ran her husband's shop, tavern, farm, or even plantation, women like Elizabeth and Nancy Spear who excelled in business and enjoyed the game of it found themselves frequently characterized as mas-culine.[138] Commerce and finance still supposedly remained outside the realm of genteel women. The legal status of coverture made clear that married women, a class that should have included almost all adult women, did not have any financial identity, let alone one as a savvy businesswoman. Though many women of this era recognized the severe and broad limitations of financial dependence, few enjoyed the circumstances not only to achieve financial independence but also to become successful in the male world of business.

Like many other men and women, Elizabeth long benefited from her class position. She used her class privileges to acquire a comfortable living and to ensure her access to capital for making profitable investments. Though a woman, Elizabeth's elite status garnered her access to the power of the state—through its courts, banks, and legislature—to further her economic interests, which secured her and her son's social and economic futures. Elizabeth was one of the fortunate independent women who received "unearned" income from interest payments on bonds, dividends from stock, and rents from her leased properties. Poorer *feme soles* usually struggled to make a living, per-forming arduous or demeaning labor to earn a few coins. Elizabeth's class as well as her gender shaped her identity and behavior in this environment. Equally important was her legal status as a *feme sole*, which allowed her to have sole control over her money and make her own financial decisions. But Eliza-beth herself played a key role in her accumulation of wealth. She once declared that she "possess[ed] instinctively some knowledge of Finance."[139] In fact, she seems to have had a better head for business than her brothers who had trained in William Patterson's merchant house.

Elizabeth was quite single-minded in the pursuit of increasing her wealth. James Gallatin, who knew Elizabeth in Europe in the 1810s and 1820s, declared that her "one god seems to be money." Her acumen in business impressed many. Gallatin's father, former Secretary of the Treasury Albert Gallatin, held "the highest opinion of her intelligence—particularly on financial matters." "He has often said had she met the Emperor Napoleon, and had joined forces with him, the fate of Europe might be quite different from what it is to-day."[140] By 1818, Elizabeth was in the top 10 percent of all wealth holders in her district.[141] Over the years, she had carefully saved and judiciously invested the monies that had come to her since her abandonment. From 1809 through 1814, Elizabeth noted, she received a total of $71,514 from the French government.[142] In 1825, her uncle Samuel Smith surmised that she was worth $100,000.[143] She had quite a diverse portfolio, owning stock in insurance companies and in the Second Bank of the United States and bonds from municipalities and states; she continued to buy American stocks and bonds while in Europe. She invested in a textile factory and was an early investor in railroads. She also owned numerous rental properties around Baltimore, including houses, shops, and warehouses near the docks, as well as an oilcloth factory and a wharf.

Elizabeth had an excellent model of a shrewd businesswoman to follow in her aunt Nancy Spear, who was renowned for her business acumen as well as her passion for politics. Henry Lee, Jr., joked in 1813 that if the British attacked Baltimore "Miss Spear, the keen Speculatrix, will be perhaps, like Archimedes, captured while profoundly pondering some intricate problem in the science not of mathematics but of stockjobbing."[144] While Elizabeth was in Europe, Spear took care of her financial affairs. Financial adviser John White, who took over the management of Elizabeth's finances in the mid-1820s, insisted that her affairs "could not be in more faithful or intelligent hands" than Spear's.[145] Writing to Elizabeth in Paris, Spear told of a new renter for one of Elizabeth's Baltimore properties, alerted her that "Stocks of all kinds have risen & landed property greatly; yours have all given dividends, except the fire Company & the falls turnpike," and encouraged her that since "dividends are daily coming in, do spend your money freely."[146] In early 1816, Spear cautioned that there had been a slight depression in the stock market because of a commercial slowdown during the winter, but the experienced businesswoman told Elizabeth not to worry.[147] Indeed, Spear chided Elizabeth for being too cautious: "You know there is not a being on earth that could make you spend your income, not even living in Paris at the Fountain of Pleasure because I know it is quite sufficient to support you like [a] Lady if you would spend it. I expect all you do lay out is packed away in little pretty things in your Trunk."

"You cannot live forever," she continued, "& you know your son has a certain resource in your fathers fortune. I hope you will profit by this scolding."[148]

Spear continued sending detailed letters about Elizabeth's rents, stocks, and bonds, interest rates, and other business affairs during her long stay in Europe in the 1820s and early 1830s. In 1827, she excitedly reported: "I suppose you know that Baltimore is about to become the very first city in the U States & all the property worth 10 times its former value by the construction of a rail road from Baltimore to the Ohio . . . and will receive to her all the trade of the West." Even Elizabeth's father, "who was never imaginative or theoretical has full faith in it" and had invested fifty thousand dollars. With investors expecting "full 10 percent for their money," "all the Maids & Widows in town have taken stock." Like Elizabeth, those *feme soles* with legal control over their money saw the railroad as a good investment. Being extremely capable, Spear was hurt when Elizabeth, in letters to her father, "constantly say you hope Miss Spear will run no risks." "I never have run any," Spear vowed.[149]

Even with her finances in Spear's capable hands, Elizabeth returned to Baltimore from Europe in 1817, 1824, and 1834 primarily to take care of her financial and business affairs. Writing from Baltimore in November 1817, she admitted to David Bailie Warden that "my property required my presence & my economy for some time."[150] Such attention appeared both in the restraint with which she spent money and the caution with which she invested it. As she informed Spear, she wanted "no risks of any kind" with her money and preferred "a moderate interest upon good security," such as federal bonds. By the late 1820s, in spite of her father's and Spear's recommendations, she "had no confidence in road stock, water stock, fire insurance, cotton manufactories, or State banks." She recognized "that a single woman like myself" would be "cheated by servants and tradespeople" more than "women who have husbands to look after their concerns." And she believed that "capital can [not] be improved by a single woman to the same advantage that it might be by men." Given these constraints, she boasted that "my affairs, considering everything, have been as well managed as they could have been by any other person in my position."[151] Elizabeth knew she had excellent business skills.

By 1830, Elizabeth was "worth *upwards* of $100,000," and her estate provided her an "income of $5000 yearly," sometimes as high as $7,000. Such an income, her financial manager believed, "when disbursed under your good management, [was] abundantly sufficient to place your establishment (as it ought to be) upon a very fashionable footing, and to afford every comfort that you can desire."[152] After her son's marriage in 1829, White encouraged Elizabeth to remain in Europe where her income would allow her to live "in enjoyment, in the respect and attentions of society, and in public esteem"—in other words, to live like an aristocratic celebrity. Since "no one else has a claim on your bounty," White thought it a wonderful plan for this independent woman.[153] Spear disagreed and pressed Elizabeth to return to Baltimore, proclaiming that she "woud be happier here & that it woud be more to your [financial] interest to return."[154] In 1831, Elizabeth agreed with her father that her money "ought to be placed in the most permanent funds and those which offer the greatest security for the future." She wanted Spear to make sure that her "floating capital" was "divided into *three* parts: *one* to be invested in five per cents. [bonds] of the city; one to be invested in five per cents. of the State [of Maryland]; the other *third* to be equally divided—*one-half* in ground rents, and the other half lent out as at present." She did not consider herself "rich enough to speculate in any way," though "many women in Europe enrich themselves in this way," preferring low-risk investments.[155] In this rare instance, Elizabeth decided not to model herself after European women.

Elizabeth's identity was based firmly on practical matters—what could gain her status and money and perhaps make her happy. Unlike many other women of this era, she did not define herself by her feelings or ties of affection for others. In fact, she found such ties to be not very useful, especially in marriage. Nor was she content to define herself, as so many of her peers did, as a conveyor and arbiter of refinement for the new nation's culture. She enjoyed being out in the social whirl, dressing in the height of fashion, conversing with men on myriad subjects, including politics and business. But she did so as a cosmopolitan celebrity with aristocratic aspirations, not as an elite American woman who found reward in her efforts to shape the culture of the new republic. Further, what made a woman a good wife in this era may have been open for discussion, but only a few thought it was a wife like Elizabeth.

Elizabeth never consciously presented herself as a model for American women, but she did consciously choose to pursue a life that was at odds with the models that other elite women offered at the time. She cultivated an image of herself, but not necessarily one that would be instructive to other women. She was a celebrity not a role model and probably vastly preferred the former identity to the latter. She never tried to embrace, even in part, the domestic roles of wife and mother, as many other elite and middling women did at the time. She wanted attention and acclaim and, like some other women, a leading place in polite society. Along with Anne Bingham, Dolley Madison, Elizabeth Monroe, and other women who did not fully follow the older prescriptions of republican society, who refused to focus only on raising virtuous citizens within the confines of their homes, Elizabeth became a social success, garnering social and cultural power in spite of her divorced status and scandalous clothes. In contrast to those women, however, she simply went too far—much farther than most of her female contemporaries—in challenging public and private gender boundaries. While never seriously offending the morals of the nation's genteel circles, as the tavernkeeper's daughter Margaret O'Neal Eaton would in the late 1820s, Elizabeth did offend their emerging nationalism, their love of country. She turned her rejection of American gender roles, even the alternative models of womanhood crafted by her elite friends, and of republican citizenship into an intense anti-Americanism. When at home in Baltimore or even in Washington instead of in Paris, Geneva, or Florence, Elizabeth felt herself to be as much in exile as any of the Bonapartes. Happiness for this modern woman, she firmly believed, could only be found in Europe.

Chapter 4

"Happiness for a Woman"
The Femme d'Esprit

In late 1816, missing her dear friend desperately, Elizabeth wrote to Lady Sydney Morgan, listing all of the people in Paris who had asked her to send their good wishes to the author, who had recently departed France. "In fact," Elizabeth noted, "if I were to write all that your admirers and friends tell me, I should never put my pen down."[1] Lady Sydney Owenson Morgan, an Irish noblewoman, and Elizabeth Patterson Bonaparte, an American divorcée, had met earlier that year on each woman's first trip to Paris, as each rose to celebrity status in Europe. As the author of some extremely popular and nationalistic novels, especially *The Wild Irish Girl* (1806), Morgan "was admired and *fêted*, and received all the intoxicating homage of a Parisian success."[2] Elizabeth assured her that "the French admire you more than any one who has appeared since the Battle of Waterloo in the form of an English woman."[3] This famous writing woman soon served as one of Elizabeth's closest confidants and truest supporters.

Just a few years apart in age and sharing a similar spirit of independence and love of attention, the two women worked together at increasing their celebrity and the number of their fashionable acquaintances on the continent. "Lady Morgan," Elizabeth recalled when she was very old, "was brilliant in wit, good-natured and flattering; short, with sparkling eyes; her hair close cut, in dark curls."[4] She had married Sir Charles Morgan when she was thirty, and the couple lived in Dublin with no children. Their marriage was based on a staunch belief in the equality of men and women and a firm commitment to the preservation of Morgan's writing career; Sir Charles had also agreed that

Figure 9. Elizabeth's closest friend, the novelist Lady Sydney Morgan, at the height of her celebrity. René Théodore Berthon, *Portrait of Lady Sydney Morgan (Sydney Owenson)*, ca. 1818, courtesy of the National Gallery of Ireland.

all the money his wife earned as a writer would remain her own.[5] Morgan reigned over her own literary salon in Dublin and, with her fame and literary reputation, easily gained access to the finest salons, both aristocratic and artistic, when she visited Paris. Her celebrity certainly helped open doors for her new friend Elizabeth. "I assure you, and you know I am sincere," Elizabeth wrote Morgan in 1817, "that you are more spoken of than any other person of the present day."[6] Knowing her cousin would spread the news to friends and family in the United States, Elizabeth boasted of her friendship with Morgan in a letter to him. "Her reputation as the best novel writer in the World," she wrote with some exaggeration, "is her passport to all the Courts of Europe & to the first circles of Rank & Fashion."[7] Yet Morgan's significance to Elizabeth went beyond what she could do for her quest for transatlantic celebrity and desire to mix with fashionable aristocrats. Morgan quickly became one of the most important women in Elizabeth's life.

Elizabeth and Morgan spent a great deal of time in each other's company in Paris, usually seeing each other every day as they visited public gardens, cafés, and boulevards in the city or toured the sights at "St. Cloud, Versailles or some other Place in the Environs of Paris" or called on friends.[8] Often unescorted by a man, the pair frequented parties, dinners, and salons, chatting about politics, books, and other intellectual or merely scandalous topics with socialites, French aristocrats, minor European royalty, scientists, writers, and artists. Both women relished finally being at the center of the fashionable and literary world among the "*gens d'esprit*."[9] Both regarded Paris as a vastly superior place to their respective hometowns. In her 1817 published account of France, Morgan stated that "the society of Paris, taken as a whole, and including all parties and factions, is infinitely superior in point of taste, acquirement, and courtesy, to that of the capital of any other nation."[10]

Many of the members of the "Beau Monde," as Elizabeth called it, found the two women charming and sought a closer relationship with them beyond mere acquaintance.[11] The fashionable *salonnières*, the Comtesse de Genlis, Madame Récamier, and Madame La Rochefoucauld-Liancourt, enjoyed their company often, as did the archaeologist Baron Vivant Denon, who entertained them in his "superb" apartments.[12] Elizabeth "attribute[d]" Denon's interest in her to the "partiality with which" Morgan had "distinguished" her, for which she was "very grateful."[13] One of the leading literary women in Paris, Voltaire's adopted daughter, the Marquise de Villette, held great affection for the two friends and frequently invited them for dinner and conversation. Often, just the three of them gathered together. On one special occasion, Morgan and Elizabeth received particular notice as "the only foreigners present at" Villette's annual "literary *déjeûner*" commemorating Voltaire.[14] The "variety" of "society" in Paris guaranteed that the two women would engage in, as Morgan described it, the "most singular combinations and unlooked-for associations" with other people. In her published work, Morgan gave the perfect example of this Parisian phenomenon, one that included "the lovely Madame Jerome Buonaparte (Mrs. Patterson)." "I was at a ball one evening, at Madame de Villette's, and leaning on Mrs. Patterson's arm," her account began, "when the Prince Paul of Wirtemberg entered into conversation" with them. He had noticed Elizabeth and, after hearing her make "some observations," asked her if she "was *an American.*" According to Morgan, Prince Paul "was not aware" that this was *"the wife* of the man, who was since married to *his own sister."*[15] The prince apparently found Elizabeth especially intriguing. Only in Paris, the locus of cosmopolitanism, could such an encounter take place.

Both Morgan and Elizabeth considered their entrée into this rarefied environment a "brilliant success."[16] They found warm welcome at all kinds of salons, in all ranges of the political spectrum. Almost every night they received invitations to exclusive dinners, parties, and even masquerade balls. The fashionable French celebrated and liked them. The two women also easily entered the circle of writers gathered in Paris and established ties with many leading authors, including Germaine de Staël. Morgan and Elizabeth formed a supportive and affectionate relationship during their first visit to Paris and clearly valued it while together and perhaps even more so later when apart. In their letters, the pair discussed a wide variety of topics, including their views on marriage, motherhood, and celebrity; the processes of writing and publishing; and their shared belief that they could only be truly happy and fulfilled in Paris. They also frequently and delightedly gossiped about friends and other celebrities. Morgan considered Elizabeth her "dearest friend" and "admired and loved [her] much."[17] Elizabeth, in turn, wrote Morgan once that she had "met few persons who possess the stability of friendship that I find in yourself. You are, in this particular, as in most others, *une personne distinguée.*"[18] It probably came as little surprise to Elizabeth that it was in Europe, not America, where she found her dearest and most compatible friend.

In the new American nation and even more so in post-Bonaparte Europe, the 1810s and 1820s constituted an era of shifting identities. National, social, and individual identities remained very much in flux, especially in a Europe trying to reconstruct itself after a quarter-century of revolution and war. In the United States and in Europe, people knew they could change their identity simply by moving across a country or an ocean or by transforming themselves through a change of economic or social status.[19] In continental Europe, Napoleon had created scores of new aristocrats who now mingled with those of older lineages, as all sought to rebuild a social structure that favored those at the top of the hierarchy. Manipulating one's own identity was far easier than creating national identities, though citizens sought to do both at the same time. After the Bonapartes, Europe, especially France, relied on social identities and a growing sense of nationalism to help restore order, stability, and peace. Europeans rebuilt their countries socially, economically, and politically, some with new constitutional monarchies. New class hierarchies appeared, often similar to those of the *ancien régime*, but including the new aristocrats and the wealthiest, non-noble families at the highest levels.[20] This was a new kind of society coming to fruition in the nineteenth century.

In this period of dislocation and change, as Europe and Europeans reinvented themselves as nations and individuals, gender definitions gained importance. With many still confused about the relevance of lineage, wealth, and merit, gender roles and definitions served as strong markers of identity for individuals and for social groups. As in the United States after its revolution, how European women behaved, dressed, thought, and learned actively shaped the reconceptualization and reorganization of post-revolutionary European society.[21]

Women on both sides of the Atlantic appeared in public spaces and helped shape the tone of society, culture, and politics in their nations. But, in Europe, ambitious women had more acceptable outlets for actively creating their own and their country's identity. They relied on a longer tradition than their American counterparts of women as writers, intellectuals, actresses, artists, *salonnières*, socialites, and even mistresses of key political or cultural figures. These women, often referred to as *femmes d'esprit* in the early 1800s and centered in Paris, rarely relied on a cloak of domesticity to legitimate their public roles, as many American women did. The *femmes d'esprit* comfortably acted in public, scholarly, and political arenas and men fully expected them to be there. While their private behavior sometimes caused such women to be labeled scandalous, many of them received admiration and respect from large numbers of European men and women. Their lives seemed to prove the adage that Paris was "the paradise of women."[22]

As Elizabeth Patterson Bonaparte viewed it, Europe offered wonderful possibilities for women, especially independent ones. Continental high society promised the life she had always wanted. Not only did it provide the aristocratic milieu in which she desperately desired to live, but it also furnished the gender norms that fostered definitions of womanhood in which she staunchly believed. "In Europe," she once assured her father, "women have fully as much their own way as the men have."[23] For Elizabeth, Europe meant freedom for women to act in ways that displayed and celebrated the talents women like her possessed, without the restraints found in the United States. Europe, she believed, offered her greater independence of thought and action. She seems to have been unaware that she wanted and actually lived a life very different from that of most of the women she knew—American or French. Though Napoleon himself was gone, the Napoleonic code remained in force to circumscribe sharply the lives of French women. Elizabeth must have known of its effects, but they had no impact on her opinion of French women's freedoms. Once in Europe, Elizabeth quickly became a part of the exclusive circles and formed close friendships with many *femmes d'esprit*. In Europe, she, too, changed her identity, reinventing herself as a cosmopolite worthy of inclusion in aristocratic society. This reinvention, however, rested heavily on her views of the possibilities available to European women and her interactions with certain kinds of them.

Neither fully American nor fully European, Elizabeth clearly took advantage of this era of shifting identities as she drew from a wide variety of gender characteristics from both sides of the Atlantic to create her own version of womanhood that could serve her well in multiple transatlantic environments.[24] The woman she became easily engaged with the Bonapartes and other European aristocrats, fully participated in the supportive and energizing circle of female intellectuals, and always appeared as a virtuous woman who was worthy of admiration, acclaim, friendship, and even sympathy.

Elizabeth's travels to Europe exposed her to a different set of women's roles as well as to alternative ideas about women. European women of the upper ranks could think and act (and dress) in ways outside of the varied social prescriptions for American women in the early 1800s. In France, Elizabeth believed, women knew how to be women—attractive, intelligent, interesting, and entertaining. They were not simply wives and mothers but were valued most as men's social counterparts. Not mere "ornaments," women were considered the intellectual equals of men. Society welcomed and encouraged women's participation, both intellectually and socially, in heterosocial spaces. The French prized mixed-gender sociability as a hallmark of their culture and made sure that this national characteristic would play a foundational role in their new post-Bonaparte society. This attitude also ensured an essential part for women in public life.[25] Robert Livingston, the American minister to France in the early 1800s, saw things much as Elizabeth would, believing the French were such happy people because "women form the rosy links of their society."[26]

Yet, in seeming opposition to these ideas, the Civil Code of 1804, later known as the Napoleonic code, regarded all women as minors and kept married women in particular in an inferior and subordinate position. The code legally defined women strictly in terms of their relationship to men, overturned the Revolutionary concept of egalitarian marriages based on happiness, and resurrected the staunchly patriarchal model of family relations. It did preserve the right to divorce but removed incompatibility as an acceptable cause. The code explicitly ordered wives to obey their husbands and reside with them; it also allowed for the legitimate use of violence against a wife. As in the United States and Great Britain, however, the legal code did not fully reflect reality. Few husbands exercised all of the rights established in the code. Furthermore, the "doctrine of 'tacit consent,' whereby a woman could act independently . . . on the assumption that all was done with her husband's unspoken authorization," ameliorated some of the code's impact.[27] Within the legal and political restrictions of the Napoleonic code, elite French women in this era enjoyed a great deal of freedom in thought and action. Captivated by these women's greater independence and social influence, Elizabeth became convinced that the gender roles and expectations of European aristocrats encouraged women to express not just what society expected of them but their real selves.

For Elizabeth, the true role for women, at least those of her class and background, was to promote sociability, and the European circles in which she moved gladly assigned to women that public role instead of a primarily domestic one. One of her financial advisers in Baltimore agreed. "Beauty or brilliancy"—the qualities Elizabeth so clearly possessed—"are not indispensable at the fireside or in the nursery," he admitted; "their natural element is scenes of splendour." "By all accounts your present residence" in Europe was most "favorable to their successful display."[28] Elite European women had a far easier time and faced far less criticism in commanding civil spaces and wielding public influence than their American counterparts. Early nineteenth-century French aristocrats possessed a more positive view of women in the public arena than many Americans, seeing them not as "an element of social disorder" but as "preeminently" performing the crucial "task of guarding social conventions and maintaining the equilibrium, and consequently, the advantages of civilized life."[29] European society expected refined women to bring together and soften the distinctions between the public and private worlds in drawing rooms, dining rooms, ballrooms, and other genteel spaces. Not surprisingly, these women exerted an acknowledged cultural and political power and enjoyed more social independence than most American women.[30]

More than any other capital on the continent, Paris gathered intellectuals and aristocrats from around Europe, and noble Russians and Poles seemed especially drawn to this capital of fashion, culture, and learning. Writers, scientists, philosophers, political theorists, and other intellectuals abounded and mixed regularly with aristocratic socialites of new and old families. Lady Sydney Morgan declared that post-Bonaparte Paris remained "the elysium of men of letters," as well as "the resort of foreigners of literary, scientific and political eminence." Nowhere else, according to Morgan, would one find "princes and potentates, who have influenced the destinies of nations," socializing "with the more valuable characters of Europe[,] whose works and names are destined to reach posterity."[31] And there were not only learned men holding forth in salons and in printed material but learned women as well. Most of the leading socialites were women, and women led most of the influential salons. Elite European culture fostered mixed-gender interaction and granted women significant space to voice their own beliefs.

European salon culture and high society were completely intertwined with not just the arts and fashion but also business and politics.[32] Significant social, economic, and political "work" was done in these quasi-public spaces, most of which were controlled by women. Indeed, as French political partisanship intensified during the Restoration, female-controlled salons became the center of "political sociability," while still remaining the center of cultural sociability because of the intellectuals, writers, and artists.[33] In 1818, for example, Sydney Morgan spent Christmas Day in Paris "talking politics over the fire till past six" with an assortment of visitors, which included the Duchess of Devonshire, the Sardinian minister "with two other Italians," and the novelist and political writer, Benjamin Constant. The following day, she and her husband "went from Constant's *salon* to the Princess Jablonowski's, where there were a number of persons, and nothing thought of but politics," as those who supported the Bourbons debated those who wanted a constitutional monarchy.[34] Though salons were less public and formal than France's legislative chambers, they held comparable influence and provided a "power base" for women through the political debates held at them.[35] The salon culture these polished women controlled remained quite partisan well after Napoleon's reign. Countess Rumford's salon, for example, was known for its ultra-royalist guests, those who sought the restoration of the *ancien régime*. The salons of Albertine de Staël, Germaine's daughter, and the Comtesse de Rémusat were known for their liberalism; such salons tended to be less exclusive than those of the ultra-royalists. The center party, the Constitutionalists, had their own salons as well. The women who held and attended these gatherings knew they were political players and often lobbied for "a particular policy or course of action."[36]

Some American women had long hoped for the kind of influence, freedoms, and respect that many French aristocratic women possessed in the late 1700s and well into the 1800s. The "republican society of manners" that genteel American women sought to construct for their new nation drew heavily from these European and courtly notions of women's behavior, notions that Elizabeth and other elite women acted on as best they could in their republican milieu. American women in their own spaces desired what European women enjoyed in their fashionable salons: "the liberty to speak speculatively about politics, religion, and philosophy and the right to exercise wit."[37] As Anne Willing Bingham wrote to Thomas Jefferson, "Parisian Ladies" were "accomplished"; Bingham, who had been to France, believed they understood "the Intercourse of society better than in any other Country." More important for Bingham, "either by the gentle Arts of persuasion, or by the commanding force of superior Attractions and Address," the "women of France" had "obtained the Rank and Consideration in society, which the Sex are intitled to, and which they in vain contend for in other Countries," including the United States. "We are therefore bound in gratitude," she reminded Jefferson, "to admire and revere them, for asserting our Privileges."[38]

For Jefferson, however, the gender relations of France and the public power of French women reflected exactly what was wrong with a monarchical Europe. In his view, France's gender definitions allowed women to indulge in political and sexual intrigues, encouraged effeminacy in men, and failed to value household economy in women or industrious labor in men, as in the United States. Jefferson considered women to be naturally domestic and thought that the best societies, such as the American republic, allowed them the right to pursue this happiness by embracing the private sphere. The political involvement and sexual freedom of French women reflected what was corrupt about aristocratic Europe. Jefferson believed aristocracy and luxury fostered "unnatural gender relations and unbridled sexuality."[39] Republicanism, on the other hand, protected what Jefferson regarded as the natural order of gender relations, with women as domestic beings and men as public ones, and ensured a wholesome sexuality based on marital fidelity. For Jefferson, such gender definitions rested at the center of national identity. As he wrote to Bingham, in France, wives did not get out of bed until noon and then spent their days dressing, visiting, wasting time on public amusements, playing cards and chatting in salons until late, and meddling in politics. In contrast, American wives spent their energies on "the society of [their] husband, the fond cares for the children, the arrangements of the house, the improvements of the grounds," filling "every moment with a healthy and an useful activity."[40] With their energies focused on domestic "cares" instead of elsewhere, Jefferson believed, American women would help maintain a virtuous republic.

This comparison between French and American women and their respective roles in each nation's civil society is important. As discussed in the previous chapter, in the early years of the nation, some American women tried to create a salon culture that supported the political arena, but their efforts never proved as effective as the *salonnières* in France. They never gained as much influence or an equal recognition of their power. Anne Bingham's salon and Dolley Madison's soirees could never compete with the Senate chamber. It was much more of a struggle for American women. Indeed, when an American woman showed too much interest in politics, she might be labeled "French."[41] While French women regained much of their earlier influence in Restoration France, American women's roles in political sociability diminished in the late 1810s and 1820s, when partisanship intensified again in the United States and more men became a part of the electorate.[42] While American women had once had a significant presence in the political arena, serving as cultural arbiters and moderators or conciliators among politicians, they increasingly performed these tasks far more in the domestic realm than in the public one. Women in France preserved their direct political influence through public sociability longer than their American counterparts.

Not surprisingly, Elizabeth's definition of womanhood did not match Jefferson's or that of many other Americans. Her choice of a husband and most of the subsequent decisions of her life made it clear that she did not want to live within the gender expectations of the new nation, as Jefferson defined them. Like some other women of her class, she could not abide the increasingly circumscribed role assigned to women as wives and mothers.[43] And she recoiled from the idea, which became increasingly popular as the century progressed, that women's modesty, morality, and piety made them uniquely suited for the domestic realm instead of the public world and privileged their duties to husband and children above all else.[44] After her experience, she saw little use for husbands. Babies, in her opinion, only ruined a woman's appearance and rendered mothers uninteresting. Salons, balls, and formal dinners—not firesides and nurseries—were, she strongly believed, the appropriate arenas for a woman with her qualities. "I can never be satisfied in America," she informed her father in 1816. "It was always my misfortune to be unfitted for the modes of existence there, nor can I return to them without a sacrifice of all I value on earth."[45] Ten years later, she still felt much the same. She thought it "quite as rational to go to balls and dinners as to get children, which people must do in Baltimore to kill time." She also believed that she "resembl[ed] every woman who has left America" in her desire never "to return there" and to the lives it offered women.[46] Ultimately, her intense hatred of the United States probably derived mainly from its gender limitations. Though she took a different course, Elizabeth, like Anne Bingham or Dolley Madison, desired and actively pursued broader "cultural horizons" (though not political ones) than American society allowed most wives and mothers in this era.[47]

With such views about the place and role of women, Elizabeth turned to Europe as her salvation. In Europe, especially France, she saw few limitations placed on elite women and thus chose to embrace that version of womanhood. There, she could escape the tightening gender constraints as well as "the insipidity of America," as she explained to Jonathan Russell, the American minister to Sweden and a regular visitor to Elizabeth's while in Washington. Already planning her return to Europe, she informed Russell that she "no longer [had] the courage to submit to the unvaried dullness of life here."[48] On the Continent, life would be vastly different, for, unlike in the United States, "the purposes of life are all fulfilled—activity and repose without monotony." According to Elizabeth's definition of womanhood—one she shared with many other Europeans—women as much as men needed to be engaged with the world, and European, especially French, society encouraged that. Elizabeth had always complained about her brothers and father "banish[ing] Society from the house."[49] In Parisian houses, "the weight of existence is lightened by intercourse *with the World*."[50] Familial (and female) isolation, animosity, and simplicity characterized America, while social engagement, happiness, and sophistication characterized Europe. Even within Europe, she drew important distinctions.

Americans were, in her words, "a dull, fat, heavy, prejudiced race" who liked "to eat, and to drink, and are cold and fuddled" because they were descended from Englishmen. The French, on the other hand, had "more vivacity, a better literature, infinitely more the art of conversation and society, are less prejudiced, more temperate, and are happier and make others happier."[51] After her second trip to Europe, she formulated a definition of "happiness for a woman": "to be handsome, to be a wit, to have a fortune, to live in Paris, and to have the freedom of the houses of the best circles there."[52]

Elizabeth's comments about motherhood, marriage, and women's social roles reflect a clear and coherent analysis of the limitations of American ideas of womanhood and their impact. Though she never wrote anything for publication or even broad circulation, she never shied away from voicing her views in letters to family and friends, at home and abroad, or at dinner parties in Europe or in Baltimore, New York, or even Washington. After dining with her one evening in the nation's capital, Reverend Horace Holley strongly suggested that she end her "playful attack upon the condition of society in our country"; she "would be a gainer," he insisted, as would "your friends," who tired of defending themselves.[53] Her dissatisfaction with the United States seems to have come more from her personal agitation with the social limitations placed on women of her qualities than from a larger sense of gender injustice. Her exposure to European views of women allowed her to conceive of a life very different from that expected of most elite American women, but after 1812, it was her legal status as a divorcée that actually gave her the rare chance to live that different life. This status set her apart from many European women as well, since it was far more difficult to obtain a divorce on the Continent and almost impossible in England.[54] With no man holding legal control over her and with sufficient wealth, she truly was an independent woman, though she never felt so.

Elizabeth traveled whenever and wherever she wanted. As a manless woman, she did not have a husband controlling her movements; and, after Bo was no longer an infant, she did not need to worry about children. Among elite Americans, it was not unheard of for women to make one or two trips to Europe. Elizabeth ultimately crossed the Atlantic eight times. Other women freed from husbands or child-care responsibilities also traveled without men in this period, but rarely as far or as often or for such long periods. Traveling women in Europe and America had some limitations on their movement and often found companions, even if just another woman, to accompany them as a shield against any unpleasantness. In 1815, Elizabeth's agent in London,

James McElhiney, worried what people would say if a woman alone rented a cottage at the famous bathing resort of Cheltenham.[55] As she grew more acquainted with Europe and its modes of travel, however, Elizabeth seems to have worried less about traveling with the "correct" companions and even took some journeys, usually short ones, alone. As at home, Elizabeth relied on a network of women for her travels in Europe. Dolley Madison asked her female friends whether Elizabeth could accompany them on voyages, and Elizabeth herself turned to women for traveling companions, including Eliza Anderson and Ann Tousard, Colonel Louis Tousard's widow. On an 1825 trip, she and Tousard found company on a ship among five English widows who "seemed to enjoy themselves quite as much as if they had been settled at home with husbands."[56] She also relied on women she met on ships to Europe or after arriving, who gladly accompanied her, sometimes with their husbands, as she moved from England to France to Italy to Switzerland. In various cities, women secured lodgings for her and invitations to parties and other amusements.

Happily for Elizabeth, Europeans were more accepting than Americans of the unaccompanied movement of women around cities and other places, both

Figure 10. Elizabeth's travel trunk made many trips with her across the Atlantic. Bonaparte traveling trunk, ca. 1802–1830. Image #XX.5.552, courtesy of the Maryland Historical Society.

indoors and out. During his trip to Europe in the late 1820s and early 1830s, James Fenimore Cooper informed his daughter that "in Europe it is not at all unusual, or in the least out of place," for even young ladies "to go everywhere without an escort."[57] Furthermore, French etiquette did not require a woman to be escorted by a man to the table or to her carriage, "rendering" French women "more independent" than American women.[58] Mrs. John Mayo, who visited Paris in 1828, pleasingly noted that "married ladies are very independent in France and can go anywhere without an escort, to balls, parties, or the theatre, and nothing is thought of it, nor are they liable to rudeness or insult." "As I have often said," she concluded, "Paris is the place for strangers, for elderly people, and for ladies."[59] Elizabeth would have completely agreed. She always thrilled at being back in the cosmopolitan center of Paris. Soon after their arrival in 1825, she and Tousard took "rooms in the gayest part of Paris & near the Public walks." The two, according to Elizabeth, would "dine out four days in the week, & go out every night to a party. . . . The Mornings we spend in the Public gardens or drive out with our friends." "We amuse ourselves as much as we can," she informed her father, "because life is short & neither of us have any time to lose." Elizabeth's ease of mobility around Europe and among her exclusive circle of cosmopolites in Paris, Geneva, Florence, and Le Havre, allowed this woman on her own to "lead a very gay life."[60]

Strangers and ladies, including Elizabeth, crowded Paris and other European cities after Bonaparte's exile. Yet Europe remained unstable throughout much of Elizabeth's long sojourn between 1815 and 1835. Into the 1830s, coups, revolts, and military confrontations in city streets continued to rock France and other nations. New or transformed individual identities matched the way new or transformed governments of the post-Napoleonic era were being reinvented. Real and fake aristocrats roamed around Europe, causing consternation for those who could not tell them apart. Attesting to the continuing importance of a noble title despite the recent republican revolutions, the early nineteenth century witnessed numerous instances of "self-enoblement," as many concocted a noble lineage and title for themselves, often by simply adding "de" to their last name. For example, Bernard François Balzac added "de" to his last name, adopted a coat of arms for decoration, and claimed ancestry from "an ancient, but long extinct, noble family."[61] His son continued the charade. In this climate of shifting identities, there was a surge of imposters around Europe, including a woman who sometimes claimed to be Elizabeth's sister, calling herself Georgiana Maria Patterson, and, at other times, to be

Elizabeth herself. As she traveled around Europe, this woman hoped that her imagined connection to or her pretended identity as Elizabeth would not only gain her status but also property and money.[62]

Elizabeth's own transformation in Europe was not so brazen as her imposter's or de Balzac's. But she liberated herself from American limitations by embracing a certain sense of aristocratic womanhood and befriending women who also followed those norms. That required manipulating or emphasizing certain parts of her identity over others, but, as an American celebrity with aristocratic style, she already excelled at that. Before she had even embarked for Europe, Elizabeth began transforming her identity. Though she had kept "Bonaparte" as her last name after her divorce, she became "Patterson" again, for her "own convenience," when she left for Europe.[63] Dropping "Bonaparte" probably protected her from any trouble and allowed her to enter France, since all of the Bonapartes closest to Napoleon had been officially exiled. Changing her last name also seems to have brought her some solace. As she explained to Dolley Madison in late 1814, she intended to "resume the name of my own Family & abandon one which produced so much unhappiness."[64] Still, many in Europe and the United States continued to refer to her as Madame Bonaparte.

Like some of the roaming European aristocrats, Elizabeth's identity was complicated even further by the vague state of her nationality or citizenship. Few in Europe would have considered her French, but neither did they generally categorize her as American. Though many Americans condemned her for being too French, Elizabeth never seems to have been officially regarded as a French citizen, even though she was married to a Frenchman at a time when many believed that American women legally adopted the citizenship of their husbands at marriage. As a result, other American women who were married to foreign men had lost not only their U.S. citizenship but also property, child custody, or other rights on occasion. With citizenship in the United States determined by the individual states rather than the federal government, confusion was rampant. Legislatures and courts in the early 1800s never clarified whether married women's citizenship relied on that of their husband or whether they were citizens in their own right. It was difficult for an American-born wife of a foreigner to predict how she would be treated by the law. Ending this uncertainty was probably one motive for Elizabeth to seek a divorce through the Maryland legislature. Not until after World War I, with the passage of the Cable Act, would uncertainty over married women's citizenship be fully resolved.[65] Questions about women's citizenship only added to the fluidity of people's identities in this period. To Elizabeth, establishing her U.S. citizenship protected her legal and economic rights; she also traveled under an American passport. But the cosmopolitan identity she had crafted rose above the national one. In her mind, she was neither French nor American. In this, she mirrored many of the other cosmopolites traveling around Europe who may have been legally citizens of one country but never felt a strong sense of national attachment to any.

Elizabeth's blindness to the political and legal limitations of French women enabled her to believe that she had found a society that valued her particular ideas about women and also admired the qualities she possessed. She clearly recognized the benefits of European gender norms, as she understood them, when compared with those in the United States. According to her, Baltimore could only be "congenial" to American women who "have no mental culture" and "consequently are not pained by unsatisfied intellectual requirements."[66] While at home in Baltimore in 1825, she likened her life there to that of Corinna, a character in one of Germaine de Staël's novels, who found "the subjects of conversation . . . limited to births, marriages, and deaths." Since Elizabeth's "opinion of them has been so long decided"—births meant "misery," marriages meant pain, and death meant "dread"—she grew "so tired of hearing these three important events discussed" all the time and often kept to her own room.[67] Europe, in contrast, fed women's intellectualism and encouraged its display. James Fenimore Cooper similarly noticed that French women possessed a wider "latitude of speech" than their American counterparts.[68] The European women that Elizabeth most admired, and with whom she formed friendships, were famous writers and thinkers; they were the *femmes d'esprit*—women who had pushed the bounds of European gender norms but had received respect for their intellectual talents.

While in the United States, Elizabeth relied on a small circle of female friends; in Europe, she found many more women who shared her ideas of womanhood, and her circle of friends expanded immensely. Those she befriended firmly believed women needed wider ties to the world than what could be found within their own family. They read widely, thought seriously about public issues, and enjoyed discussing them. They, like many of their male peers, looked beyond the private sphere for reward and satisfaction. They moved easily in the spaces created by civil society and confidently contributed their opinions, through writings or conversations, to the public sphere. In the late 1810s and 1820s, these women included the Irish novelist Sydney Morgan, the French philosopher Marquise de Villette, and the French writer Germaine de Staël. Villette had been raised by Voltaire, who had educated her and then "left her part of his Fortune & the Title of Bel-Espirit." She had made a marriage of "convenience" to the Marquis de Villette, one of Voltaire's "Literary Friends," but was a widow by the time she met Elizabeth.[69] When in Paris, Villette and Elizabeth dined together multiple times a week; when apart, they shared an affectionate correspondence. After Elizabeth's return to Baltimore in 1817, Villette missed her so much that she "had two orange trees planted in my garden: one is called 'Elisa,' and the other 'Patterson.' From time to time I go out to water them myself."[70] De Staël's reputation was so great that Elizabeth secured a letter of introduction to her before she even left England for Paris in November 1815. Elizabeth became close enough friends with De Staël that many in Elizabeth's circle believed she could convince the famous intellectual and writer to accept their invitations to parties. De Staël praised Elizabeth's beauty and virtue and enjoyed telling amusing stories about her sharp wit.

Elizabeth's most intimate female relationship was with Sydney Morgan. After their initial meeting in Paris, the letters between Elizabeth and Morgan became vehicles for true self-expression, with each woman feeling comfortable enough with the other to discuss private thoughts and sentiments. Even so, Morgan wrote on one occasion that "you are *one* of *the few women* I have known who have given me a strong impression of *professing* even *less* than they *feel*."[71] It was only to Morgan that Elizabeth revealed a self that few ever saw, including her intense love for her son. With Morgan, Elizabeth removed much of the emotional armor she wore in public, confessing her deep depressions, her lack of confidence, and even the occasions when she had thought of suicide. "Oh! My dear Lady Morgan," Elizabeth lamented in 1820, "I have been in such a state of melancholy, that I wished myself dead a thousand times—all my philosophy, all my courage, are insufficient sometimes to support the inexpressible *ennui* of existence."[72] Many of their letters bordered on the philosophical, with ruminations about the meaning of life and each woman's hopes and dreams. Neither woman, though both international celebrities, seemed very happy (except when in Paris). "There are so many hours besides those appropriated to the world, that one does not know how to get rid of," a weary Elizabeth wrote, "that I have sometimes wished to marry from *ennui* and *tristesse*." Elizabeth believed that Morgan must have "never felt *ennui* in any state, because, when absent from society, you cultivate talents which will immortalize you." Indeed, Elizabeth knew "no person so happy as yourself."[73] Morgan could not understand why Elizabeth complained so much about her unhappy life. "All things considered," Morgan once wrote to Elizabeth, "life ought to have as much charm for you as for most people; clever, handsome, independant, respected & respectable, & with such a son." But then she added, sounding very much like Elizabeth, "the fact is life *is* a dreary penalty from beginning to end. Those who enjoy it most are the fools & rogues." Just like Elizabeth, Morgan regretted that she had "only had *glympses* of the society with wh. I desired to live. The greater part of my life has been passed with the dull, the prejudiced & the ignorant, who have always looked down on me."[74] Elizabeth could have easily written the same thing about her life in Baltimore.

While in Paris, Geneva, and Florence, Elizabeth formed close relationships with many aristocratic or royal women who enjoyed her company. A Countess Hocquard, whom Elizabeth described as "full of wit, talent, & selfishness," and a Lady Bridges both invited Elizabeth to spend the summer of 1826 with them in their country houses.[75] Polish Princess Alexandre Caroline Galitzin became like a sister to her and went so far as to assign Elizabeth her own guest room, which she could decorate to her taste, at her country house outside of Geneva. In Geneva, a German countess, whom Elizabeth characterized as "a practical philosopher of the Epicurean sect," befriended her; they visited each other every day. Elizabeth reported to Sydney Morgan that the countess had tried to "*débarasser* [relieve] me of what she called *mes idées romanesques et mes grandes passions.*" Elizabeth envied this woman's "coarse common sense" and declared her to have "greater knowledge of the world, than any person I have ever known." She wished she "resembled her, because I should be more happy."[76] "The clever, the witty, the agreeable" Madame L. d'Esmenard, who was "one of the most intellectual & cultivated Persons whom I have known," also became one of Elizabeth's dear friends.[77] Elizabeth made the choice to surround herself with these friendly, intellectual women and must have relished living among such a brilliant, supportive group.

Elizabeth's circle of women included some of the leading *salonnières* as well. The Comtesse de Genlis, who reigned over a literary salon and wrote many works about education, invited her regularly to gatherings, as did Marie-Anne de Rumford—the estranged wife of the British-American scientist Benjamin Thompson, also known as Count Rumford—who held a salon that attracted liberals and intellectuals. Rumford liked Elizabeth so much that she also visited her at her own lodgings. Every Tuesday when in Paris, Elizabeth attended the salon of the aristocratic philanthropist Madame de La Rochefoucauld-Liancourt. And she held a standing invitation to Madame Récamier's salons where "men of letters & other great Persons" appeared "every Evening."[78] One of the most famous women in France and beyond for her beauty and sense of style, Récamier had returned to Paris after being banished by the Consulat for supporting De Staël. By the time Elizabeth arrived in Paris, Récamier had regained her popularity and exclusivity. According to the Duchess d'Abrantès (formerly Madame Junot), Madame Récamier "truly deserved . . . homage; she was really a pretty woman! The expression of her eyes was mild and intellectual, her smile was gracious, her language interesting; her whole person possessed the charm of native grace, goodness, and intelligence."[79] A British visitor did not share this glowing opinion of Récamier, snidely commenting that "beside being a beauty, she has pretensions to *bel esprit*: they may be as well founded as the other, yet not sufficient to burn her for a witch."[80]

Elizabeth considered herself a full member of this female society, identifying herself as continental in her character and as a *femme d'esprit* as well. With her accomplished skills and carefully constructed identity, she fit in easily, while others did not. The visiting Englishwoman Lady Blessington believed that her countrymen found salon culture difficult because they did not possess the "lightness and brilliancy" of Parisians, who "sparkle on the surface, with great dexterity, bringing wit, gaiety, and tact into play"; such conditions, she caustically added, allowed "even the ignorant [to] conceal the poverty of their minds."[81] Conversely, Elizabeth made friends with few Englishwomen, characterizing them as "cold, formal, and affected—just my antipodes."[82] The female intellectuals and *salonnières* with whom Elizabeth identified possessed warmer and more welcoming natures. Trying to explain why the Duke of Wellington preferred her former sister-in-law and rival Mary Caton Patterson to herself, Elizabeth confessed in a revealing comment that it was because he had "no taste *pour les femmes d'esprit*."[83] She clearly considered herself a full member of this group.

Elizabeth happily participated in the social whirl that centered on salons in Paris, Geneva, Florence, and Rome and easily engaged with the famous writers, artists, scientists, and other intellectuals she encountered. In Florence, she spent quite a lot of time with the French writer and leading politician Alphonse de Lamartine while he was *chargé d'affaires* for Charles X. Another very close friend was Baron Vivant Denon, the artist and famous Egyptologist.

Figure 11. Madame Juliette Récamier, known as one of the most beautiful women in Europe, reigned over a fashionable salon and befriended Elizabeth. Here, she is clothed in the revealing fabric of the fashionable Grecian style and sits in a *klismos* chair. François Gérard, ca. 1802–1805. Musée de la Ville de Paris, Musée Carnavalet, Paris, courtesy of Scala/Art Resource, New York.

In Paris, the German naturalist and explorer Baron Alexander von Humboldt began a friendly relationship with her. She exchanged letters with the philosopher Baron de Bonstetten, who appreciated the way she expressed her ideas on paper since he "seemed to see and hear" her when he read them.[84] While in Le Havre in the summer of 1825, Elizabeth attended all of the festivities for the returning Marquis de Lafayette, triumphant from his reception in the United States. Since her father was friends with Lafayette, Elizabeth spent some time with him, though she found him boring. He even invited her to La Grange, his estate outside of Paris, to see the cows her father had given him, which she did because of the social cachet attached to the visit. Her close ties with some of these people paid large dividends on occasion. For example, in early 1833, Elizabeth finally appeared at the French royal court of the "republican" King Louis Philippe, formerly the duc d'Orléans, because the Countess de Bourke, widow of a Danish ambassador and new friend of Elizabeth's, had arranged it. Able to adapt to almost any environment, Elizabeth seems to have flitted among all the salons, whether ultra-royalist, Bonapartist, or liberal, with little regard for their political affinities. After dining with Elizabeth on one occasion in a politicized salon, where she was "as usual brilliant, and kept the whole table alive with her witticisms," one Italian gentleman remarked, "'really, Madame Bonaparte, you should have been a man; you would have been a diplomatist.'"[85]

Unlike many American visitors, especially women, Elizabeth was rarely scandalized by what she witnessed in aristocratic circles. She fully accepted elite European forms of gender roles and relations. In fact, she vastly preferred European modes of marrying to those in the United States. Unlike Americans who believed in "lofty pretentions & sentimental acting," the French did "not make marriages from idleness & ennui & call them love matches." Instead, they married "rationally & sincerely for the purpose of enjoying society & spending life agreeably." She understood that such marriages—based on "natural affection" and "more friendship"—sometimes permitted adultery. But Elizabeth insisted that if vice in France "really exist[ed] in a greater degree" than in America (and she was not convinced that it did), it was "less disgusting & more polite." While she followed a strict moral code that centered on protecting her virtuous reputation and apparently never engaged in love affairs, she never denounced in her letters the morality of men and women she knew were engaging in premarital or extramarital affairs. She cared little that Americans condemned "immoral" Europeans or criticized herself for associating with them. "If they [Europeans] commit sins," she decided, "they are more agreeable as sinners than [Americans] are as saints."[86] Indeed, Elizabeth seems to have relished the gossip that circulated throughout her exclusive circle concerning the sexual escapades and romances of Europe's leading men and women, relying on friends in Paris and other places to keep her posted on new developments as she traveled. One friend in Paris, for example, responded to Elizabeth's inquiries from Geneva about some unnamed Russian "Lady & her lover."[87] Another friend from Florence excitedly informed Elizabeth that two men had almost dueled over her and then detailed which aristocrat or royal was courting whom and who had visited whose palace.[88] Combining her interest in female writers with fashionable gossip, Elizabeth asked Sydney Morgan in late 1825 what she thought of the recently published "Miss Harriet Wilson's life, written by herself," that "Every one" was reading. The scandalous Wilson had recently married "a very handsome man, who was willing to make an honest woman of her," and currently lived in Paris, "which seems," Elizabeth remarked, "to be the favourite residence of all naughty English women."[89]

It must have become well-known in her European circles that Elizabeth preferred the agreeable sinners to the virtuous saints. In 1831, her close friend, Princess Caroline Galitzin, felt perfectly comfortable giving her the last eight volumes of Casanova's scandalous memoirs. James Gallatin, the wayward son of Albert Gallatin, turned to Elizabeth in 1819 while in Geneva for advice on how "to get rid" of a married woman with whom he had had an affair.[90] Elizabeth moved in circles with women who had been marked by scandal, but she never seemed to judge them. She knew well and exchanged letters with Lord Byron's former mistress, Teresa Guiccioli, whom Elizabeth described as having "a shower of golden curls; fair, with blue eyes, unlike the typical Italian; teeth and hands perfect; naïve and sweet of temper."[91] The Comtesse d'Albany, the longtime companion of the poet Vittorio Alfieri, and Lady Fanny Jersey, the mistress of the Prince of Wales, later George IV, also became her friends. So, too, did the celebrated divorcée Anne Cavendish Bradshaw, the former Lady Westmeath. And she enjoyed Germaine de Staël's company, even though the famous writer, according to Elizabeth, pursued "a liberal system . . . through life." When it was discovered that De Staël had married a man twenty years her junior just before her death in 1817, Elizabeth agreed with her French friends that it was more "a ridicule" than a scandal.[92] She formed close relationships with many of the most notorious adulterers in Europe, including Talleyrand, with whom she enjoyed witty repartee and intellectual exchanges, and her famously philandering former sister-in-law Pauline Bonaparte Borghese. Baron de Bonstetten, a good friend, wrote to Elizabeth from Geneva slyly suggesting that she ask Pauline about "her secret remedies against ennui" promising that she would "never again suffer it, wherever you go," if she adopted Pauline's practices.[93] The baron probably knew that the cosmopolitan Elizabeth would laugh at his suggestion instead of blush.

The rare occasions when Elizabeth condemned European morals seem to have been influenced by her relationship with the Bonapartes, focusing on broken promises and money issues. "There is no French-man whose word is less brittle than pie-crust," she announced. "The people on the continent of Europe have not the most remote idea of truth or principle in any way." In Geneva, she found the Swiss "as interested and fraudulent as the French; they have more sense, but are less agreeable than the French. In Geneva, they cheat from the highest to the lowest classes, and all aid in plundering the English who go there." She discovered that "the English women pay exactly double what I do for sedan chairs, servants' wages, &c." Because Elizabeth had found out this pricing game, the Genevans showed her "great respect for my adroitness, and seem to consider me now worthy of being dealt fairly with in prices."[94] But her disappointments with some Europeans never outweighed her delight in living among them.

In Europe, especially in Paris, Elizabeth found herself "in the midst of the Brilliant & the Literati," according to an envious friend.[95] As in the United States, reading consumed elite men and women's leisure time and brought the sexes together. Conversation at salons and other social gatherings often centered on books and other printed and manuscript materials; one had to be well-read in the classics as well as more contemporary works to participate confidently. Writers filled Paris during the years Elizabeth spent in Europe, and the publishing industry thrived. There was also a rage for writing memoirs, as many realized that the years of tumult through which they had lived was of great historical importance. Significantly, women could as easily write memoirs as men, providing another public space in which women could share their political views. At the salons, newly penned works, such as plays, poems, fiction, and memoirs, were sometimes read aloud.[96] Reading and writing, together and individually, created a shared language and strong social bonds among men and women and formed the basis of many relationships. This circle of intellectuals and authors not only provided scintillating company for Elizabeth but also encouraged her to write.

Elizabeth knew many different kinds of writers who wrote on a wide variety of topics. One of her longtime friends, and a neighbor while in Paris, was David Bailie Warden, the former American consul in Paris, who began publishing his descriptions of the new nation's capital in 1816 and a history of the United States in 1819. In the 1820s, he wrote a ten-volume history of the United States and North and South America. Elizabeth also became well acquainted with Simonde de Sismondi, a Bonapartist historian living in Paris who wrote extensively on the republics of Italy, and with Baron Vivant Denon, who published chronicles of his archaeological work in Egypt. Elizabeth was even acquainted with Frances Trollope some years before she published her *Domestic Manners of the Americans* in 1832. She also interacted with Maria Edgeworth, the British-Irish novelist whose works were often critical of British policies.

Elizabeth possessed the credentials to be a member of this circle of writers in Europe. She was well educated, fluent in French, and well read. She constantly received and purchased books on her travels, for her own enjoyment and as status symbols. Books also relieved the boredom of the long trips across the ocean and the quiet times she spent alone. Elizabeth interacted with her books, frequently underlining words and sentences and commenting in the margins. During her years in Europe, Elizabeth continued to add to her library, which included many histories, essays, memoirs, and biographies; a number of philosophies; and a smaller number of fictional works. Not surprisingly, she also owned travel accounts of various European countries that provided travel tips and descriptions of customs and manners that she probably used on her many trips or to recall her own visits. She owned books in French as well as English, such Greek and Roman classics as Homer's *Iliad* and Virgil's *Aeneid*, and great works of the Enlightenment, including Edward Gibbon's *Decline and Fall of the Roman Empire* and Joseph Addison's *Spectator*, along with numerous volumes of Rousseau, Voltaire, Samuel Johnson, Alexander Pope, and even Benjamin Franklin. Some of the books in her collection reveal a romantic sensibility, such as a few works by Sir Walter Scott, including *The Lady of the Lake*, and the many volumes of Lord Byron, including one given to her by rejected suitor Samuel Colleton Graves. She later owned the complete works of Alexandre Dumas. Once Elizabeth began befriending writers in Europe, she purchased or received their writings, too, such as Germaine de Staël's essays and memoirs. Some of these works included references to or descriptions of Elizabeth. Sydney Morgan first mentioned her in *France* (1817) and later in her autobiography. The Duchess d'Abrantès chronicled in her memoirs the time she and her husband ran into Jerome Bonaparte on his way to convince the emperor to let him keep Elizabeth as his wife. On the basis of a miniature portrait of Elizabeth, d'Abrantès described her as "exquisitely beautiful," with features very similar to Jerome's sister Pauline, reputedly the most beautiful woman in Europe. The duchess also took Elizabeth's side, making clear in her memoirs that Elizabeth "really was [Jerome's] wife."[97] With works from her friends, classical authors, and leading literary giants, Elizabeth's library was that of a well-educated cosmopolite; indeed, it was more voluminous and wide-ranging than most Americans' of her time. Like many other educated women of the era, Elizabeth used her reading of and thoughts about books to gain a sense of self-identity and participate in the "transatlantic community of letters."[98]

In Europe, Elizabeth surrounded herself with women who wrote for public audiences. Though not all of them did so to earn a living, some did write for an income, including Sydney Morgan. After 1800, more European women published their writings than ever before. After the revolution, female intellectuals and *salonnières* in France sought ways to preserve their cultural and political power and seized the opportunities presented by print culture. With the decline of lineage as the key to identity in post-revolutionary France, "the reflective activities of intellectual production—reading and writing—were becoming the primary means of making a self."[99] But this was not a phenomenon restricted to French women. Many of the women writers Elizabeth knew who were not French also turned to writing not only as the "primary means for making a self" but also to find a respectable way of entering or staying in public life. Women in the United States joined in this use of print as a way to exert cultural, if not political, power. As more American women received an education after 1800, more started writing as a way to become actively involved in shaping public opinion. If their voices were no longer welcomed in political arenas, they could use print to be heard still. But female writers in the United States, unlike in Europe, were cautioned against displaying their learning or intelligence in any obvious way. As long as their public writing appeared to be for the benefit of others and not for the purpose of bringing themselves any acclaim, American women could acceptably make contributions to the national culture.[100] Female writers in Europe had far more latitude to express themselves as individuals and *as women* and to revel in any fame their writing brought. They contributed to the rise of nationalism in Europe and to the drive to return to order and stability.

For Sydney Morgan, like many other European female authors, writing meant more than earning a living; it was also about fame and a new identity. She made clear to Elizabeth that writing for the public was yet another way a woman could reinvent herself and achieve influence in the world. In February 1817, on the eve of the publication of her two-volume *France*, Morgan proclaimed that "all the world is alive about it."[101] She had included a few sentences about Elizabeth in the book, and, in doing so, she not only "told the world that I am always glad to repeat to you that you excited both my interest and admiration" but also added to her dear friend's celebrity.[102] Elizabeth responded by highlighting her friend's cosmopolitan reputation, enviously declaring, "How happy you must be at filling the world with your name as you do!"[103] For the *femmes d'esprit*, writing shaped their personal and public identities and provided a means for not only personal gratification but also public acclaim and power. The world would *know* their names and read their words.

Elizabeth and her writing friends talked frequently and in depth about writing, books, publishing, authors, critics, and the public reception of printed works. These topics regularly appeared in the letters they exchanged. Though Elizabeth never published any of her own writings, she did write often and appreciated her friends' talent and passion for writing. Elizabeth and Sydney Morgan especially focused on these literary concerns. Morgan often wrote ten hours a day when in the middle of a work. She informed Elizabeth that she had received £2,000 for her published observations on France, noting that "it is by far the best thing I ever did."[104] Elizabeth responded from Paris that the work "appeared to me, like everything you write, full of genius and taste. Its truths cannot at this moment be admitted here, but in all other countries it will have complete success." As testament to its political impact and with a sharp understanding of print culture, she added that "the violent clamour of the editors of the Paris gazettes proves that it is too well written; were it an insignificant production they would say less about it."[105] While writing the fervently nationalistic and quasi-feminist novel *Florence Macarthy: An Irish Tale* during 1818, Morgan kept Elizabeth regularly informed of her progress. When Elizabeth returned to Baltimore briefly that same year, she happily alerted Morgan that "the demand was so great" for *France* in the United States "that it went through three editions with us."[106] She also reported that *Florence Macarthy* was "the most delightful creature, and had the greatest success with us." In typical businesswoman fashion, she also counseled Morgan to discuss with her London publisher "the profits which accrue to him from the sale of your works in

America, where they are as much sought after as in Europe."[107] After Morgan published her two-volume *Italy* in 1821, Elizabeth often suggested that Morgan visit America and write a book about it as so many others were doing.

Elizabeth's friends among the group of writing women encouraged her to write her own memoirs or autobiography, or travel accounts, or other works. One of the closest friends of her years as a wife and young mother, Eliza Anderson wrote and edited a Baltimore ladies' magazine in the early 1800s, perhaps the first woman in the United States to do so.[108] Anderson regularly conducted literary business in cities along the Atlantic Coast and was one of the first women to encourage Elizabeth to write for the public. Writing in July 1808, Anderson informed Elizabeth that she had "read two or 3 sentences of your last Letter to Mrs. Craig" and that Craig had "assured" her that "the stile was not inferior to Lady Montague's & said it convinced her you had both head & heart"; in the language of the time, Elizabeth possessed Jane Austen's fashionable sense and sensibility.[109] The comparison with Montagu is not surprising. The popular and acclaimed poet and essayist, Lady Mary Wortley Montagu believed in women's intellectual equality with men, wrote about public and private topics, and was "one of the founding mothers of England's 'blue-stockings.'"[110] Though no longer an editor, Eliza Anderson Godefroy wrote Elizabeth in France in 1817 again encouraging her to publish. After reading a "very tiresome" series of letters published by Madame de Sévigné, Godefroy thought of Elizabeth and "how much celebrity you might acquire & in this splendid day of Literature by giving a volume of yours to the World." "You write with a spirit & originality that would give interest to any subject," she remarked. "The country you are now in is so prolific in matters of universal interest that joined with your own observations on Life & the contrast of manners between France & America &c &c I am sure you might produce a volume that would give you . . . fame & money."[111] Sydney Morgan regularly suggested that Elizabeth write about her life for publication, always encouraging her to remain a writing woman. After Elizabeth returned to Baltimore in 1834, Morgan, now living in London on a pension given for literary excellence, urged Elizabeth to write and publish the memoirs of her own romantic life, offering help if Elizabeth would come for a visit. Numerous correspondents commented on Elizabeth's enjoyable writing style and skill at telling stories and shaping characters. In 1816, Nancy Spear remarked that, after reading the letters Elizabeth had sent to her and her brother Edward from Europe, she had been "all most convulsed with laughter at the Wit; Sense & madness

Figure 12. This lap desk accompanied Elizabeth on her journeys and allowed her to remain a writing woman. Elizabeth Patterson Bonaparte lap desk, date unknown. Image #XX.5.252, courtesy of the Maryland Historical Society.

with which they abound." "Certain" that "they will all be published one day or other," Spear had "carefully preserved" the letters.[112]

Though almost none of her writings other than letters survive, it is clear that Elizabeth had kept extensive journals or diaries even before leaving for Europe in 1815. Her friends in Europe, however, seem to have influenced her to become an active and prolific writer—one of the *femmes d'esprit*. She owned numerous writing implements, such as a French writing desk that Jerome had given her, a portable mahogany lap desk to use while she traveled, and "a very elegant Ink stand" she purchased while in France.[113] In addition to her extensive correspondence, she kept lengthy travel diaries while in Europe, as well as voluminous journals over a course of years that must have chronicled daily events along with her opinions. She also seems to have been compiling memoirs during her stay in Europe and after for eventual publication. Many of her friends had published or planned to publish their memoirs or autobiographies, such as Madame de Genlis, the Duchess d'Abrantès, and Sydney Morgan; it would not have been at all unusual, then, for Elizabeth to contemplate writing and publishing her own. In 1835, a longtime friend, Harriet Stewart, who had lodged with Elizabeth during one of her early visits to Le Havre, inquired whether Elizabeth was writing her memoirs: "You know this was a project of yours; of which I hope you are not losing sight." Stewart had even written a preface for the planned work.[114] Soon after, Morgan invited Elizabeth to stay with her in Dublin so she could help Elizabeth complete her memoirs.[115] At some point, Elizabeth definitely penned one work of fiction, entitled *Dialogues of the Dead*, about a conversation her father and Jerome had in hell. What these writings included or revealed about Elizabeth and her times will remain a mystery, since they were destroyed or disappeared. Her travel journals might have been similar to her countryman James Fenimore Cooper's multivolume travel series but assuredly with more bite. Her voluminous diaries might have been similar to Margaret Bayard Smith's in chronicling the social world of Washington, D.C., and elsewhere but certainly with more venom. Her fiction might have been similar to Susanna Rowson's in concentrating on strong women but probably with more satire.

Elizabeth found much of what she valued reaffirmed during her years in Europe. The people she encountered and befriended there prized her qualities, cherished her friendship, and respected her notions of womanhood. Elizabeth's female friends shared her belief that Europe was the best place for women like them—women of independent spirit. Whenever she considered returning to Baltimore, Elizabeth recoiled from the idea. She confessed to her cousin John Spear Smith that, "when I think of the possibility of returning, I regret I am not a Moth, which is the most stupid & solitary insect." "Imagination, feeling, taste, intelligence are not only superfluous to such a situation" in Baltimore, she insisted; they actually "render[ed] the load of existence as insupportable as disgusting. . . . I can compare my sufferings only to those of a criminal on the wheel." The "monotonous mode of life inflicted" on her in the United States caused her "inexpressible mental pain" and even drove her to contemplate "terminat[ing] an existence which was of no value."[116] Many of her European friends encouraged her to move permanently to Europe, the center of cosmopolitanism, and stop "waisting away" the "prime of [her] life . . . in seclusion" on the American periphery.[117] Yet Elizabeth always felt drawn back to Baltimore by her business interests and her son.

In the summer of 1834, at the age of forty-nine, Elizabeth sailed for her hometown, leaving Europe for pressing financial and family reasons. Drawing on all of her courage and strength, she returned to her hated native country for what was likely to be a permanent homecoming. For nineteen years, she had enjoyed a life that encouraged her independence, intellectualism, and aristocratic ambitions. After her departure, her European friends—princesses, writers, and others—kept her abreast of the marriages, deaths, publications, travels, and intrigues of her aristocratic and fashionable acquaintances in Paris, Le Havre, Florence, Rome, London, and Geneva. These friends always encouraged her to return to Europe, particularly Paris, sure that the "gay and attractive" city's "advantages over every other residence in Europe" would allow Elizabeth, with her "fortune" and "claims to social distinction," to "make [her] self the most happy person imaginable," living "delightfully" and "in the most eligible social position."[118] They could not imagine willingly leaving the cosmopolitan center for the provincial periphery, especially knowing how much Elizabeth loathed it. Uncertain when she would see Europe again, Elizabeth arrived in Baltimore loaded with European finery, including at least twenty-two dresses made of expensive fabrics, such as chambray gauze, satin, silk, hand-painted muslin, lace, and merino. She detested American fashions as much as she detested American society.

Struggling to accommodate herself to the city she had once called an "opulous desert," Elizabeth in Baltimore was disconsolate at her "cruel exile from every pleasure & every comfort" of cosmopolitan Europe.[119] Her European friends agreed, declaring she "really & truly" was "throwing [her]self away in America."[120] Elizabeth's daily existence in her hometown little resembled her days in Europe. There were far fewer parties and dinners and even fewer cosmopolitan intellectuals, artists, writers, and fashionables with whom to socialize. Her circle included no American *femmes d'esprit*. Elizabeth seems to have revived few of the friendships she had left behind. A number of her girlhood friends, such as Henriette Pascault Reubell and Eliza Godefroy, had moved from the area or even across the Atlantic. Furthermore, being out of the country for so long had estranged her from many of her old friends, such as Dolley Madison, whom she now rarely saw; and her contentious relationships with her relatives, especially the Catons and the Smiths, meant she would find few friends among her kin. Her disagreements with Nancy Spear and her brothers meant that neither they nor their wives would provide her with much companionship. Moreover, her son's wife, Susan, remained distant and never forgave Elizabeth for her great hostility to the marriage. While she did remain close to some American friends, such as the Gallatins, Elizabeth must have felt quite lonely back in Baltimore with such a thin circle of intimates.

Probably more troubling for Elizabeth was the difficulty she had staying connected with her European friends. A stream of correspondence throughout the 1830s kept her in their thoughts and alerted her to European events. The letters back and forth across the Atlantic included gossipy details about the people she knew and continued the exchange of political and philosophical musings. Books and writing remained subjects of interest for Elizabeth and her correspondents. But the letters to and from Princess Caroline Galitzin, Charlotte Constant, Lady Westmorland, Alexandre Gortchakoff, and even Lady Sydney Morgan ultimately could not replace being with them in person. No longer roaming through Europe with her friends and acquaintances, attending glittering parties or convivial salons, and seeing the sights in Paris, Rome, Florence, Geneva, or London, Elizabeth believed that her humdrum life in Maryland gave her little to write about in her letters. Her correspondence with her European friends sharply declined after 1840.

Elizabeth's decision to return to Baltimore had necessarily meant that her cosmopolitan world would shrink, but she seemed surprised by how much her life had been transformed. While she made some summer trips to fashionable resorts, she now traveled quite infrequently compared with her days in Europe and socialized far less. As she confessed to Lady Westmorland around 1840, Washington "during the sessions of Congress" would be "a more agreeable residence" than Baltimore, as would New York City, but she "had seen nothing of either since [her] return to this Country."[121] Her unchanging views of her country and its society left Elizabeth not only morose and bored after her return but also disconnected from her European friends. She could have filled letters with comments about books, her writings, politics, or the assorted other topics that she had once discussed with her friends. She still read voraciously and wrote regularly in her memoirs and still must have been able to offer strong opinions and witty remarks about current affairs and fashionable people in the United States and Europe. But she seems to have withdrawn from these topics of correspondence. Many had considered her a wonderful letter writer, but she must have believed she no longer possessed that talent. Convinced that her mundane life specifically and events in the United States generally were of no interest to her European correspondents, she saw little reason to write about herself or them. During her "vegetation in this Baltimore" in the 1840s and 1850s, Elizabeth conceded that she "[gave] up all correspondence with [her] friends in Europe." "There is nothing here worth attention or interest," she wrote to Morgan in 1849, "save the money market." Her sentiments on the state of American society had not changed in over forty-five years. In her opinion, "society, conversation, friendship, belong to older countries, and are not yet cultivated in any part of the United States." "You ought to thank your stars for your European birth," she assured her friend.[122]

Surprisingly, Elizabeth never attempted to make Europe her home again. Her several return visits only lasted for months, not years. In 1839, she traveled to Paris to enjoy all of its pleasures once again. She returned to many of her favorite places and reunited with a few old friends—counts, princesses, and duchesses. But she also found that too many of her friends were dead or absent for her to have as good a time as before. After spending several months there, the fifty-four-year-old Elizabeth lamented that she had "grown [too] fat, old, and dull" for Parisian life.[123] Though a Paris correspondent reported to a Philadelphia newspaper that "Mrs. Jerome Bonaparte (Mrs. Patterson) has arrived in our capital, with the intention of settling definitively in France," her time in Europe was quite brief.[124] She also traveled to Italy but seems to have avoided Florence, another of her favorite cities, perhaps because a friend had informed her that Americans had "quite taken possession" of the city or, more probably, because her ex-husband Jerome and his wife now lived there.[125] Elizabeth was back in Baltimore by the summer of 1840.

She decided to make another trip to Europe in 1849, declaring to Sydney Morgan that she owed "nothing to my country; no one expects me to be grateful for the evil chance of having been born here." She regarded the trip as a way to "emancipate myself" from the "long, weary, unintellectual years inflicted on me in this my dull native country."[126] With her nephew Louis-Napoleon now the president of France's Second Republic, Paris might hold new possibilities for her. In addition to Paris, she planned to visit Morgan at her fashionable home in London. Yet, even with Louis-Napoleon in power, Paris disappointed Elizabeth again. By now, too many of her friends had died or were too old to travel around Europe and remained in their country houses far from the former cosmopolitan center. Some, such as her dear friend Prince Alexandre Gortchakoff who now held a diplomatic post for Russia, had shed their fashionable, wandering ways for more serious pursuits. Elizabeth herself truly regretted her age of sixty-four, and the stay reaffirmed her earlier notion that Paris was only for the young and beautiful.

More rewarding was her visit with Morgan in London, the first time the two friends had seen each other in decades. As before, they spent entire days together, chatting and seeing the sights. The two still shared a strong bond and easily returned to their old friendly patterns of giving and receiving support and sympathy. Presumably, these close friends also returned to their old topics of conversation—books, writing, personal issues, and gossip. Elizabeth assuredly continued sharing her feelings of suffering and loneliness and detailing the long list of abuses of various family members against her. Morgan turned to Elizabeth for emotional support as she dealt with her failing health. Since Sir Charles's death several years earlier, Morgan's health had declined. Her increasingly poor eyesight no longer allowed her to write as long or as much as before. Yet she remained committed to writing and publishing. Morgan continued to work on the second half of her feminist *Woman and Her Master*, a book very different from her earlier novels and travel accounts. In the years since she had included a chapter on the situation of women in her *France* (1817), Morgan's interest in analyzing women's place in European society had grown. In that chapter, she had recognized and criticized, unlike Elizabeth, the inequalities in French law and society regarding women. By her middle age, Morgan had developed a clear feminist consciousness. During the late 1830s, Morgan—echoing Wollstonecraft's and De Staël's earlier protestations, but in a much more pleasing tone—had begun writing the planned two-volume *Woman and Her Master*. In the first half, published in 1840, she argued that, in spite of men's "systematic subordination," women throughout the centuries had been "the real trustees of the vital and important ideas of their time" and that women were made of "'finer clay' than their so-called master, man."[127] Though Elizabeth never articulated a feminist sentiment this coherently in her extant writings, she probably would have agreed with her friend. They may have discussed the second volume during her visit. Morgan still yearned to share her voice with the reading public and encouraged Elizabeth to do so as well through her memoirs or other writings. This happy visit was the last time these two strong-spirited women would see each other. Elizabeth, however, cherished until her death her friendship with Morgan, probably one of the most nurturing relationships in her life.

Elizabeth's discovery that Europe no longer offered the attractions it had once held for her must have been a serious disappointment. Maybe it was her age or her declining beauty that made the follies and fashions of Europe less appealing; certainly the disappearance of key members in her circle of friends contributed to her disenchantment. But European society had also changed in the years since 1830. Even if Elizabeth had found a way to remain in Europe, she would not have been able to continue to live the life she had enjoyed before 1834. The world in which she lived, the world that she loved, was already disappearing by the time Elizabeth resolved to return to Baltimore. She was probably very aware of some of the changes, such as the Revolution of 1830 in France, and less aware of others, such as the waning influence of female aristocrats. Over the 1830s and 1840s, European monarchs would increasingly see their power challenged and, in some cases, including the Bourbons in France, overturned by revolutions and republics. Aristocrats lost influence as members of the middle classes, the bourgeoisie, claimed powerful political positions and increasingly shaped society to reflect their own moral code. The rise and reign of middle-class values, in Europe and the United States, brought new gender definitions to the fore.

Elizabeth's and many other elite women's expansive definitions of womanhood, on both sides of the Atlantic, were being replaced by more restrictive views. Around the time Elizabeth began criticizing American gender roles, women had already begun to retreat to more domestic identities, no longer staging parades or toasting the rights of women. By the late 1810s and 1820s, the mood of American society no longer matched Elizabeth's or Anne Bingham's or Dolley Madison's ideas that women would play more public roles and have more social independence than their mothers. In France as well, elite and upper-middle-class women, including some of the surviving *femmes d'esprit*, increasingly separated themselves from the "dangerous classes" that increasingly inhabited public culture and "chose to lead more domestic existences."[128] Just as in the United States, bourgeois ideals incrementally replaced aristocratic attitudes, including those toward women, in France. A new set of gender definitions arose and even aristocrats apparently accepted the new domestic ideology. More surprisingly, they also increasingly embraced the bourgeois sexual "double-standard" that permitted extramarital relations for men but "prescribed fidelity for wives and chastity for daughters."[129] The American middle class already held such a moral standard. The era of gender flux ended in the United States and France at almost the same time. By the 1820s, both societies began to value women foremost as mothers and homemakers and to attack as "decadent" the behavior of aristocratic or elite women. By the 1830s,

American travelers to Europe could now comfortably condemn a young woman who was widely considered *"accomplished,"* because, *"as Americans,"* they believed her education had been "sadly neglected" since she was "an entire stranger to all the duties of house-keeping" and "equally ignorant of the use of the needle."[130] In Europe and America, these changes accompanied a growing acceptance that politics was exclusively male and the gradual disappearance of the ways in which women had operated as political beings.[131] But, even as newer gender definitions emphasized women's domestic roles and foreclosed their political ones, elite women retained their right to rule polite society and set its tone. They would just do so in other ways and in less public venues.

Returning to Baltimore in 1834 required Elizabeth to acquaint herself with a new set of gender ideologies and expectations that were quite different from the ones to which she had grown accustomed as a girl in Baltimore or as a woman in Europe. Of course, Elizabeth, like other Americans, was not consciously aware of all of the transformations in her society. But she did remain keenly aware that she hated the character of American society and its definitions for women, especially as they grew more domestic. She had never sought to be the kind of divorcée, daughter, wife, or mother that American society expected, and she was not going to start now. She would always long for and look back fondly on the years she had spent living her aristocratic and independent European life. Until her death, she cherished and regularly recalled her circle of close friends in Europe. They had provided her with solace, an escape from troubling relationships with her family and kin. She had connected with them as an independent woman, and they had treated her as an equal. Yet no matter how much these female friendships had sustained her, she never gave up feeling that her glorious destiny had been thwarted by the principal men in her life: her father, her husband, and eventually her son.

Chapter 5

"So Much Agitated About This Child's Destiny"
The Mother and Daughter

When William Patterson drew up his will in 1827, he used it as a chance to state, publicly and finally, precisely what he thought about his eldest daughter, Elizabeth. After spending several pages chronicling his life, relating how he had amassed his great fortune, and providing pieces of advice in a manner similar to Benjamin Franklin's *Autobiography*, Patterson proceeded to the distribution of his vast estate. Various neighbors, friends, and civic organizations received respectable sums. To Nancy Spear, who had overseen Elizabeth's investments and lived with Patterson at times over the years, he provided a one-hundred-dollar annuity, accompanied by a reprimand for her political activity. She would only enjoy the annuity "on this express condition that she shall never after my death attend any of the sessions of Congress at Washington or elsewhere"; the money was "solely intended to provide against the calls & infirmities of old age, & not for the gratification of folly or ambition." The four Patterson sons who lived nearby received the largest plantations and country estates, as well as fairly equal divisions of the stores, warehouses, rental properties, and vacant lots in Baltimore. All five of Patterson's living sons received shares of "the Plate, Furniture, . . . Liquors & Groceries" in his possession. Patterson even included in his will his white, illegitimate daughter Matilda Summers, leaving her a house and a few properties in Baltimore. His grandsons, especially Jerome, received generous portions of real estate and stocks. He also, boldly, freed "all the slaves I may die possessed of . . . at my decease."[1]

Patterson's generosity did not extend to Elizabeth. Not only did Patterson fail to include his eldest daughter in an equal division of his property among his children, as he had promised when she married Jerome, he prefaced his limited bequest to her with a lengthy condemnation of her behavior. Except for the comment about Nancy Spear's habit of attending Congress, no other child, relative, or friend mentioned in the will received such criticism. "The conduct of my daughter Betsy," Patterson began, "has through life been so disobedient, that in no instance has she ever consulted my opinion or feelings, indeed she has caused more anxiety & trouble, than all my other children put together, & her folly & misconduct has occationed me a train of expense that first and last has cost me much money." "Under such circumstances," he believed, "it would not be reasonable, just, or proper that she should at my death inherit & participate in an equal proportion with my other children, in an equal division of my Estate." "Considering however the weakness of human nature & that she is still my Daughter," the stern and disappointed father relented somewhat, giving her the house on South Street "where she was born," another house and lots "at the Corner of Market Street Bridge," "three new adjoining Brick Houses" on Market Street, and two more new brick houses and their lots on Gay Street. Elizabeth would possess these properties "during the Term of [her] Natural life," when her son and his heirs would inherit them "forever."[2] Elizabeth was hardly cut out of an inheritance, as this potentially lucrative list of properties in downtown Baltimore makes clear. But her bequests paled in comparison to those to her brothers and even her son. Patterson added a warning to his will—most likely aimed at Elizabeth—that, if any of his heirs challenged it, he or she would forfeit everything.

After Patterson died in February 1835, at the age of eighty-three, and the will's contents were revealed to the family and the public, Elizabeth was hurt, angry, and embarrassed. She saw his comments as yet another example among many of the "falshood, persecution, injustice & calumny" that her father had heaped upon her. With the attack on her in his will, Patterson "had flattered himself that his firmness of purpose & his cunning could defraud Death of the right to freeze that torrent of injuries & of misfortunes of which [he] had been to me the first, the copious, & the unfailing Source." For her, the clause "which relates to myself betrays the embarrassment of a loaded conscience & of a bad cause." By denying his daughter her promised rights, Patterson had clearly "violated every principle of honour & of equity to make a ruin of my ambition, of my hopes, & of my happiness." The will was clear evidence, to her mind, of the "principle of human nature that men cannot forgive those to whom they have been guilty of great cruelty, perfidy, & injustice."[3] Elizabeth's

Figure 13. The stern patriarch, William Patterson, never understood his daughter's aspirations. Thomas Sully, 1821. Image #1883.1.1, courtesy of the Maryland Historical Society.

brother John, who had not fared as well as some of his brothers in the will, suggested that they both "take a little time to consider it coolly."[4] But that was not Elizabeth's nature. Armed with a copy of the marriage contract with Jerome, which stated that she would receive "a proportional distributive Share" of her father's estate, "real, personal, and mixed," equal to that of "each of his other children," Elizabeth decided to fight the will—and her brothers.[5] Her son soon joined her. Elizabeth's roles as daughter, mother, and independent woman united at this moment as she fought for not only what was rightfully hers but also what would become her son's.

Three of her brothers, Joseph, Edward, and Henry, quickly challenged her; the other two, John and George, seem to have stayed out of the battle. The three brothers argued that when the French civil authorities annulled Elizabeth and Jerome's marriage, they rendered the provisions in her marriage contract null and void. By mid-March 1835, Elizabeth had contacted an attorney, and not just any attorney. True to form, she chose the leading attorney in Maryland, the former attorney general under Andrew Jackson and soon-to-be chief justice of the Supreme Court, Roger B. Taney. After examining Elizabeth's papers, Taney reported that he considered her claim valid because "the Covenant of Mr. Patterson depended on the *Event* of *the Marriage*, & *not* the *continuance* of the Union." The marriage contract, moreover, had acknowledged the possibility of divorce, yet still granted Elizabeth and her children an equal share in Patterson's estate. Lastly, Taney concluded that, according to the laws of Maryland, Elizabeth and Jerome had still been married until the legislature passed her divorce bill in 1812. Far from overturning Elizabeth's rights, he stressed, the legislative divorce "was intended more effectually to secure" them. Therefore, in his view, Elizabeth's "right to the Distributive Share of her Father's Estate which [was] vested in her on her marriage, still exists in *Full Force*, & has not been invalidated or impaired by any thing that has since happened."[6] As Elizabeth consulted with Taney, her son Jerome traveled to Philadelphia to seek the opinions of the renowned attorneys Horace Binney and John Sergeant. They concurred that Elizabeth's divorce "did not impair the Covenant" in the marriage contract.[7] "The plain & manifest interpretation is," Sergeant concluded, "that at his death, Mrs. Patterson & her issue shall have a full child's share of his estate."[8] According to Jerome, moreover, Binney and Sergeant also professed "that in their lives, they have never read so singular a document as the will. They both asked if his mind had not been very much weakened by old age."[9]

After reading the lawyers' opinion, Edward and Joseph decided to carry the fight beyond the courts. As Elizabeth understood it, she was being blackmailed. "I have been menaced with publication of my *private* letters during the last 30 years," she informed her brother George, and with "an *exposée* of myself, drawn up by Joseph & Edward, & of the Testator's reasons for having disinherited & slandered me." The world would read letters to her father, her brothers, and Nancy Spear filled with scathing comments about her friends and relatives, her Baltimore neighbors, and American society and politics. That Spear—Elizabeth's longtime confidant and sometimes business manager—had agreed "to throw *my* letters to *her* into the family budget of Betrayed Correspondence" and had proclaimed "to many persons 'that the will was perfectly, *admirably* just'" proved especially wounding. Considering Spear the tool of her malicious brothers, Elizabeth decided not "to hold any further communication" with her. "It is understood by the public, & by myself," Elizabeth wrote George, "that *Edward* advises, & that *Joseph* executes."[10] Her youngest brother, Henry, she viewed as merely "a yelping nuisance in [her] way."[11] At the end of December, Joseph and Edward continued their attack on Elizabeth by illegally cancelling the insurance policies on several of the properties she had inherited. She demanded "entire remuneration for all expenses of new policies" and apprised her brothers that their actions had "become a subject of some notoriety & discussion" in Baltimore.[12]

The bickering with her brothers over her inheritance continued into 1836, with Taney still advising Elizabeth even after he became chief justice. In the end, Elizabeth decided not to fight her father's will in court. Perhaps the threat of an "exposée" had scared her; more likely, she had decided not to risk losing her inheritance. Taney certainly endorsed this course. "The amount of property which she will have in case she acquiesces in the will, is sufficient for her wants," he informed her son's attorneys, while "the loss of that devised to her would render her situation exceedingly uncomfortable." According to Taney, Elizabeth also believed that "the bare *possibility* of incurring the forfeiture would make her anxious & unhappy." He therefore advised her against "go[ing] through a year of anxiety & unhappiness to enforce this claim when she has enough without it to make her comfortable for the rest of her life."[13] Jerome ultimately agreed with his mother and dropped the fight as well. Not surprisingly, the breaches between Elizabeth and her brothers and between Elizabeth and Nancy Spear over the will would last until death.

In this era of shifting national and individual identities, of changing gender definitions and notions of womanhood, the function of the family in American society also shifted and changed. Transforming gender roles and identities necessarily effected a reworking of the roles and identities of parents and children. Father and mother, son and daughter—all took on new meanings in the late eighteenth and early nineteenth centuries. The expectations and feelings of family members toward each other also changed, with the family increasingly carrying different emotional weight for its members than in the past. In an 1804 letter to his wife, Virginia attorney William Wirt captured the new views of family life. His familial ideal was to be "settled at home . . . before a good warm fire, with you and our dear child by my side," to "read, converse, & listen to the prattle" of their daughter and "pass away the evenings so entirely to ourselves."[14] This newly redefined American family in its newly reconceived home emerged along with the new nation.

As many historians have shown, the transformation of the American family from a more authoritarian, public, and patriarchal household to a more affectionate, private, and permissive home was neither smooth nor quick.[15] Over the decades in which the American republic developed, the main function of the family gradually changed from pooling the labor of all members of the household for production to focusing on rearing and nurturing children. Multiple factors contributed to this transformation. Economic forces, such as the increasing separation of wage labor from the home; demographic forces, such as the migration westward and a decline in the birth rate; and social forces, such as the rise of the middle class, all helped reshape the roles of family members and the family's purpose in society. Intellectual forces played a major role as well. The questioning of all forms of authority and an emphasis on personal happiness, coming out of Enlightenment and Revolutionary thought, contributed to a decline in the power of the patriarchal father and an increase in the independence of children. An increasingly child-centered family was presided over by a newly defined mother. As affection, love, and sensibility came to be viewed as positive characteristics during the eighteenth century, women, who were believed to possess innately these attributes more than men, came to be viewed as the parent more naturally suited to educate young children, especially in Christian values and good citizenship, and to attend to their special needs. The role and power of the father diminished. Maternal love and mothers received far more praise than paternal authority and fathers. The staunch patriarch gave way to a reconceived notion of fatherhood, with a new emphasis on breadwinning outside of the home but still involving an important domestic role, in partnership with his wife, in the raising of proper children. Of course, not all families experienced these changes at the same time or in the same way. And many families suffered generational tensions as parents and children struggled over the shifting meanings of family and changing expectations for these roles.

Elizabeth Patterson Bonaparte's roles as daughter and mother and her relationships with her father and her son highlight the changing ideas of womanhood and family, though in complex and often contradictory ways. With her father and her son, Elizabeth constantly debated notions of filial obedience and parental authority. The conflict with her father—a conflict in which her own child became a central figure—partially stemmed from their different definitions of family duties and different expectations for family members. Elizabeth refused to play the role of dutiful daughter to her patriarchal father, and Patterson refused to surrender the increasingly old-fashioned notion that a father's authority should be unquestionably followed. He always kept his family "as much as possible under [his] own eye" and was "the last up at night" to secure the house, which "induced" his children "to keep regular hours."[16] Reflecting the new ideas, Elizabeth firmly believed that parents should always support their children, even when they acted independently, while Patterson remained convinced that parents should punish children for their disobedience. This familial conflict, however, was also a conflict between American and European values, between republican and aristocratic ways. Patterson's republicanism shaped his ideas about the appropriate futures for both his daughter and his grandson. In turn, Elizabeth's aristocratic beliefs meant that many of her views about marriage, parenting, and children were very traditional—even more so than her father's on occasion. These conflicts with her father over familial duties and proper values fundamentally shaped her relationship with her son.

As a daughter, Elizabeth spent much of her life fighting with her father over her right to pursue her own version of personal happiness. Yet, as a mother, she insisted on defining happiness for her son—and they fought over it. Elizabeth's goals as a mother, centered on her Bonaparte son, provided much of the motivation for her actions from Bo's birth in 1805 until the last decades of her life. Of course, her idea of a dedicated mother differed vastly from that of many American women, who saw themselves playing important social roles by raising republican children, maintaining affectionate domestic spaces, and finding personal happiness in their families. Elizabeth was not like them. She did not nurture her son so much as cultivate him, attuned to her ambitions far more than his own. At a time when evolving gender definitions increasingly lauded affectionate motherhood, Elizabeth wrote her father that, even as she hoped Bo would "reward by his success all my cares," she "rejoice[d] that I have no more children to toil after, never having envied any one the honor of being a mother of a family, which is generally a thankless position."[17] Moreover, Elizabeth deliberately presented herself as the opposite of a good "republican mother." In her aspirations, Bo was not to become a successful and respected American citizen but a proud and admired member of a European royal, or at least noble, family. She expended much of her energy—and her money—on raising her son to make him suitable for a monarchy or principality, not a republic. Even as she spent much of her life cultivating an identity that would gain her entry into exclusive circles, Elizabeth knew that her son could be the means for her to achieve her own ambitions. Like many American parents, her efforts focused on getting her child to value what she valued. But, unlike other American parents, none of whom had children whose uncle had ruled a European nation, she trained her son for the destiny she believed his imperial birth merited. If her son achieved all she hoped, then she would be able to live the life she had dreamed of when she met his father. Yet the success of these plans rested on her son sharing her values and aspirations. And when he eventually chose a path that differed from the one she had imagined for him, she reacted with fury.

After Elizabeth returned to Baltimore from England in 1805, her young son—or rather her son's future—became the main focus of her life. All of her most important decisions centered on making sure Jerome Napoleon Bonaparte had a magnificent future among European aristocrats, like the one that had been snatched from her. With this as her goal, her ideas of motherhood differed from those of most American women, and she knew that. Having no companionate husband to provide for her and share in parenting decisions and responsibilities already made her stand apart. But, more consciously, Elizabeth did not adopt the growing notion, touted in prescriptive literature, that a mother was self-sacrificing and her duties included instructing her children in good citizenship and the rudiments of learning. Instead, she followed aristocratic parenting methods, as she understood them, and carefully plotted a course that would perfectly prepare her son for his imperial destiny. For example, one of the first steps in her plan was to baptize Bo as a Catholic, the religion of his Bonaparte family and of kings, and ask Bishop John Carroll, the highest-ranking Catholic official in the United States and the man who had married Elizabeth and Jerome, to serve as his godfather. Her next step had been to try to secure Bo the title of "prince" from Napoleon when he was five. To learn gentlemanly manners, he attended balls as early as age eight. More formally, Elizabeth did not rely on her own tutoring efforts but arranged for the best teachers in Baltimore to educate Bo, including religious instruction from "Mr. DuBois, a respectable Ecclesiastic."[18] Her friends regularly encouraged her in these lofty aspirations, assuring her that "a bril-

liant destiny awaits you & the dear little Bo."[19] This is not to say she did not
deeply love her son. Writing to a friend in 1816, she made clear that she
"love[d] him so entirely" that she needed to leave her beloved Europe to return
to him. At the same time, Bo adored his "mama," writing often as a boy: "I love
you better than all the world put together."[20] But her high expectations for
their future colored her affection for her son. There was no separating the
ambition she had for him and the love she felt for him.

Though Jerome continued to push for his son to come to Westphalia until
he lost his throne in 1814, Elizabeth had firmly decided by mid-1809 against
sending Bo to his father's kingdom. This decision did delay her and her son's
appearances in the courts of Europe and, among other issues, may have stemmed
from concerns over Bo's welfare prompted by stories of the degeneracy of
Jerome's palace at Cassel. Instead, Elizabeth chose to seek Napoleon's aid over
that of her weak, dissipated, and disloyal former husband, believing that the
fulfillment of her son's destiny lay with the still-powerful emperor. She sent
Jerome a portrait of Bo instead of the real thing and followed the course she
had set for the boy.

Bo showed early signs of wanting to pursue a different life from the one his
mother was planning for him. When he struggled with Latin, he declared at
one moment, perhaps repeating something his grandfather had said, that he
should not have to learn Latin since his grandfather and Patterson uncles "had
made fortunes without it, and as he was to be a merchant, he had no more occasion for Latin than either of them."[21] What the eleven-year-old Bo did not
yet realize was that his mother would never stand for him becoming just a
merchant. In her view, the courts of Europe were his rightful place. In 1820,
when Bo was fifteen, Elizabeth purchased a copy of the just-published *A System of Education for the Infant King of Rome and other French Princes of the
Blood drawn up by the Imperial Council of State with the approbation, and under
the personal superintendence of the Emperor Napoleon*, which she assuredly used
to compare her son's education with that of his princely cousins. She already
feared, however, that "after exciting my hopes," her son would "become, like
the generality of people, mediocre and tiresome."[22] She worried incessantly
about whom Bo should marry, even while he was still a toddler. The question
became one of the focal points of her life for many years. James Gallatin was
surprised to discover in 1816 that she kept "a list of the different princesses
who will be available for him to marry: as he is only ten years old, it is looking
far ahead." Gallatin questioned whether Elizabeth had "much heart," since

money and "her son seems to be her one thought."[23] Love and affection, what came from the "heart," was supposed to characterize mothers.

While Elizabeth pursued what she considered important maternal duties, her relationship with her father worsened. Her marriage and its troubles had already produced much tension between them, and, when she returned to her father's house, with no intention of playing the role of the dutiful daughter or the self-abnegating divorcée, their conflicts continued. Elizabeth's departure for Europe in 1815 caused a real breach between them, and their misunderstandings increased. The previous years had been difficult ones for her. The Titles of Nobility Amendment furor in 1810, the turmoil of legislative divorce in 1812, and, not insignificantly, the war with England had taken their toll. The year 1814 had proven especially hard for Elizabeth. The British had briefly occupied the nation's capital, her social center, and destroyed its public buildings, and had attacked Baltimore, her hometown. More personally, in the same year, her beloved sixteen-year-old sister Caroline had died and her even younger brother Octavius had been killed in a riding accident. The biggest blow surely came when her mother, Dorcas, died in May of that year. Her mother's death alienated her from her father even more. Since his eldest daughter was no longer a wife, Patterson assumed that she would care for her now wifeless father, but Elizabeth never considered her "manless" state as a reason to remain under the paternal roof. They also continued to clash over her aristocratic preferences. He harshly criticized her for going to Europe for what he saw as whimsical reasons. He refused to pay for her to live in the style she desired in Europe, convinced that she could be happier living in Baltimore if she would just get over her foolish expectations for an aristocratic life. Furthermore, he firmly believed that his daughter should have asked his permission and that a woman should not live on her own. As Patterson informed one of his agents in England, "I by no means approve of her living in Europe under any Circumstances, for it would be highly improper and more especially in her present Situation, deprived of the protection of any of her family."[24] Believing in individual choice instead of filial obedience, Elizabeth ignored her father and managed to live in Europe on her own income.

Elizabeth's successes in European high society further strained the relationship with her father. After receiving numerous letters about the balls she had attended and the fashionable people she had met, her fiercely patriotic father warned her that she was "pursuing a wrong course for happiness." In 1815, Patterson could still "hope and pray you may soon perceive your mistake, and that you will look to your mother-country as the only place where you can be really respected." What must "the world [meaning Baltimoreans] think," he continued, of a woman who left her father's house soon after her mother's death, left her son at a boarding school, "and thought proper to abandon all to seek for admiration in foreign countries?" The only explanation for such behavior, in his opinion, was "that it must proceed in some degree from a state of insanity, for it cannot be supposed that any rational being could act a part so very inconsistent and improper."[25] But Elizabeth did not see herself as irrational. Her "fervent desire of European pleasures was not the vision of a distempered fancy," she assured her father, but "only a prophetic spirit of the fascinations which here surround existence."[26]

Her goals for her son, in addition to her desire for transatlantic celebrity and an aristocratic life, had propelled her to Europe and kept her there for years. As Elizabeth saw it, Europe, not the United States, offered both the life she wanted to live as a woman and the means for achieving the ambitions she had as a mother. After her divorce, making permanent the life she desired in Europe seemed increasingly to depend on her son, especially after Napoleon lost his empire. Her hopes for her son, she strongly believed, hinged on bringing him into contact with his Bonaparte relatives. She regarded the still-influential, still-wealthy, and still-aristocratic Bonapartes as the key to Bo's successful future and to her own. Her unreliable and financially straitened ex-husband, known now as Prince Montfort, was never a part of her calculations.

In 1817, she returned from Europe committed to the idea that Bo must receive his education in Europe, like any young aristocrat. Again, Elizabeth received plenty of encouragement from her friends but not from her family. Her father, who adored his grandson and had a close relationship with him, opposed Elizabeth on this issue on republican grounds, believing that "no one of an independent spirit could think of living in Europe after having seen & experienced the happy state of this country compared with any other in the world."[27] Her plan for Bo, however, required that he go to Europe. During this visit to the United States, Elizabeth also recognized that an enormous opportunity to advance her son awaited in New Jersey. After he fled Europe, Joseph Bonaparte, the eldest of the brothers and the former king of Spain, settled on an estate in New Jersey, near Philadelphia. Elizabeth and her friends knew that Joseph, now known as the Count of Surveilliers, could have a great impact on Bo's future. Relying on ties of female friendship, Elizabeth orchestrated the initial contact between the count and Bo through her friend Ann Tousard, the widow of Colonel Tousard, who had attended Bo. Drawing on her French connections, Tousard worked diligently but discreetly to find out whether Joseph wanted to meet his nephew. He did. Bo spent New Year's of 1819 with the count, who made a very "publick" showing of receiving his nephew.[28]

Probably with the approval of Joseph Bonaparte, Elizabeth decided that Bo should be schooled in Geneva, Switzerland. Beginning in 1819 and continuing through most of 1821, Bo attended an academy there, at an expense of about one thousand dollars a year, while his mother lived nearby. In addition to academics, he took lessons in dancing, fencing, and riding—skills any good nobleman should have. All of his lessons were in French, but Elizabeth made sure he remembered English by using it while constantly counseling him on what he should and should not be doing. While in Geneva, Elizabeth wrote to Jerome for the first time "in many years," updating him on his son's life. Jerome was hurt to have "remain[ed] in the dark about my dear child" for so long, but promised to help pay for Bo's education, though he had only a "mediocre" fortune left. He suggested that Bo learn "at the most basic, math, French, English, German, writing," and argued that, befitting the son of a former king, "Latin, drawing, horseback riding should not be neglected." Because of the current condition of the Bonaparte family, he reminded Elizabeth, Bo would need to find a profession and suggested law.[29] Elizabeth had other ideas.

Elizabeth's hopes for Bo's future must have soared when her friend John Jacob Astor informed her in March 1820 that Princess Pauline Borghese, Jerome's sister, wanted to meet Elizabeth and Bo and had invited them to stay at her palace in Rome for a lengthy visit. Astor believed that Pauline might even intend to make Bo her heir.[30] The invitation became even more tempting when former Maryland senator and Federalist vice-presidential candidate Robert Goodloe Harper forwarded Elizabeth a letter from someone "intimate with" the Bonaparte families in Rome. According to this letter, Pauline was "entirely unacquainted with the situation of her Brother Jerome's first wife." Nonetheless, she "wish[ed] to do every thing in her power for repairing the wrongs done by her family, to a lady who had been sacrificed by political errors, which reasons of state" could not "justify." Finally, a member of the Bonaparte family had acknowledged not only Elizabeth's existence and the wrongs done to her by the family but also her status as an in-law. That must have thrilled Elizabeth, but what the princess suggested next must have been beyond her wildest dreams. Princess Borghese, according to this letter, wanted to share her house with Elizabeth as well as "her fortune," detailing that if Elizabeth "compl[ied]

listed some of the "notables" he had seen in the front row at Florence's main opera house. In the "same row" as the "ex-king of Holland" (Louis Bonaparte) and "Prince de Montfort, his brother, or the ex-king of Westphalia" (Jerome), Cooper spied "Mrs. Patterson, once the wife of the last-named personage." If correct, Cooper had witnessed a remarkable occurrence since Elizabeth repeatedly wrote that she never wanted to see Jerome again, and she often left a city when she heard of his arrival. Cooper seemed quite certain in his identifications, and he was friendly with Louis and, possibly, Jerome.[44] But he also may have mistaken Pauline Borghese for Elizabeth since they were said to look so much alike. An article in *Lippincott's Magazine* suggests a different meeting, also in Florence. The tone of the article suggests that the author had interviewed Elizabeth and that she had told many stories and shared numerous personal letters. According to the author, Elizabeth and Jerome had met by chance in the galleries at the Pitti Palace in 1822. As the story was related, Elizabeth—not surprisingly "attired in her most *recherché* costume"—noticed the "eager, persistent stare of a very handsome man whom she did not recognize, but whose strange likeness to her son enchanted her. Suddenly the truth flashed to her heart: 'It is Jerome!'" Jerome reportedly wondered who the beauty was before his sister-in-law replied that it was his first wife. He "started, and with an agitated whisper" to Catherine that this was his "American wife," "left the gallery." Elizabeth and Jerome allegedly saw each other the following day as their carriages passed on the streets, and Jerome "nearly precipitated himself in a last, lingering look at the wife of his youth."[45] There is no suggestion that they ever saw each other again.

The curiosity about whether Elizabeth would remarry never ended. While she was back in Baltimore briefly in 1824 and early 1825, a "Lord H.C." wrote her a number of times, raising concern among some of her relatives, especially when she surprised them by returning to Europe in June 1825 without telling them. He was "married to another lady" but was believed to be in love with Elizabeth and capable of proving "troublesome." Even as her uncle declared that Elizabeth had "always retained her good name" and that the family could "rely confidently on her prudence in that particular," he still worried that "her character might suffer." "Some of our American ladies lead droll lives and do us no very great credit," he remarked.[46] Two years later, rumors reached Nancy Spear and others in Baltimore "that you either are or are to be married to Lord William Russel." Spear doubted them, however, and simply "suppose[d] some new flirtation has given rise to the report."[47] The speculation and the gossip continued. In 1829, minister to France James Brown wrote that "Mrs. Patterson appears wedded to Florence but is not likely to be wedded at Florence, though it is said she has had many offers," including one from the Marquis del Douro, a son of the Duke of Wellington.[48] By that time, Elizabeth, now almost forty-five, was surely too used to the life of an independent woman to consider marriage and dependence seriously. Romantic love, which many elite Americans believed in by 1800, had not played a large role in her life after Jerome, perhaps not even with him. Marriage had always been a matter of practical calculations.

Elizabeth seems to have ultimately decided to rely on her son's marriage, instead of a second one for herself, as the way to achieve what she desired. Her views of marriage supported the choices she made and differed from American ones. Elizabeth believed that elite Europeans had a superior understanding of marriage to that of her countrymen. Her experience had taught her that marriages should not be based on foolish notions of love, as in the United States, but on practical concerns. To her, the French way of marrying for financial interests, not love, was the better way.[49] In Europe, parents "make all the matches," according to Elizabeth, "and much better it should be, for they always look out for money."[50] Europeans knew that marriage was primarily about selecting an appropriate spouse, not a romantic partner, and that it took a lot of work on the parents' part and a lot of money. Some of the Americans in Europe understood this fact as well. Elizabeth clearly admired John Jacob Astor, who spent four hundred thousand dollars to "establish his daughter in Paris" and place her "in the best society" to find a suitable husband. "No one can get a husband in Paris without money," Elizabeth told her father.[51]

Elizabeth even gave great credit to her kinswoman, Mary Carroll Caton, after three out of her four daughters married high in the British aristocracy. Caton, married to an Englishman herself and the daughter of immensely wealthy Charles Carroll, apparently shared Elizabeth's view that a good marriage for one's children required hard work and plenty of money. In 1825, when Caton's widowed daughter and Elizabeth's rival and former sister-in-law, Mary Caton Patterson, married the Marquis of Wellesley, the Duke of Wellington's older brother, Elizabeth seethed with anger and also envy. Caton Patterson had already enraged Elizabeth when rumors of an affair with the Duke of Wellington made the rounds in 1820. James Gallatin heard in Paris that it was "an open secret that she is his mistress" and listened to Elizabeth regularly condemn her rival over the next few years while dining with his family.[52] Such a high-status marriage for a Maryland woman with whom she had always competed for acclaim seemed unfair to Elizabeth. She had only admiration for Caton Patterson's mother, however, and believed that she "deserved her unexampled great luck, for certainly she toiled & starved herself for years to advance her family." Mary's sisters Louisa and Elizabeth lived with Mary on Wellesley's impressive estate, guaranteeing them access to the finest circles in which to search for husbands. Even "if he had beaten them all," Elizabeth concluded, "they would still be fortunate in having made such a connexion."[53]

The three Caton sisters' marriages started an early trend of rich American heiresses marrying impoverished, yet titled men in England or on the Continent. In time, such matches became a commonplace. But, before the mid-nineteenth century, they baffled many on both sides of the Atlantic. Elizabeth's agent, Londoner James McElhiney, could not explain the "wild scheme of American women coming to Europe to look for husbands." It seemed irrational since the English nobility "look on the Americans as a people sprung from the Scum of the Earth." Americans, in McElhiney's opinion, "ought to have a more independent spirit and not come to England to sneak after greatness."[54] Yet the trend grew as more and more noble European families looked to American matches to save their family's estates and reputations. In 1826, soon after the Caton sisters began marrying titled husbands, Moncure Robinson commented to his father from Paris that "American ladies seem so far to be in fashion on this side of the water lately [that] one of them[,] Miss Astor of New York[,] exchanged some of the surplus dollars of her father for the diplomatic honours of a Hamburg Minister."[55] Elizabeth herself had once commented to the Gallatins that had she "but waited," with her "beauty and wit I would have married an English duke, instead of which I married a Corsican blackguard."[56]

Soon after Elizabeth and Bo's arrival in Rome in late 1821, Pauline Borghese, Madame Mére, and Elizabeth decided that an excellent match could be made between the impressive sixteen-year-old Bo and his cousin Charlotte, Joseph's youngest daughter, who was two years older and stood to inherit a large fortune. Charlotte had recently come to live with her father in New Jersey. In 1822, when Bo returned to the United States, many in the Bonaparte family, including Jerome, and Elizabeth expected the marriage to take place. In a not very maternal tone and with little concern for the feelings of her son, Elizabeth conceded to her father that this marriage provided "the only sure way of relieving myself of the expense he occasions me and I can illy afford."[57]

While waiting to hear whether Joseph approved of the match, Elizabeth described the kind of marriage she envisioned for her son. She would only consent to a wife of "great wealth" and could only "recognize a marriage of ambition and interest"; Bo's "name and rank require it." She believed "he owes a great deal to me, [and] a great deal to his position in society." She was convinced, moreover, that Bo accepted as much as she did "that he should never part with a single particle of his consequence, which might be lost in some boyish connection begun in folly and to end in children, obscurity, and poverty." Writing to her father, Elizabeth "beg[ged]" him to make clear to Bo just how important this match was and to "discourage all that tendency to romance and absurd falling in love which has been the ruin of your own family"—referring perhaps to herself. She also confessed that she had become "so much agitated about this child's destiny, so torn by desires and fears," that she had become ill with "continual vomiting."[58]

Bo sailed from Europe in the spring of 1822 and stopped by his uncle Joseph's estate to visit Charlotte before returning to Baltimore. Before leaving Europe, Bo had made clear he was agreeable to the match, but, for reasons that are unclear in the extant documents, the match never came off, though Bo and Charlotte remained close for the rest of her life. She would later marry another cousin, a son of Louis Bonaparte. Elizabeth's friend, Ann Tousard, who lived in Philadelphia, was one of the few who were pleased that the marriage plan had failed. She believed that it would have been "a great sacrifice" for Bo to marry Charlotte since she was "in size a dwarf and excessively ugly."[59] Elizabeth, however, reeled with disappointment, yet regarded the failed plan as another in a long line of unkept Bonaparte family promises. Over the next few years, her hopes for her son to marry well soured and so did her opinion of marriage and motherhood. On hearing of a relative's marriage in 1826, she proclaimed: "Marrying is almost a crime, in my eyes, because I am persuaded that the highest degree of virtue is to abstain from augmenting the number of unhappy beings. If people reflected, they would never marry, because they entail misery upon themselves when they bring children into the world. I have no desire to see my son married, and I hope he never will have any family"— both of which she told him repeatedly.[60]

With another plan dashed by the Bonapartes, Bo turned to his mother's second plan by enrolling at Harvard. Elizabeth was proud of his "greater intelligence," as well as his "remarkable personal beauty," and thought herself "fortunate that he was not born a fool, which two-thirds of the children brought into the world are." A foolish child, she admitted to her father, "would have embarrassed [her] exceedingly" since "it is only permitted to women to be idiots," a damning indictment of American gender expectations.[61] Elizabeth understood that Bo's class, family background, and celebrity imposed demands on him. His "position," she believed, would be "more difficult than that of any other young person" at Harvard "because it is more conspicuous and people expect more sense and better conduct from him than are exacted from the middle classes" in the United States. She readily acknowledged, moreover, that she also placed high demands on her son to realize her version of his destiny. "It requires every exertion on his part not to appear unworthy of the distinction his name gives to all who bear it." Over the years, she had "always acted on this principle in my unceasing endeavors to inspire him with elevated ideas and ambition above what might be necessary in the situation of other young people."[62] Fearing Bo might fall in with a bad crowd and besmirch his name and rank, she had let his dog, Le Loup, sail with him since she believed Le Loup would "be a safer companion" for Bo "than many others he will meet" in Cambridge. She adored the dog and deeply regretted his departure, especially after discovering he was not permitted at the college and had to live in Baltimore. If she had known Harvard would not have accepted Le Loup, she "would have insisted on keeping him with me [in Paris], as a reward for the poor beast's fidelity and many other good qualities which he possesses, not to mention his great intelligence which renders him superior to half the persons one meets in the world."[63]

Once the hoped-for marriage with Charlotte fell through, Elizabeth desperately feared Bo would make "an imprudent matrimonial connection." Seeing no one suitable for him to marry in America, she hoped he would remain single. Perhaps revealing why she had remained unmarried, she explained to her father in 1823 that "marriage offers no such comforts as to induce rational beings to give up their independence without some return of advantage." She wanted Bo to avoid marrying "some poor young woman from the caprice of the moment" and "consign[ing]" himself to "her insipid society and the torment of bringing up a family of children."[64] The popular romantic ideal of "love in a cottage," she insisted, was "even out of fashion in novels." "An amiable, prolific daughter-in-law"—a perfect match in the minds of many American parents—seemed "a very poor compensation for all the trouble and anxiety I have had with that boy." Elizabeth hoped "the amiable, scheming[,] . . . young ladies" in America would "select some other unsuspecting dupe."[65] That Bo was so handsome concerned her greatly. While in Rome, Elizabeth reported, the ladies "ran after him so much that I feared his being spoiled, although he seemed quite unconscious of it, supposing probably that women old enough to be his grandmother could not be foolish enough to fall in love with him." A German princess had even admitted that "she had followed him once in Geneva, at a ball, from room to room, to look at him, and that he was the handsomest creature she ever saw."[66] By 1826, Elizabeth declared that she would "prefer paying Bo's expenses in Siberia or Africa" to having him "married to some idiot and bringing beggars into the world every year, which is what we see every day."[67]

With his republican values, William Patterson counseled his grandson quite differently, provoking Elizabeth's ire. He saw no promise for a good life for Bo in a European bride, especially a Bonaparte, since he knew Bo preferred to live in America. "Your father's family are all on the decline and going down hill," he candidly wrote Bo at Harvard, and "will soon be . . . of no consequence whatever. . . . Should you remain in this country and make good use of your time and talents, you may rise to consequence; but in Europe you would be nothing, and must come to nothing with the other branches of your family."[68] The United States, as Patterson long knew, was the best place.

With her aristocratic longings, Elizabeth still imagined a future for Bo in Europe among the Bonapartes. In 1826, she informed her father that "every one advises me to have [Bo] sent to Leghorn [Italy] that he may spend a year with his [Bonaparte] Family" and meet his father. That was her opinion as well. "I should feel that I have not done my duty if I did not do all in my power to promote his advantage in every way," she noted, reiterating the understanding of her maternal duties that had guided her for two decades. Since his birth, she had done everything she could "to promote his advantage." She lived through her son, trusting that all of the hopes and expectations that Jerome and Napoleon had destroyed for her could be achieved for him, and through him for herself. The Bonapartes could still do much more than she could on her own to elevate her son to the heights she dreamed of for him; "they have it in their power to introduce him into the first circles in Europe which would give to his manners the polish which I fear they cannot receive in America." She also hoped that meeting Bo again would cause some of his relatives to include him in their wills. Convinced that seeing "something of the world [was] the only effectual way of improving young men," she urged her father to have Bo return to Europe. After again reminding him of the inferiority of the

United States compared with Europe, she asked her father to get Bo an American passport in the name of "Edward Patterson" so he could "avoid attention from the Police in England or Italy."[69] She also recognized that Bo needed to meet Jerome and that she would be a "very unfeeling parent if I do not let him see his father." She decided to bear the burden of all of the expenses of Bo's trip, of course. Informing her father, whose parenting attitude had been very different, that, since she "brought him into the world," it was her "duty to spend money upon him when his interest requires it, and to try to render his life as agreeable as I can."[70]

In 1826, Bo returned to Europe to meet his father as his mother wanted. Elizabeth decided to stay in Florence while Bo traveled to Rome for the visit. He had left Harvard early for this trip, receiving permission from the president of the college not only to leave that term but also to graduate early—a rare "indulgence," according to his grandfather. Patterson, however, could only see one purpose for the trip: to see if the Bonapartes "mean to do anything for" Bo. He refused to believe that his grandson could actually "settle or live with any pleasure or satisfaction in any part of Europe considering his republican education."[71] The United States was clearly the only place for his republican grandson, even if not for his defiant daughter. Born a British subject, not a French or American citizen despite his parents, Bo had never felt the lure of French citizenship. At the age of fourteen, he had already signed an "Oath of Intention to become a Citizen of the U.S."[72] As Bo, now going by his given name Jerome, prepared to return to Baltimore in July 1827 after meeting his father, his future course began to take shape. Even as she lowered her earlier expectations, Elizabeth still hoped that he might become a secretary of legation, perhaps to Great Britain or to Sweden, where the king was a relative. She thought her father and her uncle Samuel Smith could use their influence with Andrew Jackson to get Jerome the appointment, but it was to no avail.[73] Such a career would have kept her in Europe, giving her a way to remain there without abandoning her son. But, soon after his return, in September, the twenty-two-year-old Jerome gave clear evidence that he thought his future was in the United States by becoming an American citizen. He also returned to the home of his grandfather and began looking for a rich American wife.

William Patterson had hoped that Elizabeth might return with his grandson and told her so in his usual combative and patriarchal manner, which pitted his republican beliefs against her aristocratic ones. Jerome possessed "too much good sense not to think with me" that the United States was "the only country in which he can live with any satisfaction" away from the "follies of Europe," he chided. He still wondered that his daughter "insist[ed] on your own situation [in Europe] being greatly preferable to that of people in this country who live in a quiet rational way," and he saw "no rational ground for happiness in the kind of life you lead." To Elizabeth's father, "a common housekeeper" in Baltimore who "can indulge in going to methodist meeting & attend to religious duties has a much better chance of Happiness both here & hereafter than those who pass their time in idle dissipation as must be the case from your representation of the state of society in Florence." He also regarded Elizabeth and women like her as bad role models. If "all the American Ladies who visited Europe are so attached to that country & so unwilling to return again to their own," he concluded, "it is a great misfortune that they ever left America & should in future be guarded against with the rising generations."[74] Such reasoning did not persuade her to return.

In September 1829, Elizabeth exploded when she learned that her son was to marry Susan Williams of Baltimore. In its excess, her response to Jerome's marriage to a young woman who would have exceeded the expectations of most American parents encapsulates and highlights her ideas about marriage, motherhood, parental and filial duties, family, and the superiority of European modes of living. Perhaps more than any other episode from this period of her life, her son's marriage forced Elizabeth to look back at the choices she had made and evaluate them. The event would prove to be one of the major turning points in her life. Everything she had envisioned for herself and her son—everything she had fiercely pursued his whole life—came crashing down the moment he chose to wed an American. Her hatred for the ordinariness of life in the United States, for republican simplicity, and for the middling business classes merged in her response. Like his father before him, Jerome had been her ticket to the grandeur of life as European nobility, as a member of one of Europe's "public" families. His abandonment of that dream struck an excruciating blow. Her harsh response to the news makes perfectly clear how much of her sense of her own identity and of her future prospects had been destroyed. She reacted as someone in intense physical and mental anguish.

Elizabeth was confident that her father had encouraged the match, even though he had been fully aware that a bride such as Williams was incompatible with her plans for her son. After receiving news of the engagement, she began her first letter to her father: "Had I been dying my breath would have delayed long enough to allow me to *protest* against the marriage you *proposed* for my son." She further announced that her "*solemn, fixed, unchangeable* resolution is that he *never shall with my consent* marry Miss Williams or any other woman in America." Patterson and Jerome had ignored her long "expressed determination & intentions." For twenty years, she reminded her father, she had made it clear that Jerome's "education had ever for its object a residence sooner or later in Europe" and that "he ought never to marry unless it be into some of the great European families." She had done everything to prevent him from "marrying beneath his rank." Unlike her own father, she never "shirk[ed] from the duty of a Parent," believing that "when I gave birth to a child I incurred the charge of maintaining him"—a statement that highlighted her sense of herself as an independent woman since her ex-husband was removed even from their son's birth. In her view, all that the Williams family desired was to "ennobl[e] their dirty blood" by marrying their daughter to a Bonaparte. "Let them marry their daughter to one of her Equals," she seethed, but "the Nephew of Napoleon has no equal in America." Jerome's father did not matter; it was the link to the great emperor that gave him status—the same link that Elizabeth had cherished from the early days of her marriage because of the rank and fame it gave her. Since her abandonment, she herself "might have made twenty better marriages than the one proposed to him, but I never forgot that I had the honor of having made one which rendered it impossible for me to marry a Low person." She had withstood "poverty, solitude & [iso]lation, . . . three things I most abhor," but she had "never bent my spirit to the meanness of marrying unsuitably."[75]

As everything she had worked for so hard and for so long collapsed, Elizabeth became desperate. "Let him employ every means in his power" to end the engagement, she charged her father, then breathlessly listed some options: "Let him employ my name in any way or every way to break off the disgraceful engagement. Let him return to Europe. Let him say that he is obliged to consult his relations here. Let him do any thing rather than make *such* a match." If the marriage could not be prevented, she was ready to "declare in the face of the whole world that I utterly disclaim all participation in it." She believed that the Bonapartes had to be told of the disaster and she would relay to them her "affliction that so improper a marriage had been effected in my absence & in defiance of my wishes." Feeling abandoned by her son, she determined to stay in Europe and spend her money only on herself. She soon contacted Nancy Spear to arrange for all of her possessions—"the house Linen, Plate & wearing apparel left in Baltimore" and her "Box of jewels"—to be sent to her immediately. She already had enough funds to live on for a year and wanted Spear to "remit me the interest accruing from my property after paying taxes &c." in the future.[76] Since her family had defied her, she decided to have little contact with them.

By December, after having calmed down some, Elizabeth wrote to her father that she would no longer oppose the marriage since the bride had a fortune but nor would she ever accept it. She told everyone she knew that her son had spurned all of her efforts to help him achieve the life his status required. At the same time, she conceded that, despite all of her work since his birth, Jerome possessed "neither my pride, my ambition, nor my love of good company." As unimaginable as it was for her, she decided that, if he could "be satisfied with living in such a place as Baltimore" and marrying someone there (she noted that she would "rather die then marry any one in Baltimore"), she would not fight it. She had "no right," she ultimately recognized, "to make another person adopt my standard of happiness." She closed her letter by reiterating that, while she "would as soon have gone to Botany Bay [the Australian port that received British convicts] to look for a husband as to have married any man in Baltimore[,] if my son thinks it possible for him to live there, and does not feel any of my repugnance to such a connection, [then] I no longer oppose it."[77] She would, however, stop giving him his regular allowance, and she soon removed him from managing her financial affairs.

The wedding of Jerome Napoleon Bonaparte and Susan Williams took place on November 3, 1829. John Carroll's successor as archbishop of Baltimore, James Whitfield, performed the ceremony. In fact, Jerome had learned much from his mother about marriages, even though he did not choose a wife suited to Elizabeth's plans. His marriage to Susan Williams appears to have been little motivated by love. Like his mother, he accepted that marriages should be about money and connections. Jerome had shown little enthusiasm for pursuing a profession in law or government and only somewhat enjoyed business. Like his father, he enjoyed spending money but not doing the work necessary to earn it. To secure financial independence without real effort required marrying an heiress. Nancy Spear informed Elizabeth that "Jerome had the greatest conflict with himself" before the wedding, "between the dread of making you unhappy & the fear of losing an oppertunity of settling himself advantageously for life." Jerome, she said, "was unhappy because he was not independent [but] born with an unbounded love of money." The choice of Williams, with a dowry of almost two hundred thousand dollars, made perfect sense. Spear believed that Jerome had enough interest in and skill at business that his bride's "prosperity & his own [would] give him the kind of employment that is to his taste"; in "a few years more," she predicted, "he will be the richest of our citizens." Spear also reassured Elizabeth that Williams "was universally sought after & courted[;] has the finest figure you ever saw, with a beautiful complexion [and] has great ambition & industry. She was born rich & her education has been attended to." She added that Williams "has much greater pretensions than her countrywomen who have married english dukes," a clear reference to the Caton sisters.[78]

Figure 14. Elizabeth's son, Jerome Napoleon Bonaparte, disappointed his mother with his marriage to an American. Artist and date unknown. Image #CSPH 190, courtesy of the Maryland Historical Society.

Elizabeth's father certainly believed that Jerome had made the correct choice and enthusiastically consented to the match. In Patterson's thinking, "it was decidedly the best & most rational thing he could possibly do, for it was securing one of the largest fortunes in this country & making himself independent for life."[79] Jerome's "ambition did not lead him to wish for the life you wanted him to pursue in Europe," he told his daughter, "nor would anything induce him to live there in the degraded state of his [Bonaparte] family." In Baltimore, he asserted, Jerome would "hold the first rank in society," while in Europe, "he could be nothing & must be continually mortified from his situation."[80] The pleased grandfather generously bestowed on the new couple both money—about $50,000—and property, including Mount Pleasant, a plantation several miles outside of Baltimore. Elizabeth's uncle Samuel Smith concurred, delighting in the visits that Jerome and his new wife made to his house. While Elizabeth, in Smith's view, had "wanted that [Jerome] should be miserable in Europe looking up to nobility," Smith wholeheartedly supported his grandnephew's decision "to be an independant American on a footing with all men" instead of an "Idolator of Title."[81] Elizabeth had staked everything on the Bonaparte name carrying her son far in marriage and in life. For her father and uncle, the inglorious decline of the Bonapartes boded only disgrace and dishonor for Jerome. A life lived in the United States—not Europe—held the most promise for him. Patterson never tried to understand the hopes Elizabeth held for herself or her son. Instead, he scolded his wayward daughter, saying she should not blame Jerome, but should "look *back at your own* conduct in relinquishing your family & country for an imaginary consequence amongst strangers who can care little for you" and "commend" Jerome for his actions.[82]

While Elizabeth had expected the Bonapartes to share her outrage over the marriage, the family members actually rejoiced, especially Jerome's father. Cousins, aunts, and uncles sent Jerome congratulatory letters and presents, and his father sent the couple lavish gifts. What little opposition there was came not from the Bonapartes but from Elizabeth's brother Edward, who tried to prevent the marriage in her absence. In his view, "it was a *mercenary transaction* altogether, and carried through in a purely mercantile spirit and admits of *no palliation*."[83] Edward professed that he "never witnessed any thing that shewed [such] morbid greediness, less head, less heart, & less tact."[84] That it was so calculated, rather than based on affection, might actually have been reassuring to Elizabeth. "Great secrecy was observed," Edward further reported to Elizabeth, "and so intent were they upon carrying it through undisturbed that every one who shewed any disapprobation was looked upon with suspicion & avoided." Confirming Elizabeth's suspicions, Edward also remarked that "the whole business was managed by Jerome & his grand-father with George [their brother] to advise." Even as their father hoped Elizabeth would learn from Jerome's example and return home, Edward encouraged his sister to spend her "fortune," which was of her *own making*," on her own "comforts & amusements." "Think of no one situation but your own," he advised. He also reassured her that she "need not fear seeing [the couple] in Europe," since Jerome surely "must have sense enough to see that [Susan] is not in any respect *qualified* for a trip of that kind."[85] This news must have seemed inconceivable to Elizabeth. Her son had chosen a wife who lacked the necessary refinement to display herself in the aristocratic circles of Europe. How could such a thing have happened after everything she had done for him, sacrificed for him?

Both Elizabeth and her son had firmly believed in the right of a child to choose her or his own spouse. Like many young Americans in the early republic, each had pursued individual happiness with little regard for familial considerations or parental warnings. Yet neither had embraced the more modern idea of a companionate marriage based on romantic love. While Elizabeth surely was in love with her husband at the beginning, her views of marriage soon adapted to those of aristocratic France, and she ultimately rejected the entire institution for both her and her son. Her son Jerome's views of a good bride harkened back to the colonial era as he sought a woman who could bring him wealth far more than affection. Jerome, too, simultaneously possessed older and newer notions about marriage and family.

Elizabeth's dreams were completely dashed for the second time in her life. She had spent so much money educating her son "with the intention of his living in Europe." She had "always told" him "that he should never degrade himself by marrying in America." All that was left to her was to try to "content myself by the reflection that I did all that I could to disgust [Jerome] with America." Jerome had chosen America over Europe, money over grandeur. She referred to him as her "most *unnatural* heir" but still promised to leave him her fortune, believing it to be her duty as his parent, even though he had engaged in "duplicity, ingratitude," and "unnatural conduct." She also labeled her father's conduct in the marriage "unnatural" and expected his "conscience" to "reproach" him. Her failure to raise a son who shared her ambitions led Elizabeth to look back on her own father's attempts to turn her into something she was not. "A parent cannot make a silk purse of a sow's ear," she wrote her father, "and you found that you could never make a sow's ear of a silk purse." Patterson had wanted "to bend my talents and my ambition to the obscure destiny of a Baltimore housekeeper" and to have Elizabeth spend her life "in a trading town, where everything was disgusting to my tastes" and "contrasted so strongly with my wishes." After marrying the brother of an emperor, however, she had not possessed "the meanness of spirit to descend from such an elevation to the deplorable condition of being the wife of an American."[86] Now, though, she had to admit that her efforts with Jerome had failed as badly as her father's efforts with her. Neither of their parenting methods, which blended some of the traditional and some of the new in different ways, had been successful.

More than a year after the wedding, Elizabeth was still fuming in letters home to her father and still trying to adjust to this new turn in her life. She saw herself as the intended victim of her family's plotting. "Every one knew" the marriage "must . . . separate me from my son." They all must have "fores[een] and calculated," she charged, that it would be "a source of deep affliction and burning shame" to her.[87] She vowed henceforth to contact Jerome only "when there is any necessity about money affairs."[88] In typical fashion, her father criticized this attitude, warning her to stop her "constant & continued bitter remarks on account of his marriage" because they "were doing a great injury to Jerome." He also urged a reconciliation. Observing the tumultuous situation in France following the overthrow of the Bourbon King Charles X in 1830, Patterson seized yet another opportunity to point out the superiority of the United States to Europe, a republic over a monarchy. "You may see at last how every thing is turning upside down in Europe, & the confusion & distress that must be brought on before things can settle down in any regular way," he remarked. And he informed his monarchy-loving daughter, "It is not likely there will be a crowned head left except at the will of the people." Just like the Americans in 1776, Patterson firmly believed that "they are all looking forward to independence & Republicanism & nothing short of this will satisfy them." He closed his already harsh and patriarchal letter by announcing that, with her mother long dead and her brothers all married and gone from the house on South Street, he had been placed in a "disagreeable situation." A dutiful and loyal daughter would never have left him in a position where he had to ask his son Joseph and his family to live with him.[89] As an old man without a wife, he had naturally expected his eldest daughter, who did not have a husband to look after, to care for him and his house. After receiving this letter, Elizabeth did not write her father again for months.

While Elizabeth struggled to come to terms over the next few years with her son's choice and her bitter disappointment, family members regularly sent her news that made her start thinking about returning to Baltimore to live. At the end of September 1830, her brother Edward informed her that Jerome and Susan were soon to have a baby. Judging "from her make," he predicted that Susan would probably "present" Jerome "with one annually."[90] John White, Elizabeth's friend and financial manager, reported in early 1833 that Jerome had "a very fine, stout boy with Corsican features" and that the young family intended to visit Washington "sporting a coach & four, in order I suppose to excite the gaze or run down the Grandees of the Metropolis."[91] Such a showy display of status from her son, so similar to her own when she used to visit the national capital, probably made her proud and perhaps inspired hope that Jerome still shared some of her aspirations. Around the same time, Nancy Spear alerted Elizabeth to "the horrid commotions" at Patterson's house. Spear had just learned with "the utmost horror" about Patterson's illegitimate daughter, Matilda, born in 1817 (about three years after Elizabeth's mother's death) to his former housekeeper, Providence Summers, and that the young woman was actually visiting him in Baltimore. Patterson paid for Matilda to attend the expensive "George town seminary" and brought her to his house "to spend her hollidays with him." Spear reported to Elizabeth that, when she had told Patterson that "it would kill his children" if he allowed Matilda to stay in his house and that "they woud never enter his doors while she was" there, he had replied that if Elizabeth "had staid with him he never woud of thought of it." After two weeks, he sent the young woman back to her mother. To end the family scandal, Elizabeth's brothers asked Spear to live with their father, trusting, as Spear explained, that he would "hardly bring [Matilda] back if I am here." Spear was still incredulous that Patterson had committed such a public act with this illegitimate child. It had given Baltimore "a shock" that "so exemplary, self[-]denying a being, who [had] only lived to set a good example, should have wantonly thrown away character & friends."[92]

In her pleas to convince Elizabeth to return to Baltimore, Spear told her how frequently her father "talks of you to me & of your leaving him." She "wish[ed] most ardently you woud forgive him for your own sake as well as his, for he is almost childish." If Elizabeth came home and played the role of the dutiful daughter, Spear was "sure that he will give you the house he is in, with the command of everything." She also lured her with information about Jerome, his wife, and their little boy, Jerome Napoleon Bonaparte, Jr. "The boy is the handsomest and the finest child that ever was born in Baltimore," while Susan was "quite as ambitious as yourself, very fashionable & stylish looking." She further assured Elizabeth that the couple's houses, "both in town and country," were "the resort of the best company." The two "drive four horses in their Coach," which displayed the Bonaparte crest, and had "been a great deal at Joseph Bonapartes where they have acquired a great deal of knowledge of style."[93] They also spent the winter social seasons in Washington, and Spear was sure Elizabeth could join them whenever she wanted.

Elizabeth finally returned to Baltimore in the summer of 1834, after what had been an almost uninterrupted sojourn of nineteen years in Europe. Surprised, her father assumed that his daughter had concluded that "sweet Home & the natural intercourse & connexion with our family & friends is after all the only chance of Happiness in this World." More likely, Elizabeth returned out of a combination of concern over the presence of Matilda in her father's house and the state of her finances in the United States and hope that her son and daughter-in-law shared some of her values, as well as a desire to see her grandson. President Andrew Jackson had paid off the national debt, leaving few avenues for safe investments. Furthermore, her father had warned in March 1834, just before her return, that the country was "in great confusion and distress" over Jackson's "arbitrary conduct in respect to the Bank of the United States." No one knew how the crisis would end; Patterson supposed it could "ultimately bring about Revolution." Greatly alarmed, he had warned her that her return was "absolutely necessary to look after your affairs & property." Financial interests had always been a great motivator for Elizabeth and seem to have been at this time as well. She later noted that she believed she "might have lost" property if she had "deferred my departure from Europe."[94] Though certain she would find no happiness in America, she left her beloved Europe and her cherished circle of friends to return to her family and hometown. Her grandson, Jerome Napoleon, instilled a fresh round of hopes and ambition in her. Maybe this boy would succeed where her son had failed?

In Baltimore, Elizabeth monitored closely the activities of Bonaparte family members over the years and always took pleasure when they remembered Bo, as several did. The fickle Pauline Bonaparte greatly surprised Elizabeth by including Bo in her will and, therefore, recognizing him as a legitimate member of the Bonaparte family. Mother and son returned to France in 1839 to claim a legacy of fifty thousand francs left to Bo by his great-uncle Cardinal Fesch. In 1854, Elizabeth's son and eldest grandson traveled to Paris to reunite with their Bonaparte relatives, including Emperor Napoleon III. Bo and his son also spent some time with Jerome, who was delighted to meet his American grandson. The two Americans became French citizens, and the emperor recognized his cousin as a legitimate Bonaparte, even offering titles to the two, which Bo refused. Jerome Napoleon decided, at the emperor's urging, to join the French Army and fought bravely in the Crimean War, quickly becoming a much-decorated captain. Concerned about the warm welcome his American half-brother received, Prince Napoleon, Jerome's son with Princess Catherine, supported by the king of Württemberg, convinced Napoleon III to call a council of the family. Even though Bo strongly defended his claims, the council ultimately declared that the American Bonapartes could not be in the line of succession and that Bo possessed no rights as the eldest son of his father.[95] Bo returned to Baltimore and focused his energies on overseeing his investments and raising horses in the Maryland countryside. According to one newspaper account from November 1854, Bo bore his recent "honors with becoming republican simplicity."[96] His son remained in France, serving the emperor and empress.

Elizabeth's relationship with the Bonapartes remained fractious. Writing about Jerome a few years before his death and more than a half century after he had abandoned her, she wished that some day her former husband could read her "reminiscences of him" so he would know exactly what she thought of "his attributes."[97] Her early love for Jerome had turned into bitter hatred over the years. "The sentiment of contempt to old Jerome," she wrote in one of her account books, "is in my heart, & circulates with every drop of blood in my body. I look upon him as belonging to the lowest type of humanity."[98] A favorite quote was Napoleon's alleged quip to Jerome: "If the majesty of kings is imprinted on the countenance, *you* may safely travel *incognito*."[99] In her view, Jerome, whom she now called "Pere Malaparte," along with her father, had earned her eternal hatred because "they converted my life, which might have been a garden of roses, into a dreary wilderness."[100] At the same time, however, she continued to see the Bonaparte family as a route to distinction for her son and grandsons. In the quarter century after Bo and Jerome Napoleon's trip to Europe, Elizabeth focused all of the energy that she had once devoted to her son on her grandsons (the second son, Charles Joseph, was born in 1851). They, she firmly believed, would fulfill their rightful destinies. She spent the rest of her life and part of her fortune encouraging Jerome Napoleon to embrace her imperial aspirations and remain permanently in Paris. While he was named a personal protector of the Empress Eugenie shortly before the fall of the Second Empire, that was as much as the American Bonapartes ever achieved in Europe.

Elizabeth did not visit Europe from 1850 to 1860, when she returned fighting with her son by her side. Jerome had died and, true to form, had failed not only to leave a legacy to Bo but even to mention his first son in his will. Elizabeth and Bo squared off against the remaining Bonapartes and sued for his rights to a portion of Jerome's estate. While all knew there was little money at stake since Jerome had never ceased his profligate ways, Elizabeth and Bo sought for a recognition of legitimacy from the Bonaparte family. The case became a cause célèbre in France; popular opinion seemingly supported the woman whom Napoleon had treated so unfairly so many years ago. The courts, however, sided with the emperor's family by rejecting Bo's claims as a legal heir and ordering Bo and Elizabeth to pay the court costs.[101] During the months that she spent fighting for her son's rights, Elizabeth sadly discovered that Paris—the place where she had once dreamed that her true destiny awaited her—now held little charm for her. "I detest my existence here," she wrote her Baltimore banker. Once a transatlantic, cosmopolitan celebrity whose definition of happiness was to live in Paris, Elizabeth confessed: "I am too old, too ugly, & too stupid for Paris." Baltimore, the city she had long hated, now seemed more comfortable to her; she anticipated her return to "where I can buy Ennui with dollars, instead of Guineas." This woman who had once relished being the center of attention and attending the parties and salons of aristocrats and intellectuals now judged life too difficult. "I am fatigued, disheartened with the hard battle of existence, what with the B[onaparte]s & P[atterson]s. I am tired, worn out mentally & physically."[102] This disappointing—and expensive—trip would be one of Elizabeth's last.

Just as she had shaped her own definition of the proper role for women, Elizabeth shaped her roles as daughter and mother to suit her own ideas and ambitions. In this era of shifting gender definitions, before the ideal of domestic womanhood became dominant, Elizabeth took advantage of the flux to craft versions of daughter, mother, and wife that simultaneously drew on older ideas and more modern ones, as well as American and European values. This same confluence of notions also influenced her views of marriage. She followed a pattern she used frequently as a transatlantic celebrity, a would-be aristocrat, and an independent woman. Reflecting the new, more emotional sense of family ties and affectionate parenthood, Elizabeth had wanted more from her relationship with Bo than her father had from his children. She wanted them to be joined by bonds of love and even close friendship, instead of just those of parental and filial duty. But her mothering rarely focused on raising her son to be a good citizen or allowing him to choose his own path, as she had done herself. His defiance of her with his marriage choice pained her, as did the growing separation between them. Elizabeth, like her father, had strongly believed in the power of parental displeasure to shape a child's behavior. But, in line with newer ideas, she expected obedience out of love, while Patterson, holding to more traditional notions, expected obedience out of respect or fear. Yet both parents had been surprised when their child had disobeyed their wishes. Elizabeth's strong belief in personal autonomy and the pursuit of individual happiness had guided her through all of the choices in her own life as a daughter and a mother. But, when her son's definition of happiness differed from her own, she never quite recovered.

Elizabeth's conflicts with her father and her son also reveal one of the major ironies of her life—her reliance on men to achieve real independence from them. Though gender identities changed during this era, women were still defined relative to men. Elizabeth was no exception. She rebelled against her father and the notion of a dutiful daughter. She sought a husband who could help her escape her family and achieve her aristocratic ambitions. Abandoned by Jerome, she relied on her former brother-in-law for financial security and social position. And she tried to recover her lost destiny through her son and then grandsons. Though she eventually became an independent woman who supported herself, her financial position depended on property and money she had received from her father, her husband, and Napoleon. As her letters to her father and son clearly show, she also depended on men for her emotional well-being. The tension between her dependence on men and her independence from them probably produced most of the conflict in her relationships with them. In contrast, her relationships with women generally rested on feelings of equality and mutual support. Though Elizabeth was a "manless" woman by her twenties, the men in her life had powerfully influenced its quality and direction.

Epilogue

"She Belongs to History"

After her essentially permanent return to Baltimore in 1834, at the age of almost fifty, Elizabeth seemed far less concerned with playing a prominent role on the public stage, with being a celebrity. She did not attend balls, parties, and dinners as often, nor did she dress as scandalously as she had in her youth. For years, though, she continued to wear the French fashions— dresses, bonnets, jewelry, and even umbrellas—that she had stocked up on before returning to the United States. Fashions had changed dramatically by the 1830s; the revealing Grecian styles that had brought Elizabeth so much attention years earlier had completely disappeared. Elizabeth's social venues had changed, too. With few friends left in Washington, she rarely traveled to the national capital. She spent some summers at the Virginia Springs or at Rockaway Beach on Long Island, however, participating in an elite tradition in both the United States and Europe of spa-going and fashionable socializing. With her return to the United States, Elizabeth rejoined the exclusive circle of women who had the authority to set the tone and rules for elite circles in America. Whenever she visited the Virginia Springs resorts, for example, the guests granted her one of the highest places in the springs' hierarchy and looked to her as an arbiter of social rules.[1] She remained an influential presence in Baltimore society. But, by 1849, if not before, Elizabeth knew her remaining life would be spent on the periphery, not in cosmopolitan Europe; she had consigned herself to her "Baltimore obscurity."[2]

Though she believed herself to be living in obscurity, Elizabeth actually remained quite celebrated in American society. Many who met her recorded the fact in a diary or letter. Yet she no longer had to cultivate her celebrity. Instead, her former claims to public admiration and the continual fascination with her romantic life ensured her celebrated status. Strangers sought her autograph or photograph; one woman even asked Elizabeth to endorse a line of beauty products.[3] Counting on Elizabeth's celebrity to sell a story, many journalists requested interviews with her, providing another occasion to tell her tale. By the mid-nineteenth century, many historians of Maryland or the Bonapartes or of the early United States wanted to include the story of Elizabeth Patterson and Jerome Bonaparte and asked her for help.[4] References to meeting Elizabeth or comments on the dramatic events in her life appeared in numerous published memoirs and biographies, both American and European. Her marriage to Jerome and her subsequent fate also were regularly included in collected biographies of famous belles and celebrated romances, such as Alice and Phoebe Cary's *The Josephine Gallery* (1859).[5] In 1861, a distant relation wrote Elizabeth, pleading for a chance to meet the woman about whom she had heard so much "from my earliest recollection." Her "desire to see and know" Elizabeth, she admitted, "had verged on the point of romance." Like so many others, she had "heard of your beauty & graces of manner & person till it seems a fairy tale."[6] Elizabeth's celebrated life now seemed the stuff of fairy tales, not the actual history of a real woman.

In 1872, the public presentation of her life took another turn when W. T. R. Saffell acquired "a bundle of English and French letters on the subject" of Elizabeth and Jerome's marriage that had been found in one of William Patterson's warehouses. The documents included private letters of the Patterson and Bonaparte families as well as official correspondence between members of Napoleon's government and Elizabeth's family. When Saffell approached Elizabeth with his plans for publishing the documents, she responded that "'the volume was a matter of perfect indifference to her.'" Her grandson Charles Joseph Bonaparte, however, requested "that the book should not be published."[7] The volume, provocatively titled *The Bonaparte-Patterson Marriage in 1803, and the Secret Correspondence on the Subject Never Before Made Public*, appeared in 1873 and received reviews in major periodicals. Elizabeth had overcome the normally fleeting nature of celebrity and achieved fame; she was now assured of a historical legacy, something few women in the nineteenth century managed. Before her own death in 1859, Lady Sydney Morgan attested to Elizabeth's transformation from a transatlantic celebrity to an enduring historical presence: "She belongs to history; she lived with kings and princes, philosophers and artists; there is about her a perpetual curiosity and romance."[8] An 1877 newspaper article about Elizabeth's life shared this view.

"Each year adds fresh interest to this remarkable woman," it began, "whose story has been rehearsed in every land, whose personal traits still afford food for social chronicle."[9]

While many Americans still considered her a celebrity and an influence in society, Elizabeth continued to long for Europe and its aristocratic ways, detesting the "low names & lower natures [that] make up [the] motley race of this Bastard republic."[10] Writing to Morgan after the presidencies of the common man's Andrew Jackson and after the severe economic depression that the Jacksonian Democrats caused, Elizabeth assured her that "a residence of a few months in the *Etats Unis* would cure the most ferocious Republican of the mania [for] Republics." In America's too-democratic society, she explained, "we have security neither for our lives nor our persons."[11] In her view, the state of society and politics in the United States remained hopeless. Anyone who lived in and still admired republics was foolish, in Elizabeth's mind, for it was, as she informed Morgan, "only distance from republics which lends enchantment to the view of them."[12]

When her beloved France threw off its king and became a republic again in 1848, Elizabeth despaired, though she could commend French citizens for paying "homage" to Napoleon by "voting [for] an imperial president," his nephew Louis-Napoleon Bonaparte. As she informed Morgan, "I never could endure universal suffrage until it elected the nephew of an emperor for the chief of a republic." After the European revolutions of 1848, Elizabeth's last remaining hope lay with England, which she charged to "remain steady and faithful to monarchical principles, that at least some refined society may be left in the world." And, she added, she would "be charmed with universal suffrage *once* more if it insists upon their president of France becoming a monarch," essentially predicting Louis-Napoleon Bonaparte's elevation to Emperor Napoleon III.[13] Democracy could only be redeemed in her mind if its citizens voted to erect a monarchy, not to preserve a republic. In 1852, she "rejoice[d]" when France returned to "the only Government suitable for French Men" by making the Bonapartes "once again Emperors or Kings."[14] As she had thought since before her marriage to Jerome Bonaparte, monarchy ensured refinement; a republic meant the loss of it.

By the 1850s, "Madame Bonaparte" was still widely known in the United States as a woman who "professes to despise republican America and yearns for imperial sway." As one newspaper article reported, she "talks philosophy, argues politics, ridicules sentimentalists, and loves to dwell upon and recount the glories of la belle France."[15] Elizabeth became more interested in, but not more accepting of, domestic politics in this era, characterizing the United States as "nothing" but "Elections & Noise & Democracy" and defining its legal system as "all in favor of the Mobocracy."[16] Even in her later years, she privileged Europe's aristocratic society and politics over America's republican forms. After the Civil War, when a few African Americans held seats in Congress, Elizabeth harshly commented that "baboons were in the senate, and monkeys in the house, which was carrying republican principles out to their legitimate ends."[17] The Reconstruction era merely made obvious what had always been her primary problem with republics: they were based on the equality of all men. But Elizabeth had never believed that *all* men were created equal, even all white ones. She was racist, but not merely or even primarily racist. Above all else, she was elitist. By her standards, there had always been and would always be people who were better than others—and such people were the ones who should rule both nations and societies. Republics were dangerous because they placed those from the lower orders into ruling positions, a fact that had become increasingly meaningful in the United States between the early 1800s and the late 1860s.

Though still an influential celebrity and still a staunch believer in aristocratic principles, Elizabeth no longer served as a lightning rod for those concerned about the future of the republic. She simply no longer presented a threat. Two crucial factors had changed: by the early 1830s, the republic itself was more stable and secure than it had been in the early 1800s, and, equally important, gender definitions were also more stable and secure. The new nation had survived too many challenges, internal and external, to fear what Elizabeth had once represented. Her love of aristocracy and monarchy and ties to European empires no longer appeared so dangerous. Furthermore, the kind of woman Elizabeth represented no longer seriously challenged the political or social order. Americans no longer had to be anxious about fashionable, elite women exerting too much political power—that threat had gradually eroded. Such women retained great social power, but their political place and influence had been contained.

Just as she never embraced her nation's political ideals, Elizabeth never adopted its new gender definitions by becoming a model of patriotic motherhood or female domesticity. Instead, in the years after her return to Baltimore, she became well known as "a lady who understands business" and received admiration for that knowledge, in a way she had not previously. Some men turned to her for advice in business matters, including former Secretary of the Treasury Albert Gallatin.[18] In the 1840s, David Bailie Warden, still in Paris, sought Elizabeth's aid when he was having difficulties collecting debts from some Americans. The practical and experienced businesswoman urged him to take them to court, blaming Warden's old-fashioned and "too romantic a belief in the integrity of Men" and his "credulity respecting honesty & honour" for his unfortunate situation. Much had changed in American society, she informed Warden in 1843; it had been a long time since honor had enjoyed a place in the world of business. "You would only be laughed at if you were to talk of debts being sacred," Elizabeth explained. In her view, the "Experiment of Liberty & Equality" in the United States had "demoralized everyone"; it had, in other words, made them amoral. She boasted that she stood "Sentinel on my property, & will lose no more of it from confidence."[19] Attesting to her impressive business acumen, Elizabeth's friend Harriet Stewart called her a *"Man of business."*[20] Equally impressed, one of Baltimore's bankers remarked that he knew of "no man capable of creating legitimately, with so small a capital, the large fortune amassed by Mme. Bonaparte."[21] In her old age, her estate "amounted" to $1,500,000 and provided her a yearly income of "nearly one hundred thousand dollars." Since she allegedly spent only about "two thousand a year," her heirs were certain to receive a substantial fortune.[22] Even when she was nearing seventy, Elizabeth remained fiercely independent and continued to manage her business affairs, adding significantly to her fortune. "She may be frequently seen," one newspaper reported in the mid-1850s, "on the wharves, at the post office, visiting brokers, bankers and other gentlemen of business, collecting rents, buying stocks, and participating in other speculative matters."[23]

American women, at all economic levels, had long been involved in managing family finances, but few possessed the high level of business skills that Elizabeth did. Many single women controlled their own finances, but few became millionaires. Elizabeth's ability ultimately to live the kind of life she desired was largely the result of her own financial acumen. While the initial capital had come from her father, her husband, and Napoleon, she had managed her money herself, aided by savvy businesswoman Nancy Spear; made her own decisions about how to invest her funds; and turned these beginnings into an impressive estate. In the end, her financial situation, and her reputation as a skilled businesswoman, formed one of the great successes of her life.

After one final, brief trip to Europe in 1863, Elizabeth spent the last years of her life in Baltimore. She lived frugally in a boardinghouse, dressed in her now-antiquated French clothing, and subsisted on memories of her days in Europe. In 1858, Elizabeth had directed her grandson Jerome Napoleon to "buy nothing" for her while he was in Paris for she felt "too old & too ugly to care for Dress."[24] She did not socialize much anymore and had little need for stylish clothing. Clothes remained a crucial part of her public identity, but now they made her seem eccentric instead of fashionable. By the end of her life, she was renowned for wearing a "black velvet bonnet, trimmed with or-ange colored feathers," and for carrying a red parasol as she walked the streets of the city collecting her rents.[25]

Toward the end of her life, Elizabeth looked back and reevaluated some of the women in her circle of friends. In 1867, she recalled Eliza Anderson Gode-froy, whom she had dropped a half century earlier when Godefroy's drinking had caused a scandal, as her "talented good friend . . . [whom] I always shall love." "I love her Memory," Elizabeth mused, "as I do that of all who loved me & were kind to me." This image of Godefroy she now juxtaposed to that of Nancy Spear, whom she referred to as "my recreant friend of my *prosperity* alone." On a wrapper holding numerous letters from Spear, Elizabeth wrote "*Et tu Brutus!*" Sifting through Spear's letters had made her "sad" over "the death of her love for me" that had been "buried in [the] year 1835," during the great battle over William Patterson's will. Spear had been her "early Mentor, the confidante & soi disante affectionate ally of my youth." But she had joined forces with "Joseph & Edward Patterson to whom she sold my letters to her!!" Spear's traitorous act had revealed "the baseness of human nature" and had been quite "painful" for Elizabeth.[26] By the last decade or so of her life, Eliza-beth had very few close friends left. Most of those from her days in Europe were now dead, including Lady Morgan. Her most important friendships only survived in her memories.

Elizabeth remained a committed *femme d'esprit*, however. While no longer sending as many letters, she continued to write fervently, revising her story and its details in the multiple volumes of her memoirs and diaries. This en-gagement with her own past also included making extensive marginal notes in many of the saved letters and books she owned, which included various histo-ries of Napoleonic Europe and the Bonapartes. As she told her grandson, she "read five hours every day to keep my mind from rusting."[27] As she read and reread many of the volumes in her library during the decades after her return from Europe, she regularly commented on passages she found striking or rel-evant to her life. Writing and revising her history sustained her in her later years and filled the hours she had once devoted to her friends and the fashion-able world. She still worked on her two-volume fictional work, *Dialogues of the Dead*, but her memoirs appear to have received most of her time and attention. She probably relied on her journals to help with their details; in 1839, she noted that she had "12 volumes of my Journal kept in Europe from part of 1826 to, &, inclu[ding] part of [the] year 1834." By 1839, she had written five "cahiers" toward "a sketch of my memoirs."[28] By 1860, her memoirs filled thir-teen volumes.[29]

Elizabeth let many people, including journalists, know of the existence of her memoirs and of her plans to publish them. One reporter who interviewed her late in life remarked that, since Elizabeth was "very caustic of tongue and severely critical," it was "not likely that she will spare either friend or foe" in her memoirs. Best of all, in his view, the work promised to "be racy" since Elizabeth had "met almost every person since the first Napoleon" and knew many of them intimately.[30] Another writer noted that if her "diary" was "ever given to the public," it would "have the effect of a shower of cayenne." But he was sure "dis-cretion" would prevent her "*magnum opus*," the *Dialogues of the Dead*, in which "her father and King Jerome rehearse her story" in "Hades," from ever "seeing the light."[31] Having read the letters that Saffell had published in 1873, another journalist commented that Elizabeth possessed "a remarkable literary ability of a certain kind." "She was sharp, piquant and not particularly good-natured in her comments upon men, women, and manners," the journalist contended, further arguing that Elizabeth must have "caught a portion of the naivete of French memoir-writers."[32] Unfortunately, few would enjoy Elizabeth's "re-markable literary ability," as none of these works ever "saw the light."

By the 1870s, in her late eighties and early nineties, Elizabeth was rarely seen in public, except while out collecting her rents. In early 1873, after a lengthy interview, a correspondent for the *New York Herald* offered this de-scription of Elizabeth at eighty-eight: "Her complexion is still smooth and comparatively fair; while her peculiarly beautiful blue eyes are as yet un-dimmed." Though she still possessed "wonderful energy," the reporter contin-ued, "her nature is suspicious and warped by her many injuries."[33] Elizabeth had long felt that Jerome's betrayal, her father's cruelty, and her brothers' greed had left her their victim. Those whom she had relied on as family had cast her aside, she complained, in their "blind avarice and selfishness." "The cruel feelings of the injustice of those, from whom I had a right to expect affec-tion & assistance, has poisoned my whole Existence," she had written years earlier. "It is the worm, which will leave me only when I quit this disgusting world."[34]

While Elizabeth felt victimized at times, she also stayed true to the self-identity of a cosmopolitan and aristocratic celebrity she had created early in her life. And Americans continued to acknowledge that identity even in her later years. One newspaper declared that Elizabeth still possessed "a deep stoicism and unbending philosophy," as well as a marked "independence." As had long been the case, Elizabeth's "every thought" was "replete with favoritism for royalty," the article announced, and she willingly professed that republics were "common" and "ungrateful."[35] Americans also continued their ambivalence about her. Though her anti-American opinions were still well-known, Elizabeth remained a person of interest. According to a woman who rented a room in the boardinghouse where Elizabeth lived in her old age, "large parties of sightseers came . . . to see Madame Bonaparte." Elizabeth, dressed in a "black velvet dress and adorn[ed] . . . with her superb jewels, . . . would sweep down to the little parlor and hold court among her guests regaling them with anecdotes of former court days and completely captivating her audience." On other days when her fellow boarder announced the arrival of callers, Elizabeth responded: "Tell them today is not Show Day!"[36] When she did feel like putting on a show, she would welcome a few chosen visitors into her large, yet plainly furnished, bedroom where she would open her trunks, display her "ancient finery," and relate the history of particular pieces of clothing: "This was her husband's wedding coat; this dress was given her by the Princess Borghese; this one had been worn at the court of Tuscany; this one she wore at the Pitti Palace on the day she met her husband; this she wore when presented to Madame Mère, etc."[37] Not surprisingly, Elizabeth had kept much of the clothing that had played such an instrumental role in creating her cosmopolitan identity and maintaining her fashionable celebrity. Later in her life, the items evoked only past glories but still retained their power to shape how others saw her.

Elizabeth outlived her father, former husband, imperial brother-in-law, brothers, and son—all the men she had initially depended on and then used to gain her independence. Her two grandsons were the remaining important men in her life in her final years. Her eldest grandson Jerome Napoleon severely disappointed her by returning to the United States in 1871 and marrying an American divorcée. But she maintained a warm relationship with her other grandson, Charles Joseph, who oversaw her business affairs after he became a lawyer. He would later serve Theodore Roosevelt as secretary of the navy and attorney general.[38] In 1877, in a codicil to her will, she divided her estate equally between her grandsons, "share and share alike." She also left Charles "all histories of my life, written by myself, all my Diaries, my Dialogues of the Dead, the letters received by me from various correspondents, and all manuscripts whatsoever belonging to me."[39] When she died two years later, at the age of ninety-four, Elizabeth still clung to the hope that her grandsons would fulfill the aristocratic aspirations she had possessed when she married Jerome Bonaparte in 1803.

Attesting to her continued celebrity and significance to the nation, obituaries of Elizabeth appeared in newspapers across the country. Though long forgotten as a one-time threat to her country, she remained a popular, important figure. The *New-York Daily Tribune* headlined its obituary: "Madame Patterson-Bonaparte. A ROMANTIC LIFE CLOSED."[40] The widely read *Frank Leslie's Illustrated Newspaper* announced her death on its front page, under the heading "CLOSE OF A NOTABLE ROMANTIC CAREER," and included an engraving of her from her younger years, dressed in a revealing Grecian-style gown.[41] That is exactly how Elizabeth would have wanted to be remembered.

Notes

The following abbreviations appear in the notes.

DHi   Delaware Historical Society, Wilmington
DLC   Library of Congress, Washington, D.C.
EPB   Elizabeth Patterson Bonaparte
FHS   Filson Historical Society, Louisville, Ky.
JB   Jerome Bonaparte
JNB   Jerome Napoleon Bonaparte
MdHS   Maryland Historical Society, Baltimore
MHi   Massachusetts Historical Society, Boston
MiU   Clements Library, University of Michigan, Ann Arbor
NYHS   New York Historical Society, New York
PHi   Historical Society of Pennsylvania, Philadelphia
PJM:SS   Papers of James Madison, Secretary of State Series
SM   Sydney Morgan
ViHi   Virginia Historical Society, Richmond
ViU   Special Collections, Alderman Library, University of Virginia, Charlottesville
WP   William Patterson

Introduction

1. EPB, marginalia, ca. 1867, in Account Book, ca. 1840s–1850s, EPB Papers, MS142, MdHS (hereafter EPB Papers).

2. EPB, marginalia, ca. 1867, on Anne (Nancy) Spear to EPB, 30 May 1816; EPB, marginalia, ca. 1867, in Account Book, ca. 1840s–1850s, both EPB Papers.

3. EPB, marginalia, ca. 1867, in Account Book, ca. 1840s–1850s, EPB Papers.

4. Ibid.

5. Helen Jean Burn's recent biography, *Betsy Bonaparte* (Baltimore: Maryland Historical Society, 2010), is a glaring exception. Though hers is not a scholarly work, Burn meticulously researched the collections of the Maryland Historical Society and carefully chronicled the lives of Elizabeth and her family.

6. W. T. R. Saffell, ed., *The Bonaparte-Patterson Marriage in 1803, and the Secret Correspondence on the Subject Never Before Made Public* (Philadelphia, 1873), vii.

7. Eugene L. Didier, *The Life and Letters of Madame Bonaparte* (New York: Charles Scribner's Sons, 1879), viii.

8. For accounts that stress the romantic episodes of her life or simply fictionalize them, see Geraldine Brooks, *Dames and Daughters of the Young Republic* (New York: Thomas Crowell and Company, 1901), 130–75; Mary Caroline Crawford, *Romantic Days in the Early Republic* (Boston: Little, Brown, 1912), 257–65; Alice Curtis Desmond, *Bewitching Betsy Bonaparte* (New York: Nelson Doubleday, 1958); Susan Ertz, *No Hearts to Break* (New York: D. Appleton-Century, 1937); Daniel Henderson, *The Golden Bees: The Story of Betsy Patterson and the Bonapartes* (New York: Frederick A. Stokes, 1928); Virginia Tatnall Peacock, *Famous American Belles of the Nineteenth Century* (Philadelphia: J. B. Lippincott, 1901), chap. 3; and A. M. W. Stirling, *A Painter of Dreams and Other Biographical Studies* (New York: John Lane, 1916), chap. 4. This fictionalization of parts of Elizabeth's life continues even among those who state a wish to restore her to the historical record. See Claude Bourguignon-Frasseto, *Betsy Bonaparte: The Belle of Baltimore*, trans. Elborg Forster (Baltimore: Maryland Historical Society, 2003).

9. See Ruth H. Bloch, "The Gendered Meanings of Virtue in Revolutionary America," *Signs* 13 (Autumn 1987): 37–59; and Jan E. Lewis, "The Republican Wife: Virtue and Seduction in the Early Republic," *William and Mary Quarterly* 44 (October 1987): 689–721.

10. For the power of women in Philadelphia, see Susan Branson, *These Fiery Frenchified Dames: Women and Political Culture in Early National Philadelphia* (Philadelphia: University of Pennsylvania Press, 2001). For women in early Washington, D.C., see Catherine Allgor, *Parlor Politics: In Which the Ladies of Washington Help Build a City and a Government* (Charlottesville: University Press of Virginia, 2000). See also citations in chapter 3.

11. See especially Rosemarie Zagarri, *Revolutionary Backlash: Women and Politics in the Early American Republic* (Philadelphia: University of Pennsylvania Press, 2007); and Branson, *Fiery Frenchified Dames*. See also Allgor, *A Perfect Union: Dolley Madison and the Creation of the American Nation* (New York: Henry Holt, 2006); Joanne Freeman, *Affairs of Honor: National Politics in the New Republic* (New Haven, Conn.: Yale University Press, 2001); Nancy Isenberg, *Sex and Citizenship in Antebellum America* (Chapel Hill: University of North Carolina Press, 1998); Mary Kelley, *Learning to Stand and Speak: Women, Education, and Public Life in America's Republic* (Chapel Hill: University of North Carolina Press, 2006); Simon P. Newman, *Parades and the Politics of the Street: Festive Culture in the Early American Republic* (Philadelphia: University of Pennsylvania Press, 1997); and David Waldstreicher, *In the Midst of Perpetual Fetes: The Making of American Nationalism, 1776–1820* (Chapel Hill: University of North Carolina Press, 1997).

12. See Linda K. Kerber, *No Constitutional Right to Be Ladies: Women and the Obligations of Citizenship* (New York: Hill and Wang, 1998), especially 37–41.

13. For works that examine some elite women who pursued alternatives to republican womanhood, see Allgor, *Perfect Union* and *Parlor Politics*; Branson, *Dangerous to Know: Women, Crime, and Notoriety in the Early Republic* (Philadelphia: University of Pennsylvania Press, 2008) and *Fiery Frenchified Dames*; Wendy Anne Nicholson, "Making the Private Public: Anne Willing Bingham's Role as a Leader of Philadelphia's Social Elite in the Late Eighteenth Century" (M.A. thesis, University of Delaware, 1988); Sheila Skemp, *First Lady of Letters: Judith Sargent Murray and the Struggle for Independence* (Philadelphia: University of Pennsylvania Press, 2009); Susan M. Stabile, *Memory's Daughters: The*

Material Culture of Remembrance in Eighteenth-Century America (Ithaca, N.Y.: Cornell University Press, 2004); and Zagarri, *Revolutionary Backlash* and *A Woman's Dilemma: Mercy Otis Warren and the American Revolution* (Wheeling, Ill.: Harlan Davison, 1995).

14. EPB, marginalia, ca. 1867, in Account Book, ca. 1840s–1850s, EPB Papers.

15. EPB, marginalia, 16 January 1867, on bottom of James McElhiney to EPB, 16 April 1816, EPB Papers. For more on the disappearance of Elizabeth's papers and on the donation of some of her papers and personal objects to the Maryland Historical Society, see Burn, *Betsy Bonaparte*, 256–58.

16. Much of the discussion of American simplicity versus European luxury has focused on the Revolutionary period, not on the early decades of the nineteenth century. Some good examples of recent trends in early republic historiography include Doron Ben-Atar and Barbara B. Oberg, eds., *Federalists Reconsidered* (Charlottesville: University Press of Virginia, 1998); Marshall Foletta, *Coming to Terms with Democracy: Federalist Intellectuals and the Shaping of an American Culture* (Charlottesville: University Press of Virginia, 2001); and Jeffrey L. Pasley, Andrew W. Robertson, and David Waldstreicher, eds., *Beyond the Founders: New Approaches to the Political History of the Early American Republic* (Chapel Hill: University of North Carolina Press, 2004).

17. For a more thorough account of Elizabeth's life and family, see Burn, *Betsy Bonaparte*.

18. WP, will, 20 August 1827, WP Papers, MS145, MdHS.

19. Napoleon Bonaparte to JB, 6 Messidor, year X [6 June 1802], in D. A. Bingham, *The Marriages of the Bonapartes*, 2 vols. (London: Longmans, Green, 1881), 2:156.

20. E. Dentu, ed., *Mémoires et Correspondance du Roi Jérome et de La Reine Catherine*, 2 vols. (Paris: Libraire de la Société des Gens de Lettres, 1861), 1:129. For an account of Jerome's earlier years, see Glenn J. Lamar, *Jérôme Bonaparte: The War Years, 1800–1815* (Westport, Conn.: Greenwood, 2000).

21. James Gallatin, *A Great Peacemaker: The Diary of James Gallatin, Secretary to Albert Gallatin, 1813–1827* (New York: Charles Scribner's Sons, 1914), 62. Most accounts of Elizabeth and Jerome's meeting and marriage are either overly romanticized and unsupported or simply fictional. Neither left a surviving account of how they met. Henriette Pascault did marry Jean-Jacques Reubell.

22. Samuel Smith to WP, 26 October 1803, EPB Papers.

23. Louis André Pichon to JB, 27 October 1803, and Pichon to WP, 28 October 1803, in Dentu, *Mémoires du Roi Jérome*, 1:233–35.

24. Anonymous to WP, [ca. 5 November 1803], in Saffell, *Bonaparte-Patterson Marriage*, 29–30.

25. Quoted, without citation, in Didier, *Life and Letters*, 7–8.

26. Soon after the ceremony, Carroll confided that he could not "help fearing that [Elizabeth] may not find all the comforts hereafter, which she promised herself" (John Carroll to James Barry, 26 December 1803, in Thomas O'Brien Hanley, ed., *The John Carroll Papers*, vol. 2 [South Bend, Ind.: University of Notre Dame Press, 1976], 428).

Chapter 1. "Nature Never Intended Me for Obscurity"

1. Margaret Bayard Smith to Mrs. Kirkpatrick, 23 January 1804, in Gaillard Hunt, ed., *First Forty Years of Washington Society* (New York: Charles Scribner's Sons, 1906), 46.

2. Rosalie Stier Calvert to Madame H. J. Stier, 2 March 1804, in Margaret Law Callcott, ed., *Mistress of Riversdale: The Plantation Letters of Rosalie Stier Calvert, 1795–1821* (Baltimore: Johns Hopkins University Press, 1991), 78.

3. Margaret Bayard Smith to Kirkpatrick, 23 January 1804, in Hunt, *First Forty Years*, 46–47.

4. Calvert to Madame H. J. Stier, 2 March 1804, in Callcott, *Mistress of Riversdale*, 78.

5. Margaret Bayard Smith to Kirkpatrick, 23 January 1804, in Hunt, *First Forty Years*, 46–47.

6. Thomas Law, enclosed in Calvert to Madame H. J. Stier, 2 March 1804, in Callcott, *Mistress of Riversdale*, 78–79. In the version that reached Rosalie Calvert, Law had deleted two lines following "her limbs revealed her bosom bare."

7. Calvert to Madame H. J. Stier, 2 March 1804, in ibid., 78–79.

8. Law, enclosed in Calvert to Madame H. J. Stier, 2 March 1804, in ibid., 79. Calvert remarked that Law had to write this second part "in order to keep his eyes," a possible reference to Elizabeth's nature.

9. Calvert to Madame H. J. Stier, 2 March 1804, in ibid., 78.

10. Sally McKean Yrujo to EPB, 14 February 1804, EPB Papers, MS142, MdHS (hereafter EPB Papers). For others who viewed her portrait in Stuart's studio, see Anna Maria Brodeau Thornton Diary, 14 February and 5 March 1804, William Thornton Papers, DLC.

11. See Joanne Freeman, *Affairs of Honor: National Politics in the New Republic* (New Haven, Conn.: Yale University Press, 2001), xx. See also Douglass Adair, "Fame and the Founding Fathers," in *Fame and the Founding Fathers: Essays by Douglass Adair*, ed. Trevor Colburn (New York: Norton, 1974).

12. See Patricia Brady, *Martha Washington: An American Life* (New York: Viking, 2005); and Catherine Allgor, *A Perfect Union: Dolley Madison and the Creation of the American Nation* (New York: Henry Holt, 2006).

13. See Adair, "Fame and the Founding Fathers," 8. A few women were motivated by a historical reputation. Allgor persuasively shows that Dolley Madison desired "historical renown" and actively constructed her historical legacy, like Elizabeth (Allgor, *Perfect Union*, 385).

14. For a man who became celebrated in the 1820s without virtuous public service, see Paul E. Johnson, *Sam Patch, The Famous Jumper* (New York: Hill and Wang, 2003).

15. Sarah Gales Seaton to unknown friend, ca. 1814, quoted in Anne Hollingsworth Wharton, *Salons Colonial and Republican* (Philadelphia: J. B. Lippincott, 1900), 203.

16. For the celebrity of the Decaturs, see James T. De Kay, *A Rage for Glory: The Life of Commodore Stephen Decatur, USN* (New York: Free Press, 2004); and Robert J. Allison, *Stephen Decatur: American Naval Hero, 1779–1820* (Amherst: University of Massachusetts Press, 2005). See also note 30 below.

17. Seaton to unknown friend, ca. 1814, in Wharton, *Salons*, 203.

18. Catherine Allgor refers to Dolley Madison as "famous," but not as a celebrity for she believes this era was "an age before the modern cult of celebrity" (*Perfect Union*, 5). While celebrity in the early republic certainly differed from that in our own time, it was not the same as fame and was recognized as such. Dolley, I would argue, was both famous and celebrated. Allgor discusses the ways Dolley constructed her public persona in *Perfect Union*, chap. 12.

19. John Quincy Adams to Louisa Catherine Adams, 1 February 1807, Adams Papers, MHi (microfilm edition).

20. For Wollstonecraft, see Rosemarie Zagarri, *Revolutionary Backlash: Women and Politics in the Early American Republic* (Philadelphia: University of Pennsylvania Press, 2007), 41. For Hayley, see Amanda Bowie Moniz, "A Radical Shrew in America: Mary Wilkes Hayley and Celebrity in the Early United States," *Common-Place* 8 (April 2008); available at www.common-place.org (accessed 10 April 2008).

21. Amanda Vickery, *The Gentleman's Daughter: Women's Lives in Georgian England* (New Haven, Conn.: Yale University Press, 1998), 11. Though Vickery is not referring to female celebrities here, her point about the rewards women could gain from the proper performance of their roles is apt.

22. For more on the "performative understanding of selfhood" in the early republic, see Jay Fliegelman, *Declaring Independence: Jefferson, Natural Language, and the Culture of Performance* (Stanford, Calif.: Stanford University Press, 1993), quote on 2. See also C. Dallett Hemphill, "Class, Gender, and the Regulation of Emotional Expression in Revolutionary-Era Conduct Literature," in *An Emotional History of the United States*, ed. Peter N. Stearns and Jan Lewis (New York: New York University Press, 1998), 33–51.

23. After her name and birth and death dates, the first word in Elizabeth's entry for the *American National Biography Online* is "celebrity" (Lewis L. Gould, "Bonaparte, Elizabeth Patterson," *American National Biography Online*; available at www.anb.org [accessed 17 May 2007]).

24. Judith Sargent Murray, *The Traveller Returned*, in *The Gleaner* (Boston: I. Thomas and E. T. Andrews, 1798; reprint, Schenectady, N.Y.: Union College Press, 1992), 670. My thanks to the anonymous reader at the *Journal of Women's History* who suggested this passage.

25. For Bingham's influence in the 1790s, see Margaret Louise Brown, "Mr. and Mrs. William Bingham of Philadelphia, Rulers of the Republican Court," *Pennsylvania Magazine of History and Biography* 61 (July 1937): 286–324; Wendy Anne Nicholson, "'Making the Private Public': Anne Willing Bingham's Role as a Leader of Philadelphia's Social Elite in the Late Eighteenth Century" (M.A. thesis, University of Delaware, 1988); and Susan Branson, *These Fiery Frenchified Dames: Women and Political Culture in Early National Philadelphia* (Philadelphia: University of Pennsylvania Press, 2001), chap. 4.

26. Abigail Adams to Abigail Adams Smith, 26 December 1790, in Charles Francis Adams, ed., *Letters of Mrs. Adams* (Boston: Little and Brown, 1848), 351.

27. EPB to WP, 2 September 1815, in Eugene L. Didier, *Life and Letters of Madame Bonaparte* (New York: Charles Scribner's Sons), 45.

28. See Anne Leakin Sioussat, *Old Baltimore* (New York: Macmillan, 1931), 157.

29. Isaac Coles to Joseph C. Cabell, 1 November 1804, Cabell Family Papers, ViU.

30. Catherine Carroll Harper to Robert Goodloe Harper, ca. 1804, Robert Goodloe Harper Papers, MdHS (microfilm edition). For more on the Decaturs, especially Susan, see also Charles Carroll to Mary Caton, 13 November 1800, Charles Carroll Papers, MdHS (microfilm edition); Henry St. George Tucker to Cabell, 27 December 1803, Cabell Family Papers, ViU; Richard Caton to Robert Goodloe Harper, 23 December 1815, Robert Goodloe Harper Papers, MdHS; and Mary Crowninshield to her mother, 2 January 1816, in Francis Boardman Crowninshield, ed., *Letters of Mary Boardman Crowninshield, 1815–1816* (Cambridge, Mass.: Riverside Press, 1905), 36.

31. *Kentucky Gazette and General Advertiser* (Lexington), 9 April 1805. This exhibit may easily have included a figure of Elizabeth among the Baltimore beauties since she had already achieved much renown.

32. E. Dentu, ed., *Mémoires et Correspondance du Roi Jérome et de La Reine Catherine* (Paris: Libraire de la Société des Gens de Lettres, 1861), 134.

33. [Harman Blennerhassett Jr.], "Blennerhassett," [1844], p. 10, Harman Blennerhassett Papers, DLC. Blennerhassett did not explain what the "gross insult" was but did record that Jerome preferred signing a written apology to dueling, "a flow of ink to that of his haughty blood."

34. Augustus John Foster to Elizabeth Foster, 30 December 1804, Augustus John Foster Papers, DLC.

35. Samuel Smith to John Hollins, 25 October 1803, Carter-Smith Family Papers, ViU. Smith continued: "God grant it may prove better than appearances justify."

36. "Madame Patterson-Bonaparte," *Lippincott's Magazine of Popular Literature and Science* 20 (September 1877): 310. The anonymous author of this article seems to have interviewed Elizabeth.

37. Quoted in Clarence Edward Macartney and Gordon Dorrance, *The Bonapartes in America* (Philadelphia: Dorrance, 1939), 23.

38. "Madame Patterson-Bonaparte," 310.

39. Louis André Pichon to Charles-Maurice Talleyrand-Périgord, 2 November 1803, in Dentu, *Mémoires du Roi Jérome*, 244. Jerome also borrowed vast sums from his countryman Victor du Pont de Nemours and never repaid him, which helped cause du Pont's bankruptcy in 1805; see Betty-Bright P. Low, "The Youth of 1812: More Excerpts from the Letters of Josephine du Pont and Margaret Manigault," *Winterthur Portfolio* 11 (1976): 175.

40. James Madison to Robert R. Livingston, 28 October 1803, in Robert J. Brugger, et al., eds., *The Papers of James Madison: Secretary of State Series*, 8 vols. (Charlottesville: University Press of Virginia, 1986–), 5:586 (hereafter *PJM:SS*). For Franco-American relations in this period, see Clifford Egan, *Neither Peace nor War: Franco-American Relations, 1803–1812* (Baton Rouge: Louisiana State University Press, 1983); and Peter Hill, *Napoleon's Troublesome Americans: Franco-American Relations, 1804–1815* (Dulles, Va.: Potomac, 2005).

41. Thomas Jefferson to Livingston, 4 November 1803, in Andrew A. Lipscomb and Albert Ellery Bergh, eds., *The Writings of Thomas Jefferson* (Definitive Edition), 20 vols. (Washington, D.C.: Thomas Jefferson Memorial Association, 1905–1907), 10:424–25.

42. See Robert Patterson to WP, 12 March 1804, in W. T. R. Saffell, ed., *The Bonaparte-Patterson Marriage in 1803, and the Secret Correspondence on the Subject Never Before Made Public* (Philadelphia: W. T. R. Saffell, 1873), 36–39. In late 1804, the new minister to France noted that "the *matrimonial* connection of Jerome" was one source of Napoleon's "*irritation*" and "*temper*" (John Armstrong to Madison, 24 December 1804, in *PJM:SS*, 8:416–17).

43. Dentu, *Mémoires du Roi Jérome*, 161.

44. Ibid., 150.

45. See Jane Turner Censer, *North Carolina Planters and Their Children, 1800–1860* (Baton Rouge: Louisiana State University Press, 1984), chap. 4; Charlene Boyer Lewis, *Ladies and Gentlemen on Display: Planter Society at the Virginia Springs, 1790–1860* (Charlottesville: University Press of Virginia, 2001), 175–86; and Stephen M. Stowe, *Intimacy*

and Power in the Old South: Ritual in the Lives of the Planters (Baltimore: Johns Hopkins University Press, 1987), chap. 2. According to Jerome's memoirs, "all of Baltimore's society, flattered by a choice which did it honor, conspired to encourage their mutual devotion" (Dentu, *Mémoires du Roi Jérome*, 138; as translated in Sydney Alexander Mitchell, *A Family Lawsuit: The Story of Elisabeth Patterson and Jérôme Bonaparte* [New York: Farrar, Straus, and Cudahy, 1958], 36).

46. Lord John Russell, ed., *Memoirs, Journal, and Correspondence of Thomas Moore*, vol. 1 (London: Longman, Brown, Green, and Longmans, 1853), 158. When the *New-York Evening Post* discovered that Moore had mentioned Elizabeth in his travel journal, it "sincerely congratulate[d] that lady that she was not made the subject of lascivious verses which afterwards found their way into the newspapers" ("English Tourists," *New-York Evening Post*, 10 November 1806).

47. The goal of a good wife, whether in the eighteenth or early nineteenth century, was anonymity. As Laurel Thatcher Ulrich has concluded, a wife's goal was "not public distinction but private competence" (*Good Wives: Image and Reality in the Lives of Women in Northern New England, 1650–1750* [New York: Oxford University Press, 1982], 14). Catherine Allgor discusses the growing middle-class emphasis on public anonymity for women by the 1820s in *Parlor Politics: In Which the Ladies of Washington Help Build a City and a Government* (Charlottesville: University Press of Virginia, 2000), chap. 5.

48. *Federal Gazette* (Baltimore), 25 January 1804.

49. Vickery, *Gentleman's Daughter*, 291.

50. Pichon to Talleyrand, 20 February 1804, in Dentu, *Mémoires du Roi Jérome*, 266.

51. EPB, marginalia, in her copy of Dentu, *Mémoires du Roi Jérome*, 138.

52. Account Book, 1875, EPB Papers.

53. For fashion in this period, see Elisabeth McClellan, *Historic Dress in America, 1607–1870*, vol. 2 (New York: Benjamin Blom, 1904–10); Dixon Ryan Fox, "American Fashions and French Influences 150 Years Ago," *Légion d'Honneur Magazine* 10 (April 1940): 389–400; and Branson, *Fiery Frenchified Dames*, chap. 2.

54. See McClellan, *Historic Dress*, 24.

55. Samuel Latham Mitchill to Catherine Mitchill, 9 February 1807, Samuel Latham Mitchill Papers, MiU.

56. Benjamin Henry Latrobe to Joshua Gilpin, 20 February 1804, in John C. Van Horne and Lee W. Formwalt, eds., *The Correspondence and Miscellaneous Papers of Benjamin Henry Latrobe*, vol. 1 (New Haven, Conn.: Yale University Press, 1984), 434.

57. Charles Carroll to Charles Carroll, Jr., 14 February 1804, Charles Carroll Papers, MdHS.

58. Simeon Baldwin to his wife, 12 January 1804, in Simeon E. Baldwin, ed., *Life and Letters of Simeon Baldwin* (New Haven, Conn.: Tuttle, Morehouse, and Taylor, n.d.), 345.

59. Aaron Burr to Theodosia Burr Alston, 17 January 1804, in Matthew L. Davis, *Memoirs of Aaron Burr*, vol. 2 (New York: Harper, 1836–37), 269.

60. Louisa Catherine Adams to Abigail Adams, 11 February 1804, Adams Papers, MHi.

61. Catherine Carroll Harper to Robert Goodloe Harper, 20 January [1804], Robert Goodloe Harper Papers, MdHS.

62. Baldwin to his wife, 12 January 1804, in Baldwin, *Life and Letters*, 345.

63. Waller Holladay to Huldah Holladay, 9 April 1804, Holladay Family Papers, ViHi.

64. Jacob Johnson, *The Way to Get Married: And the Advantages and Disadvantages of the Marriage State* (Philadelphia: Jacob Johnson, 1806), 49.

65. As Diana Crane has observed, clothing serves as "an indication of how people in different eras have perceived their positions in social structures and negotiated status boundaries" (*Fashion and Its Social Agendas: Class, Gender, and Identity in Clothing* [Chicago: University of Chicago Press, 2000], 1). See also Fred Davis, *Fashion, Culture, and Identity* (Chicago: University of Chicago Press, 1992).

66. See Carole Turbin, "Refashioning the Concept of Public/Private: Lessons from Dress Studies," *Journal of Women's History* 15 (Spring 2003): 48.

67. Calvert to H. J. Stier, 2 March 1804, in Callcott, *Mistress of Riversdale*, 77.

68. Huldah Holladay to Waller Holladay, 22 April 1804, Holladay Family Papers, ViHi.

69. S. Morton to EPB, 12 August 1804, EPB Papers. The Baltimore *American* published the poem on 24 August 1804. Women also wrote odes to her loveliness; see Louisa Catherine Adams to Abigail Adams, 11 February 1804, Adams Papers, MHi.

70. Henry M. Brackenridge, *Recollections of Persons and Places in the West* (Philadelphia: J. Kay, Jun., and Brother, 1834), 131. Brackenridge added that he "met her thirty years afterward, but how changed! She was then short and dumpy, and very unlike the famous statue."

71. "Important and Interesting to the Ladies: Alexander C. D. Lavigne," *American and Commercial Daily Advertiser* (Baltimore), 19 January 1807.

72. Dentu, *Mémoires du Roi Jérome*, 165.

73. For a detailed discussion of the exchange between Napoleon and Pope Pius VII concerning the annulment and its consequences, see D. A. Bingham, *The Marriages of the Bonapartes* (London: Longmans, Green, 1881), 168–88.

74. Captain Bentalou to Robert Patterson, 17 October 1805, in Saffell, *Bonaparte-Patterson Marriage*, 218. Napoleon also implied that he considered Elizabeth nothing more than Jerome's mistress.

75. Contrary to legend, the ship was not owned by Patterson. See William Stevenson Journal, 1805, DLC; and Dorothy M. Quynn and Frank F. White, Jr., "Jerome and Betsy Cross the Atlantic: Account of the Passage by the Captain of the *Erin*," *Maryland Historical Magazine* 48 (September 1953): 204–14.

76. Thomas Barclay to Captain Bradley, 23 June 1804, in George Lockhart Rives, ed., *Selections from the Correspondence of Thomas Barclay* (New York: Harper, 1894), 170.

77. Denis Decrès to Pichon, 20 April 1804, in Saffell, *Bonaparte-Patterson Marriage*, 67.

78. Quoted in Didier, *Life and Letters*, 25.

79. Augustus John Foster to Elizabeth Foster, 30 December 1804, Foster Papers, DLC. For others who kept an eye on the drama of Elizabeth and Jerome, see, for example, Eldred Simkins to Creed Taylor, 10 August 1804, Creed Taylor Papers, ViU; Elizabeth Drinker Diary, 4 September 1806, in Elaine Forman Crane, ed., *Diary of Elizabeth Drinker*, vol. 3 (Boston: Northeastern University Press, 1991), 1,962; and Louisa Catherine Adams to John Quincy Adams, 6 July and 25 November 1806, Adams Papers, MHi.

80. "Jerome Bonaparte," *National Intelligencer and Washington Advertiser* (D.C.), 11 February 1805.

81. *Columbian Centinel* (Boston), 3 April 1805.

82. "Latest European Intelligence," *Scioto Gazette* (Chillicothe, Ohio), 29 July 1805.

83. Stevenson Journal, 1805, DLC.

84. *Scioto Gazette*, 29 July 1805 and 18 September 1806. See also *Pittsburgh Gazette* (Pa.), 12 August 1806; and "Jerome Bonaparte," *Impartial Review and Cumberland Repository* (Nashville, Tenn.), 6 September 1806.

85. James McElhiney to EPB, 12 March 1806, EPB Papers.

86. EPB to WP, 14 August 180[5], Ferdinand J. Dreer Autograph Collection, PHi.

87. Decrès to Jerome Bonaparte, 20 April 1804, in Saffell, *Bonaparte-Patterson Marriage*, 73–78.

88. Dentu, *Mémoires du Roi Jérome*, 168.

89. Augustus John Foster to Elizabeth Foster, 27 November 1806, Foster Papers, DLC.

90. Ibid.

91. Louisa Catherine Adams to John Quincy Adams, 25 November1806, Adams Papers, MHi.

92. EPB to WP, 14 August 1805, Dreer Autograph Collection, PHi.

93. Eliza Anderson to EPB, 8 [August] 1808, EPB Papers.

94. Sophia May to Abigail May, 11 December 1806, Sophia May Letters, American Antiquarian Society, Worcester, Mass.

95. "Jerome Bonaparte's Bigamy," *Virginia Argus* (Richmond), 16 October 1807. See also "Jerome Bonaparte's Marriage," *New-York Evening Post*, 13 October 1807; and "Jerome Bonaparte's Marriage," *Mirror* (Russellville, Ky.), 1 December 1807.

96. "To Eliza," *Observer* 2 (26 December 1807): 394–95.

97. Anderson to EPB, 4 June 1808, EPB Papers. See also Anderson to EPB, 2 July 1808, ibid.

98. Anderson to EPB, 8 [August] 1808, ibid.

99. Fredrika J. Teute, "The Spectacle of Washington: Creating Public Celebrity in the New Nation" (paper presented at the annual meeting of the Omohundro Institute of Early American History and Culture, Santa Barbara, Calif., 25 June 2005), 1. I thank Fredrika for permission to quote from this work.

100. Catherine Mitchill to Margaret Miller, 28–30 December 1808, Samuel Mitchill Papers, MiU.

101. See Teute, "Spectacle of Washington"; Allgor, *Parlor Politics* and *Perfect Union*; and Freeman, *Affairs of Honor*.

102. Margaret Bayard Smith to Kirkpatrick, 13 March 1814, in Hunt, *First Forty Years*, 95.

103. George B. Milligan to "Aunt," 16 February [1812], DHi.

104. Catherine Mitchill to Margaret Miller, 21 November 1811, Catherine Mitchill Papers, DLC. See also Anna Maria Brodeau Thornton Diary, entries from 1810 to 1813, William Thornton Papers, DLC. Spear was certainly related to Elizabeth's mother, Dorcas, but whether she was a sister or a cousin is not entirely clear. I have chosen to refer to her as Elizabeth's aunt.

105. Abijah Bigelow to his wife, 28 November 1811, in Clarence S. Brigham, ed., "Letters of Abijah Bigelow, Member of Congress, to His Wife, 1810–1815," *Proceedings of the American Antiquarian Society* 40 (October 1930): 318.

106. Elbridge Gerry to EPB, 22 April 1814, EPB Papers.

107. Milligan to "Aunt," 16 February [1812], Milligan-McLane Papers, DHi.

108. Jonathan Russell to EPB, 20 February 1814, EPB Papers. See also Samuel Smith to Mary B. Mansfield, 6 November 1811, Carter-Smith Family Papers, ViU.

109. For more on Dolley Madison's relationships with younger women, see Allgor, *Perfect Union*.

110. Dolley Madison to EPB, 24 November 1813, EPB Papers.

111. Anderson to EPB, 8 [August] 1808, ibid.

112. Lydia Hollingsworth to Ruth Tobin, 12 August 1809, Hollingsworth Papers, MdHS.

113. JB to EPB, 21 November 1805, JB Papers, MS143, MdHS.

114. See EPB, Account Book, ca. 1804–1815, EPB Papers; and List of Collections Donated by Mrs. Charles Joseph Bonaparte (Ellen Channing Day), 1922, Accession Number XX.5, MdHS.

115. Catharine Mitchill to Margaret Akerly Miller, 21 November 1811, in Carolyn Hoover Sung, ed., "Catharine Mitchill's Letters from Washington, 1806–1812," *Quarterly Journal of the Library of Congress* 34 (July 1977): 184.

116. Phoebe Morris to [Rebecca Morris], 17 February 1812, as quoted in Wharton, *Social Life in the Early Republic* (Philadelphia: J. B. Lippincott, 1903), 147.

117. Dolley Madison to Edward Coles, 13 May [18]13, in David B. Mattern and Holly C. Shulman, eds., *The Selected Letters of Dolley Payne Madison* (Charlottesville: University of Virginia Press, 2003), 176–77.

118. Mary Caton Smith to EPB, as quoted in Alice Curtis Desmond, *Bewitching Betsy Bonaparte* (New York: Nelson Doubleday, 1958), 3.

119. Catharine Mitchill to Miller, 21 November 1811, in Sung, "Catharine Mitchill's Letters," 184.

120. Samuel Colleton Graves to EPB, 14 May 1809, EPB Papers.

121. "Nicholas Nemo" to EPB, 25 October 1812, ibid. Nicholas Nemo was the pseudonym for a Mr. Cuttings who resided in Washington. For other poems, see also Catherine Mitchill to Miller, 8 April 1812, Samuel Latham Mitchill Papers, MiU; Eli Kneeberry, David Canutmore, Josiah Isaac to EPB, 22 August 1812, EPB Papers; Mr. [Gold] of the Senate to EPB, [9 January] 1813, ibid.; and William Johnson, Jr., to EPB, 28 March 1814, ibid.

122. Maria Carr to Hetty Carr, 6 April [1818], Carr-Cary Family Papers, ViU.

123. Horace Holley to Mary Austin Holley, 12 and 13 March 1818, Holley Papers, MiU; and Horace Holley to EPB, 2 April 1818, EPB Papers.

124. Horace Holley to Mary Austin Holley, 16 March 1818, Holley Papers, MiU.

125. Seaton to unknown, 2 January 1813, as quoted in Josephine Seaton, *William Winston Seaton of the "National Intelligencer"* (Boston: James R. Osgood, 1871), 90.

126. Louisa Catherine Adams to Abigail Adams, 11 February 1804, Adams Papers, MHi. For other women's jealousy of Elizabeth, see Horace Holley to Mary Austin Holley, 17 March 1818, Holley Papers, MiU.

127. Jonathan Mason Diary, 6 December 1804, in George E. Ellis, ed., "Diary of the Hon. Jonathan Mason," *Proceedings of the Massachusetts Historical Society*, 2d ser., 2 (March 1885): 12.

128. Johnson, *Way to Get Married*, 65.

129. Joseph D. Fay to Ethan A. Brown, 13 January 1807, Ethan A. Brown Papers, Ohio Historical Society, Columbus (microfilm edition).

130. *Republican; or Anti-Democrat* (Baltimore), 21 December 1803.

131. "On Fashion," *Impartial Observer* (Richmond, Va.), 19 July 1806. For a similar sentiment, see "The Maid with Elbows Bare," *Weekly Messenger* (Washington, Ky.), 23 June 1803.

132. Abigail Adams to Mary Cranch, 15–18 March 1800, in Stewart Mitchell, ed., *New Letters of Abigail Adams, 1788–1801* (Boston: Houghton Mifflin, 1947), 241–42. The Federalist Harrison Gray Otis reported that, through her thin muslin dress, he had "been regaled with the sight of" Marie Bingham's "whole legs for five minutes together" (Harrison Gray Otis to his wife, 18 January 1800, in Samuel Eliot Morison, ed., *The Life and Letters of Harrison Gray Otis, Federalist, 1765–1848*, vol. 1 [Boston: Houghton Mifflin, 1913], 137).

133. John Quincy Adams to Louisa Catherine Adams, 1 February 1807, Adams Papers, MHi. Louisa considered the poem "the sauciest lines I ever perused" (Louisa Catherine Adams to John Quincy Adams, 17 February 1807, ibid.).

134. "An Extract," *Western American* (Louisville, Ky.), 14 May 1806.

135. See Robert Wilson Torchia, "Eliza Ridgely and the Ideal of American Womanhood, 1787–1820," *Maryland Historical Magazine* 90 (Winter 1995): 413–16.

136. D. Fraser, *The Mental Flower Garden: Or, an Instructive and Entertaining Companion for the Fair Sex* (New York: Southwick and Hardcastle, 1807), 178.

137. *American*, 18 September 1804.

138. Milligan to "Aunt," 16 February [1812], Milligan-McLane Papers, DHi.

139. Horace Holley to Mary Austin Holley, 16 March 1818, Holley Papers, MiU. See also Reverend Horace Holley Journal, 11 March 1818, MiU.

140. See Allgor, *Perfect Union*.

141. For example, in the early 1800s, the wives of British diplomats Anthony Merry and Francis James Jackson and of French general Jean Victor Moreau all served as models of cosmopolitan style.

142. Hollingsworth to Tobin, 10 January 1810, Hollingsworth Papers, MdHS.

143. EPB to Dolley Madison, 29 December 1814, William Patterson Papers, MdHS.

144. Robert Gilmor to Madame Liccama, 10 April 1815, EPB Papers.

145. John Willink to William Willink, 17 April 1815, ibid.

146. Jefferson to EPB, 24 April 1815, ibid.

147. Washington Irving to Henry Brevoort, 8 September 1815, in Ralph M. Adermann, et al., eds., *Letters*, vol. 1 (Boston: Twayne, 1978), 422.

148. EPB to WP, 2 September 1815, in Didier, *Life and Letters*, 44–45.

149. Ibid., 44.

150. McElhiney to WP, ca. 15 September 1815, enclosed in McElhiney to EPB, 15 September 1815, EPB Papers.

151. Anne (Nancy) Spear to EPB, 30 May 1816, ibid.

152. EPB, as quoted in Wharton, *Social Life*, 147. Elizabeth played with the words *belle*, which means beautiful, and *belle soeur*, which means sister-in-law. My thanks to my colleague Kathy Smith for pointing out this double meaning.

153. John Spear Smith to EPB, 18 April and 25 May 1816, EPB Papers.

154. McElhiney to EPB, 16 April 1816, ibid.

155. EPB to Mary (Caton) Patterson, 7 November 1816, in "Unpublished Letters," *Maryland Historical Magazine* 20 (June 1925): 123–24.

156. Edward Patterson to EPB, 15 December 1815, EPB Papers.

157. See Torchia, "Eliza Ridgely," 406–7.

158. Richard Lalor Sheil, as quoted in Mary Caroline Crawford, *Romantic Days in the Early Republic* (Boston: Little, Brown, 1912), 253–54.

159. Reverend Horace Holley Journal, 12 and 19 March 1818, MiU.

160. John Spear Smith to EPB, 18 April and 25 May 1816, EPB Papers.

161. See, for example, Mary (Caton) Patterson to EPB, 15 November 1815, ibid.; Spear to EPB, 17 November [1815 or 1816], ibid.; Eliza (Anderson) Godefroy to EPB, 29 March 1816, ibid.; and Edward Patterson to EPB, 5 May 1816 and 6 March 1817, ibid.

162. Spear to EPB, 1 May 1816, ibid.

163. Edward Patterson to EPB, 15 December 1815, ibid.

164. Mary (Caton) Patterson to EPB, 18 December 1815, ibid.

165. Godefroy to EPB, 29 March 1816, ibid.

166. Spear to EPB, 17 November [1815 or 1816], ibid. In fact, nearly all of Elizabeth's letters to Spear have been lost.

167. Edward Patterson to EPB, 20 September 1816, ibid.

168. Hollingsworth to Tobin, 31 August 1816, Hollingsworth Papers, MdHS.

169. Samuel Smith to Mansfield, 28 May 1825, Carter-Smith Family Papers, ViU.

170. Horace Holley to Mary Austin Holley, 20 March 1818, Holley Papers, MiU.

171. JNB to WP, 25 May 1825, in Didier, *Life and Letters*, 161.

172. EPB to WP, 23 September 1815, in Didier, *Life and Letters*, 48.

Chapter 2. "The Duchess of Baltimore"

Portions of this chapter were previously published in Leonard J. Sadosky, Peter Nicolaisen, Peter S. Onuf, and Andrew J. O'Shaughnessy, eds., *Old World, New World: America and Europe in the Age of Jefferson* (Charlottesville: University of Virginia Press, 2010).

1. See John Spear Smith to Samuel Smith, 9 January 1810, Samuel Smith Papers, DLC; and Sally McKean Yrujo to Dolley Madison, 20 June 1812, in David B. Mattern and Holly C. Shulman, eds., *Selected Letters of Dolley Payne Madison* (Charlottesville: University of Virginia Press, 2003), 167.

2. *New York Gazette*, 24 November 1809.

3. *National Intelligencer and Washington Advertiser* (D.C.), 10 November 1809.

4. *New York Gazette*, 24 November 1809.

5. *Statesman* (Newburyport, Mass.), 28 December 1809.

6. [Margaret] McHenry to "Mrs. Henry," ca. March 1810, James McHenry Papers, DLC (microfilm edition).

7. Deborah Onderdonk to Henry U. Onderdonk, 20 November 1809, Society Collection, PHi (emphasis added). Onderdonk must have read this fact in a newspaper for her language is almost exactly that of a contemporary newspaper clipping in Elizabeth's clipping book at MdHS.

8. As quoted in W. H. Earle, "The Phantom Amendment and the Duchess of Baltimore," *American History Illustrated* 22 (November 1987): 37.

9. Lydia E. Hollingsworth to Ruth Tobin, 10 January 1810, Hollingsworth Papers, MdHS.

10. *National Intelligencer*, 31 January 1810.

11. Ibid., 16 February 1810.

12. Timothy Pickering, notes on "Amendment of Constitution[:] Mr. Reid resolution— with an *Addition*," [ca. 1810], Timothy Pickering Papers, MHi (microfilm edition).

13. *Enquirer* (Richmond, Va.), 4 November 1806.

14. For recent work on disunion see, for example, David C. Hendrickson, *Union, Nation, or Empire: The American Debate over International Relations, 1789–1941* (Lawrence: University Press of Kansas, 2009); James E. Lewis, Jr., *The American Union and the Problem of Neighborhood: The United States and the Collapse of the Spanish Empire, 1783–1829* (Chapel Hill: University of North Carolina Press, 1998) and *The Louisiana Purchase: Jefferson's Noble Bargain?* (Charlottesville, Va.: Thomas Jefferson Foundation, 2003); and Peter S. Onuf, *Jefferson's Empire: The Language of American Nationhood* (Charlottesville: University of Virginia Press, 2000).

15. My discussion of refinement rests on Richard Bushman's brilliant *The Refinement of America: Persons, Houses, Cities* (New York: Vintage, 1993). For pre-1800 Americans' ambivalence about refinement, see chap. 6.

16. *Enquirer*, 4 November 1806.

17. "On Luxury," *Enquirer*, 19 April 1805.

18. See, especially, Gary J. Kornblith and John M. Murrin, "The Dilemmas of Ruling Elites in Revolutionary America," in *Ruling America: A History of Wealth and Power in a Democracy*, ed. Steve Fraser and Gary Gerstle (Cambridge, Mass.: Harvard University Press, 2005), 27–63; and the essays in James Horn, Jan Ellen Lewis, and Peter S. Onuf, eds., *The Revolution of 1800: Democracy, Race, and the New Republic* (Charlottesville: University of Virginia Press, 2002).

19. See Eve Kornfeld, *Creating an American Culture, 1775–1800: A Brief History with Documents* (Boston: Bedford/St. Martin's, 2001), vii.

20. See Marshall Foletta, *Coming to Terms with Democracy: Federalist Intellectuals and the Shaping of an American Culture* (Charlottesville: University Press of Virginia, 2001).

21. Catherine Allgor has stated that the Revolution did not destroy "the American commitment to aristocratic forms" but rather inspired "vigorous debate as to what place they should have" (*A Perfect Union: Dolley Madison and the Creation of the American Nation* [New York: Henry Holt and Company, 2006], 169). Similarly, David Shi has argued that, by the early 1800s, the prosperity and "happiness of American society negated republican simplicity" as Americans decided they did not want to live without British luxuries and increased their importations of them (*The Simple Life: Plain Living and High Thinking in American Culture* [New York: Oxford University Press, 1985], 88). Daniel Kilbride has persuasively shown that the "leisure class," especially Southern planters, remained a powerful presence in the new republic and fought valiantly in the "ongoing struggle" between "privilege and democratization" (*An American Aristocracy: Southern Planters in Antebellum Philadelphia* [Columbia: University of South Carolina Press, 2006], 7).

22. See Gordon S. Wood, *The Radicalism of the American Revolution: How a Revolution Transformed a Monarchical Society into a Democratic One Unlike Any That Had Ever Existed* (New York: Alfred A. Knopf, 1992).

23. For similar arguments, see Kilbride, *American Aristocracy*, and Harvey Levenstein, *Seductive Journey: American Tourists from Jefferson to the Jazz Age* (Chicago: University of Chicago Press, 1998).

24. Charles Royster, *A Revolutionary People at War: The Continental Army and American Character, 1775–1783* (Chapel Hill: University of North Carolina Press, 1979), 353–58 (quotes on 356 and 354).

25. For more on these contentious issues, see Joanne Freeman, *Affairs of Honor: National Politics in the New Republic* (New Haven, Conn.: Yale University Press, 2001), chap. 1; Alan Taylor, *Liberty Men and Great Proprietors: The Revolutionary Settlement on the*

244 Notes to Pages 68–73

Maine Frontier, 1760–1820 (Chapel Hill: University of North Carolina Press, 1990) and *William Cooper's Town: Power and Persuasion on the Frontier of the Early American Republic* (New York: Vintage, 1995); and Gordon S. Wood, *The Creation of the American Republic, 1776–1787* (New York: W. W. Norton, 1972).

26. D. Fraser, *The Mental Flower Garden: Or, An Instructive and Entertaining Companion for the Fair Sex* (New York: Southwick and Hardcastle, 1807), 176.

27. Allgor, *Perfect Union*, 68. See also Jan E. Lewis, "The Republican Wife: Virtue and Seduction in the Early Republic," *William and Mary Quarterly* 44 (October 1987): 689–721; Freeman, *Affairs of Honor*, 47; and Kornfeld, *Creating an American Culture*, 55–65. For a general history of the concept of luxury, primarily in eighteenth-century England, see John Sekora, *Luxury: The Concept in Western Thought, Eden to Smollett* (Baltimore: Johns Hopkins University Press, 1977).

28. EPB to John Spear Smith, 22 August 1816, EPB Papers, MS142, MdHS (hereafter EPB Papers).

29. See Susan Branson, *These Fiery Frenchified Dames: Women and Political Culture in Early National Philadelphia* (Philadelphia: University of Pennsylvania Press, 2001); and Rosemarie Zagarri, *Revolutionary Backlash: Women and Politics in the Early American Republic* (Philadelphia: University of Pennsylvania Press, 2007).

30. William Lee to Susan Palfrey Lee, 17 December 1809, in Mary Lee Mann, ed., *A Yankee Jeffersonian: Selections from the Diary and Letters of William Lee of Massachusetts* (Cambridge, Mass.: Harvard University Press, 1958), 97.

31. John Quincy Adams to Louisa Catherine Adams, 19 July 1804, in Worthington Chauncey Ford, ed., *Writings of John Quincy Adams*, vol. 3 (New York: Macmillan, 1913–17), 43.

32. *The Gentleman's Magazine* (London), 95 (January 1804): 78. I thank Karen Racine for sending me a copy of this article.

33. Ralph Izard, Jr., to Alice DeLancey Izard, 18 April 1804, Ralph Izard Papers, South Carolina Historical Society, Charleston.

34. John Quincy Adams Diary, 7 January 1804, in Charles Francis Adams, ed., *Memoirs of John Quincy Adams: Comprising Portions of His Diary from 1795 to 1848*, vol. 1 (Philadelphia: J. B. Lippincott, 1874–77), 284–85.

35. Transcript of conversation with Lucien Bonaparte, in Paul Bentalou to WP, 16 March 1804, in W. T. R. Saffell, ed., *The Bonaparte-Patterson Marriage in 1803, and the Secret Correspondence on the Subject Never Before Made Public* (Philadelphia: W. T. R. Saffell, 1873), 53.

36. Cuneo D'Ornano to JB, 20 January 1805, in ibid., 146.

37. "Jerome Bonaparte," *American and Commercial Daily Advertiser* (Baltimore), 30 July 1804. See also ibid., 6 August 1804.

38. Transcript of conversation with Lucien Bonaparte, in Bentalou to WP, 16 March 1804, in Saffell, *Bonaparte-Patterson Marriage*, 53–54 (emphasis added).

39. E. Dentu, ed., *Mémoires et Correspondance du Roi Jérome et de La Reine Catherine* (Paris: Librairie de la Société des Gens de Lettres, 1861), 138.

40. Yrujo to EPB, 14 February 1804, EPB Papers.

41. Catherine Mitchill to Margaret Miller, 16 February 1811, Catherine Mitchill Papers, DLC.

42. William Eaton to Thomas Dwight, 14 August 1804, Gratz Collection—American Miscellaneous Papers, PHi.

43. Similarly, Rosalie Stier Calvert lived her life negotiating between two cultural identities (Belgian and American); she, too, had "little enthusiasm for republican government." See Lorri M. Glover, "Between Two Cultures: The Worlds of Rosalie Stier Calvert," *Maryland Historical Magazine* 91 (Spring 1996): 85–94 (quote on 91). See also Margaret Law Callcott, ed., *Mistress of Riversdale: The Plantation Letters of Rosalie Stier Calvert, 1795–1821* (Baltimore: Johns Hopkins University Press, 1991).

44. See Seth Rockman, *Scraping By: Wage Labor, Slavery, and Survival in Early Baltimore* (Baltimore: Johns Hopkins University Press, 2009), population statistic on 27.

45. Jonathan Mason Diary, 21 December 1804, in George E. Ellis, ed., "Diary of the Hon. Jonathan Mason," *Proceedings of the Massachusetts Historical Society*, 2d. ser., 2 (March 1885): 15.

46. John Melish, *Travels in the United States of America, in the Years 1806 & 1807, and 1809, 1810 & 1811*, 2 vols. (Philadelphia: Thomas and George Palmer, 1812), 1:184.

47. JB to EPB, 21 November 1805, JB Papers, MS143, MdHS (hereafter JB Papers).

48. Anna Kuhn to EPB, 24 November 1807, EPB Papers.

49. *Pittsburgh Gazette* (Pa.), 12 August 1806.

50. A. M. Hollingsworth to Tobin, 14 November 1809, Hollingsworth Papers, MdHS.

51. EPB to Mr. Gilmor, 26 January, ca. 1805, Gratz Collection—Notable American Women, PHi; Lydia E. Hollingsworth to Tobin, 10 January 1810, Hollingsworth Papers, MdHS. Similarly, George and Rosalie Stier Calvert drove around Maryland in a coach with four horses and "two postilions in yellow jackets, leather pantaloons, and black velvet caps with gold lace trim" (Rosalie Stier Calvert to Madame H. J. Stier, November 1803, in Callcott, *Mistress of Riversdale*, 63).

52. Inventory, collection donated by Mrs. Charles Joseph Bonaparte, 1922, MdHS.

53. EPB, List of Jewels Taken to France, June 1825, EPB Papers.

54. See Carole Turbin, "Refashioning the Concept of Public/Private: Lessons from Dress Studies," *Journal of Women's History* 15 (Spring 2003): 43–51.

55. Kathleen M. Brown, *Good Wives, Nasty Wenches, and Anxious Patriarchs: Gender, Race, and Power in Colonial Virginia* (Chapel Hill: University of North Carolina Press, 1996), 293. For excellent discussions of the connections between clothing and political identity, see Wendy Perkins, ed., *Fashioning the Body Politic: Dress, Gender, Citizenship* (New York: Berg, 2002).

56. See Branson, *Fiery Frenchified Dames*, especially chap. 2.

57. Joan B. Landes, *Visualizing the Nation: Gender, Representation, and Revolution in Eighteenth-Century France* (Ithaca, N.Y.: Cornell University Press, 2001), 22. See also James McMillan, *France and Women, 1789–1914: Gender, Society, and Politics* (New York: Routledge, 2000), chap. 3; and Timothy Wilson-Smith, *Napoleon and His Artists* (London: Constable, 1996).

58. See, especially, the essays in Donald R. Kennon, ed., *A Republic for the Ages: The United States Capitol and the Political Culture of the Early Republic* (Charlottesville: University Press of Virginia, 1999). See also Donald R. Kennon, ed., *The United States Capitol: Designing and Decorating a National Icon* (Athens: Ohio University Press, 2000); and Donald R. Kennon and Thomas P. Somma, eds., *American Pantheon: Sculptural and Artistic Decoration of the United States Capitol* (Athens: Ohio University Press, 2004).

59. See Jay Fliegelman, *Declaring Independence: Jefferson, Natural Language, and the Culture of Performance* (Stanford, Calif.: Stanford University Press, 1993); and Freeman, *Affairs of Honor*, especially chap. 1.

60. See Freeman, *Affairs of Honor*, 38; and Nancy Isenberg, "The 'Little Emperor': Aaron Burr, Dandyism, and the Sexual Politics of Treason," in *Beyond the Founders: New Approaches to the Political History of the Early American Republic*, ed. Jeffrey Pasley, Andrew W. Robertson, and David Waldstreicher (Chapel Hill: University of North Carolina Press, 2004), 129–58.

61. Edward Patterson to EPB, 23 April 1817, EPB Papers.

62. "Sacharissa," "To Samuel Saunter, Esq.," *Republican; Or, Anti-Democrat* (Baltimore), 30 December 1803.

63. For the importance of fashion in constructing a "self-narrative," see Diana Crane, *Fashion and Its Social Agendas: Class, Gender, and Identity in Clothing* (Chicago: University of Chicago Press, 2000), quote on 10. See also Fred Davis, *Fashion, Culture, and Identity* (Chicago: University of Chicago Press, 1992). Linzy A. Brekke has explored the links between fashion and patriotism in the new republic in "The 'Scourge of Fashion': Political Economy and the Politics of Consumption in the Early Republic," *Early American Studies* 3 (2005): 111–39. For the importance of male fashion, especially Jefferson's robe and slippers, and political identity in the early republic, see David Waldstreicher, "Why Thomas Jefferson and African Americans Wore Their Politics on Their Sleeves: Dress and Mobilization Between American Revolutions," in Pasley et al., *Beyond the Founders*, 79–103.

64. Thomas Law, poem, enclosed in Calvert to Stier, 2 March 1804, in Callcott, *Mistress of Riversdale*, 78–79.

65. Simeon Baldwin to his wife, 12 January 1804, in Simeon E. Baldwin, ed., *Life and Letters of Simeon Baldwin* (New Haven, Conn.: Tuttle, Morehouse, and Taylor, n.d.), 345.

66. "Female Dress," *Alexandria Daily Advertiser* (D.C.), 9 September 1807. For a few more examples, see editorials and letters in *Western Spy* (Cincinnati), 9 December 1806; *Enquirer*, 3 February 1807; and *People's Friend* (New York), 15 May 1807.

67. Lydia Hollingsworth to Tobin, 8 February 1815, Hollingsworth Papers, MdHS.

68. Waller Holladay to Huldah Holladay, 9 April 1804, Holladay Family Papers, ViHi.

69. Huldah Holladay to Waller Holladay, 22 April 1804, ibid. For a similar response, see Catherine Carroll Harper to Robert Goodloe Harper, 30 January [1804], Robert Goodloe Harper Papers, MdHS (microfilm edition).

70. Allgor, *Perfect Union*, 9.

71. William Burwell to Letitia Burwell, 10 January 1813, William A. Burwell Collection, DLC.

72. Margaret Bayard Smith Diary, [end of 1804] and 23 March 1806, Margaret Bayard Smith Diary, DLC.

73. Joseph C. Cabell to Isaac Coles, 17 February 1807, Cabell Family Papers, ViU.

74. "To Madame Jerome Bonaparte," *American*, 24 August 1804.

75. "Jerome Bonaparte," *Columbian Centinel* (Boston), 3 April 1805; and the *Telegraph and Daily Advertiser* (Baltimore), 26 July 1806. American media vehemence against Jerome and the Bonapartes ran deep and long. See, for an example from three years later, *The American Register: or, General Repository of History, Politics, and Science*, vol. 2, *Annals of Europe and America for 1807* (Philadelphia, 1808), 58–59.

76. "Jerome Bonaparte," *American*, 30 July 1804.

77. EPB to Mary Caton Patterson, 7 November 1816, in "Unpublished Letters," *Maryland Historical Magazine* 20 (June 1925): 123–24.

78. JB to EPB, 16 May 1808, and JB to WP, 16 May 1808, JB Papers.

79. Eliza Anderson to EPB, 2 July 1808, EPB Papers. In an earlier letter, 31 May 1808, Anderson told Elizabeth that she had heard from a French gentleman that Napoleon intended making her a "Duchess Regent of some place." That may be the origin of Elizabeth's later demand of the emperor. For a summary of Elizabeth's letter to Turreau, see Sydney Alexander Mitchell, *A Family Lawsuit: The Story of Elisabeth Patterson and Jérôme Bonaparte* (New York: Farrar, Straus, Cudahy, 1958), 166.

80. Oakley was the son of Sir Charles Oakley, the former governor of Madras, India.

81. Napoleon Bonaparte to Louis-Marie Turreau, 18 November 1808, as quoted in Mitchell, *Family Lawsuit*, 167. At the end of the letter, Napoleon ordered that "this affair must be quietly and secretly handled."

82. JB to EPB, 22 November 1808, JB Papers.

83. EPB to Alexandre Gortchakoff, 19 February [*sic*, 21 January] 1861, EPB Papers; and EPB, as quoted in Eugene L. Didier, *Life and Letters of Madame Bonaparte* (New York: Charles Scribner's Sons), 197. Elizabeth later admitted that Jerome's "ire" over her preference for Napoleon's help gave her "satisfaction & some amusement" (EPB to M. H. Torrens McCullogh, 24 January 1861, EPB Papers).

84. Turreau to Napoleon Bonaparte, April 1809, as quoted in Mitchell, *Family Lawsuit*, 167.

85. Notes, 9 July 1808, EPB Letterbook, EPB Papers.

86. EPB to Mary Caton Patterson, 7 November 1816, in "Unpublished Letters," 123–24.

87. EPB to John Armstrong, 17 March 1809, EPB Papers.

88. Turreau to Louis Tousard, 24 November 1809, in Mitchell, *Family Lawsuit*, 168–69.

89. Richard M. Johnson to Joseph Hamilton Daveiss, 20 February 1810, Joseph Hamilton Daveiss Papers, FHS.

90. *Statesman*, 28 December 1809, Clippings Booklet, EPB Papers. It is unclear exactly when Tousard abandoned his post. He was still with Elizabeth and her son in November 1810, but left soon after the arrival of the new French minister.

91. "The Bonaparte Family," *Republican and Savannah Evening Ledger* (Ga.), 23 November 1809.

92. Samuel Taggart to John W. Taylor, 12 February 1810, in "Letters of Samuel Taggart, 1803–1814," *Proceedings of the American Antiquarian Society* 33 (April–October 1923): 345.

93. Thomas Truxton, as quoted in *Guide to Truxton-Biddle Papers*, PHi, 21–22.

94. Henry Clay to George Thompson, 14 March 1810, in James F. Hopkins, ed., *Papers of Henry Clay*, vol. 1 (Lexington: University of Kentucky Press, 1959), 458.

95. [Margaret] McHenry to "Mrs. Henry," ca. March 1810, James McHenry Papers, DLC (microfilm edition).

96. Pickering, notes on "Amendment of Constitution[:] Mr. Reid resolution—with an *Addition*," [ca. 1810], Pickering Papers, MHi (microfilm edition).

97. Curt E. Conklin, "The Case of the Phantom Thirteenth Amendment: A Historical and Bibliographical Nightmare," *Law Library Journal* 88 (Winter 1996): 121–27 (quote on 124); Jol A. Silversmith, "The 'Missing Thirteenth Amendment': Constitutional Nonsense and Titles of Nobility," *Southern California Interdisciplinary Law Journal* 8 (Spring 1999):

577–611 (quote on 583). See also David E. Kyvig, *Explicit and Authentic Acts: Amending the U.S. Constitution, 1776–1995* (Lawrence: University Press of Kansas, 1996), 117.

98. In his *Amending America: If We Love the Constitution So Much, Why Do We Keep Trying to Change It?* (New York: Random House, 1993), Richard B. Bernstein remarks that Jerome Bonaparte's "liaison with a Baltimore prostitute named Betsy Patterson, whom he made pregnant," was a partial impetus for the amendment (178). That a historian could describe her as a prostitute attests to Elizabeth's troubled historical legacy. Silversmith, "The 'Missing Thirteenth Amendment,'" and John R. Vile, *Encyclopedia of Constitutional Amendments, Proposed Amendments, and Amending Issues, 1789–2002* (Santa Barbara, Calif.: ABC-CLIO, 2003), 454–55, present the threat of Elizabeth and her son as one possible reason for the amendment, but both conclude that the hatred of foreigners on the eve of war was the more likely cause.

99. Conklin, "Case of the Phantom Amendment," 124. See also Tom Pendergast, Sara Pendergast, and John Sousanis, eds., *Constitutional Amendments: From Freedom of Speech to Flag Burning*, vol. 3 (Detroit: UXL Imprint of Gale Group, 2001). Only W. H. Earle solidly places the cause of the amendment on "the lovely, witty, tragic, vain, ambitious, calculating 'Duchess of Baltimore'" ("The Phantom Amendment and the Duchess of Baltimore," *American History Illustrated* 22 [1987]: 33).

100. Johnson to Daveiss, 20 February 1810, Daveiss Papers, FHS.

101. Taggart to Taylor, 12 February 1810, in "Letters of Samuel Taggart," 345.

102. Eaton, Speech at Brimfield, Mass., Town Meeting, [ca. Fall 1808], in Charles Prentiss, *The Life of the Late Gen. William Eaton* (Brookfield, Mass.: E. Merriam, 1813), 415.

103. [John Randolph], *Letters of Mutius, Addressed to the President of the United States*, (Washington, D.C., 1810), 10–11.

104. Ibid., 9–11.

105. "Marius" [Wilson Cary Nicholas], "To Mucius," *Enquirer*, 9 March 1810.

106. *Cooperstown Federalist* (New York), 18 November 1809.

107. *Boston Gazette*, 13 November 1809.

108. "Our Liberties in Danger!!," *Raleigh Register or North-Carolina Weekly Advertiser*, 29 March 1810 (accessed in 19th Century U.S. Newspapers, Gale Digital Collections, available at http://gdc.gale.com/). The newspaper linked Jefferson to Elizabeth's uncle Robert Smith through Jefferson's son-in-law John Wayles Eppes, but Jefferson was also related to Elizabeth through Smith's sister, who was married to Peter Carr, Jefferson's nephew.

109. "The Bonaparte Family," *Republican*, 23 November 1809.

110. William Jenks, *Memoir of the Northern Kingdom, Written A.D. 1872, by the Late Rev. Williamson Jahnsenykes, Ll.D., and Hon. Member of the Royal American Board of Literature, in Six Letters to His Son* (Boston, 1808); reprint, Ed White, ed., *Journal of the Early Republic* 30 (Summer 2010): 320–22.

111. See Lewis, *American Union*, 32–40. For concerns in Washington at this time, see Richard Cutts to Thomas Cutts, 5 January 1809, in Henry S. Burrage, "Some Letters of Richard Cutts," *Collections and Proceedings of the Maine Historical Society* 9 (1898): 31–32.

112. As quoted in Earle, "Phantom Amendment," 37.

113. Augustus John Foster, *Jeffersonian America: Notes on the United States of America Collected in the Years 1805–6–7 and 11–12*, ed. Richard Beale Davis (San Marino, Calif.: Huntington Library, 1954), 67.

114. J. C. A. Stagg, *Borderlines in Borderlands: James Madison and the Spanish-American Frontier, 1776–1821* (New Haven, Conn.: Yale University Press, 2009), 281, n. 21. Stagg is referring to a letter from Onís to Francisco Saavedra, 2 February 1810.

115. Amendment, 26 April 1810, in *Annals of Congress*, Senate, 11th Cong., 2d sess., 671.

116. Robert Bayly to John Payne, 14 December 1811, John Payne Papers, DLC.

117. Mitchill to Miller, 21 November 1811, Catherine Mitchill Papers, DLC.

118. Samuel Smith to Mary B. Mansfield, 6 November 1811, Carter-Smith Family Papers, ViU.

119. EPB to Lescallier, 10 October 1811, EPB Papers.

120. George B. Milligan to "Aunt," 16 February [1812], Milligan-McLane Papers, DHi.

121. See Anna Maria Brodeau Thornton Diary, February 1810–December 1813, William Thornton Papers, DLC.

122. Samuel Smith to Mansfield, 6 November 1811, Carter-Smith Family Papers, ViU.

123. EPB to WP, 2 September 1815, in Didier, *Life and Letters*, 45.

124. See Silversmith, "The 'Missing Thirteenth Amendment,'" 585.

125. EPB to Madison, 29 December 1814, WP Papers, MS1084, MdHS (hereafter WP Papers).

126. Jonathan Russell to EPB, 20 February 1814, EPB Papers.

127. See EPB to Caroline Eustis, 6 March 1815, ibid. How much longer the annuity continued after Napoleon's return to power in March 1815 and his second exile to St. Helena is unclear.

128. EPB to Madison, 29 December 1814, WP Papers.

129. Eustis to Madison, 11 May 1815, in Holly C. Shulman, ed., *The Dolley Madison Digital Edition* (Charlottesville: University of Virginia Press, version 2009.06).

130. EPB, "Some Autobiographical Notes," ca. 1805, EPB Papers.

131. Emily Caton to Robert Goodloe Harper, 12 March 1816, Robert Goodloe Harper Papers, MdHS. EPB's love of aristocratic distinction caused Caton to respond: "poor woman! what will she be on her death bed!!"

132. EPB to WP, 22 August 1815, in Didier, *Life and Letters*, 41.

133. Anonymous [probably Samuel Colleton Graves] to EPB, 2 September 1815, EPB Papers.

134. See Steven Kale, *French Salons: High Society and Political Sociability from the Old Regime to the Revolution of 1848* (Baltimore: Johns Hopkins University Press, 2004). For a discussion of Napoleon's new nobility, see William Doyle, *Aristocracy and Its Enemies in the Age of Revolution* (New York: Oxford University Press, 2009).

135. James Gallatin Diary, July 1821, in James Gallatin, *The Great Peacemaker: The Diary of James Gallatin, Secretary to Albert Gallatin, 1813–1827* (New York: Charles Scribner's Sons, 1914), 190.

136. For the creation of this community of cosmopolitan intellectuals in eighteenth-century France, see Dena Goodman, *The Republic of Letters: A Cultural History of the French Enlightenment* (Ithaca, N.Y.: Cornell University Press, 1994).

137. My thanks to Dena Goodman for sharing her insights with me about the changing character of European cosmopolitanism and the impact of nationalism in the early nineteenth century.

138. Similarly, James McMillan has found that in mid-nineteenth-century France "the world of high society . . . no longer centered on the Court but on the haunts of the rich . . . which brought together the new elites of money, power, and talent" (*France and Women*, 57). Steven Kale has found that aristocratic émigrés established salons outside of France during their exile and that Restoration salons "mixed old aristocrats, newer elites, foreigners, and men of letters," "combining tradition and innovation" (*French Salons*, 143). See also Philipp Ziesche, *Cosmopolitan Patriots: Americans in Paris in the Age of Revolution* (Charlottesville: University of Virginia Press, 2010).

139. Washington Irving to Henry Brevoort, 8 September 1815, in Ralph M. Adermann, et al., eds., *Letters*, vol. 1 (Boston: Twayne Publishers, 1978), 422.

140. Some of these arguments come out of discussions with Dena Goodman. I am indebted to her for helping me clarify what I was seeing in EPB's writings. See her important and influential *Republic of Letters* and "Enlightenment Salons: The Convergence of Female and Philosophic Ambitions," *Eighteenth-Century Studies* 22 (Spring 1989): 329–50. An interesting question, which I cannot answer here, is how merchants and global commercialism fit with this reformed cosmopolitan community.

141. EPB to WP, 2 September 1815, in Didier, *Life and Letters*, 43.

142. Mary Caton Patterson to EPB, 2 August [1816], EPB Papers. See also Gallatin, *Great Peacemaker*, which includes numerous references to EPB and her admirers.

143. All three quotes are in Didier, *Life and Letters*, 76.

144. Gallatin Diary, 14 August 1816, in Gallatin, *Great Peacemaker*, 90–91. Gallatin added that EPB "was much gratified" to hear this.

145. EPB to WP, 2 September 1815, in Didier, *Life and Letters*, 43.

146. EPB to WP, 25 April 1820, in ibid., 63.

147. JNB to WP, ca. 1820 and 6 November 1820, in ibid., 73 and 74.

148. EPB to WP, 23 September 1815, in ibid., 47 and 49.

149. Margaret Manigault to Josephine du Pont, 19 June 1814, in Betty-Bright P. Low, ed., "The Youth of 1812: More Excerpts from the Letters of Josephine du Pont and Margaret Manigault," *Winterthur Portfolio* 11 (1976): 201.

150. Edward Patterson to EPB, 11 January 1817, EPB Papers.

151. Edward Patterson to EPB, 15 December 1815, ibid. (emphasis added).

152. Charles Carroll to Elizabeth Caton, 22 May 1817, Charles Carroll Papers, MdHS (microfilm edition).

153. EPB to WP, 6 October 1825, in Didier, *Life and Letters*, 167.

154. Gallatin Diary, 19 December 1815, 15 January 1822, and 30 November 1822, in Gallatin, *Great Peacemaker*, 81, 196, and 224.

155. EPB to WP, 4 December 1829, in Didier, *Life and Letters*, 218–19.

156. EPB to John Spear Smith, 22 August 1816, EPB Papers.

157. EPB to WP, 11 and 24 December 1822, in Didier, *Life and Letters*, 114, 116. Indeed, according to Elizabeth, Le Loup "was the admiration of all who saw him here [in Geneva], and every one knew him. When he walked with me, many unknown to me used to call him by his name and bid him good day" (116).

158. EPB to Gortchakoff, ca. 1832, as quoted in Claude Bourguignon-Frasseto, *Betsy Bonaparte: The Belle of Baltimore*, trans. Elborg Forster (Baltimore: Maryland Historical Society, 2003), 241.

159. EPB to SM, 14 March 1849, in Didier, *Life and Letters*, 253.

160. Kilbride, *American Aristocracy*, 2.

161. Harman Blennerhassett Diary, 18 October 1807, in Raymond E. Fitch, ed., *Breaking with Burr: Harman Blennerhassett's Journal, 1807* (Athens: Ohio University Press, 1988), 134. Blennerhassett added that Randolph had "cordially hoped, whenever [Aaron] Burr or anyone else, again attempted to do anything, the Atlantic States would be comprised in the plan" (135). Blennerhassett had just been released from prison after being indicted as one of Burr's co-conspirators.

162. Benjamin Henry Latrobe to Philip Mazzei, 19 December 1806, in John C. Van Horne and Lee W. Formwalt, eds., *The Correspondence and Miscellaneous Papers of Benjamin Henry Latrobe*, 4 vols. (New Haven, Conn.: Yale University Press, 1984–88), 2:330. In his *Coming to Terms with Democracy*, Marshall Foletta has similarly found more conservative Americans in the 1810s and 1820s who despaired of the United States ever producing genteel society or great literature because the "egalitarian structure of American society" and "the daily life of a republican society contained [not] enough romance, intrigue, and adventure" (82). Eve Kornfeld, in *Creating an American Culture*, has concluded that after 1815, "American intellectual leaders came to see more excitement than danger in European culture" and dismissed American culture as "too small . . . and provincial" (78).

163. Gallatin Diary, 29 January 1823, 4 July 1823, and 30 November 1822, in Gallatin, *Great Peacemaker*, 235, 244, and 224.

164. EPB to WP, 21 December 1829, in Didier, *Life and Letters*, 221.

165. James Fenimore Cooper, *Gleanings in Europe: France* (reprint, Albany: State University of New York Press, 1983), 18.

166. EPB to WP, 22 May 1823, in Didier, *Life and Letters*, 142.

167. EPB to Mary Caton Patterson, 7 November 1816, EPB Papers.

168. EPB to WP, 4 December 1829, in Didier, *Life and Letters*, 219.

169. Anne (Nancy) Spear to EPB, 17 November [1816], EPB Papers.

170. EPB to John Spear Smith, 22 August 1816, ibid.

171. Spear to EPB, 20 May 1816, ibid.

172. EPB to John Spear Smith, 22 August 1816, ibid.

173. Edward Patterson to EPB, 6 March 1816, ibid. Harvey Levenstein has noted that many Americans traveled to Europe in the first half of the nineteenth century for the status a visit there would bring them. See *Seductive Journey*, 28.

174. Minnie Clare Yarborough, ed., *The Reminiscences of William C. Preston* (Chapel Hill: University of North Carolina Press, 1933), 60.

175. See Daniel Kilbride, "Travel, Ritual, and National Identity: Planters on the European Tour, 1820–1860," *Journal of Southern History* 69 (August 2003): 549–84; Levenstein, *Seductive Journey*; and William W. Stowe, *Going Abroad: European Travel in Nineteenth-Century American Culture* (Princeton, N.J.: Princeton University Press, 1994).

176. EPB to John Spear Smith, 22 August 1816, EPB Papers.

177. Fanny W. Hall, *Rambles in Europe: Or, a Tour Through France, Italy, Switzerland, Great Britain, and Ireland, in 1836*, vol. 1 (New York: E. French, 1839), 151–52.

178. James Brown to Samuel Smith, 12 March 1829, Samuel Smith Papers, DLC.

179. Eliza Godefroy to EPB, 29 March 1816, EPB Papers.

180. EPB to John Spear Smith, 22 August 1816, ibid.

181. John Spear Smith to EPB, 18 April 1816, and Spear to EPB, 1 May 1816, ibid.

182. Godefroy to EPB, 10 May 1817, ibid. See also Emily Caton to Robert Goodloe Harper, 12 March 1816, Robert Goodloe Harper Papers, MdHS.

183. EPB to WP, 2 September 1815, in Didier, *Life and Letters*, 44–45.

184. Cooper to Mrs. Peter Augustus Jay, 26 July 1830, in James Franklin Beard, ed., *The Letters and Journals of James Fenimore Cooper*, vol. 1 (Cambridge, Mass.: Harvard University Press, 1960), 427. Cooper described Jerome's wife Catherine as "a good natured, fat personage" who was "a little absurd on account of her airs of Royalty."

185. EPB to John Spear Smith, 22 August 1816, EPB Papers.

186. James McElhiney to EPB, 18 September 1817, ibid.

Chapter 3. "A Modern *Philosophe*"

1. Benjamin W. LeCompte, note, ca. December 1812, as quoted in "Betsy Patterson's Petition for Divorce Found in Desk," unidentified newspaper clipping, 17 or 18 December 1933, in Newspaper Clipping File, MdHS.

2. William B. Barney to EPB, 2 December 1812, EPB Papers, MS142, MdHS (hereafter EPB Papers).

3. William Burwell to Letitia Burwell, 20 December 1812, William A. Burwell Collection, DLC.

4. EPB to Pierre Antoine Berryer, 3 December 1857, EPB Papers. According to Elizabeth, "none of the papers or proofs in the case were ever preserved" (EPB to Berryer, 3 June 1858, ibid.). Her papers include copies of her petition for the divorce, the original committee bill, some extracts of the assembly's proceedings, and the final bill.

5. EPB, Account Book, ca. 1858, ibid.

6. EPB, draft petition for divorce, [ca. November 1813], enclosed in Barney to EPB, 2 December 1812, ibid. The words "Brother" and "Napoleon" had been crossed through.

7. "Extracts—Acts & Proceedings of House of Delegates & Senate of Maryland on Act No. 130 annulling Marriage of JB & EB," ibid.

8. Barney to EPB, 2 December 1812, ibid.

9. Barney to EPB, 16 December 1812, ibid.

10. Barney to Robert Patterson, 15 December 1812, ibid.

11. John F. Mifflin to Thomas Law, 16 December 1812, Thomas Law Papers, DLC.

12. William Burwell to Letitia Burwell, 20 December 1812, William A. Burwell Collection, DLC.

13. William Burwell to Letitia Burwell, 10 January 1813, ibid.

14. Both Rosemarie Zagarri, in *Revolutionary Backlash: Women and Politics in the Early American Republic* (Philadelphia: University of Pennsylvania Press, 2007), and Sarah Fatherly, in *Gentlewomen and Learned Ladies: Women and Elite Formation in Eighteenth-Century Philadelphia* (Bethlehem, Pa.: Lehigh University Press, 2008), examine the phenomenon of "female politicians," though Fatherly locates it earlier, well before the Revolution. Mary Kelley, in *Learning to Stand and Speak: Women, Education, and Public Life in America's Republic* (Chapel Hill: University of North Carolina Press, 2006), explores the ways in which women functioned as key members of civil society. Some of the classic works on republican wives and mothers include Linda Kerber, *Women of the Republic: Intellect and Ideology in Revolutionary America* (Chapel Hill: University of North Carolina Press, 1980); Mary Beth Norton, *Liberty's Daughters: The Revolutionary Experience of American Women, 1750–1800* (Boston: Little, Brown, 1980); Jan Lewis, "The Republican Wife: Virtue and Seduction in the Early Republic," *William and Mary Quarterly* 44 (Oc-

tober 1987): 689–721; Kerber, et al., "Beyond Roles, Beyond Spheres: Thinking About Gender in the Early Republic," *William and Mary Quarterly* 46 (July 1989): 565–85; and Zagarri, "Morals, Manners, and the Republican Mother," *American Quarterly* 44 (June 1992): 26–43. See also Sheila L. Skemp's introduction to *Judith Sargent Murray: A Brief Biography with Documents* (New York: Bedford, 1998).

15. Susan Branson, *These Fiery Frenchified Dames: Women and Political Culture in Early National Philadelphia* (Philadelphia: University of Pennsylvania Press, 2001), 5.

16. See Zagarri, *Revolutionary Backlash*, 2; and Kelley, *Learning to Stand and Speak*, 26. See also Jan Lewis's important essay, "Politics and the Ambivalence of the Private Sphere: Women in Early Washington, D.C.," in *A Republic for the Ages: The United States Capitol and the Political Culture of the Early Republic*, ed. Donald R. Kennon (Charlottesville: University Press of Virginia, 1999), 122–51.

17. For examples of other women who were playing with, violating, and creating new gender parameters, see Branson, *Dangerous to Know: Women, Crime, and Notoriety in the Early Republic* (Philadelphia: University of Pennsylvania Press, 2008); Marion Rust, *Prodigal Daughters: Susanna Rowson's Early American Women* (Chapel Hill: University of North Carolina Press, 2008); and Sheila Skemp, *First Lady of Letters: Judith Sargent Murray and the Struggle for Independence* (Philadelphia: University of Pennsylvania Press, 2009). Mary Kelley also finds that the decades after the Revolution were marked by "relatively fluid gender distinctions," but became "increasingly freighted with ideological determinism" by the beginning of the antebellum era (*Learning to Stand and Speak*, 52).

18. Lewis, "Politics and the Ambivalence of the Private Sphere," 124–25.

19. Carolyn Eastman, review of Zagarri, *Revolutionary Backlash*, on H-SHEAR, available at http://by111w.bay111.mail.live.com (accessed 11 September 2008). Kelley's *Learning to Stand and Speak* has also greatly shaped my understanding of civil society in this era.

20. See Mary Catherine Moran, "From Rudeness to Refinement: Gender, Genre and Scottish Enlightenment Discourse" (Ph.D. diss., Johns Hopkins University, 1999). See also Fatherly, *Gentlewomen and Learned Ladies*, and Steven Kale, *French Salons: High Society and Political Sociability from the Old Regime to the Revolution of 1848* (Baltimore: Johns Hopkins University Press, 2004).

21. Christopher L. Doyle, "The Randolph Scandal in Early National Virginia, 1792–1815: New Voices in the 'Court of Honor,'" *Journal of Southern History* 69 (May 2003): 304. Doyle examines the response to Nancy Randolph, another woman whose "manless" freedom led her beyond the acceptable bounds of womanhood in the new nation, though in a very different way than Elizabeth. See also Victoria Bynum, *Unruly Women: The Politics of Social and Sexual Control in the Old South* (Chapel Hill: University of North Carolina Press, 1992), and Cynthia Kierner, *Scandal at Bizarre: Rumor and Reputation in Jefferson's America* (New York: Palgrave Macmillan, 2004).

22. See Kelley, *Learning to Stand and Speak*, especially chap. 3.

23. See Kelley, *Learning to Stand and Speak*, and Lucia McMahon, "'Of the Utmost Importance to Our Country': Women, Education, and Society, 1780–1820," *Journal of the Early Republic* 29 (Fall 2009): 475–506.

24. See Caroline Winterer, "The Female World of Classical Reading in Eighteenth-Century America," in *Reading Women: Literacy, Authorship, and Culture in the Atlantic World, 1500–1800*, ed. Heidi Brayman Hackel and Catherine E. Kelly (Philadelphia:

University of Pennsylvania Press, 2008), 105–23. Some of the important works on women and reading in this period include Cathy N. Davidson, *Revolution and the Word: The Rise of the Novel in America* (New York: Oxford University Press, 1986); Kelley, *Learning to Stand and Speak*; Catherine Kerrison, *Claiming the Pen: Women and Intellectual Life in the Early American South* (Ithaca, N.Y.: Cornell University Press, 2006); Ruth Perry, *Women, Letters, and the Novel* (New York: AMS Press, 1980); and Skemp, *First Lady of Letters*.

25. Eugene L. Didier, *The Life and Letters of Madame Bonaparte* (New York: Charles Scribner's Sons, 1879), 5.

26. Kelley has noted that De Staël served as a model for many young, educated women through the mid-nineteenth century (see *Learning to Stand and Speak*, 171–72 and 233).

27. Rosalie Stier Calvert to Madame H. J. Stier, November 1803, in Margaret Law Callcott, ed., *Mistress of Riversdale: The Plantation Letters of Rosalie Stier Calvert, 1795–1821* (Baltimore: Johns Hopkins University Press, 1991), 62.

28. Eliza Godefroy to EPB, 8 June [1815], EPB Papers.

29. I found helpful Katherine Gray, "'A Brilliant Assemblage of Both Sexes': Youthful Heterosociability and the Magazine in the Early Republic," and Lucia McMahon, "'The Union of Reason and Love': Reading and Writing Courtship in the Early American Republic" (papers presented at the annual meeting of the Society for Historians of the Early American Republic, Springfield, Ill., 17 July 2009). See also John Fea, *The Way of Improvement Leads Home: Philip Vickers Fithian and the Rural Enlightenment in Early America* (Philadelphia: University of Pennsylvania Press, 2008); Charlene Boyer Lewis, *Ladies and Gentlemen on Display: Planter Society at the Virginia Springs, 1790–1860* (Charlottesville: University of Virginia Press, 2001), chap. 3; and Lucia McMahon, "'While Our Souls Together Blend': Narrating a Romantic Readership in the Early Republic," in *An Emotional History of the United States*, ed. Peter N. Stearns and Jan Lewis (New York: New York University Press, 1998), 66–90.

30. E. Smith and Smith Nicholas to EPB, February 1802, EPB Papers.

31. Ibid.

32. *Baltimore Patriot and Evening Advertiser*, 23 May 1814.

33. Eliza Southgate to Moses Porter, [ca. 1800], in [Clarence Cook, ed.], *A Girl's Life Eighty Years Ago: Selections from the Letters of Eliza Southgate Bowne* (New York: Charles Scribner's Sons, 1887; reprint, Williamstown, Mass.: Corner House Publishers, 1980), 37–38.

34. Samuel Smith to John Hollins, 25 October 1803, Carter-Smith Family Papers, ViU.

35. Calvert to Stier, November 1803, in Callcott, *Mistress of Riversdale*, 62.

36. Robert Patterson to WP, 28 March 1804, in W. T. R. Saffell, ed., *The Bonaparte-Patterson Marriage in 1803, and the Secret Correspondence on the Subject Never Before Made Public* (Philadelphia: W. T. R. Saffell, 1873), 64.

37. JB to EPB, 7 and 16 October 1805, in Sydney Alexander Mitchell, *A Family Lawsuit: The Story of Elisabeth Patterson and Jérôme Bonaparte* (New York: Farrar, Straus, Cudahy, 1958), 102–103.

38. JB to EPB, 23 May 1806, in ibid., 106.

39. Ibid.

40. "Jerome Bonaparte," *Scioto Gazette* (Chillicothe, Ohio), 2 September 1805.

41. Newspaper clipping, ca. 1805–1810, Newspaper Clipping File, EPB Papers. In 1806, Eliza Southgate Bowne compared another American woman recently married to a

Frenchman to "Madame Jerome Buonoparte and many other poor Madames that have founded their hopes on the fidelity of a Frenchman" (*A Girl's Life Eighty Years Ago* [Boston: Charles Scribner's Sons, 1887; reprint, Williamstown, Mass: Corner House, 1980], 214.)

42. EPB to Mrs. M. H. Torrens McCullogh, 24 January 1861, ibid.

43. EPB, Account Book, ca. 1858, ibid.

44. EPB to WP, 4 December 1829, in Didier, *Life and Letters*, 218.

45. Eliza Anderson to EPB, 4 June 1808, EPB Papers.

46. See Catherine E. Kelly, *In the New England Fashion: Reshaping Women's Lives in the Nineteenth Century* (Ithaca, N.Y.: Cornell University Press, 1999).

47. EPB to [Eliza Monroe], ca. July–August 1805, EPB Papers.

48. James Monroe to EPB, 6 November 1808, ibid.

49. EPB to James Monroe, 15 October 1808, James Monroe Papers, DLC (microfilm edition).

50. James Monroe to EPB, 6 November 1808, EPB Papers.

51. EPB to Auguste Le Camus, 17 March 1809, ibid.

52. EPB to Napoleon Bonaparte, ca. 1809, as quoted in Claude Bourguignon-Frasseto, *Betsy Bonaparte: The Belle of Baltimore*, trans. Elborg Forster (Baltimore: Maryland Historical Society, 2003), 90.

53. EPB to Napoleon Bonaparte, ca. 1811, as quoted in ibid., 93.

54. EPB to McCullogh, 24 January 1861, EPB Papers.

55. EPB, notes on conversation with Louis-Marie Turreau, 24 March 1809, ibid. Of course, she blamed this on Jerome who "ought to have, when he bartered me for the Crown of Westphalia[,] made a pecuniary provision for me, which would have saved me from the insolent pretensions of Turreau as well as the horrible treatment of my father & his Sons Robert & John" (EPB, marginalia, 1 May 1857, "Notes," 9 July 1808, EPB Letterbook, EPB Papers).

56. Louis Sérurier to Duc de Bassano, 24 July 1811, in Mitchell, *Family Lawsuit*, 171.

57. See Lee Virginia Chambers-Schiller, *Liberty a Better Husband: Single Women in America: The Generations of 1780–1840* (New Haven, Conn.: Yale University Press, 1984); Clare A. Lyons, *Sex Among the Rabble: An Intimate History of Gender and Power in the Age of Revolution, Philadelphia, 1730–1830* (Chapel Hill: University of North Carolina Press, 2006); Kirsten Wood, *Masterful Women: Slaveholding Widows from the American Revolution Through the Civil War* (Chapel Hill: University of North Carolina Press, 2004); and Karin Wulf, *Not All Wives: Women of Colonial Philadelphia* (Philadelphia: University of Pennsylvania Press, 2000).

58. James Wilkinson to Samuel Smith, 2 November 1808, James Wilkinson Papers, Darlington Memorial Library, University of Pittsburgh, Pennsylvania.

59. Samuel Colleton Graves to EPB, 16 May 1808, EPB Papers.

60. Lydia Hollingsworth to Ruth Tobin, 12 August 1809, Hollingsworth Papers, MdHS.

61. John Carroll to Elizabeth Carroll, 18 August 1809, in Thomas O'Brien Hanley, ed., *The John Carroll Papers*, vol. 3 (South Bend, Ind.: University of Notre Dame Press, 1976), 92.

62. Joseph Patterson to EPB, 25 April 1812, EPB Papers.

63. Henry Lee, Jr., to EPB, 19 March 1813, ibid.

64. William Johnson, Jr., to EPB, 28 March 1814, ibid.

65. Washington Irving to James Renwick, 18 December 1812, in Ralph M. Adermann et al., eds., *Letters*, vol. 1 (Boston: Twayne, 1978), 350.

66. For Martha Ballard, see Laurel Thatcher Ulrich, *A Midwife's Tale: The Life of Martha Ballard, Based on Her Diary, 1785–1812* (New York: Vintage, 1990); for Elizabeth Wirt, see Anya Jabour, *Marriage in the Early Republic: Elizabeth and William Wirt and the Companionate Ideal* (Baltimore: Johns Hopkins University Press, 1998).

67. Aaron Burr to Theodosia Burr Alston, 17 January 1804, in Matthew L. Davis, *Memoirs of Aaron Burr: With Miscellaneous Selections from His Correspondence*, vol. 2 (New York: Harper and Brothers, 1836–37), 269.

68. F. Calsey to Pierre Van Cortlandt, Jr., 27 June 1812, in Jacob Judd, ed., *Correspondence of the Van Cortlandt Family of Cortlandt Manor, 1800–1814*, vol. 3 (Tarrytown, N.Y.: Sleepy Hollow Restorations, 1978), 540–42.

69. Jeremiah Mason to Mrs. Mason, 12 December 1813, in G. J. Clark, *Memoirs of Jeremiah Mason* (Boston: Boston Law Book, 1917), 68. Clark mistakenly identified the "Madame Bonaparte" who had a house near Mason's lodgings as Josephine Beauharnais Bonaparte.

70. Elbridge Gerry to Ann Gerry, 1813, in "Letters of Elbridge Gerry, 1797–1814," *Proceedings of the Massachusetts Historical Society* 47 (1914): 485, 487.

71. Horace Holley to EPB, 2 April 1818, EPB Papers.

72. Quoted in Mitchell, *Family Lawsuit*, 169. Frances Few described Turreau as "a tall thin man with enormo[u]s whiskers and long cue both of which he loads with powder and pomatum—he paints his eye-brows and had altogether a most firocious appearance" (Frances Few Diary, 2 December 1808, in Noble E. Cunningham, Jr., ed., "The Diary of Frances Few, 1808–1809," *Journal of Southern History* 29 [August 1963]: 352–53).

73. B. Smith to John Spear Smith, 24 December [1810], Samuel Smith Papers, DLC (microfilm edition).

74. EPB, marginalia, 1 May 1857, "Notes," 9 July 1808, EPB Letterbook, EPB Papers.

75. Catherine Carroll Harper to Robert Goodloe Harper, 18 February 1805, Robert Goodloe Harper Papers, MdHS.

76. Godefroy to EPB, [ca. 1810], EPB Papers.

77. William Burwell to Letitia Burwell, 20 December 1812, Burwell Collection, DLC.

78. B. M. to EPB, 26 January 1816, EPB Papers.

79. EPB to Admiral Graves and Samuel Colleton Graves, 16 May 1809, ibid.

80. EPB to WP, 2 September 1815, in Didier, *Life and Letters*, 45.

81. EPB to SM, 11 August 1817 and 23 May 1818, in W. Hepworth Dixon, ed., *Lady Morgan's Memoirs*, vol. 2 (London: W. H. Allen, 1862; reprint, New York: AMS Press, 1975), 66, 81.

82. Godefroy to EPB, 8 June [1815], EPB Papers.

83. See Glenda Riley, *Divorce: An American Tradition* (New York: Oxford University Press, 1991), 34. For divorce in Maryland, see James S. Van Ness, "On Untieing the Knot: The Maryland Legislature and Divorce Petitions," *Maryland Historical Magazine* 67 (Summer 1972): 171–75.

84. See Riley, *Divorce*, 54.

85. Anonymous, memoirs, quoted in Samuel Eliot Morison, ed., *The Life and Letters of Harrison Gray Otis, Federalist, 1765–1848*, vol. 1 (Boston: Houghton Mifflin, 1913), 137. Maria Bingham later married Henry Baring, who then divorced her after her affair with another man. After this second divorce, she married a French nobleman in Napoleon's service.

86. See Riley, *Divorce*, 54.

87. Anonymous note, ca. December 1812, as quoted in "Betsy Patterson's Petition for Divorce Found in Desk," newspaper clipping, 17 or 18 December 1933, in Newspaper Clipping File, MdHS.

88. Anderson to EPB, 4 June 1808, EPB Papers.

89. Anderson to EPB, 8 June [probably August] 1808, ibid.

90. Edward Patterson to EPB, 7 April 1817, ibid.

91. Ann Tousard to EPB, ca. 7 December 1818, ibid.

92. Catherine Carroll Harper to Robert Goodloe Harper, ca. 1804, Harper Papers, MdHS.

93. Elbridge Gerry to Ann Gerry, 1813, in "Letters of Elbridge Gerry," 487.

94. Margaret Bayard Smith to Mrs. Andrew Kirkpatrick, 17 October 1804, Margaret Bayard Smith Papers, DLC.

95. Sally McKean Yrujo to Dolley Madison, 20 June 1812, in David Mattern and Holly C. Shulman, eds., *Selected Letters of Dolley Payne Madison* (Charlottesville: University of Virginia Press, 2003), 167.

96. EPB to David Bailie Warden, 1 April 1818, David Bailie Warden Papers, MdHS.

97. See Riley, *Divorce*, and Lyons, *Sex Among the Rabble*.

98. See Lyons, *Sex Among the Rabble*, and Wulf, *Not All Wives*.

99. Kelley, *Learning to Stand and Speak*, 78.

100. Ibid., 7. See also David S. Shields and Fredrika Teute, "The Republican Court and the Historiography of a Women's Domain in the Public Sphere" (paper presented at the annual meeting of the Society for Historians of the Early American Republic, Boston, 15 July 1994), 2–3. My thanks to David and Fredrika for allowing me to cite their paper.

101. Zagarri, *Revolutionary Backlash*, 5. See also Catherine Allgor, *Parlor Politics: In Which the Ladies of Washington Help Build A City and a Government* (Charlottesville: University of Virginia Press, 2000), and *A Perfect Union: Dolley Madison and the Creation of the American Nation* (New York: Henry Holt, 2006).

102. Known as the "undisputed queen of the Republican Court," Bingham's status rested on her experiences in England and her importation of manners and style from there to the United States (Morison, *Life and Letters of Harrison Gray Otis*, 1:134). See also Branson, *Fiery Frenchified Dames*, 133–36; Wendy Anne Nicholson, "Making the Private Public: Anne Willing Bingham's Role as a Leader of Philadelphia's Social Elite in the Late Eighteenth Century" (M.A. thesis, University of Delaware, 1988); and Caroline Winterer, *The Mirror of Antiquity: American Women and the Classical Tradition, 1750–1900* (Ithaca, N.Y.: Cornell University Press, 2007), 113–15. For other women who led salons as a part of their role in shaping the new nation, see Daniel Kilbride, "Cultivation, Conservatism, and the Early National Gentry: The Manigault Family and Their Circle," *Journal of the Early Republic* 19 (Summer 1999): 221–56.

103. Robert C. Alberts, *The Golden Voyage: The Life and Times of William Bingham, 1752–1804* (Boston: Houghton Mifflin, 1969), 142–47, as quoted in Branson, *Fiery Frenchified Dames*, 134.

104. Margaret Bayard Smith Diary, 17 September 1806, Margaret Bayard Smith Papers, DLC.

105. Margaret Bayard Smith Diary, 23 March 1806, ibid.

106. See David S. Shields, *Civil Tongues and Polite Letters in British America* (Chapel Hill: University of North Carolina Press, 1997), 320–22, and his comments at "Whither the Early Republic: A Roundtable Prognostication" (presented at the annual meeting of the Society for Historians of the Early Republic, Providence, Rhode Island, 24 July 2004). See also Patricia Brady, *Martha Washington: An American Life* (New York: Viking, 2005), chaps. 9 and 10.

107. See Allgor, *Parlor Politics*, chap. 4, and *Perfect Union*. See also Winterer, *Mirror of Antiquity*, chap. 4. As David Shields and Fredrika Teute have noted, these American *salonnières* created a national style that "married the manners of European gentility with the morals of post-revolutionary American republicanism" ("Republican Court," 4).

108. Winterer, *Mirror of Antiquity*, 109. For Margaret Bayard Smith's influence specifically, see Fredrika J. Teute, "Roman Matron on the Banks of Tiber Creek: Margaret Bayard Smith and the Politicization of Spheres in the Nation's Capital," in Kennon, *Republic for the Ages*, 89–121.

109. For a discussion of the many significant elements of these Grecian-style portraits, see Winterer, *Mirror of Antiquity*, chap. 4.

110. Winterer has noted that this style of dress little resembled actual female gowns of ancient Greece and that these gowns pushed women's breasts up into "two high, distinct orbs, as though announcing the new republican vogue for breast-feeding" (*Mirror of Antiquity*, 122–24 [quote on 122]).

111. Quoted in Elisabeth McClellan, *Historic Dress in America, 1607–1870*, vol. 2 (New York: Benjamin Blom, 1904–10), 26.

112. William Plumer, Jr., to Margaret F. Mead, 13 January 1820, William Plumer, Jr., Papers, NYHS.

113. Jeremiah Mason to Mrs. Mason, 23 January 1814, in Clark, *Memoirs of Jeremiah Mason*, 73.

114. Isaac Coles to Joseph C. Cabell, 4 February 1807, Cabell Family Papers, ViU. Cabell held similar sentiments about fashionable women; see Cabell to Coles, 17 February 1807, ibid.

115. *A Series of Letters on Courtship and Marriage* (Hartford, Conn.: Lincoln and Gleason, 1806), 117–18.

116. Daniel Kilbride, "Avoiding a 'Little, Mean [and] Despicable' Republic: Privileged Women and the Cultural Work of the Grand Tour in the Post-revolutionary Era" (paper presented at the annual meeting of the Society for Historians of the Early American Republic, Buffalo, N.Y., July 2000). I thank Dan for permission to quote from this work.

117. Horace Holley to Mary Austin Holley, 3 April 1818, Horace Holley Papers, MiU.

118. EPB to John Spear Smith, 22 August 1816, EPB Papers. The passing of apples and nuts was a common evening entertainment in American households. See Mary Guion Diary, 5 November 1804, Mary Guion Diary, NYHS.

119. EPB to SM, 23 May 1818, in Dixon, *Lady Morgan's Memoirs*, 81.

120. Horace Holley Diary, 19 March 1818, Holley Papers, MiU. In this entry, Holley recorded a dinner conversation he had had with Elizabeth, noting that she "talked with great raciness."

121. Branson, *Fiery Frenchified Dames*, 142. See also Allgor, *Parlor Politics*, and Lewis, "Politics and the Ambivalence of the Private Sphere."

122. Mary Caton Patterson to EPB, 10 February 1816, EPB Papers.

123. See John Law to Mrs. Law, 15 March 1806, Thomas Law Family Papers, MdHS; Frances Purviance to Mary Anne Breckinridge, 25 February ca. 1819, Breckinridge-Watts Family Papers, ViU; and James Brown to Samuel Smith, 10 October 1826, Samuel Smith Papers, DLC.

124. Catherine Mitchill to Margaret Miller, 21 November 1811, Catherine Mitchill Papers, DLC.

125. Jeremiah Mason to Mary Mason, 25 December 1813, in Clark, *Memoirs of Jeremiah Mason*, 73.

126. James Brown to Samuel Smith, 10 August 182[7], Samuel Smith Papers, DLC.

127. Brown to Samuel Smith, 28 January 1828, ibid.

128. Mitchill to Miller, 3 April 1806, Mitchill Papers, DLC.

129. Few to Maria Nicholson, 29 January 1809, in Cunningham, "Diary of Frances Few," 355 n. 45.

130. Jeremiah Mason to Mary Mason, 23 January 1814 and 2 November 1814, in Clark, *Memoirs of Jeremiah Mason*, 73, 97.

131. Augustus John Foster, *Jeffersonian America: Notes on the United States of America Collected in the Years 1805-6-7 and 11-12*, ed. Richard Beale Davis (San Marino, Calif.: Huntington Library, 1954), 280.

132. Mary Caton Patterson to EPB, 10 February 1816, EPB Papers.

133. John White to EPB, 23 January 1833, ibid.

134. White to EPB, 27 April 1833, ibid.

135. [Anne (Nancy) Spear] to EPB, 6 April 1833, ibid.

136. White to EPB, 23 January 1833, ibid.

137. [Spear] to EPB, 6 April 1833, ibid.

138. For the acceptance of the former, see Lyons, *Sex Among the Rabble*; Wood, *Masterful Women*; and Wulf, *Not All Wives*.

139. EPB to Alexandre Gortchakoff, ca. 1858, EPB Papers.

140. James Gallatin Diary, March 1819, in James Gallatin, *A Great Peacemaker: The Diary of James Gallatin* (New York: Charles Scribner's Sons, 1914), 145.

141. "Mrs. Patterson (formerly Mrs. Bonaparte)," 1818 Assessment, Ward 7, City Assessor Tax records, Record Group 452, reel 196, Baltimore City Archives.

142. EPB, notes regarding pension from French Government, 1809–1812, EPB Papers.

143. Samuel Smith to Mary B. Mansfield, 28 May 1825, Carter-Smith Family Papers, ViU.

144. Lee to EPB, 19 March 1813, EPB Papers.

145. White to EPB, 26 October 1830, ibid.

146. Spear to EPB, [1815], ibid.

147. Spear to EPB, 14 January [1817], ibid.

148. Spear to EPB, 19 September [1816], ibid.

149. Spear to EPB, 12 April 1827, ibid.

150. EPB to Warden, 8 November 1817, Warden Papers, MdHS.

151. EPB to WP, 28 November 1826, in Didier, *Life and Letters*, 191–92.

152. White to EPB, 26 October 1830, EPB Papers.

153. White to EPB, 14 April 1833, ibid.

154. Spear to EPB, 19 May 1833, ibid.

155. EPB to WP, 24 September 1831, in Didier, *Life and Letters*, 234–35.

Chapter 4. "Happiness for a Woman"

1. EPB to SM, 28 November 1816, in W. Hepworth Dixon, ed., *Lady Morgan's Memoirs*, vol. 2 (London: W. H. Allen, 1862; reprint, New York: AMS Press, 1975), 45.

2. Dixon, editorial introduction, ibid., 40.

3. EPB to SM, 23 September 1816, ibid., 42.

4. "Madame Patterson-Bonaparte," *Lippincott's Magazine of Popular Literature and Science* 20 (September 1877): 318.

5. See Mary Campbell, *Lady Morgan: The Life and Times of Sydney Owenson* (London: Pandora, 1988); and Elizabeth Suddaby and P. J. Yarrow, eds., *Lady Morgan in France* (Newcastle upon Tyne, U.K.: Oriel, 1971).

6. EPB to SM, 8 May 1817, in Dixon, *Lady Morgan's Memoirs*, 63.

7. EPB to John Spear Smith, 22 August 1816, EPB Papers, MS142, MdHS (hereafter EPB Papers).

8. Ibid.

9. EPB to SM, 28 November 1816, in Dixon, *Lady Morgan's Memoirs*, 2:45.

10. SM, *France* (1817), quoted in Suddaby and Yarrow, *Lady Morgan in France*, 72.

11. EPB to Mary Caton Patterson, 12 February 1816, EPB Papers.

12. EPB to John Spear Smith, 22 August 1816, ibid.

13. EPB to SM, 8 May 1817, in Dixon, *Lady Morgan's Memoirs*, 62.

14. SM, *France*, 2 vols. (London: Colburn, 1817), 2:412.

15. Ibid., 412–13.

16. EPB to SM, 8 May 1817, in Dixon, *Lady Morgan's Memoirs*, 63.

17. SM to EPB, 13 January 1826, EPB Papers.

18. EPB to SM, 22 September 1839, in Dixon, *Lady Morgan's Memoirs*, 454.

19. See Andrew Cayton, comment on "Secession in Early Kentucky" panel (paper presented at the Fourth Academic Conference of the Filson Institute, Louisville, Ky., 22 October 2010).

20. See William Doyle, *Aristocracy and Its Enemies in the Age of Revolution* (New York: Oxford University Press, 2009); Philip Mansel, *Paris Between Empires, 1814–1852* (London: John Murray, 2001); and Isser Woloch, *The New Regime: Transformations of the French Civic Order, 1789–1820s* (New York: Norton, 1994).

21. See Denise Z. Davidson, *France After Revolution: Urban Life, Gender, and the New Social Order* (Cambridge, Mass.: Harvard University Press, 2007), 2.

22. Mansel, *Paris Between Empires*, 140.

23. EPB to WP, 6 October 1825, in Eugene L. Didier, *The Life and Letters of Madame Bonaparte* (New York: Charles Scribner's Sons, 1879), 168.

24. For other independent women who successfully crafted transatlantic, or even global, identities in this era, see Patricia Cleary, *Elizabeth Murray: A Woman's Pursuit of Independence in Eighteenth-Century America* (Amherst: University of Massachusetts Press, 2003); and Linda Colley's brilliant *The Ordeal of Elizabeth Marsh: A Woman in World History* (New York: Anchor, 2007).

25. See Davidson, *France After Revolution*, 4. Davidson recognizes that "ideas about gender complementarity could force women into roles that were as narrowly defined as those put forth in domestic ideology" (138).

26. Robert R. Livingston to Samuel Baird, 28 May 1802, as quoted in George Dangerfield, *Chancellor Robert R. Livingston of New York, 1746–1813* (New York: Harcourt, Brace, 1960), 321.

27. James F. McMillan, *France and Women, 1789–1914* (New York: Routledge, 2000), 36–41. McMillan notes that "some lawyers, indeed, feared that . . . the whole spirit, let alone the letter, of the Code was constantly subverted" (39).

28. John White to EPB, 26 October 1830, EPB Papers.

29. Steven Kale, *French Salons: High Society and Political Sociability from the Old Regime to the Revolution of 1848* (Baltimore: Johns Hopkins University Press, 2004), 13.

30. European women's historians generally arrive at the same conclusions drawn by Elizabeth. See, for example, Amanda Foreman, *Georgiana: Duchess of Devonshire* (New York: Random House, 2000); Dena Goodman, *The Republic of Letters: A Cultural History of the French Enlightenment* (Ithaca, N.Y.: Cornell University Press, 1994); and Amanda Vickery, *The Gentleman's Daughter: Women's Lives in Georgian England* (New Haven, Conn.: Yale University Press, 1998).

31. SM, *France* (1816), quoted in Suddaby and Yarrow, *Lady Morgan in France*, 72.

32. See Goodman, *Republic of Letters*, and Kale, *French Salons*.

33. See Kale, *French Salons*, chap. 4; and McMillan, *France and Women*, chaps. 3 and 4.

34. SM to Lady Clarke, 25 December 1818, in SM, *Passages from My Autobiography* (New York: D. Appleton, 1859), 267–69.

35. See Mansel, *Paris Between Empires*, 120–22.

36. McMillan, *France and Women*, 57.

37. David S. Shields and Fredrika Teute, "The Republican Court and the Historiography of a Women's Domain in the Public Sphere" (paper presented at the annual meeting of the Society for Historians of the Early American Republic, Boston, 15 July 1994), 2–3. I thank David and Fredrika for allowing me to cite their paper.

38. Anne Willing Bingham to Thomas Jefferson, 1 June 1787, in Julian P. Boyd, ed., *The Papers of Thomas Jefferson*, vol. 2 (Princeton, N.J.: Princeton University Press, 1955), 392–93.

39. Brian Steele, "Thomas Jefferson's Gender Frontier," *Journal of American History* 95 (June 2008): 17–42 (quote on 24).

40. Jefferson to Bingham, 7 February 1787, in Boyd, *Papers of Thomas Jefferson*, 2:122–23.

41. Fisher Ames to Rufus King, 24 September 1800, in W. B. Allen, ed., *Works of Fisher Ames*, vol. 2 (Indianapolis: Liberty Classics, 1983), 1385.

42. See Rosemarie Zagarri, *Revolutionary Backlash: Women and Politics in the Early American Republic* (Philadelphia: University of Pennsylvania Press, 2007), chaps. 4 and 5.

43. For the increasing limitations on women's activities in the civic arena after 1800 and the turn toward women influencing the public sphere mainly as wives and mothers, see Susan Branson, *These Fiery Frenchified Dames: Women and Political Culture in Early National Philadelphia* (Philadelphia: University of Pennsylvania Press, 2001); Rosemarie Zagarri, "Gender and the First Party System," in *Federalists Reconsidered*, ed. Doron Ben-Atar and Barbara Oberg (Charlottesville: University Press of Virginia, 1998), 118–34; and Zagarri, *Revolutionary Backlash*, especially chaps. 4 and 5.

44. Important works on separate spheres include Nancy F. Cott, *The Bonds of Womanhood: "Woman's Sphere" in New England, 1780–1835* (New Haven, Conn.: Yale University Press, 1977); Linda K. Kerber, "Separate Spheres, Female Worlds, Woman's Place: The Rhetoric of Women's History," *Journal of American History* 75 (June 1988): 9–39; and Carroll Smith-Rosenberg, "The Female World of Love and Ritual: Relations Between Women in Nineteenth-Century America," *Signs* 1 (August 1975): 1–29. Mary Kelley reminds us that, while antebellum America's gender ideology prized women in their domestic duties, women did not abandon their role in civil society or quit influencing public opinion; indeed, they became more involved as "educators, writers, editors, and reformers" (see *Learning to Stand and Speak: Women, Education, and Public Life in America's Republic* [Chapel Hill: University of North Carolina Press, 2006], quote on 246).

45. EPB to WP, 22 February 1816, in Didier, *Life and Letters*, 52–53.

46. EPB to WP, 12 February 1827, in ibid., 202.

47. Vickery wonderfully describes the "cultural horizons" within which gentlewomen of eighteenth-century England lived in *Gentleman's Daughter* (quote on 9).

48. EPB to Jonathan Russell, 27 January 1814, in "Letters to Jonathan Russell, 1801–1822," *Proceedings of the Massachusetts Historical Society* 47 (March 1914): 303.

49. Samuel Smith to Mary B. Mansfield, 28 April 1825, Carter-Smith Family Papers, ViU.

50. EPB to John Spear Smith, 22 August 1816, EPB Papers.

51. Horace Holley Diary, 19 March 1818, Horace Holley Papers, MiU. In this entry, Holley recorded a dinner conversation he had had with Elizabeth.

52. Horace Holley to Mary Austin Holley, 20 March 1818, ibid.

53. Horace Holley to EPB, 2 April 1818, EPB Papers.

54. See Glenda Riley, *Divorce: An American Tradition* (New York: Oxford University Press, 1991), 52.

55. James McElhiney to EPB, 15 September 1815, EPB Papers.

56. EPB to WP, 10 July 1825, in Didier, *Life and Letters*, 162.

57. James Fenimore Cooper to Caroline De Lancey, 3 December 1831, in James Fenimore Cooper, ed., *Correspondence of James Fenimore Cooper* (New Haven, Conn.: Yale University Press, 1922), 250.

58. James Fenimore Cooper, *Gleanings in Europe: France* (reprint, Albany: State University of New York Press, 1983), 215.

59. Mary Mayo Crenshaw, ed., *An American Lady in Paris, 1828–1829: The Diary of Mrs. John Mayo* (Boston: Houghton Mifflin, 1927), 18.

60. EPB to WP, 20 April [1826] (mistakenly filed under 1825), Gratz Collection—Royalty France, PHi.

61. Mansel, *Paris Between Empires*, 205.

62. See Bemy Stappaerts to Hope and Company, 16 August 1819; Mr. VanderHoop to EPB, 19 August 1819; and unknown correspondent to EPB, 28 August 1819, EPB Papers. That Elizabeth had an imposter also appeared in print in the United States. See *Orleans Gazette, and Commercial Advertiser* (La.), 31 December 1819.

63. EPB to Mrs. M. H. Torrens McCullogh, 24 January 1861, EPB Papers.

64. EPB to Dolley Madison, 29 December 1814, WP Papers, MS 1084, MdHS.

65. See Linda K. Kerber, *No Constitutional Right to Be Ladies: Women and the Obligations of Citizenship* (New York: Hill and Wang, 1998), especially 37–41.

66. EPB, Account Book, ca. 1858, EPB Papers.

67. EPB to SM, ca. 1825, in Didier, *Life and Letters*, 160.

68. Cooper, *Gleanings in Europe: France*, 217.

69. EPB to John Spear Smith, 22 August 1816, EPB Papers.

70. Marquis de Villette to EPB, as quoted in Claude Bourguignon-Frasseto, *Betsy Bonaparte: The Belle of Baltimore*, trans. Elborg Forster (Baltimore: Maryland Historical Society, 2003), 154.

71. SM to EPB, 9 (*sic*, 29) October 1816, EPB Papers.

72. EPB to SM, 30 September 1820, in Dixon, *Lady Morgan's Memoirs*, 141.

73. EPB to SM, 11 August 1817, in ibid., 66–67.

74. SM to EPB, 14 October 1821, EPB Papers.

75. EPB, marginal note on Countess Hocquard to EPB, 23 May 1823, EPB Papers; and EPB to WP, 20 April 1826, Gratz Collection—Royalty France, PHi.

76. EPB to SM, 30 September 1820, in Dixon, *Lady Morgan's Memoirs*, 142.

77. L. d'Esmenard to EPB, 26 July and 21 December 1824, EPB Papers.

78. EPB to John Spear Smith, 22 August 1816, ibid.

79. Duchesse d'Abrantès, *Memoirs of Madame Junot*, vol. 3 (Boston: Dana Estes, n.d.), 47 and 48.

80. "Miss Berry," as quoted in "Madame Patterson-Bonaparte," 313.

81. Countess Marguerite Blessington, *The Idler in France* (1841), as quoted in Mansel, *Paris Between Empires*, 133.

82. EPB to SM, 30 September 1820, in Dixon, *Lady Morgan's Memoirs*, 142.

83. EPB to SM, 8 May 1817, in ibid., 63.

84. Baron de Bonstetten to EPB, ca. 1821, as quoted in Bourguignon-Frasseto, *Betsy Bonaparte*, 191.

85. James Gallatin Diary, 29 January 1822, in James Gallatin, *A Great Peacemaker: The Diary of James Gallatin* (New York: Charles Scribner's Sons, 1914), 200.

86. EPB to John Spear Smith, 22 August 1816, EPB Papers.

87. Ann Tousard to EPB, 10 August 1830, ibid.

88. E. Hamilton to EPB, 10 December 1833, ibid.

89. EPB to SM, 28 November 1825, in Dixon, *Lady Morgan's Memoirs*, 223.

90. Gallatin Diary, 10 January 1819, in Gallatin, *Great Peacemaker*, 138.

91. "Madame Patterson-Bonaparte," 318.

92. EPB to SM, 11 August 1817, in Dixon, *Lady Morgan's Memoirs*, 2:67.

93. Baron de Bonstetten to EPB, ca. 1821, as quoted in Bourguignon-Frasseto, *Betsy Bonaparte*, 191.

94. EPB to WP, 6 May 1823, in Didier, *Life and Letters*, 139–40.

95. E. Hamilton to EPB, 10 December 1833, EPB Papers.

96. See Mansel, *Paris Between Empires*, 308–15.

97. D'Abrantès, *Memoirs of Madame Junot*, 4:33 and 290.

98. Kelley, *Learning to Stand and Speak*, 167.

99. See Carla Hesse, *The Other Enlightenment: How French Women Became Modern* (Princeton, N.J.: Princeton University Press, 2001), 30–38.

100. See Kelley, *Learning to Stand and Speak*, 65 and 100.

101. SM to EPB, 6 February 1817, EPB Papers.

102. SM to EPB, 26 May 1817, ibid.

103. EPB to SM, 8 May 1817, in Dixon, *Lady Morgan's Memoirs*, 63.

104. SM to EPB, 6 February 1817, EPB Papers.

105. EPB to SM, 11 August 1817, in Dixon, *Lady Morgan's Memoirs*, 65–66.

106. EPB to SM, 23 May 1818, in ibid., 80.

107. EPB to SM, 1 October 1819, in ibid., 110.

108. See Natalie Wexler, "'What Manner of Woman Our Female Editor May Be': Eliza Crawford Anderson and the Baltimore *Observer*, 1806–1807," *Maryland Historical Magazine* 105 (Summer 2010): 100–31.

109. Eliza Anderson to EPB, 2 July 1808, EPB Papers.

110. Sheila L. Skemp, *First Lady of Letters: Judith Sargent Murray and the Struggle for Female Independence* (Philadelphia: University of Pennsylvania Press, 2009), 24.

111. Eliza Godefroy to EPB, 10 May 1817, EPB Papers.

112. Anne (Nancy) Spear to EPB, 19 September [1816], ibid.

113. Robert White to EPB, 20 January 1818, ibid. Customs agents noted that the box with the inkstand also contained "a manuscript." This may have been her memoirs or the *Dialogues of the Dead* or some other document.

114. Harriet Gore Stewart to EPB, 13 October 1835 and undated, ibid.

115. SM to EPB, 20 April 1836, ibid.

116. EPB to John Spear Smith, 22 August 1816, ibid.

117. Ann Tousard to EPB, 6 February [*sic* March] 1819, ibid.

118. S. Harris to EPB, 14 April 1838, ibid.

119. EPB to Mary Caton Patterson, 7 November 1816, ibid.

120. Stewart to EPB, 15 August 1840, ibid.

121. EPB to Lady Westmorland, ca. January 1839, ibid.

122. EPB to SM, 14 March 1849, in Didier, *Life and Letters*, 253.

123. EPB to SM, 22 September 1839, in Dixon, *Lady Morgan's Memoirs*, 455.

124. *North American* (Philadelphia), 15 October 1839.

125. E. Hamilton to EPB, 8 May 1837, EPB Papers.

126. EPB to SM, 14 March 1849, in Didier, *Life and Letters*, 253.

127. Campbell, *Lady Morgan*, 231.

128. Davidson, *France After Revolution*, 15.

129. McMillan, *France and Women*, 43, 39.

130. Fanny W. Hall, *Rambles in Europe: or, A Tour Through France, Italy, Switzerland, Great Britain, and Ireland, in 1836*, 2 vols. (New York: E. French, 1839), 2:117.

131. See Davidson, *France After Revolution*, 15–16; and McMillan, *France and Women*, chaps. 3 and 4. For the United States, see Zagarri, *Revolutionary Backlash*, chaps. 4 and 5.

Chapter 5. "So Much Agitated About This Child's Destiny"

1. WP, Will, 20 August 1827, WP Papers, MS145, MdHS, Baltimore (hereafter WP Papers).

2. Ibid.

3. EPB, notes regarding William Patterson's Will, undated, EPB Papers, MS142, MdHS (hereafter EPB Papers).

4. John Patterson to EPB, 15 February 1835, ibid. Years later, Elizabeth sarcastically noted on this letter that "the amiable Father left him . . . an equal portion with his sons of Brandy & wine[.] A Joke with which to amuse the Public because John was a Drunkard & known to be such."

5. Articles of Agreement and Settlement, 24 December 1803, ibid.

6. Roger Taney, copy o f Mr. Taney's Opinion, 27 March 1835, ibid.

7. Horace Binney to JNB, 4 April 1835, JNB Papers, MS144, MdHS (hereafter JNB Papers).

8. John Sergeant to JNB, 4 April 1835, ibid.

9. JNB to EPB, 31 March 1835, ibid.

10. EPB to George Patterson, 12 August 1835, EPB Papers.

11. EPB, marginalia in Account Book, ca. 1840s–1850s, ibid.

12. EPB to Joseph W. and Edward Patterson, 24 February [1836], ibid.

13. Taney to Sergeant and Binney, 6 May 1835, ibid.

14. William Wirt to Elizabeth Wirt, 21 October 1804, as quoted in Anya Jabour, *Marriage in the Early Republic: Elizabeth and William Wirt and the Companionate Ideal* (Baltimore: Johns Hopkins University Press, 1998), 55.

15. For some key works on the history of the American family, see Carl N. Degler, *At Odds: Women and the Family in America from the Revolution to the Present* (New York: Oxford University Press, 1980); Jay Fliegelman, *Prodigals and Pilgrims: The American Revolution Against Patriarchal Authority, 1750–1800* (Cambridge: Cambridge University Press, 1982); Stephen M. Frank, *Life with Father: Parenthood and Masculinity in the Nineteenth-Century American North* (Baltimore: Johns Hopkins University Press, 1998); and Steven Mintz and Susan Kellogg, *Domestic Revolutions: A Social History of American Family Life* (New York: Free Press, 1988).

16. WP, Will, 20 August 1827, WP Papers.

17. EPB to WP, 10 April 1820, in Eugene L. Didier, *The Life and Letters of Madame Bonaparte* (New York: Charles Scribner's Sons, 1879), 56–57.

18. EPB to Dolley Madison, 29 December 1814, WP Papers.

19. Eliza Anderson to EPB, 4 June 1808, EPB Papers.

20. EPB to SM, 28 November 1816, in W. Hepworth Dixon, ed., *Lady Morgan's Memoirs*, 2 vols. (London: W. H. Allen, 1862; reprint, New York: AMS Press, 1975), 2:447; JNB to EPB, 26 December 1813, JNB Papers.

21. Mary Caton Patterson to EPB, 15 November 1815, EPB Papers.

22. EPB to SM, 11 August 1817, in Dixon, *Lady Morgan's Memoirs*, 2:68.

23. James Gallatin Diary, 11 August 1816, in James Gallatin, *A Great Peacemaker: The Diary of James Gallatin* (New York: Charles Scribner's Sons, 1914), 90.

24. James McElhiney to EPB, 16 April 1816, EPB Papers.

25. WP to EPB, 13 December 1815, in Didier, *Life and Letters*, 50–51.

26. EPB to WP, 23 September 1815, in ibid., 48.

27. WP to EPB, 23 April 1827, WP Papers.

28. Ann Tousard to EPB, 31 December 1818 and 1 January 1819, EPB Papers.

29. JB to EPB, 5 May 1821, JB Papers, MS143, MdHS.

30. John Jacob Astor to EPB, 15 March 1820, EPB Papers.

31. Robert Goodloe Harper to Anne (Nancy) Spear, 17 February 1820, ibid.

32. EPB to WP, 20 April 1820, in Didier, *Life and Letters*, 57.

33. "Madame Patterson-Bonaparte," *Lippincott's Magazine of Popular Literature and Science* 20 (September 1877): 318. For more on Pauline Bonaparte, see Flora Fraser, *Pauline Bonaparte: Venus of Empire* (New York: Anchor, 2009).

34. EPB to WP, 28 November 1821, in Didier, *Life and Letters*, 82.

35. EPB to WP, 12 July 1823, in ibid., 145.

36. Mary Caton Patterson to EPB, 2 August [1816], EPB Papers.

37. Spear to EPB, 19 September [1816], ibid.

38. EPB to David Bailie Warden, 12 May 1818, David Bailie Warden Papers, MdHS.

39. Mary Caton to Catherine Carroll Harper, 16 August 1818, Robert Goodloe Harper Papers, MdHS (microfilm edition).

40. EPB to Warden, 12 May 1818, David Bailie Warden Papers, MdHS.

41. EPB to WP, 23 September 1815, in Didier, *Life and Letters*, 48.

42. SM to EPB, 22 March 1826, EPB Papers.

43. SM to EPB, 6 February 1817, ibid.

44. James Fenimore Cooper, *Gleanings in Europe: Italy* (reprint, Albany: State University of New York Press, 1981), 26, 307.

45. "Madame Patterson-Bonaparte," 317. There are many published accounts of this meeting, but this one seems the most accurate since it is apparently based on Elizabeth's own words. There are no primary sources describing this brief encounter.

46. Samuel Smith to Mary B. Mansfield, 9 June 1825, Carter-Smith Family Papers, ViU.

47. Spear to EPB, 12 April 1827, EPB Papers.

48. James Brown to Smith, 27 June 1829, Samuel Smith Papers, DLC.

49. Elizabeth's judgment on this was keen. Historian James F. McMillan argues that "family strategies" were paramount to "romantic attachments" when it came to marriages in France in this period (*France and Women, 1789–1914* [New York: Routledge, 2000], 49).

50. EPB to WP, 15 February 1823, in Didier, *Life and Letters*, 129.

51. EPB to WP, 20 April 1826, Gratz Collection—Royalty France, PHi.

52. Gallatin Diary, September 1820, in Gallatin, *Great Peacemaker*, 165.

53. EPB to WP, 20 April 1826, Gratz Collection—Royalty France, PHi.

54. McElhiney to EPB, 18 September 1817, EPB Papers.

55. Moncure Robinson to John Robinson, 10 February 1826, in "Letters of Moncure Robinson to His Father, John Robinson, of Richmond, Va., Clerk of Henrico Court," *William and Mary Quarterly* 8 (April 1928): 85–86.

56. Gallatin Diary, 18 February 1815, in Gallatin, *Great Peacemaker*, 62.

57. EPB to WP, 8 January 1822, in Didier, *Life and Letters*, 87.

58. EPB to WP, 29-30 January and 8 March 1822, in ibid., 91, 97, 98.

59. Tousard to WP, ca. 1822, in ibid., 110.

60. EPB to WP, 20 December 1826, in ibid., 194.

61. EPB to WP, 11 and 24 December 1822, in ibid., 113, 115.

62. EPB to WP, 5 February 1823, in ibid., 122.

63. EPB to WP, 3 August and 15 September 1822, in ibid., 105–6, 111.

64. EPB to WP, 5 February 1823, in ibid., 122.

65. EPB to WP, 9 November 1823, in ibid., 147–48.

66. EPB to WP, 6 May 1823, in ibid., 137.

67. EPB to WP, 10 July 1826, in ibid., 186.

68. WP to JNB, 14 August 1825, in ibid., 165.

69. EPB to WP, 20 April 1826, Gratz Collection—Royalty France, PHi.

70. EPB to WP, 23 January 1826, in Didier, *Life and Letters*, 175.

71. WP to EPB, 12 June 1826, WP Papers.

72. Certificate of Oath of Intention, 29 April 1819, JNB Papers.

73. EPB to WP, 30 May 1828, in Didier, *Life and Letters*, 210–11.

74. WP to EPB, 23 April 1827, WP Papers.

75. EPB to WP, 9 September 1829, EPB Papers. It is unclear whether Elizabeth sent this letter, but it is very similar to other letters she sent family members during this period of crisis.

76. Ibid.

77. EPB to WP, 4 December 1829, in Didier, *Life and Letters*, 219–20.

78. Spear to EPB, 29 August 1830, EPB Papers.

79. WP to EPB, 24 July 1829, WP Papers.

80. WP to EPB, 26 November 1829, ibid.

81. Smith to Mansfield, 2 February 1830, Carter-Smith Family Papers, ViU.

82. WP to EPB, 4 November 1829, WP Papers.

83. Edward Patterson to EPB, 5 March 1830, EPB Papers.

84. Edward Patterson to EPB, 28 September 1830, ibid.

85. Edward Patterson to EPB, 5 March 1830, ibid.

86. EPB to WP, 21 December 1829, in Didier, *Life and Letters*, 221–22.

87. EPB to WP, 22 December 1830, in ibid., 226–27.

88. EPB to WP, 25 April 1830, in ibid., 225.

89. WP to EPB, 27 November 1830, WP Papers.

90. Edward Patterson to EPB, 28 September 1830, EPB Papers.

91. John White to EPB, 23 January 1833, ibid.

92. Spear to EPB, 26 November 1833, ibid.

93. Spear to EPB, 4 August 1833, ibid.

94. WP to EPB, 10 and 18 March 1834, WP Papers. Elizabeth's comment was written on the bottom of this letter on 9 March 1867.

95. For more on Napoleon III and Jerome, see Helen Jean Burn, *Betsy Bonaparte* (Baltimore: Maryland Historical Society, 2010), 226–32.

96. "The Baltimore Bonapartes," 18 November 1854, Newspaper Clipping File, EPB Papers.

97. EPB to Jerome Napoleon Bonaparte, Jr., 2 September 1858, ibid.

98. EPB, Account Book, ca. 1858, ibid.

99. Newspaper clipping, undated, Newspaper Clipping File, ibid.

100. EPB to Jerome Napoleon Bonaparte, Jr., 2 September 1858, ibid.

101. See Burn, *Betsy Bonaparte*, 234–39; and Sydney Alexander Mitchell, *A Family Lawsuit: The Story of Elisabeth Patterson and Jérôme Bonaparte* (New York: Farrar, Straus, and Cudahy, 1958).

102. EPB to Henry White, 13 February 1861, EPB Vertical File, MdHS.

Epilogue

1. See Louisa Emmerson Remembrances, [pre-1860], Louisa Emmerson Papers, ViU; and Mary J. Windle, *Life at the White Sulphur Springs; or, Pictures of a Pleasant Summer* (Philadelphia: J. B. Lippincott, 1857), 26.

2. EPB to SM, 14 March 1849, in Eugene L. Didier, *The Life and Letters of Madame Bonaparte* (New York: Charles Scribner's Sons, 1879), 25.

3. See EPB to unknown, 12 August 1864; Libbie McCabe to EPB, 14 January 1878; and Cora C. Rogers to EPB, 27 March 1878, EPB Papers, MS142, MdHS (hereafter EPB Papers).

4. John Spear Smith to EPB, 11 September 1849, ibid. For other writers who sought information from her or her son, see EPB to editors of the *New American Encyclopedia*, ca. post-1852, ibid.; and C. Edwards Lester and Edwin Williams to JNB, 5 May 1852, JNB Papers, MS144, MdHS. Later in the century, Henry Adams devoted several pages to Elizabeth and Jerome's wedding and its impact in his *History of the United States of America During the Administrations of Thomas Jefferson* (New York: Library of America, 1986), 558–60. See also Anne Hollingsworth Wharton, *Social Life in the Early Republic* (Philadelphia: J. B. Lippincott, 1903), 145–47.

5. Alice and Phoebe Cary, eds., *The Josephine Gallery* (New York: Derby and Jackson, 1859), 269–70. See also the works cited in the Introduction, note 8.

6. Virginia Mosby to EPB, 15 January 1861, EPB Papers.

7. W. T. R. Saffell, *The Bonaparte-Patterson Marriage in 1803, and the Secret Correspondence on the Subject Never Before Made Public* (Philadelphia: 1873), v–vi.

8. SM, as quoted in "Madame Patterson-Bonaparte," *Lippincott's Magazine of Popular Literature and Science* 20 (September 1877): 309.

9. "Madame Patterson-Bonaparte," *Lippincott's Magazine*, 309.

10. EPB to unknown, 31 August 1842, EPB Papers. This line is from a short poem written below the letter, in EPB's hand.

11. EPB to SM, 22 September 1839, in W. Hepworth Dixon, ed., *Lady Morgan's Memoirs*, vol. 2 (London: W. H. Allen, 1862; reprint, New York: AMS Press, 1975), 454.

12. EPB to SM, 14 March 1849, in Didier, *Life and Letters*, 253.

13. Ibid., 253–54. Elizabeth added that even her beloved Florence "was to be *travestie en Republique!*"

14. EPB to James Gallatin, 4 May 1852, EPB Papers.

15. "The Baltimore Bonapartes," 18 November 1854, Newspaper Clipping File, ibid.

16. EPB to James Gallatin, 3 November 1852, and EPB to Jerome Napoleon Bonaparte, Jr., 2 September 1858, ibid.

17. EPB, as quoted in Didier, *Life and Letters*, 265.

18. Albert Gallatin to EPB, 10 October 1840, EPB Papers; EPB to Albert Gallatin, 14 October 1840, Gallatin Papers, NYHS (microfilm edition).

19. EPB to David Bailie Warden, 29 May 1843, David Bailie Warden Papers, MdHS (microfilm edition).

20. Harriet Stewart to EPB, 26 September [1842], EPB Papers.

21. "Madame Patterson-Bonaparte," *Lippincott's Magazine*, 319.

22. Didier, *Life and Letters*, 261.

23. "The Baltimore Bonapartes," 18 November 1854, Newspaper Clipping File, EPB Papers.

24. EPB to Jerome Napoleon Bonaparte, Jr., 2 September 1858, EPB Papers.

25. Clarence Edward Macartney and Gordon Dorrance, *The Bonapartes in America* (Philadelphia: Dorrance, 1939), 42.

26. EPB, notes on letter wrappers, undated, EPB Papers.

27. EPB to Jerome Napoleon Bonaparte, Jr., 2 September 1858, ibid.

28. EPB, memorandum, 1 July 1839, ibid.

29. Helen Jean Burn, *Betsy Bonaparte* (Baltimore: Maryland Historical Society, 2010), 245.

30. Newspaper clipping, undated, Newspaper Clipping File, EPB Papers.

31. "Madame Patterson-Bonaparte," *Lippincott's Magazine*, 319.

32. "Madame Patterson-Bonaparte," *New-York Daily Tribune*, 5 April 1879.

33. "The Baltimore Bonapartes," *The Sun* (Baltimore), 17 January 1873.

34. EPB, marginalia, Account Book, ca. 1850s, EPB Papers.

35. Newspaper clipping, undated, Newspaper Clipping File, ibid.

36. Adelia Leftwich Harrison, "Memoirs of Madame Bonaparte," ca. 1930, p. 6, unpublished manuscript, Adelia Leftwich Harrison Collection, Southern Historical Collection, University of North Carolina, Chapel Hill. Harrison noted that her father, a Presbyterian minister, was with Elizabeth at her death.

37. Didier, *Life and Letters*, 264.

38. For a detailed history of the Bonaparte descendants in the United States, see Macartney and Dorrance, *Bonapartes in America*. For Charles Joseph Bonaparte, see also Joseph Bucklin Bishop, *Charles Joseph Bonaparte: His Life and Public Services* (New York: Charles Scribner's Sons, 1922).

39. EPB, Last Will and Testament, 2 September 1871, and Codicil, 8 November 1877, Charles J. Bonaparte Papers, DLC. Out of all of the listed manuscripts, only the letters remain in the archives at the MdHS.

40. "Madame Patterson-Bonaparte," *New-York Daily Tribune*, 5 April 1879.

41. "The Late Madame Bonaparte," *Frank Leslie's Illustrated Newspaper* (New York), 26 April 1879.

Index

Adams, Abigail, 5, 9, 25, 50
Adams, John, 21, 70
Adams, John Quincy, 22, 51, 70, 71
Adams, Louisa Catherine, 22, 138–39, 241
    n.133; on Elizabeth Patterson Bonaparte,
    33, 41, 49
Allgor, Catherine, 7
Anderson, Eliza. *See* Godefroy, Eliza Anderson
aristocracy, 10, 83, 89, 138, 186, 194;
    Americans' views of, 65–70, 87, 102–3, 108,
    161–62; European aristocrats, 9, 66–69, 93,
    95–98, 105, 139, 156–61, 166, 186. *See also*
    Elizabeth Patterson Bonaparte, as aristocrat
Armstrong, John, 85, 236 n.42
Astor, John Jacob, 103, 199, 200, 203–4

Baldwin, Simeon, 33, 79
Balzac, Bernard François, 166
Barney, William B., 110, 112
Bayly, Robert, 92
Bigelow, Abijah, 44
Bingham, Anne, 72
Bingham, Anne Willing, 8, 50–51, 72, 115,
    133, 139, 152, 163, 186; as *salonnière*, 25,
    137–38, 142, 162, 257 n.102; views on
    women, 161–62
Bingham, Maria (Marie), 72, 133, 241 n.132,
    256 n.85
Bingham, William, 25, 72, 103, 133
Binney, Horace, 191
Blennerhassett, Harman, 102, 251 n.161, 236
    n.33
Blessington, Lady, 171
Bonaparte, Bo (son of Elizabeth Patterson
    Bonaparte). *See* Jerome Napoleon Bonaparte

Bonaparte, Catherine (second wife of Jerome),
    99, 107, 184, 202, 218, 252 n.184; marriage
    to Jerome, 41–42, 74–75, 110, 113
Bonaparte, Charles Joseph (second grandson of
    Elizabeth Patterson Bonaparte), 10–11, 218,
    222, 228–29
Bonaparte, Charlotte, 204–6
Bonaparte, Elizabeth Patterson: and business,
    116, 146–52, 178, 182, 211, 217, 224–25;
    and clothing, 1, 5–6, 17–20, 28, 31–35,
    42–50, 53–54, 57, 69–70, 75–76, 79–81, 92,
    108, 182, 221, 225–26, 228; and fashion,
    5–6, 20, 23, 28, 32–35, 43, 45–46, 49–50,
    60, 69, 78–80, 93, 107, 141, 151, 155,
    182–83, 221, 229; and jewelry, 35, 42, 46,
    57, 75–76, 92, 107, 228; and her dogs, 56,
    101–2, 206, 250 n.157; and female friends,
    44–45, 53, 57, 59, 99, 107, 123–24, 134,
    153–58, 165–71, 174–75, 181–83, 187, 220,
    226; and male friends, 119, 130–31, 171–75,
    182–83, 187; and gossip, 19–20, 41–42, 45,
    47, 71, 86, 112–13, 120–21, 128, 156, 174,
    201–3; and scandal, 17–19, 46, 53–54, 60,
    62–64, 79, 109, 134, 152; appearance of,
    18–19, 32–35, 46–50, 53–54, 81, 92, 227,
    238 n.70; as aristocrat, 11, 29–32, 40, 43,
    56–57, 61, 65, 68–70, 75–76, 79, 82–93,
    104, 107–9, 123, 132–33, 142, 151, 155, 167,
    182, 195, 207, 219–20, 228; as celebrity in
    Europe, 54–60, 98–99, 109, 153, 169, 178,
    198, 219; as celebrity in U.S., 5–6, 9, 11,
    17–20, 23–24, 29–31, 33–36, 39–49,
    52–54, 60–61, 68–69, 74–80, 86, 109,
    122–23, 132–34, 141, 151, 167, 210, 221–24,
    226–29; as cosmopolitan, 23, 27, 35, 42, 49,

Bonaparte, Elizabeth Patterson (*continued*)
53, 55, 58, 60, 69, 73, 75, 83, 93, 104, 107–9,
151, 158, 166, 168, 177 183, 219, 228; as
daughter, 11, 124, 126, 187–95, 197–98,
205, 209–20, 227, 255 n.55; as independent
woman, 110–13, 116–17, 121, 124–27,
132–33, 146–53, 164, 170, 181–82, 187,
190, 197, 210, 220, 225, 228; as mother, 11,
44, 96, 116, 120, 123–26, 131–33, 146, 182,
187, 190, 193–200, 204–11, 219–20; as
threat to the republic, 6, 62–65, 68–70,
79, 82–95, 108–9, 116–17, 133, 224, 229;
as writer, 10, 59–60, 176–84, 226–27;
biographies of, 3, 222–23; birth of son, 39,
123, 194; books read by, 26, 117–18, 120,
176–77; competition with Caton sisters, 27,
52, 57–59, 203–4; concerns about historical
legacy, 1–2, 226–28; death of, 11, 229, 269
n.36, divorce of, 11, 41, 110–13, 124, 127,
131, 133–36, 167, 191, 197; girlhood of,
12–14, 24–27, 117–18, 123; her imposter,
166–67; honeymoon of, 17–20, 28, 30–31,
36; influence of, 49–50, 52, 57–58, 60, 69,
79, 82, 92–93, 109, 116–17, 121, 140–41,
221–23, 228–29; papers and writings of,
1–4, 10–11, 178, 180–81, 226–27, 229, 264
n.113; plans for son, 195–200, 204–8,
210–11, 214, 220; poems about, 18–19, 35,
42–43, 47, 82, 129, 234 n.6; relationship
with Jerome, pre-marriage, 13–16, 27–28,
120, during marriage, 16–20, 28, 30–31, 33,
36–37, 68, 71, 94, 120–21, 191, 209, 222,
225, 229, abandonment, 38–42, 73, 110–11,
118, 121–24, 133, 207, 209, 220, post-
abandonment, 41, 125, 131, 196, 199, 201–2,
227–28; relationship with Napoleon, 44, 56,
102, 125–26, 207, 210, 220; relationships
with European aristocrats, 95, 98–99,
103–4, 107, 154–56, 158, 166, 168–77,
181–84, 187; seeks title and annuity, 62–65,
82–93, 126, 195–96, 225, 249, n.127; suitors
of, 45, 47, 49, 119, 127–31, 200–203; travels
in and to Europe, 6, 9–10, 37–40, 54–60,
93–107, 123, 127, 153, 158, 164–67, 197,
217–19, 225; views on aristocracy, 6–7, 9, 26,
31, 56, 69, 95–97, 101, 107–8, 141–42, 159,
173–75, 194–95, 197, 223–24, 228; views on
Europe, 6, 69, 95–109, 141–43, 152, 155,
157–59, 173–75, 186, 198, 203, 207–15,
219, 223; views on family, 2, 126, 143,
188–92, 209–15, 219, 227–28; views on

father, 2, 96, 188–92; views on Jerome, 2,
102, 218; views on marriage, 31, 115–16,
119–20, 132, 162–64, 168, 173, 200–215;
views on men, 129–30; views on motherhood, 115–16, 119, 125, 143, 151–52,
162–64, 168, 194–95, 198, 205–6, 209–15,
220; views on republican government, 6, 73,
96, 101–3, 108, 147, 184, 223–24; views on
U.S., 31, 69, 73–74, 79, 85, 97, 100–109,
141–43, 152, 163–64, 182, 184, 187, 209,
223–24, 228; views on women, 7–8, 69, 101,
116, 119–20, 123, 132–33, 141, 151–52,
162–64, 181, 187, 194, 198, 215, 219–20;
views on women in Europe, 9, 95, 157–60,
162–66, 168–69, 201; wedding of, 16, 28,
70, 120, 233 n.26

Bonaparte, Jerome (husband of Elizabeth
Patterson Bonaparte), 10–12, 30, 70, 87,
94–95, 107, 134,180, 184, 198, 200, 210,
236 n.33, 236 n.39; abandonment of EPB,
38–42, 110–11, 118, 121–23, 207; as King
of Westphalia, 41–42, 83, 111–12, 124;
background of, 14–15; courtship of EPB,
13–16, 27–28; death of, 219; marriage to
Catherine, 41–43, 74–75, 83, 110–13, 151;
marriage to EPB, 6, 8–9, 16–20, 28, 31, 33,
36–37, 71, 94, 113, 120–21, 222; relationship with Bo, 83–84, 110, 121, 124, 196,
199, 208, 213, 218; relationship with EPB
post-abandonment, 41, 75, 84, 196, 201–2

Bonaparte, Jerome Napoleon (Bo; Elizabeth
Patterson Bonaparte's son), 62, 64, 74, 112,
217; and William Patterson's will, 191–92;
as imperial heir, 68–70, 83, 90–91, 133;
birth of, 39, 123; childhood of, 125,
195–200; education of, 94, 96, 195–96,
198–200, 205–6, 208, 210; in Europe,
99–100, 198–200, 204–5, 208, 217–19;
marriage of, 209–17; relationship with
Bonapartes, 198–200, 204–8, 210, 213,
217–19; relationship with father, 83, 208,
213, 218–19; relationship with grandfather,
150, 188, 196, 207–8; relationship with
mother, 100, 193–200, 209–15, 219; views
of Europe, 99–100, 214

Bonaparte, Jerome Napoleon, Jr. (first grandson
of Elizabeth Patterson Bonaparte), 217–19,
226, 228

Bonaparte, Joseph (brother of Jerome), 91,
198–99, 204–5, 217

Bonaparte, Josephine, 77

Bonaparte, Letizia (Madame Mère; mother of Jerome), 200, 204, 228
Bonaparte, Louis (brother of Jerome), 88, 202, 205
Bonaparte, Louis-Napoleon (later Napoleon III), 184, 218, 223
Bonaparte, Lucien (brother of Jerome), 29, 72
Bonaparte, Napoleon (brother of Jerome; later Napoleon I), 26, 27, 29, 70, 75, 77, 89, 93, 95–97, 102, 127, 130–31, 145, 149, 156, 198, 200, 207, 218, 222, 227; and EPB's annuity and title, 6, 62–65, 83–85, 128; and marriage of EPB and Jerome, 16, 19, 28–30, 36–40, 71–72, 83, 111–12, 121, 236 n.42; relationship with Jerome, 14–15, 40–41
Bonaparte, Napoleon (son of Jerome and Catherine), 218
Bonaparte, Susan May Williams (wife of Bo), 183, 209–12, 214, 216–17
Bonaparte family, 70, 82, 97, 134, 145, 152, 157, 167, 207, 222; EPB's connections with, 23, 39, 56, 64, 68, 71, 75, 87, 88, 90–91, 107, 199–200, 204–8, 218–19
Bonaparte-Patterson Marriage in 1803, The, 222
Bonstetten, Baron de, 173, 175
Borghese, Pauline Bonaparte (sister of Jerome), 57, 175, 177, 202, 204, 217, 228; Elizabeth Patterson Bonaparte's visit with, 199–200
Bourke, Countess de, 173
Brackenridge, Henry M., 35, 238 n.70
Brown, Ann, 105–6
Brown, James, 105–6, 144, 203
Burr, Aaron, 15, 18, 33, 89, 127, 129, 251 n.161
Burwell, William, 81, 110, 113, 131

Cabell, Joseph, 26, 82, 140
Cable Act, 167–68
Cadwalader, Frances, 72
Calvert, Rosalie Stier, 17–19, 34, 118, 120, 234 nn. 6, 8, 245 nn. 43, 51
Carr, Hetty, 47
Carroll, Charles, 27, 32–33, 101, 203
Carroll, John, 16, 128, 195, 211, 233 n.26
Catherine of Württemberg. *See* Bonaparte, Catherine
Caton, Elizabeth, 58, 60, 73, 100–101, 104, 107, 123, 212; rivalry with Elizabeth Patterson Bonaparte, 27, 52, 57, 204
Caton, Emily, 249 n.131

Caton, Louisa, 27, 58, 60, 73, 104, 107, 204
Caton, Marianne (Mary). *See* Patterson, Mary Caton
Caton, Mary Carroll, 134, 203
celebrity, 5–6, 10, 20–27, 33–34, 52, 61. *See also* Elizabeth Patterson Bonaparte, and celebrity
Chase, Maria (Mary), 25, 27
civil society, 113–15, 117, 129, 136, 140, 162, 168
Clay, Henry, 86, 147
Clinton, Cornelia, 72
clothing, 4, 22, 25, 34, 50–53, 76, 139–40. *See also* Elizabeth Patterson Bonaparte, clothing of; Elizabeth Patterson Bonaparte and fashion; fashion
Coles, Isaac, 26, 82, 140
Constant, Benjamin, 160
Constant, Charlotte, 160, 183
Cooper, James Fenimore, 101, 103, 107, 166, 168, 181, 201–2
cosmopolitanism, 23, 67, 81, 97–98, 103, 107, 109, 140, 156, 168, 181. *See also* Elizabeth Patterson Bonaparte, as cosmopolitan
Custis, Eliza Parke, 18, 135–36

d'Albany, Comtesse, 174
d'Este, Captain, 200
d'Orsay, Countess, 99
David, Jacques-Louis, 76–77
debate over American culture, 4–7, 9, 12, 60–61, 64–70, 81–83, 108, 194
Decatur, Stephen, 21, 22
Decatur, Susan Wheeler, 16, 22, 27; as celebrated belle, 26, 131
Demidoff, Nicolas, 99
Denon, Vivant, 49, 155, 171, 176
divorce, 133–36, 159, 164
Donegal, Marchioness of, 123
dress. *See* clothing; Elizabeth Patterson Bonaparte, and fashion; clothing of; fashion
Du Pont, Josephine, 100
Du Pont de Nemours, Victor, 25, 236 n.39

Eaton, Margaret (Peggy) O'Neale, 60–61, 127, 152
Eaton, William, 73, 89
Edgeworth, Maria, 176
Elgin, Lady, 123
Eustis, Caroline, 94
Eustis, William, 54, 94

fame, 6, 10, 20–24
family, 192–95, 214, 220
fashion, 4–5, 22, 32–33, 35, 50–51, 59, 67,
    76–81, 103, 115, 137–41, 160, 172, 186.
    See also clothing; Elizabeth Patterson
    Bonaparte, and fashion; clothing of
fatherhood, 193–94
Fay, Joseph, 50
"female politicians," 113, 116, 119, 137–38,
    144–46
femmes d'esprit, 9, 155, 157–58, 168, 171, 178,
    180–82, 186, 226
Fesch, Joseph, 218
Few, Frances, 145, 256 n.72
Florence Macarthy, 178
Foster, Augustus John, 28, 41, 91, 145
France: concerns about influence of, 5, 50, 63,
    70–71, 79, 81, 89–91; pro-French sentiment,
    26, 70
France, 176, 178, 185
Franklin, Benjamin, 176, 188
Fraser, D., 51–52

Galitzin, Alexandre Caroline, 59, 98, 99, 170,
    174, 183
Gallatin, Albert, 55, 72, 103, 145, 149, 183, 225
Gallatin, Hannah Nicholson, 72, 101
Gallatin, James, 101–2, 148–49, 174, 196–97,
    203–4
Garnier, Dr., 37
Genlis, Comtesse de, 98, 155, 170, 181
Gerry, Elbridge, 44, 130, 135
Gilmor, Robert, 54, 105
Godefroy, Eliza Anderson, 43, 45, 59, 106–7,
    122, 131–32, 165, 182, 226, 247 n.79; as
    writer, 179; divorce of 134–35; travels with
    Elizabeth Patterson Bonaparte, 37, 123
Godefroy, Maximilian, 43, 123, 134–35
Gortchakoff, Alexandre, 99, 102, 183–84
Graves, Samuel Colleton, 47, 128, 131–32, 176
Guiccioli, Teresa, 59, 174

Hall, Fanny, 105
Hamilton, Alexander, 68
Harper, Catherine Carroll, 26, 33, 131, 135
Harper, Robert Goodloe, 145, 199
Hayley, Mary Wilkes, 22
heterosociality, 118–19, 129, 143, 146, 158, 160
Hocquard, Countess, 170
Holladay, Huldah, 34, 81
Holladay, Waller, 81

Holley, Horace, 47–49, 52, 59, 130, 164, 258
    n.120
Hollingsworth, A. M., 75
Hollingsworth, Lydia, 45, 53, 60, 80, 128
Hughes, Laura, 101
Humboldt, Alexander von, 173

Irving, Washington, 55, 98, 127, 129
Izard, Ralph, Jr., 71

Jackson, Andrew, 144, 146–48, 191, 208, 217,
    223
Jefferson, Thomas, 15, 21, 26, 55, 66–68, 70,
    72, 90, 248 n.108; and Elizabeth Patterson
    Bonaparte's marriage, 28, 29, 38; views on
    women, 161–62
Jenks, William, 91
Jersey, Fanny, 174
Johnson, Richard, 85, 88
Johnson, William, Jr., 128–29
Josephine Gallery, The, 222
Junot, Laure (Duchess d'Abrantès), 171,
    176–77, 181

Kelley, Mary, 7
Kinson, Francois-Joseph, 108
Kuhn, Anna, 75

La Comte (or Lacombe), Madame, 25, 26
Lafayette, Marquis de, 55, 173
Lamartine, Alphonse de, 171
La Rochefoucauld-Liancourt, Madame, 155, 171
Latrobe, Benjamin Henry, 32, 102
Law, Thomas, 18–19, 78–79, 82, 135, 146, 234
    nn. 6, 8
Le Camus, Alexandre, 15–16, 28, 37
Le Camus, Auguste, 125
Lee, Henry, Jr., 128, 149
Livingston, Robert R., 28, 29, 159
Louis XVIII, 56, 94–95, 99, 102
Louis Philippe, 173
luxury, 4, 10, 65–68, 80–81, 83, 87–89, 105–6,
    108, 115, 139, 161

Madison, Dolley, 8, 21–22, 52, 63, 81, 115,
    137–38, 144, 152, 162–63, 186, 234 n.13;
    and fashion, 5, 32, 45, 53, 139; friendship
    with Elizabeth Patterson Bonaparte, 44–45,
    53–54, 93, 124, 165, 167, 182
Madison, James, 21–22, 28–29, 38, 89–91,
    138, 144

Manigault, Margaret, 100
Mansfield, Mary, 101
marriage: in Europe: 159, 204; in U.S., 120, 129, 132–33, 138, 140–41, 193
Mason, Jeremiah, 130, 140, 144–45
Mason, Jonathan, 50, 73–74
Mason, Mary, 145
Mason, Steven, 130
Massot, Firmin, 76, 142
May, Sophia, 42
Mayo, Mrs. John, 166
McElhiney, James, 56, 164–65, 204
McHenry, Margaret, 63, 86
Melish, John, 74
Mental Flower Garden, The, 51–52, 68
Mercer, Major, 104
Merry, Elizabeth, 34, 241 n.141
Mifflin, John, 113
Milligan, George, 44, 52, 92
Mitchill, Catherine, 43, 73, 144–45; opinion of Elizabeth Patterson Bonaparte, 44, 46–47, 49, 92
Mitchill, Samuel, 32, 43
Monroe, Eliza, 123
Monroe, Elizabeth, 8, 138–39, 142, 152
Monroe, James, 123–25, 145
Montagu, Mary Wortley, 179
Moore, Thomas, 31, 237 n.46
Morgan, Charles, 153–54, 185
Morgan, Sydney, 143, 153–56, 160, 174, 184, 201, 223; as celebrity, 178; as writer, 98, 169, 176–79, 181; friendship with Elizabeth Patterson Bonaparte, 59, 99, 169–70, 183, 185, 222, 226
Morris, Phoebe, 46
motherhood, 158–59, 186, 193–200
Murray, Judith Sargent, 6, 8, 24–25, 115

Napoleonic code, 158–59
nationalism, 76, 97, 156–57; in Europe, 177; in U.S., 5, 7, 66–69, 76, 78, 105–6, 108, 113–14, 136–43, 152, 161
newspapers, 25–26, 75; stories about Elizabeth Patterson Bonaparte, 31, 38–40, 42, 56, 58, 61, 63, 82, 85–86, 90–91, 121, 184, 202, 222–25, 227–29
Newton, William John, 57

Oakley, Charles, 45, 84, 86, 128, 247 n.80
O'Neale, William, 127, 130

Onís, Luis de, 91
Otis, Harrison Gray, 241 n.132

Patterson, Caroline (sister of Elizabeth Patterson Bonaparte), 197
Patterson, Dorcas Spear (mother of Elizabeth Patterson Bonaparte), 10, 13–14, 118–19, 197, 239 n.104
Patterson, Edward (brother of Elizabeth Patterson Bonaparte), 10, 13, 58–59, 105, 135, 179; and Bo's marriage, 213–14, 216; and father's will, 190–92, 226
Patterson, George (brother of Elizabeth Patterson Bonaparte), 190–92, 214
Patterson, Henry (brother of Elizabeth Patterson Bonaparte), 190–92
Patterson, John (brother of Elizabeth Patterson Bonaparte), 10, 190, 255 n.55, 264 n.4
Patterson, Joseph (brother of Elizabeth Patterson Bonaparte), 11, 13, 128, 215; and father's will, 190–92, 226
Patterson, Mary Caton, 27, 59–60, 73, 103–4, 107, 123, 171; second marriage of, 58, 203–4, 212
Patterson, Octavius (brother of Elizabeth Patterson Bonaparte), 197
Patterson, Robert (brother of Elizabeth Patterson Bonaparte), 10, 13, 27, 104, 255 n.55; sent to France, 29, 37, 121
Patterson, William (brother of Elizabeth Patterson Bonaparte), 13, 37
Patterson, William (father of Elizabeth Patterson Bonaparte), 148, 150–51, 222; and Elizabeth Patterson Bonaparte's marriage, 16, 28–29, 37; background of, 12–13; mistress and illegitimate daughter of, 10, 188, 216; relationship with Bo, 150, 188, 196, 198, 207–9, 213–14; relationship with Elizabeth Patterson Bonaparte, 2, 122, 188–95, 197–98, 208–9, 213–17; will of, 188–92, 226
Pichon, Louis André, 15–16, 28, 31, 38
Pickering, Timothy, 64–65, 87, 89, 92
Pine, Robert Edge, 13–14
Pius VII, 36–37
Plumer, William, 140
polite society, 8, 115, 117–19, 135–46, 152, 161–62, 187
Potemkin, Princess, 98–99
Preston, William C., 105

Randolph, John, 44, 251 n.161; and Titles of Nobility, 89–90
Randolph, Mary, 102
Randolph, Nancy, 253 n.21
Récamier, Jeanne-Françoise, 56, 80, 98, 104, 171–72; friendship with Elizabeth Patterson Bonaparte, 57, 59, 99, 155
Reed, Philip, 64, 89
Rémusat, Comtesse de, 98, 161
republican government, 3, 7, 18, 65–70, 72, 76, 81, 105–6, 114–15, 138–40, 146, 161–62, 194
Reubell, Henriette Pascault, 15–16, 25, 100, 123, 182, 233 n.21
Reubell, Jean-Jacques, 15, 100, 233 n.21
Richardson, Samuel, 121
Ritchie, Thomas, 65
Robinson, Moncure, 204
Rowson, Susanna, 6, 8, 25, 181
Rumford, Marie-Anne de, 98, 161, 170–71
Russel, William, 99, 202
Russell, Jonathan, 44, 94, 163

Saffell, W. T. R., 222, 227
Saint-Criq, Vicomte de, 200–1
salonnières, 8–9, 25, 98, 137, 155–57, 162, 170–72, 177
salons, 143, 154, 160–61, 173, 175
Sans Souci Club, 68
Scott, Winfield, 57, 78, 131
Seaton, Sarah Gales, 22, 49
Sergeant, John, 191
Series of Letters on Courtship and Marriage, A, 141
Sérurier, Louis, 127–28
Sheil, Richard Lalor, 58
Sismondi, Simonde de, 176
Smith, John Spear, 59, 62, 181
Smith, Margaret Bayard, 17–18, 44, 82, 137–39, 181
Smith, Margaret Spear, 13, 144, 146–47
Smith, Robert, 26, 71, 88–90, 144, 248 n.108; winter ball of, 17–19, 33, 82
Smith, Samuel,13, 26, 55, 60, 92–93, 103, 144–45, 149, 202; and Bo, 208, 213; and Elizabeth Patterson Bonaparte's marriage, 16, 71, 120, 236 n.35; and Titles of Nobility, 88–90
Society of the Cincinnati, 67
Southgate, Eliza, 120, 254 n.41

Spear, Anne (Nancy), 11, 59–60, 126–27, 179–80, 191, 200, 202, 212, 239 n.104; as businesswoman, 148–51, 225; as female politician, 44, 119, 144–48, 189; relationship with Elizabeth Patterson Bonaparte, 112, 123, 182–83, 191–92, 210–11, 217, 226; relationship with William Patterson, 188, 216
Staël, Albertine de, 161
Staël, Germaine de, 56, 98, 118, 168, 171, 185; friendship with Elizabeth Patterson Bonaparte, 59, 99, 156, 169, 174, 176
Stevenson, William, 39
Stewart, Harriet Gore, 181, 225
Stuart, Gilbert, 19–20, 128, 139
Summers, Matilda, 10, 188, 216–17
Summers, Providence, 10, 216

Taggart, Samuel, 88–89
Talleyrand-Périgord, Charles-Maurice de, 36, 56, 99, 174
Taney, Roger, 191–92
Thornton, Anna Maria Brodeau, 127, 138
Titles of Nobility Amendment, 64–65, 83–94, 108, 123, 132, 197
Tousard, Ann, 165–66, 198–99, 201, 205
Tousard, Louis, 63, 85–86, 247 n.90
Traveller Returned, The, 24
Truxton, Thomas, 86
Turreau, Louis-Marie, 36, 38, 126, 128, 130–31, 255 n.55, 256 n.72; and Elizabeth Patterson Bonaparte's title, 62, 83–85

Van Cortlandt, Pierre, Jr., 130
Villette, Marquise de, 98; friendship with Elizabeth Patterson Bonaparte, 56, 59, 99, 155–56, 169

War of 1812, 46, 80–81, 87, 93, 128, 197
Warden, David Bailie, 150, 176, 201, 225
Washington, George, 21, 25, 135
Washington, Martha, 5, 8–9, 18, 21, 25, 138
Wellesley, Marquis of, 58, 103, 203–4
Wellington, Duke of, 52, 56, 58–60, 95, 99, 171, 203–4
West, Benjamin, 95
Westmeath, Lady, 98, 174
Westmorland, Lady, 99, 183
Wheeler, Susan. *See* Decatur, Susan Wheeler
White, John, 147, 149, 151, 216
Whitfield, James, 211

Wilkinson, James, 89, 127–28

Williams, Susan May. *See* Bonaparte, Susan May Williams

Willink, John, 55

Wilson, Harriet, 174

Wirt, William, 129, 192

Wollstonecraft, Mary, 22, 118, 185

Woman and Her Master, 185

womanhood: definitions of in Europe, 139, 157–58, 160–64, 186; definitions of in U.S., 3, 7–8, 10, 21–25, 31, 33, 50–54, 113–20, 124–48, 151–52, 157–58, 161–66, 186, 193–94, 220, 224–25

women: American marrying European men, 72–73, 87, 203–4; and American culture, 4–5, 68–69, 100–101, 114–15, 117, 136–44, 152, 161–63, 221, 224; and American politics, 12, 43–44, 70, 76, 78, 113–15, 119, 137–38, 143–46, 162, 187, 224; and citizenship, 7, 167–68; and divorce, 133–36, 159, 164; and European culture, 98, 158–64; and European politics, 76–77, 161–62, 168–69, 187; and reading, 117–18, 122, 168, 175; and writing, 153–56, 168, 175–81, 185. *See also* female politicians, *femmes d'esprit, salonnières*

Wright, Fanny, 61

Yrujo, Carlos Fernando Martinez de, 72

Yrujo, Sally McKean, 19, 63, 72–73

Zagarri, Rosemarie, 7

Acknowledgments

It is such a pleasure to be able finally to thank all of the people and institutions who have made my work on this book much easier. Over the years, and at two different academic homes, the generosity I have encountered has been simply amazing.

One of my greatest debts of gratitude is owed to Helen Jean Burn and the archival staff at the Maryland Historical Society, the repository of most of Elizabeth Patterson Bonaparte's papers. I luckily met Helen Jean on my first visit to the archives. At work on her own book about Elizabeth, Helen Jean generously shared both notes, including those on Elizabeth's book collection, and insights. The archival staff members, especially Mary Herbert, were extremely helpful and attentive. I would also like to thank the staffs of the various archives listed in the endnotes, particularly the Manuscript Division, Library of Congres s; Clements Library, University of Michigan; and Special Collections, University of Virginia. Holly Shulman, editor of the Dolley Madison Papers, has also been encouraging from start to finish. Fellowships from the International Center for Jefferson Studies, the National Endowment for the Humanities, Widener University, and Kalamazoo College gave me time and money for researching and writing. Kalamazoo also granted me a much-needed sabbatical to finish the manuscript.

Many other friends and colleagues listened to my endless ruminations about Elizabeth and offered helpful comments. Among these, I would like especially to thank Catherine Allgor, Jen Einspahr, Elizabeth Manwell, Lucia McMahon, and Janelle Werner. Dena Goodman deserves special mention not only for her enthusiasm for this project but also for her brilliant insights into European cosmopolitanism. My conversations with her are always enlightening. Catherine

Allgor, Susan Branson, Brendan McConville, and Frederika Teute commented on conference papers and helped me think about Elizabeth's larger significance. Peter Onuf read part of this work and, as usual, offered perceptive analysis and insightful comments. Seth Rockman, one of the few who already knew of Elizabeth, kindly sent me a number of important Baltimore sources. Suzanne Cooper Guasco gave me her list of Elizabeth sightings, for which I am indebted. For their excellent translations of early nineteenth-century French documents, I would like to thank Jessica Pearson and Caitlin Cornell. I am extremely grateful to Rosemarie Zagarri, who read the entire manuscript and offered her enthusiastic as well as incredibly helpful suggestions for the revisions. Another enormous debt of gratitude is owed to Robert Lockhart, my editor extraordinaire at the University of Pennsylvania Press. He is everything an author wants in an editor and has become a good friend in the process.

If Elizabeth Patterson Bonaparte had the family I do, her life would have turned out quite differently. My stepfather and various in-laws, particularly Brian, have long been some of my staunchest supporters. The spirited women in my family, my mother and my sisters, have always offered me the love, understanding, and support that Elizabeth desperately wanted from her family. I am so lucky to have them—and their laughter—in my life. There are few words that can express my gratitude and my love for my husband, James, who gave so generously of his time, while working on his own book, to help me over the many years of this project. His commanding knowledge of this era, obscure references to Elizabeth, and consummate editorial skills made this a much better book. Thank you for your patience, humor, encouragement, and love—and for taking care of our new puppy, Quincy, while I finished the last revisions.